An Astrological Guide
to Parenting

CHILD
SIGNS

M. J. Abadie

LONGMEADOW PRESS
Stamford, Connecticut

Jacket design by Kelvin P. Oden

Jacket art by Frank Mayo

Interior Design by Pamela C. Pia

ISBN:0-681-00643-9

Printed in the United States of America
First Longmeadow Press Edition
0 9 8 7 6 5 4 3 2 1

Other Titles by M. J. Abadie

Finding Love
(with Sally Jessy Raphael)

Love Planets
(with Claudia Bader)

Multicultural Baby Names

Your Psychic Potential

To
Claudia Bader
with love and appreciation
for all you are and have done

CONTENTS

ACKNOWLEDGMENTS

My thanks go, first, to Claudia Bader — friend, fellow astrologer, co-author — for initially persuading me to "go professional" as an astrologer and for generously permitting me to enrich this work by adapting for it her brilliant work on key word concepts, a unique contribution.

To my dear friend and fellow Capricorn Mary Orser, astrologer/author, I also extend gratitude, not only for inspiring me with her comprehensive work on key words, but for her support and encouragement over the years.

I acknowledge my debt to the Swiss astrologer Alexander Ruperti for his illuminating lectures and for his wonderful work on cycles, published in *Cycles of Becoming*, both sources of profound inspiration and learning for me.

There have been many teachers who have given me much in my years of astrological studies. They are too numerous to list here, but I would especially like to thank Robert Hand, Liz Greene, Stephen Arroyo, Alan Oken, the late Dane Rudhyar, Donna Cunningham, and Tracy Marks for their works which have been such a source of information and insight.

My thanks go to Florida astrologer and friend Kathryn Milkey for providing an out-of-print source.

And to my research assistant, Alan Erdheim, I proffer a bushel full of thanks for his serendipitous way of finding what's needed, for cheerfully trekking here and yon, and for stoutly taking on the tedious task of computing the necessary ephemerides in Appendix I.

I thank Pamela Altschul Liflander, the editor who originally commissioned this book, for recognizing its potential and for her enthusiastic encouragement.

And to E. J. McCarthy, who had the task of taking over in the middle, I say a heartfelt "thank you," for seeing this book through the press.

My nephew, Vic Abadie, deserves kudos for providing lots of long-distance strokes, irony, and humor.

Number two nephew, Paul Abadie, is appreciated for his thoughtfulness and caring support.

John Knox was always there for me when I needed a shoulder massage, window blinds installed, or just to talk.

To Gregory Mowrey, my fairy godfather, my thanks for being skilled at converting pumpkins to golden coaches.

Maya Serkova helped in countless ways that lessened the weight of the task of composition and deserves applause.

And it is proper to acknowledge the spiritual sources who preside over endeavors such as this.

But most of all I thank *you* the reader for sharing my vision of a better tomorrow for all children.

WHY THIS BOOK?

PREFACE

"We are born at a given moment, in a given place, and, like vintage years of wine, we have the qualities of the year and of the season in which we are born."

—Carl G. Jung

Children are the inheritors of humanity's past and the bearers of its future. They stand poised between what was and what will be. The future of generations to come depends on decisions they will be called upon to make. This has always been the case, but never more so than now. Coping in the coming era of the "Global Village" — a world economy, information superhighways, and rapidly changing political structures worldwide — will be a demanding task for everyone.

In these times of rapid and often bewildering change all about us, all over the world, our children need all the help they can get on their path toward maturity. The problems that loom so dauntingly for the human race are multifold and complex — their solutions will require the best minds, sturdiest characters, stablest emotions. On these adults of tomorrow — on their developing brains, bodies, emotional and spiritual capacities — rests no less a task than the preservation of our Planet and the balancing of the natural environment with the demands of an increasing population. An awesome responsibility!

As you, as a parent, look down into your infant's innocent face or contemplate the unborn child still in the womb, you of course wonder how you are going to do your best for your child. There are many questions yet to be asked about this new person, who, contrary to some beliefs, has *not* come into the world a *tabula rasa*, or blank tablet, but from the moment of birth is already equipped with needs, desires, opinions, tendencies — all the human characteristics.

At birth, each child is already distinct. *Who is he or she?* The astrological chart provides a guide to the answering of this all-important question, one vital to your child's healthy development on all levels — mental, emotional, physical, spiritual.

All life is a journey through time. The chart, calculated for the exact time and place of birth is like a snapshot of the heavens at the precise moment of birth. And each of these, called *horoscopes*, after the hour, is induplicable as a thumbprint and bears within individual characteristics stamped upon it by Time itself. Thus, the chart might be called your celestial fingerprint. And, as each of us moves along our personal timeline into the future, we carry with us this inner roadmap to our destination.

My purpose in writing this book is to provide a significant guide to those responsible for preparing children for adulthood and the enormous tasks it will bring. These children, so full of bright promise, will carry the twenty-first century's burdens of world leadership, scientific advance, ethical determination, and spiritual resolve. They will face the unprecedented task of bringing the world fully into the long-awaited Age of Aquarius.

It is also my aim to help you to *enjoy* your child. Oftimes a small adjustment can make all the difference, and bring comfort to both child and parent. For example, one young mother with her first baby consulted me because she felt she could not handle her child's temperament. The two were already at war even though the baby was only a few weeks old. After reading the baby's chart, I gave the mother some simple advice on how to soothe her daughter's outbursts. Later, she called me, crying tears of joy. "It works!" she exulted triumphantly. "And it was so *easy*. I kept trying to comfort her the same way I like to be comforted and it was dreadful. Now I realize her needs and wants are entirely different from mine. I'm letting her be who she is and now she is a delightful baby."

Though I'm not saying that astrology can solve all the problems of child-raising, I have written this book in the belief that the information it contains, properly applied, can make an enormous difference to ourselves, our children, and to our world. I offer it to the reader in a spirit of hope for the future. In the words of Emily Dickinson,

> *If I can stop one heart from breaking,*
> *Or ease one pain,*
> *Or help one fainting robin*
> *Into his nest again,*
> *I shall not have lived in vain.*

I hope you will share this information with your child's teachers and any others who are significant — such as therapists and those who counsel children — for they will benefit from greater knowledge about the inner workings, innate proclivities, and unique talents of your child, and of all children.

You, as a parent or caregiver, would not be reading this book unless your intentions were of the best. So I salute you for your loving heart which is leading you to make this effort, and I sincerely hope this book will provide you with the means to better understand and guide your child into a healthy and productive adulthood.

M. J. Abadie
New York City, 1994

HOW TO USE
THIS BOOK

INTRODUCTION

Something of the Sun
In an apple.
Something of the Moon
In a rose.
Something of the Golden Pleiades
In everything that grows.

—D. H. Lawrence

Astrology is a complex and deep subject, one that considers the *whole person*. Inside each of us are many and varied planetary energies, symbolized by the mythological characters from whom the names of the Planets are taken. The energies of all ten Planets are the actors in our personal life drama, they are our cosmic connection, they reflect the richly variegated beings that we all are.

This book deals with *all* the components of the chart, not just the Sun sign — that's what you answer when someone asks, "What's your sign?" — yet it requires absolutely no previous knowledge of or experience with astrology. Everything you need is here. Knowledge of a child's *individual* complexity, which exists even in tiny babies, can provide parents, caregivers, teachers, and concerned others with a potent means of guiding children toward the rewarding, healthy development upon which successful adulthood depends.

My suggestion, even if you are not entirely new to astrology, is to read through the entire book before looking up your child's planetary placements or attempting to interpret them. The book functions as a teaching program, first introducing the component parts of the horoscope and their different thematic concepts, then expanding on each to demonstrate the interweaving of the parts into the whole.

Like the chart itself, the book falls into twelve segments and, like the chart, the segments both relate to and form the whole — which is always greater than the sum of its parts.

Astrology is based upon the *movement* of the *Planets* through the *Signs* of the Zodiac. As everything, including our Earth, is constantly in motion around the Sun, changes occur at every moment in time. It is this ever-changing pattern that results in *every Planet at all times occupying one or another of the Signs of the Zodiac*. This continual transiting of the Signs colors each Planet's effect upon the individual chart. Thus, comprehension of the symbolic significance of the Signs is essential to an understanding of the energies of the Planets themselves. And, as the Planets transit the Signs, which divide the Zodiac's 360 degrees into twelve segments of 30 degrees each, *they form angular relationships to each other*. Where each Planet falls in the celestial circle gives the horoscope its unique character, for no two charts are *exactly* the same.

As all the Signs are represented in an individual chart, even when no particular Planet occupies a given Sign, I believe that a grasp of the symbolic meanings of *all* the Signs is fundamental to the proper use of a chart.

Ordinarily, astrologers deal with a fully-formed adult who books a consultation, usually when some trouble arrives in a person's life. Children do not frequent astrologers, but parents with an understanding of their children's charts are better equipped to guide developing children along the lines that will most enable them to become what innately they *already are*, rather than forcing the growing human spirit into a preconceived pattern of development.

Here's what you will find in the book.

Chapter I introduces you to THE BASICS, a concise precis of the fundamentals of astrology: the Signs, the Planets, the Elements, the Modes, the Ascendant, and the Houses. This is an important chapter — especially for those new to the study of astrology — for each component of the chart strikes a theme and all finally resonate together.

Chapter II examines THE SIGNS in detail with the focus on how their energies express in children's lives at different ages. Also, the effect each Sign has on each of the *personal Planets* (Sun, Moon, Mercury, Venus, Mars) is discussed in brief using a system of *key words* to quickly acquaint the reader with the planetary functions as they relate to the Signs.

Chapter III, THE PERSONAL PLANETS, describes ego development, emotional needs, learning patterns, likes and dislikes, activities, and how these relate to the child's different developmental stages.

Chapter IV, THE INTERMEDIATE PLANETS, covers the relationship of the cycles of Jupiter and Saturn to the stages of growth — infancy, pre-school, pre-puberty, puberty, adolescence, and young adulthood — with their predictable crises, which are marked by these "timer" Planets.

Chapter V, THE OUTER PLANETS, deals with Uranus, Neptune, and Pluto, whose energies affect entire generations.

Chapter VI, THE ASCENDANT, takes up the most personal point in the chart, which functions as the "cusp" or beginning of the first House.

Chapter VII examines THE HOUSES, which symbolize the areas of life in which the personality is developed and expressed.

Chapter VIII, THE ELEMENTS, looks at how yet another of the characteristics of the Signs weights the chart and affects the person.

Chapter IX, THE MODES, continues this elaboration of the Signs from the point of view of the Earth's seasons.

Chapter X. You learn to interpret THE ASPECTS which are the already mentioned angular relationships between the Planets.

Chapter XI, FAMILY DYNAMICS, reveals how children perceive their parents and tells how to compare the charts of children with their parents, or with siblings, to further understand the harmonies and disharmonies of family life.

Chapter XII, PLANETS RETROGRADE, discusses how the retrograde effect, or "backward movement," operates on the Personal Planets.

The Appendix provides all the tables necessary for learning what Signs the Planets are in from 1950 to 2010, so that you can look up your own and your spouse's placements as well as those of your children, comparing similarities and differences as you go along. The Appendix also includes a Recommended Reading list, as well as information on how to obtain computer-calculated astrological charts.

We have also provided a sample horoscope blank and you can photocopy as many blanks as you need and fill in the spaces as you look up individual planetary placements. Then, with all the Planets in place in their Signs and the Houses, you are ready to return to the different chapters in the book and read the sections applicable to and your child. It will be an exciting, enlivening, and wondrous trip for you both!

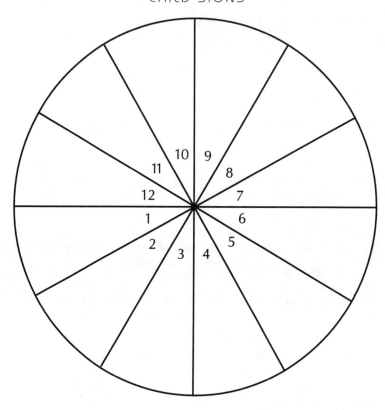

ASTROPOINTS

⊙ SUN

☽ MOON

♀ VENUS

♂ MARS

THE NATURAL ORDER OF THE SIGNS

♈ ARIES   ♎ LIBRA

♉ TAURUS   ♏ SCORPIO

♊ GEMINI   ♐ SAGITTARIUS

♋ CANCER   ♑ CAPRICORN

♌ LEO   ♒ AQUARIUS

♍ VIRGO   ♓ PISCES

THE BASICS

Anatomy
of a
Horoscope

CHAPTER 1

THE ZODIAC

The *Zodiac* is a band of the sky with the Sun's ecliptic at its center. It is divided into twelve sections, known as the *Signs*, which are named for constellations. As the *Planets* move on their orbits through the sky, they pass in turn through each of the Signs in the great wheel of the Zodiac, so that at any given time each Planet occupies one of the Signs.

THE SIGNS

The twelve Signs of the Zodiac symbolize certain unique characteristics, and they follow a "natural" order that never varies.

ARIES	symbolizes	*beginnings.*
TAURUS	symbolizes	*manifestation.*
GEMINI	symbolizes	*mentality.*
CANCER	symbolizes	*emotions.*
LEO	symbolizes	ego *development.*
VIRGO	symbolizes	*perfection.*
LIBRA	symbolizes	*relationships.*
SCORPIO	symbolizes	*reqeneration.*
SAGITTARIUS	symbolizes	*idealization.*
CAPRICORN	symbolizes	*reality.*
AQUARIUS	symbolizes	*experimentation.*
PISCES	symbolizes	*transcendence.*

Each Sign rules a part of the body, has a planetary ruler, and is represented by a zodiacal image and a thematic principle. In addition, each Sign has an *Element* and a *Mode*, which will be explained later. Another facet of each sign is its *polarity*. This is usually expressed as *positive / negative* or *masculine / feminine*, but because of the confusing connotations of these terms I prefer to use *active / receptive*, which is comparative to *yang / yin*. Also, some Signs have special relationships to different Planets in what is called the "exhaltation" of the Planet.

A Planet in the Sign of its exhaltation is in its most powerful position and influences the meaning of that Sign. For example, the Moon is exhalted in Taurus, giving Taurus a strong connection to lunar symbolism as well as to that of Venus, its ruler.

It is important to remember that the Signs apply to *all* ten Planets, not just to the Sun, which is what most people think of as their Sign. Astrology, like human beings, is much more complex than the Sign occupied by the Sun in a chart. All twelve Signs are represented in everyone's chart, whether or not each is occupied by a specific Planet. The Sign position of each Planet indicates *how* that basic energy operates.

In Chapter II we will discuss the Signs in detail and how they affect the energies of the different Planets.

THE PLANETS

There are two "lights," the Sun and the Moon, and eight Planets, listed here in the order of their distance from our Sun.

Mercury
Venus
Mars
Jupiter
Saturn
Uranus
Neptune
Pluto

Although technically the Sun and the Moon are not Planets — astrologers call them "luminaries" — for purposes of discussion we will group them here with the Planets.

Earth is also a Planet, but astrologers do not generally take the Earth into consideration in reading a chart. This is because astrology as we practice it is *geocentric* rather than *heliocentric*, which means it is based on what we *see* from the vantage point of Earth, as if Earth were indeed the center of our solar system and everything revolved around *it*. Of course, we know that the Sun is the actual center (hence, heliocentric) and that all of the Planets, including Earth, orbit around it. Thus, when we speak of a Planet as *rising* what we actually mean is that we *see* it coming over our horizon. And when we say that the Sun is passing through one or other of the Signs of the Zodiac, we mean that from our position on Earth the Sun *appears* to be in motion, when in fact it is the Earth's movement around the Sun that gives the effect of the Sun's rising and setting. Similarly, with *retrograde* motions we refer to a Planet's "backward" motion. It isn't actually moving backward; that's just how it appears to us from Earth.

Everyone contains the energies of all ten Planets, but only the "luminaries," the Sun and the Moon, and the first three Planets closest to our Sun — Mercury,

Venus, and Mars — are considered to be *personal*, due to their short orbits. As the distance from our Sun increases, the planetary orbits get longer and those further out, having the longest orbits, are less personal in their effect upon individuals, influencing whole generations of people. The longer the orbit of the Planet, which is to say the number of years it takes for the Planet to transit all twelve Signs, the more of a generational effect it will have. Pluto, for example, the outermost Planet, with its irregular orbit takes from 13 to 32 years to pass through just *one* Sign, more than 200 years to pass through all twelve! The Sun, on the other hand, passes through the entire Zodiac every year and the Moon does so each month. Thus, the Moon is actually the most personal of the personal Planets and the one which children, especially in the pre-verbal stage, *feel* the most.

Each Planet represents or *symbolizes*, different facets of the human character, basic energies common to us all.

SUN	symbolizes	*consciousness*, the "I Am" principle.
MOON	symbolizes	*the emotional body*, fundamental needs.
MERCURY	symbolizes	*the mind*, learning and communicating.
VENUS	symbolizes	*the love nature*, the attracting principle.
MARS	symbolizes	*energy*, the action principle.
JUPITER	symbolizes	*expansion*, the integrative principle.
SATURN	symbolizes	*limitation*, the reality principle.
URANUS	symbolizes	*the unexpected*, the intuitive.
NEPTUNE	symbolizes	*the unseen*, the visionary.
PLUTO	symbolizes	*transformation*, the regenerator.

This symbolism is discussed in detail in Chapters III–V.

THE ASCENDANT

The twelve Signs of the Zodiac are like an ever-turning celestial clock, containing all 24 hours of the diurnal cycle. Every two hours a different Sign appears on the horizon. This Sign is known as the *Ascendant,* or rising Sign. The Ascendant symbolizes the significance of an infant's first breath, that instant when he or she leaves behind the undifferentiated water-world of the mother womb to become an individual entity who must now rely on his own air-breathing lungs for survival in this material world.

Prior to birth, the unborn infant carries *all the energies of the planets* within, but it is only at the time of birth that the child receives the imprint of the Ascendant, which marks the gateway through which the infant enters earthly life. That moment in time and its particular attributes are forever imprinted as a deeply internal individuality.

Thus the Ascendant, which will be fully examined in Chapter VI, is the most personal point of the entire chart, one which determines the arrangement of the planets around the horoscope in what we call the Houses.

THE HOUSES

The Ascendant marks the beginning (*cusp*) of the first House and acts as the ruler of that House. The horoscope is then divided from the point of the Ascendant into twelve pie-shaped Houses, which organize the chart by placing a different sign of the zodiac, following the "natural order" given on page 3, on the cusp, or beginning, of each House. For example, Cancer on the cusp of the first House, or a Cancer Ascendant, would give Leo on the second House cusp, Virgo on the third, and so on.

The Houses describe the areas of life's activities and needs. They are the *field of encounter* for the expression of the energies of the Planets. The Sign tells *how* and the House tells *where* the energy is expressed.

The Houses and how the Planets express in them are examined in Chapter VII.

THE ELEMENTS

The Zodiac connects us to the four fundamental principles of life, the *Elements*. They refer to the most basic energies we know, not only abstract concepts but real physical phenomena. We could not live without them.

Since there are three Signs to an Element, these groupings are known as the "triplicities."

Fire (Aries, Leo, Sagittarius) is *radiant*, excitable, enthusiastic.
Earth (Taurus, Virgo, Capricorn) is *stable*, physical, practical.
Air (Gemini, Libra, Aquarius) is *ephemeral*, shifting, insubstantial.
Water (Cancer, Scorpio, Pisces) is *flowing*, intuitive, imaginative.

Also, the four Elements represent inner, spiritual energies deeply embedded in our psyches. The oft-quoted phrase, "out of his element," is an indication of how we can feel when we are elementally out of tune, so to speak.

The Elements are, in effect, the flow of energies that comprise the universal life pattern in each individual as well as in the cosmic whole. We can view this as pattern, flow, and transmutation of energy, with each of us relating variously to the four energies symbolized by the Elements, depending on how they are distributed in the chart.

In Chapter VIII we will discuss the balance of the Elements singly and in combination.

THE MODES

The *Modes* tie us to the annual cycle of seasons, to which we all instinctively respond at our most profound levels, dividing the chart into groups of four each, or "quadruplicities."

As everything else in astrology, they march around the Zodiac in a regular order.

Cardinal Signs *initiate*. They are Aries (fire), Cancer (water), Libra (air), and Capricorn (earth).

Fixed Signs *conserve*. They are Taurus (earth), Leo (fire), Scorpio (water), and Aquarius (air).

Mutable Signs *change*. They are Gemini (air), Virgo (earth) Sagittarius (fire), and Pisces (water).

Notice that there is one Sign in each of the four Elements with the result that there is *Cardinal Fire, Cardinal Water, Cardinal Air, Cardinal Earth,* and so on through the Fixed and Mutable Signs.

In Chapter IX we will examine the Modes and the personal traits they indicate and define both singly and in combination.

THE ASPECTS

Put simply, the *aspects* are the angular relationships between the planets. As the horoscope forms a 360 degree circle, the angles are those we commonly know in geometry.

There are *major* and *minor* aspects, which refer to the number of degrees apart the planets are when they form the aspects. (There are 30 degrees to each of the twelve Zodical Signs which equals the 360 degree circle.)

In this book, we will discuss only the *major* aspects, which are

Conjunction (0 degrees apart)
Opposition (180 degrees apart)
Trine (120 degrees apart)
Square (90 degrees apart)

The Moon's monthly cycle easily lets us see how planetary aspects form, for the Moon's aspect to the Sun is shown by how much light it reflects. At the New Moon, the Moon is in *conjunction* with the Sun, which is why it is dark. At the full Moon, the Moon is in *opposition* to the Sun reflecting its full light. At each quarter, the Moon is in *square* aspect to the Sun. These two squares, one while the moon is waxing and one while it is waning, represent the so-called upper and lower squares between planets.

Sometimes entire generations are born under a single, powerful aspect which will color the attitudes and experiences of a large part of the population. For example, children born from 1992 to 1995 are under the great conjunction of Uranus and Neptune in Capricorn. Just what this will mean for their futures is uncertain and will depend on individual charts, but it is already clear that the entire world will be vastly changed by the time these children reach active adulthood. It was under this conjunction that we witnessed the demise of the Soviet Union (a Capricorn country) and the fall of the Berlin Wall, which resulted in the reunification of Germany. Just what these momentous events portend in the years to come is unknown, but what we do know is that whatever world changes result it is the children of today who will have to deal with them tomorrow.

In Chapter X we will discuss planetary compatibility and explain how to determine aspects.

THE
ZODICAL SIGNS

How They Affect
the Planets

Now constellations, Muse and signs rehearse;
In order let them sparkle in thy verse;
First Aries, glorious in his golden wool,
Looks back, and wonders at the mighty Bull,
Whose hind parts first appear, he bending lies,
With threatening head, and calls the Twins to rise;
They clasp for fear, and mutually embrace,
And next the Twins with an unsteady pace
Bright Cancer tolls; then Leo shakes his mane
And following Virgo calms his rage again.
Then day and night are weighed in Libra's scales,
Equal awhile, at last the night prevails;
And longer grown the heavier scale inclines,
And draws bright Scorpio from the winter signs.
Him Centaur follows with an aiming eye,
His bow full drawn and ready to let fly;
Next narrow horns, the wisted Caper shows,
And from Aquarius' urn a flood o'erflows.
Near their lov'd waves cold Pisces take their seat,
With Aries join, and make the round complete.

—Marcus Manilius (Roman poet)

REMEMBER: *Each Planet is at all times occupying one of the twelve Signs of the Zodiac.* The Planet represents a *basic energy* and the Sign which the Planet occupies (*is transiting*) indicates our attunement to that particular inner energy.

CHAPTER II

ARIES

Element: Fire
Mode: Cardinal
Planetary Ruler: Mars
Zodiacal Image: The Ram
Body Part: The Head
Thematic Principle: I Am
Key Idea: The Individual
Exhaltation: The Sun
House Affinity: The First
Polarity: Active

Aries symbolizes the awareness of being different and separate from others. It is the individual surging through life, the ego, consciousness of self.

As the first Sign of the Zodiac, Aries relates to beginnings of all kinds, the primary energy that gets things going. Aries says clearly, "I want to be what I am." It is like the baby absorbed in the dawning consciousness of itself, totally absorbed with its own fingers and toes.

Full of Fire energy, and a Cardinal, or initiator, Sign, Aries is a self-starter. Willful and with a strong desire to be first, Aries is always looking for the next adventure, challenge, project, or experience. Intent on the preservation of its individuality, Aries may display a preference for doing things alone at an early age, firmly insisting, "I can do it *myself*, mother." It's best to give Aries as much latitude as is possible, within the bounds of safety, allowing it to learn from mistakes, for Aries will resent you for imposing your will on it. Try not to be either amused or angered by Aries's intense need for independence. Humiliation will produce combativeness.

The inner drive to be itself strictly on its own terms can lead to asocial behavior because Aries has less need than other signs for social approval and reinforcement. As long as Aries can do exactly as it pleases, it doesn't much care what others think. When relating to a group, Aries likes to be the leader, the bringer of ideas, but isn't especially interested in finishing up what is started, being just as happy to leave the details to more pragmatic Signs.

Aries has the soul of the pioneer, tending to leap first and think afterward, a veritable whirlwind of energy with little regard for the consequences of action.

As long as the *self* is being expressed, considerations like prudence and practicality are immaterial. Thus, Aries must learn the lesson, "Finish what you start."

More a sprinter than a long-distance runner, Aries needs to be made mindful of the need for rest, for Fire's energy burns fast and can easily exhaust itself. Aries' short, sudden bursts of energy are followed by fatigue and lassitude.

A talker rather than a listener, Aries dislikes dealing with emotions, and can have frequent outbursts, especially when frustrated, as a way of releasing tension. Fortunately, temper tantrums don't last long once the energy has been expended and happy smiles return quickly. Not one to pack a load of resentments and grudges, Aries forgives easily, liking to brighten up the atmosphere.

Patience is a virtue unknown to Aries, who finds waiting for *anything* difficult if not impossible, a trait guaranteed to try the parental patience. It helps to remember that Aries' characteristic *first* translates to *now*.

Naturally honest, Aries hates to be compromised. Send little Aries to the store with a dollar for a quart of milk and you'll get your change to the penny. There's a downside to truthtelling, however, if you put great store in politeness. Aries doesn't appreciate "little white lies" and will be quick to take offense at being asked to become part of a cover-up.

Aries key characteristics:

Outgoing	Aggressive
Active	Pushy
Adventurous	Foolhardy
Pioneering	Egotistical
Energetic	Impulsive
Independent	Self-centered
Enthusiastic	Headstrong

PLANETS IN ARIES

Like the first horse out of the stall at the races, Aries is always raring to go, with more thought to *starting* than to finishing. Aries energizes. Thus, Planets in Aries are prone to action even against their intrinsic natures, acting more quickly and spontaneously than they might otherwise.

KEY CONCEPTS
SUN

My purpose is to move bravely ahead at all times, meeting all challenges head-on.

I am courageous, impulsive, innocent, humorous, vital, enthusiastic, aggressive, insensitive, headstrong, inspired, one-pointed.

The Sun is exalted in Aries and thus has a special relationship to it. See Chapter III: Sun.

MOON

I need activity, adventure, stimulation, directness, competitiveness, enthusiasm, being first, seeking challenge.

I feel cared for when I am given room to move, dealt with directly, made to feel unique.

I am most comfortable in environments where there is a lot of action and stimulation.

MERCURY

My mind works quickly, impulsively, originally, inspiredly, one-pointedly, freshly, impractically.

I learn when I am enthusiastic and when I am challenged.

I communicate brusquely, directly, suddenly, aggressively, enthusiastically.

VENUS

I express love through enthusiasm, excitement, fighting and making up, being stimulating, playing.

I want stimulation, energy, challenge, action, vitality, immediate responses, new experiences.

My taste is for the new, loud, colorful, obvious, unique.

I feel loved by special attention, having time spent with me.

MARS

I act heroically, quickly, punctually, impulsively, selfishly, competitively, rashly.

I am motivated by challenge, self-interest, originality.

I get angry instantaneously, intensely, actively.

My libido is ardent, romantic, dominant, initiating.

Mars, Aries' ruler, is similar in nature. Both symbolize the expression of raw energy on its way to finding a vehicle for its expression, asserting the right to be exactly who and what they are. Mars in Aries is a powerhouse.

TAURUS

Element: Earth
Mode: Fixed
Planetary Ruler: Venus
Zodical Image: The Bull
Body Part: The Throat and Neck
Thematic Principle: I Have
Key Idea: The Material Plane
Exhaltation: The Moon
House Affinity: The Second
Polarity: Receptive

Taurus symbolizes connection to the material plane with its reliance on the physical senses and, by extension, accumulation of possessions.

The second sign of the Zodiac, Taurus provides the matrix (a word related to mother) for the primary energies of life to come to being on the physical plane.

Earthiest of the Earth Signs, Taurus is symbolic of the soil of Mother Earth herself, and, a fixed Sign, Taurus is concerned with conservation of energies. The receptive nature of Taurus is like the nature of Earth, which receives the seed, contains it, and causes it to grow.

Gifted with patience, Taurus lets things happen in their own time. Like a good gardener, Taurus is content to wait until the right time comes along, knowing there's no point in pulling up the radishes to see if they are ready.

The most fixed of the fixed Signs, Taurus's patience may seem like slowness, but it is the slowness of certainty and self-confidence. Taurus rests secure in the knowledge that tomorrow is another day and that excess motion will not make the sun rise any earlier.

Rooted in the physical world, Taurus appreciates creature comforts that minister to the five senses. Pleasing textures, sounds, smells, tastes, and sights comfort Taurus and provide a sense of warm security. Even as tiny babies, Taureans respond to the sensual in their environment. Natural nurturers, Taurus children will soothe their siblings, or even adults, with a hug or a cookie.

Venus-ruled, Taurus enjoys being attractive and is susceptible to beauty which is of solid quality and endures the test of time. Little Taurus wants a sturdy toy that will last, not some instant gratifier meant to be thrown away the next day.

Overeating may be a problem, due partly to the sheer enjoyment of the physical experience, partly because Taurus, like the great bull calmly munching grass in the pasture, isn't much inclined to the kind of racing around and expending of energy that we call exercise. A board game will do much better than a ball game.

But don't count Taurus out on the athletic field. There's a lot of stamina there, and when the sprinters have fallen by the wayside, Taurus will be settling in for the long haul.

Both boys and girls tend to be robust of constitution with abundant endurance. Don't let that fool you into relaxing the rules for proper bedtime and rest, however, as Taurus rules the throat and an overtired Taurus can easily come down with a sore throat.

Extremely affectionate, Taurus suffers if deprived of physical contact and affection, needing lots of hugs, pats, and touching. A basically even-tempered Sign, Taurus is slow to anger. But, once riled, look out. The Bull can be a charger. And anger can be followed by a fit of the sulks. Still, it's easy to make up with a Taurus. Just offer some genuine affection and some tasty tidbit and the sun will shine again.

Taurus children don't usually have much trouble interacting with other children, but they are not especially social either, being quite content to be by themselves and experience their own reality. Sharing is not a problem for Taurus but possession is important. Taurus may be quite happy to let a chum play with its fire engine so long as the vehicle's ownership is clearly recognized.

Related to the second House of money and valuables, materialistic Taurus's natural instinct is to accumulate and preserve *things*, but this is combined with a generous nature.

Taurus key characteristics:

Practical	Materialistic
Determined	Stubborn
Affectionate	Possessive
Sensuous	Self-indulgent
Loyal	Rigid
Patient	Unyielding
Persevering	Unimaginative

PLANETS IN TAURUS

In Taurus the effort is bent toward the practical with the result arrived at by methodical intent. Remember that Taurus, like a growing plant, takes its time, seeing no need to rush matters to a premature conclusion. This is occasionally a liability, but Taurus' energy can achieve much if allowed to work at its own pace.

KEY CONCEPTS

SUN

My purpose is to hold onto everything of value by not changing.

I am stable, security conscious, beauty-loving, grounded, sensual, relaxed, immovable, fixated, conservative, materialistic, placid.

MOON

I need stability, food, comfort, financial security, touching, loving, relaxing, peacefulness, conservativeness.

I feel cared for when I am given practical help, dealt with honestly, hugged and petted, made physically comfortable, given ample food.

I am most comfortable in environments where it is secure, sensuous, physically comfortable, convenient.

The Moon is exalted in Taurus and thus has a special relationship to it. See Chapter III: Moon.

MERCURY

My mind works slowly, steadily, practically, rigidly, obsessively, retentively, thoroughly.

I learn when I see a practical outcome of what I'm learning and when I can go at something at my own pace.

I communicate unambivalently, clearly, conservatively, cautiously, concretely.

VENUS

I express love through possessions, affection, sensuality, physicalness, nurturing, reliability.

I want security, stability, money, calm, comfort, beauty, luxury.

My taste is for the conservative, classical, natural, practical, solid.

I feel loved by financial and emotional security, physical and emotional contact.

Venus, Taurus's ruler, is especially well-placed in this Sign, though she tends to luxuriate to excess. Taurus's relationship to this most feminine of the goddesses is an expression of love for the fertile abundance of Nature itself and all living things.

MARS

I act dogmatically, resistantly, peacefully, slowly, conservatively, possessively, realistically, kindly.

I am motivated by security, love, money, comfort, changelessness.

I get angry slowly, physically, smolderingly, totally, unappeasably.

My libido is earthy, sensual, enduring, affectionate, protective.

GEMINI

Element: Air
Mode: Mutable
Planetary Ruler: Mercury
Zodiacal Image: The Twins
Body Part: The Hands, Arms, Lungs, Chest, Nervous System
Thematic Principle: I Think
Key Idea: Dualism
Exhaltation: None
House Affinity: The Third
Polarity: Active

Gemini symbolizes the dualistic character of humanity and the polarity of our mental processes (for example, left brain/right brain).

The third Sign of the Zodiac, it symbolizes the development of the life energy on the mental plane. Like Air, its Element, mental processes are abstract. The mind can move independently of the time/space limitations of the physical world.

Gemini's nature is to flit from place to place rapidly, like a bee gathering nectar from a field of flowers, sampling life's endless variety for the sheer joy of the experience. A collector of information for it's own sake, Gemini is unconcerned with end or use, which gives a surface quality — the sense that there is a lack of depth here. And, it is true that Gemini's insatiable curiosity about most everything in the Universe doesn't usually leave the time for examination or appreciation of the deeper aspects of any experience.

The most mutable of the mutable signs, Gemini's nature is to change. Represented by the Twins, it's duality is clearly evident. It's said that a Gemini never rises in the morning the same person who went to bed at night. Some people, especially parents who are earthy, can find this Geminian trait quite exhausting, for Geminians want more and newer experiences constantly.

The speed at which Gemini changes can be daunting. But the easy sociability of Gemini is charming and the high level of energy which this mutable Sign gives off can be as refreshing as a whiff of pure oxygen.

The need for constant mental stimulation makes boredom a major problem. Bright and quick, but not long on consistency and constancy, Gemini, like the wind, tends to go around obstacles rather than confront them directly.

Gemini loves games and tricks, including the complex social games people play involving gossiping and intrigue. These tricks are not so much intended to deceive as they are the mental response to any attempt to solidify this airy Sign. Air must be allowed to move freely or it becomes stagnant.

Free-spirited Gemini believes that everything belongs to everybody, so honesty is a flexible issue. It's important for Gemini to learn the rules of property and that "borrowing" also means putting back. However, I caution you that disciplining Gemini is a little like trying to bottle the wind.

Gemini key characteristics:

Communicative	Superficial
Quick-witted	Scattered
Curious	Trite
Variety-seeking	Distracted
Mobile	Fickle
Spontaneous	Nervous
Mental	Insubstantial

PLANETS IN GEMINI

Geminian energy is fast and variable. The most mental of the Signs, the airiest of the Air Signs, its energy enlivens and quickens. Lacking emotional sensitivity, Gemini's effect on Planets naturally sensitive and sympathetic can be detrimental because it causes them to function against their natural grain. Moon, for example, will think about emotions abstractedly rather than actually feel them.

Key Concepts
SUN

My purpose is to learn all I can and make connections using the information.

I am versatile, witty, verbal, logical, mental, changeable, social, devious, perceptive, inconsistent, amoral.

MOON

I need socializing, intellectual activity, interactive relationships, versatility, lightness, mental stimulation, talkativeness, gathering information.

I feel cared for when I am appreciated for my wit and intelligence, freed from routine, communicated with verbally.

I'm most comfortable in environments where there is mental stimulation going on at all times, where there is more than one thing going on, where it is highly sociable.

MERCURY

My mind works rapidly, changeably, flexibly, associatively, logically, curiously, superficially, eclectically.

I learn when my curiosity is provoked, when I can socialize.

I communicate easily, verbally, nervously, brilliantly, with versatility, eagerly, nonstop.

As the ruler of Gemini, Mercury is most at home in this Sign. Both Sign and Planet represent the quest for connections between Self and the environment. Mercury and Gemini both seek knowledge and enjoy change.

VENUS

I express love through talking, playing, witticisms, doing unusual things, bringing new and interesting information.

I want mental stimulation, lightness, repartee, change, freedom, flirtations, communication.

My taste is for the intellectual, literary, changeable, multifaceted, popular.

I feel loved by being interactive, given space, communicated with verbally.

MARS

I act flexibly, intelligently, light-heartedly, inconsistently, changeably, superficially, socially.

I am motivated by information, ideas, communication.

I get angry unpredictably, intellectually, logically, verbally, inconsistently.

My libido is flirtatious, playful, verbal, uncommitted, facile.

CANCER

Element: Water
Mode: Cardinal
Planetary Ruler: Moon
Zodical Image: The Crab
Body Part: The Breasts, Stomach
Thematic Principle: I Feel
Key Idea: The Mother
Exhaltation: Jupiter, Neptune
House Affinity: The Fourth
Polarity: Receptive

Cancer symbolizes the sheer tenacity of the life-force. Its image, the Crab, is known for the ability to hold on. It is the World Mother who brings forth abundant life, even in the face of death.

The quintessential Sign of nurturance — of family, home, roots, tradition — the fourth Sign of the Zodiac symbolizes the emotional faculties at the wellspring of all human existence, which are exemplified by the mother-child bonding process. This inherent trait of nurturance gives Cancer a mothering quality and Cancerians enjoy taking care of others.

The first Water Sign, Cancer represents emotional relatedness. Highly sensitive, Cancer constantly monitors the environment to assess the feeling tone. No matter what façades are put up, Cancer will know if bad "vibes" are about, for it feels without rationalizing, flowing as water flows.

Emotional security is a primary need for Cancer. Without it, this Sign develops patterns of fear and dependency, and it's tenacity can become clinginess. Deprived of the love and nurturing it needs, Cancer may withdraw into itself or revert to infantile behavior. Cancer needs a quiet place all its own for those times when the world gets to be too much, especially if the atmosphere is saturated with negative feelings.

The security of the home is absolutely vital to Cancer's development. A secure Cancer is happy, loving, and giving. An insecure Cancer is miserable, clinging, and demanding, which can be interpreted as selfish but in reality is a pitiful attempt to hold on to a sense of security when love is perceived to be in short supply.

Moon-ruled Cancer is moody and changeable, "going through phases," and needs old familiar things around, especially when there is emotional turmoil, to symbolize the security of home. Some adult Cancers still sleep with a much-loved teddy bear from childhood! Sometimes Cancer collects material possessions of a sentimental nature as a substitute for the nurturing it feels is lacking.

Food-oriented Cancer's body parts, the breasts and stomach, are the source of nourishment for new life and the place where nutrients are processed to sustain life. Round of face (Moon-faced) and body, soft of flesh and feature, in times of stress, Cancer will soothe itself with "comfort food" and weight gain can become a problem.

Cancer loves family outings and occasions — birthdays, holidays, anniversaries — that call for getting together and reliving the past, especially when food is a part of the celebration.

In today's increasingly fragmented culture, with home and family disrupted by divorce or distance, Cancerians often suffer greviously because their intense need for intimate connection to family goes unfulfilled. As a result, they forge family-type relationships with friends.

Cancer key characteristics:

Sensitive	Oversensitive
Nurturing	Dependent
Intuitive	Illogical
Traditional	Living in the past
Comfort-loving	Acquisitive
Food-oriented	Self-indulgent
Tenacious	Clinging

PLANETS IN CANCER

Cancer emotionalizes, and planets which symbolize the emotional realm do well here, but when mental faculties are colored by emotional response, rational judgement may be lacking. Cancer has the beneficial effect of softening harsher planetary energies.

KEY CONCEPTS
SUN

My purpose is to feel deeply, care strongly, nurture.

I am sensitive, shy, domestic, old-fashioned, imaginative, psychic, intimate, security conscious, tenacious, fearful, cranky.

MOON

I need security, comfortableness, ample food, humor, nurturing, intimacy, home, sentiment, protection.

I feel cared for when I am fed the food I love, babied, made to feel secure.

I'm most comfortable in environments where it's cozy and quiet and I feel safe with familiar things around me.

There is an exceptionally close relationship between Cancer and its ruler, the Moon. Both are represented by the lunar symbolism of the World Mother. Moon in Cancer amplifies the Cancerian nature.

MERCURY

My mind works psychically, historically, intuitively, emotionally, tenaciously, illogically, worriedly.

I learn when I have a personal interest in a subject, when my imagination is fired.

I communicate personally, creatively, non-verbally, sensitively, opportunistically.

VENUS

I express love through nurturing, remembering little things, holding on, wanting to set up a home and family.

I want closeness, sensitivity, security, nurturance, home, children, safety.

My taste is old-fashioned, sentimental, classical, personal, imaginative.

I feel loved by being nurtured and being intimate.

MARS

I act protectively, sensitively, imaginatively, moodily, parentally, indirectly, babyishly.

I am motivated by safety, nurturance, closeness, family, familiarity.

I get angry emotionally, sullenly, privately, moodily.

My libido is romantic, intimate, nurturing, imaginative.

LEO

Element: Fire
Mode: Fixed
Planetary Ruler: Sun
Zodical Image: The Lion
Body Part: The Heart
Thematic Principle: I Create
Key Idea: I Express
Exhaltation: Pluto
House Affinity: The Fifth
Polarity: Active

Leo, like the heart which represents it, symbolizes the center where the life-force emanates, from which all energy flows and returns. It is the creative individual energizing potential into reality.

As the natural occupant of the fifth House, which concerns children and pleasures, Leo has a delightful — or irritating, depending on your point of view — childlike quality and strong needs for self-expression and admiration. Full of the joys of discovering life and brimming with confidence, Leo demands praise and recognition. An audience of one will do if it must, but audience Leo must have. Many actors have a strong Leo, which is understandable considering Leo's need for applause.

This intense need for personal recognition is sometimes interpreted as egotism or showing off, but in truth it is the need to appear impressive for one's deeds. Leo's zodiacal image is the lordly Lion, king of the beasts, and Leo fancies itself as King, or Queen. Like the Sun, its ruler, Leo sees itself as the lighted center of the universe. Still, there is no real arrogance to the cries of "Look at me!," for Leo at any age gives off the warmth of the Sun for others to bask in. Though the Leo personality desires the limelight, once it has claimed center stage it makes room for everyone else and hands out favors with regal grace and generosity.

Though sometimes seeming to be a braggart, Leo takes pride in personal integrity and is scrupulously honest. Be sure to have your facts straight before accusing a Leo of any dishonesty, for if honor is wrongly impugned, Leo will react with massive disdain. A Leo in a sulk is magnificent to behold. Remember that Leo is a fixed Sign and that fixity, while giving persistence and perserverance, can also result in stubbornness. An injured lion is a dangerous beast.

Straightforward and direct, Leo's needs are fairly simple and easy to meet, for Leo does not carry the subtleties and complexities of some of the other Signs. Leo dislikes being alone and needs others, if only for their acknowledgment of its efforts, and usually can be found at the center of an adoring mob. Leo makes friends easily, often attracting shyer types who bask in the limelight Leo generates. Loyal Leo can be fiercely protective of those taken under its wing.

The absolute worst thing anyone can do to a Leo is to withhold approval and praise. I do not advise any parent to attempt to control a Leo child by this method, for it will only lead to resentment and withdrawal. High-spirited and strong-willed, though something of a show-off, Leo is warm-hearted and generous, bestowing boons upon all.

A natural leader, once a goal is set, Leo, not easily discouraged because of the desire to be important, will follow up with a great deal of persistence and devotion.

Leo key characteristics:

Dramatic	Attention-seeking
Generous	Dominating
Honorable	Keeping up appearances
Courageous	Self-glorifying
Fun-loving	Self-centered
Self-expressive	Insensitive
Warm	Overbearing

PLANETS IN LEO

A fixed Sign, Leo tends to stabilize. Planets in Leo have a lot of steady energy and behave honorably. Pride, self-esteem, and a sense of the importance of what one does are issues.

KEY CONCEPTS
SUN

My purpose is to unself-consciously and creatively express the Self.

I am noble, open, warmhearted, demonstrative, unsuspicious, generous, playful, creative, attention-seeking, tyrannical.

The Sun is Leo's ruler and although the correspondence between Planet and Sign is apt, unlike the Sun, which is the center of our solar system, Leo is *not* the center of the Zodiac.

MOON

I need creativity, playfulness, nobility, loyalty, grandness, respect, affection, notice, praise.

I feel cared for when I am given special attention and feedback, appreciated for my creative efforts, played with.

I'm most comfortable in environments where it is elegant, grand, personally self-expressive.

MERCURY

My mind works broadly, vitally, clearly, cogently, dogmatically, conceitedly, vividly, forcefully, pridefully.

I learn when my heart is in it, when I get positive feedback.

I communicate dramatically, convincingly, enthusiastically, warmly, energetically, opinionatedly.

VENUS

I express love through generosity, passion, loyalty, showing off, being complimentary and protective.

My taste is stylish, bold, individualistic, expensive, attention-getting.

I want glamour, affection, excellence, power, self-expression, attention, praise, appreciation.

I feel loved when I'm the center of attention and catered to.

MARS

I act grandly, honorably, openly, romantically, courageously, playfully, affectionately, egocentrically, temperamentally.

I am motivated by love, loyalty, power.

I get angry dramatically, loudly, vehemently, stubbornly.

My libido is romantic, passionate, demonstrative, playful.

VIRGO

Element: Earth
Mode: Mutable
Planetary Ruler: Mercury
Zodical Image: Young Woman Carrying a Sheaf of Grain
Body Part: The Abdomen and Intestines
Thematic Principle: I Learn and Analyze

Key Idea: The Craftsman
Exhaltation: None
House Affinity: The Sixth
Polarity: Receptive

Virgo symbolizes the quest for perfection, the Ideal which resides in the divine essence and the knowledge that is harvested from the fields of experience.

The most mental of the earth Signs, work is its hallmark, duty its cannon. Virgo pays attention to detail, sometimes to the point of excessive caution, and places a high value on orderliness and neatness. Rarely is Virgo sloppy. In fact, the Virgo child may be quite openly critical of its elders' messy habits.

Quality of workmanship is paramount to Virgo, which needs little praise or acknowledgment for its efforts. Being satisfied with the knowledge that the job has been done well, Virgo will work long and hard to meet its own high standards. Once it has done so, criticism from others is irrelevant. Virgo is exemplar of the motto, "Anything worth doing is worth doing well," and won't attempt a task unless confident of doing the job right. Consequently, Virgo's work is far more careful and craftsmanshiplike than that of others. The downside of this excellent quality is that Virgo may become disheartened when it fails to live up to its own expectations and give up in dismay. Timely encouragement can turn the tide by showing Virgo that someone cares, for rarely does Virgo ask openly for help, preferring to struggle through and work out a problem without bothering others.

Excellent critical faculties make Virgo very hard on itself and on others as well. Self-critical in the quest for perfection, it can criticize others faults only too easily. Virgo needs to learn that others don't necessarily appreciate having their flaws pointed out to them.

Interested in learning all there is to know about the world, with an emphasis on practical skills and how to use tools, Virgo has little or no trouble with school. Learning is a positive pleasure and the many details that must be mastered are fascinating to the Virgo. One reason Virgo enjoys developing skills is that it likes being useful to others.

Virgo tends to be self-effacing. Honesty is another Virgo characteristic. In fact, it can be honest to a fault, going overboard in critical self-evaluation and not giving itself credit for its own virtues, which it finds small-scale. Secretly, Virgo knows that perfection is not possible in this imperfect world (though that does not stop it from trying as hard as it can) and the knowledge gives a sense of humility which can sometimes escalate into timidity and lack of confidence. Although Virgo will work hard without approval, feedback, or praise, it does need to know that others accept it for itself.

Ego-building is difficult for this Sign and mastering skills is an excellent tool for this difficult task. Virgo is already adept at self-criticism and self-analysis. What it needs is to be effective in the real world of things and to feel accepted.

Though Virgo has high esthetic standards, there must be a use for its work. Art for art's sake doesn't interest this practical Sign, which always looks toward that which serves a purpose. Totally serious, Virgo aims at what will be effective, not what will be fun. Virgos need to learn that "All work and no play makes Jack a dull boy," or Jill a dull girl. Play that serves a learning purpose works well.

Often super-concerned about health, Virgo worries about sickness, sometimes to the point of hypochondria. Being taught the rules of good health and gently nursed when sick will ease this problem. Virgo also needs to know that health routines will be scrupulously followed and will insist they be performed in the right order. Being allowed to do personal hygienic tasks in a regular order helps give Virgo a sense of security where health is concerned.

Virgo key characteristics:

Intelligent	Worrying
Discriminating	Fussy
Analytical	Nit-picking
Logical	Boring
Orderly	Routinized
Critical	Self-effacing
Differentiating	Lacking perspective

PLANETS IN VIRGO

Like the shy person who never wants to go first, Virgo is deferential and tones down the planetary energies, making them function in a more precise and orderly manner than usual, restricting and bending all to a practical end. Playful or pleasure-loving planets find Virgo, ruler of the sixth House of work and duty, an uneasy fit. Venus, for example, will often express as devotion to duty, not passion.

KEY CONCEPTS
SUN

My purpose is humbly to be of service through exacting discriminations.

I am methodical, practical, thorough, modest, hardworking, uptight, perfectionistic, critical, sensible, orderly, exact.

MOON

I need to be analytical, detailed, modest, perfect, useful, helpful, precise, kind, sensible.

I feel cared for when I am noticed for my effectiveness, appreciated for my skill and insight, nursed when sick, given healthy food, kept on a routine.

I'm most comfortable in environments where things are in their proper place, regular order prevails, I'm clean and neat, and things make sense to me.

MERCURY

My mind works thoroughly, practically, specifically, sequentially, detailedly, critically, rationally, ingeniously.

I learn when I see the sense of it, when it is of service to someone, when there is order to the process.

I communicate logically, factually, humbly, self-effacingly, precisely, intellectually.

Mercury, Virgo's ruler, functions especially well here. While Mercury in Gemini collects knowledge with no particular purpose in mind, in Virgo, Mercury's knowledge is sorted and analyzed in order to be put to practical use.

VENUS

I express love through care taking, attention to detail, noticing small things, being useful, offering helpful criticism.

I want perfection, practicality, purity, thoroughness, discernment, cleanliness, order, organization.

My taste is exacting, clean, simple, orderly, detailed.

I feel loved by attention, being catered to, being provided with an orderly environment.

MARS

I act properly, helpfully, practically, thoroughly, manipulatively, uptightly, detailedly, healthfully.

I'm motivated by perfection, practicality, health, useful endeavor.

I get angry logically, analytically, quietly, critically.

My libido is knowledgeable, earthy, repressed, bawdy.

LIBRA

Element: Air
Mode: Cardinal
Planetary Ruler: Venus
Zodical Image: The Scales
Body Part: The Kidneys and Lumbar Region
Thematic Principle: I Unite
Key Idea: Relationship
Exhaltation: Saturn
House Affinity: The Seventh
Polarity: Active

Libra symbolizes the striving for balance in all things and, by extension, relationships, from the personal to the abstract.

The seventh Sign of the Zodiac, ruled by Venus, Libra has a strong love for whatever is harmonious, from love to the arts, and presides over both marriage and esthetics.

A natural romantic, Libra is forever on the lookout for a partner and feels the "urge to merge" at an early age. Libra without an intimate relationship suffers the pangs of loneliness acutely and may have a series of "best friends," for Libra is not good at being alone and will seek a companion for any task or activity, such as studying or going shopping.

Like its element, Air, Libra needs to circulate constantly. The main characteristic of Libra is that it cannot consider itself without being in relationship to someone or something. It is very much the "I-thou" Sign, exemplifying "people who need people," with its pleasant warmth and affectionate nature.

Naturally charming and graceful, gentle Libra recoils from anything that is unpleasant or ugly. When it encounters such, it will make a valiant effort to restore balance and harmony. Concerned with appearances, refined Libra pays careful attention to dress and looks. Not mere vanity, this is an extension of the Libran love of beauty and harmony.

Adept at getting along with others, Libra is often the mediator or negotiator. Getting along can appear to be giving in, but Libra, rather like an insect that changes its coloration to blend in with the environment, by adapting protects itself without changing its real nature.

A Cardinal Sign, Libra takes the initiative, but this process may be so subtle as to go unnoticed, for Libra can lead by following or rule by consensus.

While Librans may not have artistic talent themselves, they greatly appreciate the arts but prefer that which is classical or traditional and not disturbing either to the intellect or the senses. Intense feelings throw Libra off balance. Lovers of beautiful objects, Librans are drawn to color and fine clothing and are fond of trinkets.

The Libran desire for perfect harmony results in an inability to make decisions. In the effort to balance the scales, Libra sees both sides of the question with great clarity and has trouble weighing one or the other enough to be decisive. Watching a Libran struggle with even-handedness is like watching a tennis match in progress. Therefore, it's best not to impose decision-making on Librans before they are mature enough to take responsibility. However, with Libra there is always another side, and this trait makes Libra, who abhors argument, a superb peacemaker. Diplomats and others whose job it is to pour oil on troubled waters frequently have a Libra component in their charts.

Libra key characteristics:

Relating	Approval-seeking
Peaceful	Procrastinating
Diplomatic	Indecisive
Refined	Insipid
Impartial	Inconsistent
Artistic	Conventional

PLANETS IN LIBRA

Ego-oriented Planets suffer here while the relationship-oriented ones do very well. Generally speaking, Planets in Libra will bend toward getting along with others even at their own expense, taking on Air qualities, which makes Libra placements seem superficial and concerned only with appearances instead of with deeper issues.

Libra shows Venus, its ruler, at her best — bringer of love and patron of the arts. As Saturn, the planet of endurance, is exalted here, the combination makes Libra the marriage Sign. Thus, Libra relates to the greater social world, which accounts for the accusation of superficiality and peace-at-any-price.

KEY CONCEPTS
SUN
My purpose is to fairly and gracefully reconcile opposites and see both sides of all issues, to establish harmony whenever possible.

I am fair, gracious, beauty-loving, mental, kind, sensitive, analytical, vacillating, indecisive, conflict-avoiding.

MOON
I need harmony, art, grace, fairness, balance, sociability, intellectuality, calmness, diplomacy.

I feel cared for when I am appreciated for my social diplomacy, respected for my judgement, acknowledged for my fairness, given focused attention.

I'm most comfortable in environments where there is harmony and beauty, graciousness and well-being, a sense of balance.

MERCURY
My mind works balancedly, aesthetically, intellectually, fairly, judiciously, cooperatively, indecisively, waveringly.

I learn in a non-competitive situation, when I have one-to-one contact, when my aesthetic sense is stimulated, when I feel I am being treated fairly.

I communicate with grace, diplomacy, persuasion, gentleness, sophistication, hesitation, by examining both sides of an issue.

VENUS
I express love through being accommodating, making things lovely and pleasant, affection, giving attention, discussion, careful weighing of both sides of an issue.

My taste is harmonious, balanced, graceful, comfortable, sensual, charming.

I want beauty, harmony, fairness, intimacy, socializing, give and take.

I feel loved when I am given affection, allowed to share pleasure and beauty, treated fairly, not subjected to argument, protected from strife.

MARS
I act well-balanced, well-mannered, diplomatically, fairly, gracefully, conciliatorily, indecisively, passive-aggressively, selflessly.

I am motived by balance, harmony, fairness, beauty, affection, approval.

I get angry inconsistently, verbally, with difficulty, defensively, passive-aggressively.

My libido is unselfish, gentle, conventional, affectionate.

SCORPIO

Element: Water
Mode: Fixed
Planetary Ruler: Pluto
Zodiacal Image: The Scorpion (or Serpent), The Eagle
Body Part: The Sexual and Execretory Organs
Thematic Principle: I Will
Key Idea: Transformation
Exhaltation: Uranus
House Affinity: The Eighth
Polarity: Receptive

Scorpio symbolizes the process of transformation. It deals with life's ultimate mysteries — sex and death, rebirth and regeneration.

The eighth Sign of the Zodiac, Scorpio is concerned with the processes of destruction and renewal. It is the most powerful Sign, and its efforts will be on a high or low level depending on the motivation involved.

Transformation may seem an odd word to use in connection with children, but Scorpio at any age is vitally interested in the transformative process, of which sex and death are but the two most obvious physical manifestations. Even small Scorpios are intensely involved with their inner lives. There is always a lot going on underneath what you see on the surface.

Sensitive to the point of being psychic, Water Sign Scorpio is aware of the feeling-tone of the atmosphere and may seem to have X-ray vision, looking straight inside another person and seeing what is meant to be concealed, which can be disconcerting to say the least.

Most misunderstood of the Signs, Scorpio may seem to be self-involved and brooding, but this is usually because Scorpio discovers early that depth and breadth of feeling are subject to derision, rightly concluding that silence is better than ridicule.

Intensity is the most evident characteristic of Scorpio, which represents the desire principle, and what is desired is craved fiercely. This intensity can be frightening to those who do not share it. Scorpio possesses immense will and the tremendous emotional force behind everything Scorpio wants or does often makes emotional expression difficult. The result may be a quiet child who likes to spend a lot of time alone, just thinking, trying to figure out the puzzle of life. There's not much a parent can do about this except to allow the child time and space to be alone without demanding to know what the matter is. The intensity of Scorpio's feelings should never be underestimated.

Well-known as the Sign of sexuality, the Scorpio vibration sometimes causes parents to wonder about their child, who, theoretically at least, does not possess sexuality yet. There is a relationship between Scorpio and sexuality, but it is less concerned with the sexual act than the sheer power of human sexuality, which spawns the most potent of human emotions. It is these depths that fascinate Scorpio.

Sex and death are the ultimate human mysteries, and Scorpio loves mysteries of all kinds. A natural detective, Scorpio will track down whatever information is needed to solve a particular puzzle, putting the pieces together with both patience and enjoyment. Its watery quality allows it to flow freely while its fixed quality gives perseverance.

Scorpio does not love lightly and can be seriously injured by those who have no respect for the feelings of others. Though extremely sensitive, Scorpio won't slink off and hide when hurt. It will fight back, vehemently.

Luckily, Scorpio is slow to anger and unless there is repeated torment is unlikely to use that famous sting. Still, it is well to be aware that Scorpio's feelings do not fade away quickly. When deeply hurt, Scorpio can carry the wound for a lifetime. For this reason, Scorpio is cautious when making friends and will prefer a few trusted and long-time buddies to the crowd.

Respect is important to Scorpio, but approval less so. Not that Scorpio doesn't appreciate praise, it's just that usually it is too involved with inner matters to notice or care what others think.

Scorpio is often attracted to the supernatural and the arcane. Gothic stories and tales of vampires will be the chosen reading material and there is a taste for horror movies. This isn't a love of gore, however, but a thirst to know what goes on in other people's minds, to understand human nature at its most basic. Scorpio may become interested in psychology and the occult arts, having no fear of the darker side of human nature, but wanting to explore it.

Scorpio key characteristics:

Passionate	Possessive
Secretive	Paranois
Intense	Brooding
Mysterious	Impenetrable
Sexual	Compulsive
Fierce	Vindictive
Regenerating	Power abusing

PLANETS IN SCORPIO

Scorpio tends to increase both emotionality and inflexibility, bending planetary energies to its prime goal of transformation, energizing the relationship-oriented Planets toward transforming the partner. Because Scorpio personalizes, Planets here will be affected by an emotional intenseness which can hinder the perceptual and cognitive ones.

KEY CONCEPTS
SUN

My purpose is to probe the mysteries by going to the limit, falling apart, and rebuilding.

I am intense, sexual, perceptive, private, suspicious, committed, extreme, vengeful, catalytic, magical, healing.

MOON

I need intensity, commitment, emotions, depth, safety, intimacy, perception, control, power.

I feel cared for when I am appreciated for my intense perceptions, allowed to take my time trusting, seen as deeply fascinating, not forced to communicate verbally until I am ready to speak.

I'm most comfortable in environments where my intensity doesn't bother others, my feelings are respected even if they are not understood, I'm allowed to have my emotions.

The Moon is the sphere of the unconscious and Scorpio is deeply concerned with piercing the secrets of the fathomless inner world. It is said by some that the Moon suffers when in Scorpio, but this seems to me to be only because here the Moon expresses herself with a great intensity of feeling, which threatens those who routinely hide their feelings.

MERCURY

My mind works deeply, sensitively, perceptively, suspiciously, unerringly, determinedly, analytically, emotionally, psychically, retentively.

I learn when I see the need, when there is a hidden factor or a puzzle involved, when I'm fascinated by the subject, when I'm left alone to understand in my own way.

I communicate diffusely, cryptically, sarcastically, reticently, succinctly, confrontationally.

VENUS

I express love through passion, commitment, renewal, sexuality, trust, transforming, probing, experiencing to the fullest.

I want intensity, commitment, passion, control, power, feelings, total intimacy.

My taste is extreme, complicated, aware, definite, bizarre, personal.

I feel loved when I have deep intimacy on all levels, my emotions are understood, my intensity is respected and not feared.

MARS

I act passionately, seductively, intensely, with dedication, dangerously, riskily, suspiciously, obsessively, with discipline.

I'm motivated by power, self-discipline, taking risks, proving myself,

self-transformation, esoteric knowledge, extreme experiences.

I get angry smolderingly, intensely, slowly, vengefully, destructively, powerfully.

Prior to the discovery of the Planet Pluto and its subsequent assignment to the rulership of Scorpio, Mars was considered to be Scorpio's ruler and some today call it the co-ruler of the Sign. In any case, Mars still has a special relationship to Scorpio. Here, Mars' energy combines combustively with Scorpio, intensifying what is already intense.

SAGITTARIUS

Element: Fire
Mode: Mutable
Planetary Ruler: Jupiter
Zodiacal Image: The Archer, or Centaur
Body Part: The Thighs
Thematic Principle: I Seek
Key Idea: Freedom
Exhaltation: None
House Affinity: The Ninth
Polarity: Active

Sagittarius symbolizes the seeker after truth. It is concerned with all manifestations of the higher mind and universal values.

The ninth Sign of the Zodiac, ruled by magnificent, magnanimous Jupiter, Sagittarius signifies the religious and intellectual institutions that bind society together and advance learning and morals. The Archer loves personal liberty and intellectual freedom and looks for the absolute truth underlying all causes, for the unifying principle at the center that binds all things into a single whole.

The third mutable Sign is far-reaching conceptually and intellectually, eclectic in the quest for knowledge. Able to switch from subject to subject not only with ease but with a speed that can make more restrictive Signs dizzy, Sagittarius' curiosity is neverending. It wants to know the answer to every question it can think of, and it can think of some you never thought of! Thus, Sagittarius appreciates older people for their wisdom and experience and can frequently be found exploring the library's treasures for the answers to those burning questions about the Universe and everything in it. Though learning fascinates this Sign, it is too concerned with the broad picture to bother with the details.

Eager as it is to learn about everything, Sagittarius doesn't like to stay with anything forever. Its mutable nature is quickly ready to move on to another field of knowledge. Thus, Sagittarius may have trouble settling down to a single area of learning. It wants to roam through the stacks at the library and see what's there. Sagittarius does not like to be fenced-in or tied down. Commitment comes hard here.

Sagittarius enjoys sports and games of all kinds. Attracted to the outdoors, the Sign likes to be active physically and chafes at restrictions on movement. Despite its fiery nature, Sagittarians have their feet firmly on the ground and can ordinarily be trusted to exercise discipline and self-control over their actions. Sagittarius needs the freedom to wander where and when it will and to travel, even if it's only to the grocery store and back. They want their own wheels as soon as soon as possible, even if that means only a bicycle.

Sagittarian study habits tend toward sloppiness. Prone to jumping to conclusions without taking time to peruse the matter sufficiently to warrant a conclusion, Sagittarius often finds it has to back down because of missing a few facts along the way.

Don't expect Sagittarius to keep the environment neat as a pin. Though personal cleanliness is not an issue, Sagittarians are perpetually on the way to somewhere else and find the details of room-keeping too tedious to bother with. Why hang up those jeans and fold that sweater when you know you are going to wear them again soon? Better to spend the time with a friend or a book. It's the big picture that counts.

Like its image, the Archer, Sagittarius shoots his arrows as high as they will go, out of sight, in search of the ends of being and ideal grace.

Sagittarius key characteristics:

Outgoing	Opinionated
Expansive	Careless of details
Optimistic	Deluded
Ethical	Judgemental
Freedom-loving	Commitment phobe
Exploratory	Exaggerating
Straightforward	Blunt

PLANETS IN SAGITTARIUS

Sagittarius brings optimism and lightheartedness, freeing up the stodgy. It's desire for freedom works best with the fast-moving energies, but Planets of relationship and feeling get short shrift here as they aren't allowed to operate according to their true natures. Jupiter-ruled Sagittarius confers high ethical standards.

KEY CONCEPTS
SUN

My purpose is to move toward an ideal goal, positively affirm life, and optimistically shoot for the stars.

I am optimistic, adventurous, humorous, philosophical, open, seeking, metaphysical, clumsy, blunt.

MOON

I need freedom, learning, adventure, laughter, travel, optimism, playfulness, honesty.

I feel cared for when I am allowed to roam free, acknowledged for my wisdom, played with, laughed with, taken to new places.

I'm most comfortable in environments where there is learning going on, no limits are placed on me, it's fun, I can go somewhere.

MERCURY

My mind works broadly, eclectically, inspiredly, openly, farsightedly, scatteredly, undisciplinedly.

I learn when I'm interested, when there's a philosophical content, on a broad scale, when I travel.

I communicate wordily, lengthily, bluntly, zealously, openly, with humor.

Mercury, though said to be in "detriment" in Sagittarius, seems to suffer only in that Sagittarius doesn't like dealing with details. But fleet Mercury is not unhappy in mutable Sagittarius, for there it can communicate quickly and without restriction.

VENUS

I express love through being joyous and generous, giving the other person lots of space and freedom, sharing its adventures, communicating its wisdom, engendering laughter.

My taste is spirited, outdoorsy, learned, classical, exotic.

I want freedom, adventure, good times, travel, meaning, soul-growth.

I feel loved when I can laugh, have fun, and be free.

MARS

I act positively, zealously, extravagantly, humorously, spiritedly, uncommittedly, recklessly.

I'm motivated by knowledge, freedom, the big picture, adventure, experience in foreign countries, an ideal world.

I get angry extravagantly, humorously, energetically, philosophically.

My libido is open, adventurous, playful, uncommitted, idealistic.

CAPRICORN

Element: Earth
Mode: Cardinal
Planetary Ruler: Saturn
Zodiacal Image: The Goat
Body Part: The Knees
Thematic Principle: I Use
Key Idea: The Builder
Exhaltation: Mars
House Affinity: The Tenth
Polarity: Receptive

Capricorn symbolizes father, authority, the social order, pragmatism, and the slow but sure ascent to the top of the heap.

Driven by ambition to succeed according to the world's rules, the Goat endures. Like the tortoise in the story of the hare and the tortoise, Capricorn is still going long after the fleet of foot have dropped by the wayside. The knee, that joint so vital to the upward climb, is appropriately Capricorn's body part.

The tenth Sign of the Zodiac, Capricorn builds what is practical and useful to society, looking to authority figures to determine the right way of doing things, wanting to know exactly what the rules are. Then, while meticulously sticking to the game plan, Capricorn glories in success.

Seeming old even when young, Capricornians are mature beyond their calendar age, looking upon life as extremely serious business. Even in play, they will give off the concentrated air of an adult busy at real work. Often there is attraction to older persons who can teach Capricorn something, or those higher up the socioeconomic ladder who can be helpful to Capricorn's ambitions. Capricorn has no time or patience for foolish pursuits.

Efficiency is Capricorn's watchword. What works is accepted and applauded, what does not work is discarded without a backward glance because everything must serve the same end: usefulness. Thus, feelings will be tempered with reality. Capricorn asks, even of love, "Will this work?" and if the answer is, "No," it turns away.

Capricornians don't mind making mistakes, for they learn by them, but they expect valid direction from adults responsible for setting the standards. Quick to spot flaws in the system of authority, Capricorns either fill in the blanks themselves or take over the system. Disorganized or indecisive parents may find a little martinet-in-the-making systemizing their lives.

The main problem here is that adults easily become accustomed to the pseudo-adult behavior of young Capricorns. Coming to rely on it, they expect it as a given, thus depriving the Capricorn child of the real parenting it needs. Though Capricorn children enjoy being taken seriously and given responsibility, when the burden is too great they notice that other children don't work so hard and become envious. Capricorn must be allowed to be a child. Playtime may have to be scheduled so that it fits in with an organized way of life, but play Capricorn must, for this Sign produces workaholics.

Taking responsibility is natural to this Sign, and the young can easily shoulder more than their share, more than they are really capable of handling. The wise parent of a Capricorn child will not allow this to happen, no matter how eager the child seems for responsibilities. Adult decisions should not be made by children. Big mistakes can be made by a child required to make adult decisions and the results of these mistakes can be quite damaging to the child's development.

That being said, Capricorn must still be allowed to channel its drive for importance and achievement into projects that it can be proud of and claim as its own. Aimlessness hath no charm for Capricorn.

In school, Capricorn usually excels at those subjects which have a practical end in mind, leaving fantasy to others. Capricorn doesn't want anything that is not real.

Capricorn key characteristics:

Organized	Overstructuring
Serious	Worrying
Practical	Restricting
Ambitious	Materialistic
Disciplined	Rigid
Achieving	Overworking
Methodical	Stiff

PLANETS IN CAPRICORN

Capricorn is more concerned with social values than freedom and innovation. Planets found in this Sign will display an orientation toward reality and being down-to-earth. This doesn't set well with the relationship planets, as feelings aren't famous for pragmatism.

KEY CONCEPTS
SUN

My purpose is to do what must be done in a disciplined and structured way to achieve a practical, useful result.

I am responsible, serious, organized, successful, wry, profound, realistic, conservative, materialistic, status-conscious, repressed.

MOON

I need to be useful, spartan, ambitious, hardworking, organized, down-to-earth, productive, disciplined, controlled.

I feel cared for when I am appreciated and praised for my accomplishments, my feelings are catered to in a practical manner, I am clearly told the rules I must obey.

I'm most comfortable in environments where I feel that things are stable and I can be effective and productive.

MERCURY

My mind works practically, methodically, profoundly, wisely, pointed slowly, ambitiously, ironically.

I learn when I'm given a clear methodology to follow and when I see the use of what I'm learning in the real world.

I communicate dryly, conscientiously, seriously, ironically, carefully, boringly, stiffly.

VENUS

I express love through being useful and helpful, providing security, reliability, attention to duty, helping to achieve.

I want status, meaning, organization, results, money, success, usefulness.

My taste is conservative, elegant, simple, basic, classical, quality-oriented, quiet.

I feel loved when I am made to feel secure and relaxed, when I am appreciated for my practical approach to life.

MARS

I act well-organized, responsible, ethically, seriously, ambitiously, conservatively, dutifully, politically, practically.

I'm motivated by security, integrity, success, usefulness, recognition.

I get angry purposefully, sarcastically, with guilt, or when my efforts fail.

My libido is conservative, earthy, concealed, pagan.

Mars has a special relationship to Capricorn due to its exhaltation there. In Capricorn, Mars' fiery energy is harnessed and disciplined and put to use for practical ends. The smithy forging steel at his furnace is a good image.

AQUARIUS

Element: Air
Mode: Fixed
Planetary Ruler: Uranus
Zodical Image: "The Waterbearer," (A Man Pouring from a Jug)
Body Part: The Ankles
Thematic Principle: I Experiment
Key Idea: The Innovator
Exhaltation: Mercury
House Affinity: The Eleventh
Polarity: Active

Aquarius symbolizes the idea of the individual as a cooperative member of the larger whole, which fosters the understanding that all humanity is one coherent family, a concept which can be grasped only intuitively.

Friendship is the prime concept, for Aquarius sees everyone in the humanitarian spirit of brotherly love, relishing group activity with a social dimension.

Detachment is another faculty of Aquarius, conferring the ability to deal with large issues that would be painful to others by being objective and not getting emotionally involved. This trait makes it difficult for Air Sign Aquarius to handle personal emotions. Aquarians prefer to rationalize feelings rather than to put up with the messy bother of actually feeling them, with the concomitant lack of control that implies. Aquarians love humanity but feel ill at ease in one-on-one relationships of a close personal nature.

However, the ability to separate personal needs from the needs of the group and opt for the larger good, a mental resolution, can serve many positive ends. Aquarians will stand up for what they believe is right and fight against the system for the underdog. Fair-minded, they are good advocates and like to take up causes or work to correct some perceived social ill.

Aquarius tends to be radical and forward-looking, even futuristic, and will go out of its way for new experiences. Traditional ways of thinking and being bore Aquarius, which wants to shape the future in its own vision of how things should be. Aquarius will seek out unusual companions with unusual ideas and thrive in their company.

Though strongly individualistic, Aquarius isn't comfortable unless identified with a group or a cause and makes a commitment to society — and to reforming society — readily and early in life. Although a rebel and a free spirit, Aquarius prefers to reform within the structure of the larger group and is rarely a loner.

Fixed air is a contradiction in terms, as the nature of air is to flow freely and the nature of a fixed Sign is to remain stable. Thus, Aquarius presents a somewhat double-faced picture, a confusing combination, of one forever seeking the new and different while at the same time being extremely difficult to change.

Aquarius may show interest very early in science and politics or activities of an experimental type. Willing to try anything just for the experience, Aquarians especially enjoy the company of those of different races or backgrounds. Prejudice is alien to its nature. To Aquarius, people are people and boundaries and borders are just lines drawn on a map with no real meaning. Equality is Aquarius' battle cry. Perhaps this is because Aquarians secretly feel they are alien to this planet.

Aquarius key characteristics:

Humanitarian	Emotionally cool
Innovative	Rebellious
Independent	Disruptive
Friendly	Uninvolved
Visionary	Impractical
Tolerant	Perverse
Unusual	Unreliable

PLANETS IN AQUARIUS

Aquarius gives stability and stamina. Before Uranus was discovered, rulership of Aquarius was assigned to Saturn, which also has fixed qualities. This Sign can be surprisingly stubborn and inflexible for an Air Sign. Aquarius famed detachment dries out the emotional Planets. The Sun is said to be in detriment in Aquarius, which seems to give a problem with development of the self.

KEY CONCEPTS
SUN

My purpose is to experiment with all established structures, cross all man-made boundaries, experience the new and unusual.

I am unconventional, friendly, humanitarian, original, intuitive, analytical, eccentric, objective, scattered, remote, unfeeling.

MOON

I need uniqueness, objectivity, detachment, open-mindedness, sincerity, rebellion, knowledge, friendship.

I feel cared for when I am appreciated for my intellect, acknowledged as being unique, respected for my unconventionality, treated as a special person.

I'm most comfortable in environments where I can be as unusual as I like, I am not criticized for my tastes, everyone is friendly.

The Moon has a struggle in Aquarius as its native emotionalism feels restricted and confined by Aquarius mental nature and emotional detachment. Moon is naturally attached to the past and what's familiar, while Aquarius is attracted to what is new and unusual, even bizarre.

MERCURY

My mind works originally, intuitively, intellectually, impersonally, brilliantly, rigidly, openly, fixedly.

I learn when I'm intrigued with the unusualness of the subject, I'm allowed to look for an experimental approach.

I communicate readily, logically, intelligently, verbally, dynamically, coldly, detachedly, precisely.

Mercury is exhalted in Aquarius and thus has a special relationship to it. See Chapter III: Mercury.

VENUS

I express love through friendship, being interested and interesting, sharing unusual ideas, understanding the other's position, loyalty.

My taste is avant-garde, scientific, futuristic, humanistic, reformist, eclectic.

I want objectivity, distance, originality, experimentation, friendship, rebellion, universality.

I feel loved when I am given space, friendship, freedom, unusual experiences, new ideas.

Venus in Aquarius tends toward the buddy relationships rather than romantic ones. A pal, or better yet a lot of pals, is preferable to commitment to a steady.

MARS

I act objectively, analytically, coolly, unpredictably, unconventionally, rebelliously, humanely, intuitively.

I'm motivated by the realization of an ideal vision for society and humanity.
I get angry mentally, analytically, coldly, unpredictibly.
My libido is changeable, detached, friendly, unconventional.

PISCES

Element: Water
Mode: Mutable
Planetary Ruler: Neptune
Zodical Image: Two Fish Swimming in Opposite Directions
Body Part: The Feet
Thematic Principle: I Merge
Key Idea: Spiritual Harmony
Exhaltation: Venus
House Affinity: The Twelfth
Polarity: Receptive

Pisces symbolizes that which is most ephemeral in human nature, the desire to unite with the cosmic consciousness.

It represents the urge toward self-sacrifice to a Higher Cause and the soul's struggle with the imperfections of the material plane. Its image of two fish swimming in opposite directions suggests the dichotomy inherent in the fusion of the material and spiritual realms.

Pisces is the most receptive of the receptive Signs, the most watery of the Water Signs, the most mutable of the Mutable Signs. Although this can lead to passivity and inaction, a sort of cringing in the background of life, it can also give a desire to know the deep spiritual truths. Pisces is concerned with and connected to the invisible realm, a psychic sponge that picks up all sorts of information but may have trouble sorting it out.

Therefore, impressionable Pisceans sometimes do not know the difference between their own feelings and what is coming in from the outside, which makes ego development a problem. This Sign identifies with the pain of those around it and Pisceans need to be protected from being around others who are experiencing negative emotions, such as anger, grief, or depression.

In flight from the harshness of the outside world, Pisces takes refuge in fantasy. This should not be construed as lying but as a manifestation of creativity. Although it is important to teach Pisces that there is a difference between the two, it is equally vital not to trample on the delicate inner world of this supersensitive being.

Pisces' compassionate nature reaches out to everything in the Universe that lives and, hating to see any life form hurt, will mount rescue operations, even to the point of saving bugs and flowers. Many a little Pisces has brought home a wilted plant discarded by a careless gardener and gently nursed it back to health.

There is an otherworldly quality to Pisces. They may be absolutely angelic, with a wispy, sweet manner, and faces that are the essence of innocence and purity.

Their dreamy quality sets them apart from the more earthy or materialistic types, and they are fascinated by their feet, which are likely to be especially well-formed, even if delicate. They love to dance and caper about nimbly like wood nymphs. Water attracts them and the occasion of a bath is a time of joyousness.

Religion is often uppermost in Pisces' thoughts. They want answers to mega-questions about where God is and why there is so much suffering in the world. Drawn to the concept of martyrdom in a romantic way, Pisces may become a victim out of a misplaced desire to serve a higher purpose. They need to learn that they are just as good and important as anyone else, that their needs are deserving of being met, and that there should be a limit on helpfulness so that it does not reach the point of self-denial or victimization.

The Piscean nature is extremely easy to manipulate and their eagerness to help can be misused by adults who become dependent on it. Being helpful should not be permitted to spill over into being exploited. Pisces children can safely channel their compassionate energies into caring for a pet or occasionally visiting an ailing older relative, but caution should be exercised not to burden the Pisces child with caring for others beyond its strength.

Tears come easily to Pisces, even the boys, who should definitely not be teased about sensitivity. Pisceans should be encouraged to make appropriate friends, but not coerced into playing with rough children who may frighten or intimidate them.

Shyness is another Piscean trait. If a Pisces child invites you into its private and protected world, go gently. It will be a magical treat.

Pisces key characteristics:

Sensitive	Vulnerable
Imaginative	Escapist
Compassionate	Sentimental
Subtle	Vague
Visionary	Impractical
Artistic	Illusory
Psychic	Self-deceiving

PLANETS IN PISCES

Pisces sensitizes Planets, making them empathetic and receptive to the needs of others. At the same time, it reduces the forcefulness of their energies, especially those concerned with the ego and individuality. Planets here take on an ephemeral quality, which gives them creativity and imaginative ability but may thwart their basic natures. Those planets already attuned to the feeling realm have their natural bent exaggerated, which may weaken their sense of reality. Pisces ruler Neptune is a symbol of egolessness and the yearning to merge into the boundless, undifferentiated depths of Being.

KEY CONCEPTS
SUN

I act to sensitively flow into all things, experiencing the oneness of the All.

I am kind, imaginative, creative, compassionate, idealistic, healing, sweet, attuned, addictive, evasive, unrealistic, self-sacrificing.

MOON

I need sensitivity, devotion, escapism, inspiration, merging, imagination, evasion, attunement, compassion.

I feel cared for when I am allowed to be dreamy, apreciated for my sensitivity, understood, treated gently, protected from negativity.

I'm most comfortable in environments where I can flow into whatever is happening and still feel safe.

MERCURY

My mind works sensitively, non-verbally, whimsically, psychically, indiscriminately, creatively, fantastically, illogically.

I learn when my imagination is stimulated, I love what I'm learning, the atmosphere is gentle and caring.

I communicate with imagination, non-verbally, intuitively, creatively, compassionately, shyly, indistinctly, foggily.

VENUS

I express love through romance, sensitivity, self-sacrifice, eroticism, affection, caring, gentleness.

I want love, romance, blending, peacefulness, fluidity, the ideal.

My taste is sublime, nature-oriented, soft, sensitive, delicate, erotic.

I feel loved when I am in a safely intimate situation, shown kindness and understanding, am allowed to shift and change.

Venus, being exhalted in Pisces, has a special relationship here. Her romantic qualities are exaggerated and idealized. There is a craving for the ideal love which is almost mystical. The idea that love can transcend any obstacle makes this Venus capable of totally selfless dedication.

MARS

I act sensitively, passively, evasively, non-confrontationally, sulkily.

I'm motivated by union, the ideal situation, creativity.

I get angry passively, emotionally, weepily, non-verbally.

My libido is erotic, adoring, sensitive, flowing, psychic.

THE PERSONAL PLANETS

Sun
Moon
Mercury
Venus
Mars

As we all know, science began with the stars, and mankind discovered in them the dominants of the unconscious, the "gods," as well as the curious psychological qualities of the Zodiac: a complete projected theory of human character.

—Carl G. Jung

CHAPTER III

ONE

SUN

The Light of the Soul

Astrologically speaking, the Sun in the chart represents *individuality*, or the essence of Spirit. In metaphysical terms, it is significant of each person's individual connection to the Light Source of the Divine. Psychologically, the Sun represents the archetypal Father concept, which may not have a direct relationship to the actual parent. But the Sun's Sign placement and position in the chart will affect on how the child perceives that parent. In physical terms, which is most often how we observe the Sun in children, it is *vitality*, the state of general health and well-being.

As the Sun is at the center of the solar system, it is at the heart of the chart, telling us what we are *potentially*, not what we will actually become. The Sun determines the *conscious* sense of Self, which is concerned with the life-purpose derived from the life-giving energy of the Divine Source, and the process of coming to consciousness is one that lasts a lifetime. It is readily apparent from the Sun's function as our sense of Self that a person *grows slowly into the Sun Sign*. Thus, the latent Sun Sign energy has only a limited expression in children. That's why following astrological advice based solely on the Sun Sign often does not seem to apply.

However, the solar energy is always present and the child constantly strives toward its proper expression.

When you think of *why* you are here on Earth, *where* you are going in life, and *what* makes you feel important, you are in the Sun's territory, as it is the *purpose in life* and the sense of *"I am."*

Sun key characteristics:

Individuality	Egotistical
The Father Spirit	Authoritarian

Consciousness	Lacking instincts
Vitality	Grandiose
Will	Prideful
Drive	Dictatorial
Creative potential	Self-conscious

The Sun is in its *dignity* in Leo, which it rules, and there is where it most easily expresses itself.

The Sun is in its *exhaltation* in Aries, where it expresses itself most powerfully in terms of intensity of energy. Aries Sun people have tremendous vitality and seemingly inexhaustible energy.

MOON

The Emotional Body

The Moon is a metaphor for all that is instinctive and automatic. The Moon *reacts*. It is feelings, moods, internal physical rhythms, bodily functions and processes. It is response at a pre-verbal, survival level — from the circulation of the blood to "gut" reactions.

Being more connected to their feelings and bodily impulses, and having no other way to express themselves, children resonate emphatically to their Moon Signs, especially during the first seven years. Thus, the Moon is unquestionably the most important factor in a child, and it remains basic to the adult who always retains the "child within," no matter how efficiently the Sun has developed in later life.

Emotional health is a primary area of interest when one gives thought to the rearing of children. Successful adulthood is extremely difficult for children who are emotionally stunted or deprived of love and understanding. Children whose Moon needs are taken care of gradually grow out of their dependence, learning to take care of themselves naturally and properly. On the other hand, children who are *not* cared for in accordance with their deepest inner needs may never learn to respect those needs and honor them in adult life.

This is why the Moon is so important in the lives of children, who, if deprived of the fulfillment of their Moon needs, become immature adults, either forever "needy" or afflicted with self-deprivation. They will thus be unable to form successful relationships because unmet needs go underground where they continue to live in the dark, causing grievous harm.

Cyclical and constantly changing, the Moon is called "the Soul of Life," mediator between the planes of the spiritual (Sun) and material (Earth), reflecting back to us the light of the Sun which it has received into itself. Thus, the Moon is also a metaphor for receptivity, the *yin* principle in oriental philosophy, and is emblematic of the *container* of life, that matrix which nourishes the process of manifestation. It is that protective surrounding which shields the growing, developing entity — be it a seed in the soil, the embryo in an egg, or the fetus in the womb — during its period of gestation. The Moon, of course, is linked with the female menstrual cycle and both complete the cycle in the same 28 days. Thus, the Moon symbolizes our experience, positive or negative, of being *mothered* — nurtured, supported, protected, and loved.

As it is receptive, so it is feminine. The Moon is mother in both the sense of the archetypal Great Mother and the personal mother. The Moon's house, the fourth, represents not only that home in which we were raised; it is the home to which we come at day's end for sustenance, rest, nourishment, and replenishment. Thus, metaphorically speaking, the Moon is where you go when you "go home," and it represents what comforts us and makes us feel secure. It is that knee-jerk place within where reside deepset needs that are paramount to our sense of well-being and security.

Because the Moon shows how and what bonds one person to another, the Moon in the chart of a child and the Moons in the charts of the parents form a powerful triangular matrix. Incompatible Moons make interpersonal relations difficult at a fundamental, almost primordial, level for it is here that we resonate in tune or with disharmony. Understanding the Moon's significance will give you the confidence to fulfill your child's primary needs and develop a smooth emotional relationship.

The Moon represents what we *need*, what makes us feel *loved and cared for*, what is *most comfortable* in our environments. It is where we derive our sense of security.

Moon key characteristics:

Unconscious	Unaware
Feeling-oriented	Oversensitive
Instinctive	Automatic response
Mothering	Dependency
Nurturing	Needy
Changeable	Moody
Fundamental	Reactive

The Moon rules Cancer and there is an exceptionally close relationship between the Planet and the Sign. Both are in contact with the instinctive nature, the realm of the World Mother, and all that is implied by that symbolism. Emotional security is an issue for both. It follows that when the Moon itself is in Cancer there is a strongly lunar nature. All of the typical Cancerian needs are amplified. Moon in Cancer people often have a delightful "loony" sense of humor.

The Moon is *exhalted* in Taurus, which gives it great strength and power. People with this placement are known for robust health and endurance and are real emotional powerhouses. Often they attract special possessions, not necessarily of monetary value, of which they become very fond. In addition, the Moon in Taurus is extremely practical and down-to-earth.

MERCURY

The Light of the Mind

Mercury is multifaceted. A god of many attributes, he governs all aspects of communication — writing, speaking, learning, commerce, and messages of all sorts. The Planet quintessentially of the *mind*, Mercury in a child's chart has to do with learning and mental faculties. It is a prime indicator of intellectual interests and abilities. Thus, Mercury will become more evident in the personality of children as they begin to talk and express themselves verbally. Its influence will increase as they start to learn language skills and to process information mentally instead of instinctively, usually around age seven.

As Mercury in the horoscope relates to the mental development and expression of innate mental qualities, understanding your child's Mercury is equally as valuable as assessing the Sun or Moon. Sign and House position reveal under what circumstances and in which environments a particular child learns best, where the mental interests lie, and how information is assimilated.

In psychological terms, Mercury determines our level of ability to communicate both what we think and what we feel. As Mercury illustrates the process by which we link our internal realm both of feeling and thought to the external world of other people, and how we distinguish between emotion and thinking, he affects our ability to identify and express our feelings, to verbalize emotion. An impaired or restricted Mercury can have difficulties performing these basic functions. Though many astrologers pay little attention to Mercury, perhaps for the very reason that he is quick to change and hard to pin down, I believe a study of the Mercury in a chart, especially one of a child, to be extremely relevant in today's world of ever more sophisticated communications systems, when the arts of communication are vital to everyday life in a way never before known.

The wave of our media-oriented future, with its network of global transport and high-speed forms of communication, makes Mercury, which is exhalted in the Sign of Aquarius, in my opinion the Planet for the Aquarian Age we are now entering.

Mythologically, Mercury is the messenger of the gods, personified as being fleet of foot and quick of mind. On the metaphysical level, Mercury mediates, or delivers messages, between the conscious mind, altered states of consciousness, and the unconscious mind. Dual in nature and the most human of the gods (he had a mortal mother), Mercury represents the archetypes of both the Eternal Youth and the Wise Old Man. Far more complex than generally given credit for, he is, in addition, known as the Trickster God — a thief, liar, and master of deception.

On a spiritual level, Mercury is Thoth-Hermes, guide of souls and purveyor of wisdom. As Lord of the Roads, he occupies a special place concerning travel and commerce, which explains why these areas of life are adversely affected when he is in retrograde motion.

A vital link between child and parents/teachers, Mercury can tell us about the styles of communication between them. If the basic communication style of the adult or the learning environment is in conflict with the child's innate gift, problems arise. These can be overcome by paying attention to the Mercury placement of both child and parent and adjusting accordingly. This is especially important for teaching. Awareness of a child's Mercury component will put the parent or teacher in a better position to facilitate the child's learning process.

For example, Water Sign Mercuries find logical, straight-line (called "left brain") thinking foreign to their diffuse natures and will do better when allowed to learn in their own intuitive way. Conversely, Air Sign Mercuries do best in a strictly mental venue.

It is my opinion that a teacher who knows a child's Mercury proclivities is in a superior position vis-à-vis helping the child to learn. Children are very different from one another, and the same learning environment does not work for all. I believe that many school problems are a result of the uniformity of teaching methods, which results in a lot of square pegs struggling to fit into round holes. As the great fourteenth-century doctor/philosopher Paracelsus wrote, "He that thinks all fruits ripen at the same time knows nothing of strawberries," and this maxim can be applied to how children learn. Those who are allowed to mature in their individual ways, rather than being held to some charted standard, learn more readily and more profoundly.

Caring parents, naturally concerned with their child's mental development, can call on Mercury to put them in a position to open a clear channel for their child's development of the faculty of thought. The process of learning to think is vital and ought to be the primary goal of education. As Plato wrote, "Thoughts rule the world." To quote astrologer Lois Rodden, "All experience stems from thought. Thought is the basis of the universe, the origin of creation, and the doorway of expression. It is not only the instigator of motive but the release mechanism of action."

As parents are the child's first teachers, the pattern of communication in the home sets the tone for what follows with school. Parents who have difficulty communicating with their children can ameliorate the difficulty by checking the Mercury connection between them.

Lois Rodden says, in her excellent book *The Mercury Method of Chart Comparison*, that Mercury "opens the gates between two people," showing a "clear picture of both the attitude and the circumstances" between them. She states, "Mercury is the Planet that carries the awareness, or level of communication, from one *person to another*" (pp. 1–2).

For example, if the child's Mercury is in an Air Sign and the parent's in an Earth sign, their markedly different native styles of thinking and verbalizing sometimes make it seem that these two will never understand each other. But, just knowing where the problem lies is already half the solution. Once the parent understands that its possible to tune in to the child by switching to another channel, so to speak, an easier flow can be attained. Luckily, Mercury, being a mental Planet, is susceptible to adjustment if an effort is made. Since his purpose is to think, analyze, and understand, and since his medium is logic and his tool verbalization, Mercury does not present the difficulties of the murky, emotional Moon realm.

Mercury represents *how the mind works, how we learn,* and *how we communicate.*

Mercury key characteristics:

Idea producer	Overintellectual
Logical	Pedantic
Communicator	Gossip
Messenger	Gadabout
Teacher	Clever
Analyzer	Superficial
Adaptable	Nervous

Mercury rules both Gemini and Virgo. In Gemini, Mercury gathers information, and in Virgo the information is sorted and analyzed.

Mercury's *exhaltation* in Aquarius relates to the cosmic consciousness and it attains to great power in this Sign. Mercury in Aquarius is inspired intuitively by the Higher Self and often experiences flashes of insight.

VENUS

The Desire Nature

Venus represents the *affections,* symbolizes what we *value,* and describes the *social nature.* Its placement reveals how a child loves and wants to be loved, what is important both in material and spiritual terms, what environment is most conducive to socializing, what is appreciated artistically, and in what direction the romantic feelings flow. The process of Venus is through relating — to others, to one's own desire nature, to things, to the outside world.

The Goddess of Love, and Eros, her son, familiar as Cupid but a much more powerful figure, are actually two sides of the same principle. Venus *attracts* — draws toward us by means of Eros (desire) — representing both the qualities in us that attract others and what we find attractive in another person, place, or thing.

The Venus placement governs not only the creation of beauty, but the enjoyment of it, for she is appreciation as well as creation. Venus indicates how we enjoy or appreciate the sensual, the sexual, the romantic, and the beautiful.

In children, Venus begins to express her energies around age four or five when they first begin to have preferences for such matters as how they look, what clothes they wear, what friends they see. When this happens, there is usually the start of an outward reaching and the sense of sharing. At this time, children often spontaneously exhibit artistic effort — drawing, painting, creative building, music making. These products may be offered as gifts, evidencing the Venusian function of giving.

Though clues to the Venus expression may be visible during the early school years, it is when puberty is approaching and the child is first dealing consciously with sexuality that Venus's energy really kicks in. Now, what to wear and how to look are not only a personal preference but are geared to the attracting of others. Both sexes begin to preen, preparing themselves for the experience of the "other" in relationship terms. This is the time of crushes and puppy love, intense same-sex friendships, awareness of and fixation on the physical body, exposure and response to the peer group, and a whole range of emerging wants springing from the innate desire nature.

One of life's great mysteries is what attracts two people to one another romantically. What makes one person stimulate us and another leave us indifferent? This curious human process fascinates us all, but in the teen years and beyond to young adulthood it is of primary concern, leaving much youthful agony in its wake. Venus acts as the *transformer*, not only changing the innocent with no knowledge of sex by giving him or her "carnal knowledge," but the goddess transforms the person *psychologically*.

Who has not seen a teenager become suddenly aware of the opposite sex, previously considered an intruder, suddenly discarding ragged jeans for spiffier wear and treating formerly despised activities such as bathing as all-important rituals? Now, personal hygiene, clothes, and cosmetics become a focus and the teen gazes anxiously and often into the mirror, trying to discover if the felt inner changes are visible. Countless hours are spent both in the bathroom and on the phone in this adventure of discovery of the "other."

Venus represents the deeply feminine part of each of us, male as well as female, telling of our capacity to reach out to others in a loving and affectionate way, not just sexually or erotically.

Venus represents *how we express love, what we want, our taste,* and *what makes us feel loved.*

Venus key characteristics:

Values	Self-indulgence
Attraction	Sentiment
Desires	Cravings
Affections	Dependency

Sexual Love	Promiscuity
Artistic	Superficial
Love of beauty	Vanity

Venus rules Taurus and Libra, both of which exhibit affection and love of beauty. In Taurus she expresses herself in a more earthy, sensuous way, while in Libra she exposes her more refined and artistic side.

Venus in Pisces is *exalted* and works with the transcendental vibrations of Neptune to make love the most transcendent of experiences. Here, romantic love is rendered more altruistic, singing in tune with the harmony of the spheres. Venus in Pisces is inspired, artistic, and often musically talented.

MARS

The Fire of Energy

Mars is known as the god of war because it is his function to create *separateness* in contrast to the function of Venus which is to create unity. Mars is *energy*, most particularly physical energy. It is everything we traditionally think of as masculine — assertiveness, aggressiveness, action, drive, ambition, initiative, combativeness, and courage. Mars is where our primary energy to get things done resides.

When we are feeling angry, that is our Mars energy. When we want to kill for whatever reason, Mars has been engaged. How we express anger and what makes us angry is a function of Mars.

Mars is also identified with masculine sexuality, the forward thrust that is man engaged in sex — or war. This is an energy of unrefined power, like crude oil. In order to be useful for more than procreation and killing, it needs to be regulated, just as a furnace does. A powerful Mars can be used constructively or destructively. Active sports such as the body-contact ones of football, soccer, hockey, polo, and basketball are exhibits of Mars' energy used in a way that simulates the masculine urge toward warlike action without the deadly results. The popularity of these sports shows that many people, especially men, are able to vicariously vent their own aggressive energies through identification with the rough-and-tumble of the players.

Children with a highly active Mars should be encouraged to work out their need to push and shove by participating in active sports. Mars, however, is not particularly concerned with *sportsmanship* or the niceties of how the game is played. He is concerned with one thing only: victory. Sometimes at any price.

The connection between this kind of sports activity and sexual pursuits is obvious but sexuality beyond mere lust will be moderated by other factors, such as Venus and the Moon.

Mars also represents courage and forthrightness. In this guise he is exemplar of all the traditional positive aspects of the male of the species: sexual prowess, courage, energy, action, protectiveness, and valor. He is the valiant warrior-prince, not only aggressor but also protector.

Mythologically, Mars is forever linked with Venus, though this couple was not married. One of the fruits of their cohabitation was Eros, the potent and beautiful young god of love from whom we get the word *erotic*. In Eros, Mars and Venus energies combine to unite lust with love. And one without the other is an imbalance, for both are needed for healthy human development and a satisfying adult life.

Love without lust is tame and tepid, and often unrequited or unfulfilled, no more than a dreamy yearning for an unrealizable ideal, given to fantasizing and idealizing, fraught with unrealistic expectations. Girls with a weak Mars placement are especially prone to this psychic disturbance, but it can affect the boys as well, turning them into poetic dreamers instead of men of action.

On the other hand, lust without love is equally unsatisfactory, a mere temporary release of sexual energy which is solely physical and denies and demeans the spiritual center of the person. It is this Mars lust-only energy that produces antisocial actions such as crime.

Symbolically, then, Mars has to learn to love. His aggression must be tempered by the energy of Venus, for the Goddess always returns us to life no matter how much killing has been accomplished. When studying the chart, it is important to keep the significance of this pair in mind and to be aware of the relationship between them.

Though Mars is the primal male energy, we all have Mars in us, both males and females, just as we all have the Sun, Moon, Venus, and the rest of the planets in our charts. Women as well as men have aggressive feelings, get angry, feel passion. And woman can be warriors, leaders, athletes. Today, they can even fly combat missions in highly sophisticated military aircraft, once unthinkable for a female. What is interesting about this development of Mars energy is not that the male-dominated military establishment permits women to fly in combat, but that *women want to do it*, which proves that, given a chance, women can express Mars' energy as forcefully as men do.

Mars' sheer physical energy will be evident in babies and small children, especially around the time the child can get about somewhat independently by crawling and toddling. Mars shows what sort of activity appeals to the child and can be seen most readily when the child is in motion — doing, making, building, fighting, or defending. Mars has to do with setting and pursuing goals and is therefore much concerned with the choice of vocation.

But the real power of Mars that is derived from its relationship with sexuality will become evident with the onset of puberty, increasing in strength as sexual maturity develops. There is a clear connection between hormonal maturity and the expression of Mars' energy, especially aggressive behavior. Where Mars is active there is the possibility of aggression and where it is passive there is the possibility of being victimized.

Mars represents *how we act, what motivates us, how we get angry*, and *the libido*.

Mars key characteristics:

Motivation	Self-projection
Drive	Aggression
Physicality	Impetuous
Action	Violence
Sexuality	Hostility
Bold	Anger
Upfront	Argumentative

Mars is in *dignity* in Aries, which it rules. Interestingly, Aries was the Greek word for Roman Mars. In many ways the Planet and the Sign are similar, and Mars in Aries expresses itself exceptionally forcefully.

Mars in Capricorn is *exhalted* and here the aggressive energy of Mars is put to useful, practical ends. The fiery energy of Mars is at its best when combined with a constructive goal. Mars in Capricorn people have much ambition and often achieve worldly success.

THE
PERSONAL PLANETS
Through the Signs

CHAPTER III

TWO

SUN

Through the Signs

Tim

ARIES Sun babies have a direct and impatient nature, and even infants can show aggressive behavior. When they reach the toddler stage, Aries children want to explore everything independently and they will resent their freedom being restricted or curtailed. Like the little Rams that they are, they will butt their small heads against whatever stops their explorations.

As they reach a level of more locomotion, their need for independence will assert itself and careful supervision will become necessary to prevent injury as they charge headlong into all kinds of adventures. Head injuries should be especially guarded against. As impulsivity outruns their skills, they can take some hard tumbles. They are born pioneers.

One way to protect Aries children from hurting themselves is by distraction. As they'd rather start something than finish it, if one activity isn't suitable, another will interest them.

School is usually a delight for Aries Sun children, who love the many new challenges it presents. Stimulating their sense of curiosity is a fine way of promoting learning. However, make certain homework is finished! *ha!*

Physical activity is important for Aries at any age, but especially for teens, as they can be quite rambunctious when their energies are pent-up. Also, they need sufficient activity to make them tired enough to sleep soundly.

See page 12 for key concepts of Sun in Aries.

Me

TAURUS Sun babies are quiet and may not show much activity. They don't like change, especially sudden change, and should be moved about slowly and reassuringly. They may have throat problems, and their necks should be kept *as a* warm in cold weather. Though they are sturdy of constitution, being upset or *child* overtired can bring on a sore throat.

Little Taurus Sun will have a pleasant voice, even at the gurgling stage, and may surprise you by singing on key at an early age. When they begin to talk, they will use speech as a means of getting their way, sometimes talking the opposition right into the ground. Persistence and stamina are Taurean traits which can turn into stubbornness.

Taureans are patient, slow, and steady. A fixed Sign, Taurus resents being rushed or having plans or routines changed, especially suddenly, needing time to adjust. Comfort is important to small Taurus Sun, whose love of ease may appear to be laziness. Exercise should be encouraged to offset a tendency to gain weight.

Materialistic Taurus can seem greedy, but this is usually because they are so attached to their comforts and conveniences.

In school, Taurus will work carefully and slowly and not tire easily. Whatever the task, Taurus will finish it. Even-tempered and slow to anger, they nevertheless should not be pushed too far because their anger, once roused, burns with a steady fire that's hard to put out.

Tactile, Taureans respond to affection, hugging, patting, and stroking. In a difficult situation, touching a young Taurus will often turn the tide.

See page 15 for key concepts of Sun in Taurus.

GEMINI Sun babies are sparkling as a twinkling star, bright, quick, and full of action. Intensely interested in their surroundings, they like a lot of activity and are quickly bored. Agile as a monkey, your Gemini child will want to talk as soon as possible and, once started, may never stop.

A veritable question box, Geminians want the answers to a myriad of questions, but their attention will quickly flit elsewhere unless there's a fast answer.

When school starts, Gemini will be happy with all the new learning experiences but has a short attention span. Always wanting something new, Gemini Sun has to be taught to pay attention and to concentrate on the task at hand until it is finished.

Geminians love to read and enjoy books of the short variety, but they learn best through verbal communication. They also love games and do well in a playful environment. Moods change quickly. If they are unhappy or sad, being given something new and interesting to do will bring on a smile. The major problem with school is boredom, for Gemini can't abide rote learning.

Discipline is best administered by *explanation*. When this very mental child understands the *why* of something, natural logic gets it to go along with the program.

Respiratory ailments such as colds and asthma can be a problem and proper nutrition and rest are essential for this airy, floaty, ungrounded type.

See page 17 for key concepts of Sun in Gemini.

CANCER Sun babies are supersensitive to their surroundings from day one. Loud noises may frighten and upset them and they may try to scrunch up and hide from any disturbance. It's best to give Cancerians a protective environment, quiet and secure. They feel everything and if mother is sad, baby may cry out of sheer empathy. This infant is an emotional sponge and soaks up whatever feelings are in the atmosphere. Because of this response, Cancer Sun may have nervous stomach aches. They should be soothed with bland, milky foods and never forced to eat.

School may be traumatic for little Cancer, who loves *home* above all else and is usually very attached to mother. If at all possible, Cancer Sun should not be pushed out into the world of school any earlier than necessary and then given much reassurance that home is still there. A Cancer child should be allowed to take a favorite object along to school, especially at first, and should never have attachment to the old and familiar ridiculed.

Cancerians can become whiny and demanding if they feel insecure, so a sense of security must be carefully built from within. Emotional support is absolutely essential to young Cancer, who is basically loving and generous unless there appears to be a shortage of love. When this happens, Cancer will retreat into a shell and prying out an insecure Cancer can be quite a daunting task.

Home and family will always be of paramount importance to Cancer, even at college age. Make sure to have many family activities with your Cancer Sun child.

See page 20 for key concepts of Sun in Cancer.

LEO Sun babies are buoyant right from the start, attracting attention and loving it. From birth, a natural positive self-esteem seems to emanate from them and they exude warmth and lovingness. However, being exclaimed over and praised excessively can make Leo Sun claim the center of attention as an exclusive right. Tantrums can result if Leo is deprived of accustomed attention.

A natural show-off, partly for the sheer joy of acting, partly for the attention-getting effect, Leo demands recognition. In the school years, Leo will be spirited and strong-willed and exhibit leadership abilities. Naturally warm and affectionate, Leo Sun attracts many friends, who appreciate Leo's open-heartedness. Respect is also important to Leo Sun, who believes inherently in openness as a way of life. You'll have no trouble with fibbing from this child.

Leo Sun likes to make a good impression on others, and to this end craves fine clothes and other luxuries. Any shabbiness mortifies regal Leo, for whom self-respect is all important. Leo responds to praise and, when discipline is necessary, it's always best to praise first, criticize later. An injured Leo is a snarly beast and may retaliate by going off in a massive sulk.

If encouraged, Leo will work harder than most to turn in an excellent performance and bask in your praise.

See page 22 for key concepts of Sun in Leo.

VIRGO Sun babies seem like every mother's dream of the perfect infant — they make little fuss as long as they are kept warm and dry and fed regularly. They respond best in well-ordered surroundings and like to be kept on a regular schedule, especially with bathing. Little Virgos really like to be clean and tidy and when they reach the toddler stage they will amaze you with their eagerness to wash hands and take baths.

Virgo Sun will quickly begin to help out around the house, doing even boring chores cheerfully and well. Great with *detail*, if given a shopping list Virgo will make sure that every item bought matches the list exactly. Virgo Sun has a lot of mental power, an ability to concentrate totally, and a retentive memory. Rarely do you have to repeat an instruction for it to be carried out to the letter. If Virgoans do not understand something, they will ask logical questions in a calm and quiet way.

Self-criticism is the major problem with this child, and parental criticism only makes things worse. Think twice before you disparage, for the Virgo Sun youngster will take your words to heart and self-esteem will plummet. Being helpful to you makes Virgo Sun feel loved.

Health and diet are important to Virgo Sun, as is proper rest. This teen won't keep late hours and will follow a precise routine of personal hygiene. Sometimes finicky about food, Virgo may want to supervise the preparation of what's going to be eaten. Plain food suits them best and experimentation doesn't get very far.

See page 25 for key concepts of Sun in Virgo.

LIBRA Sun babies are an immediate delight. Sociable from the start, friendly and open, this infant will win everyone with smiles and gurgles. Even at the pre-verbal stage, little Libra is a social animal and loves to please. There's a warm and communicative gaze that charms. Interactions with family and others will be easy and pleasant, for this child has an uncanny ability to adapt to almost any situation or environment.

Beginning school is usually not a problem, as Libra Sun loves people and wants to be around them, interact with them. Likely to be talkative early, young Libra manages easily in public and quickly learns the necessary social skills. In fact, so poised are Librans that they may prefer the company of older people to peers.

Warm and affectionate, Libra wants to be part of the "gang" and hates feeling left out. Depriving Libra of social activities is an effective form of punishment but should not be over done, for a society-starved Libra can show another side and become willful and dominating.

Libra hates argument and strife of all kinds and will work hard to be the peacemaker, but decision-making is difficult, because Libra sees both sides with utter clarity, and therefore tends to go back-and-forth constantly.

Lovers of all that is beautiful, Librans needs pretty and peaceful surroundings and will appreciate any activity involving sharing and cooperating, happy when doing something with someone else.

See page 27 for key concepts of Sun in Libra.

SCORPIO Sun babies don't cry easily. This child may fix you with a penetrating stare that promises to redress any transgression. Even at a tender age, Scorpions seem to know what you are thinking, and they have been known to intimidate their parents. Try to remember that this is a *baby*, but don't assume your child isn't thinking.

Intensity and strong feelings characterize Scorpio, who is sensitive and easily hurt. Special attention and love needs to be given to this child to overcome the tendency to go it alone. School may be difficult at first, especially if there is any teasing or a sense of being *different*. Young Scorpio is likely to develop a defense system early and formidably as protection from emotional injury. As a teen, Scorpio needs to be given positive channels for the expression of negative energies, or trouble could result. The caliber of friends should also be overseen by parents, for Scorpions can be attracted to bad company.

Not easy to understand, young Scorpio suffers mostly alone, and every effort should be made to draw out this complex personality at an early age. Brooding is normal, especially in the teen years, but care should be taken that brooding does not turn to depression.

Any tendency toward vindictiveness should be recognized and curbed early by openness and honesty in all dealings. To enlist yourself as an ally is to gain Scorpio's fierce loyalty!

See page 30 for key concepts of Sun in Scorpio.

SAGITTARIUS Sun babies respond well to new experiences and seem nearly always to be full of spirit and enthusiasm. Physical activity benefits them and early attempts at walking are common. This super-energetic child needs the outdoors, physical freedom, and lots of fresh air.

School is just another venue for exploration where curious Sagittarius Sun is likely to be popular and make friends easily. Eager to learn all there is to know about the world, young Sagittarius won't mind hitting the books, but there needs to be ample time for sports and play as well as study. Innately logical, Sagittarius learns easily.

Outgoing and impulsive, Sagittarius can have an abrupt temper, but it burns out quickly leaving no residue of resentment. Exercise is usually the cure for what ails them. Neither shy nor timid, young Sagittarians will tell you what they think, often bluntly. Honesty is their first policy. Freedom-loving Sagittarians are willing to take responsibility to earn that freedom.

Attuned to the big picture, Sagittarius likes to expand its interests constantly and will enjoy and profit by travel, especially to foreign countries. This type makes an excellent exchange student and can master foreign languages. Naturally lucky, Sagittarius may get into some scrapes but these are likely to be minor. Relations with the opposite sex are likely to be platonic, for Sagittarius values friendship and freedom over commitment and emotional bounds.

See page 33 for key concepts of Sun in Sagittarius.

CAPRICORN Sun babies are serious and responsible even when very small. Infants can look preternaturally wise and solemn, like little old people. They seem to be adults who are working their way backward to childhood and can act in astonishingly mature ways at a very young age, assuming responsibilities and giving advice to their elders.

Capricorn may develop a quirky sense of humor in order to compensate for an overly serious approach to life. As soon as Capricorns can walk and talk, they want to do something important and may carry on surprisingly adult conversations with those who offer guidance. Because of all this seriousness, young Capricorn needs to be encouraged to play. Forms of play that teach while reaching a practical result are the best. School is approached in an organized fashion. Pessimism is a problem, and Capricorn needs help to see the brighter side.

Ambition will surface in the school years and goal-oriented Capricorn will work very hard to excel. Praise is not very important to the Capricorn student, but recognition for real achievements is vital. Since they tend to focus on establishment-oriented topics and time-tested methods, Capricorn's favor politics and history. Reading about successful people serves as inspiration.

Preferring the administrative and executive side of life, Capricorn may not show much enthusiasm for sports and physical activities. This teen is more likely to be the student council president than captain of an athletic team.

See page 36 for key concepts of Sun in Capricorn.

AQUARIUS Sun babies have a quality of unpredictability. They may suddenly cease to respond to a regular routine of feeding and sleeping, causing much concern. The answer here may be to change the routine, as Aquarius follows inner patterns of response. Experimentation will likely provide the solution.

Aquarius likes new things and new ideas and will evidence a free spirit quite early, making it easy for a parent to feel rejected. At an age when other children cling to their parents, this youngster may show a preference for independence. Often there is a sudden dislike of what was pleasing yesterday, but don't take it personally. It's just Aquarius Sun's natural nonconforming nature at work.

Objective and logical, Aquarius has a mental approach to life and therefore school rarely presents a difficulty. In fact, the kindergarten Aquarius may well show surprising independence and resent being escorted to school! This is an individualistic youngster — unconventional, unique, valuing the freedom to do and go without restriction. This child will bring home unusual friends, pets, and projects. Patience on the part of more orthodox parents is necessary in order to avoid alienating the child, who may be labeled a rebel. But forcing conformity will only backfire. Aquarius will simply conceal forbidden activities. Guidance is necessary, and though coercion won't work, appealing to logic and reasonableness will.

See page 38 for key concepts of Sun in Aquarius.

PISCES Sun babies are born flower children who want life to be beautiful, serene, loving, and peaceful. Loud noises and angry faces terrify them. This is a highly sensitive baby who needs lots of love and affection from the moment of birth. After the safety and warmth of the watery womb, Pisces finds life to be a shock and needs time to adjust.

Pisces Sun will bond to Mother and hate to be apart from this island of security in a scary world. Tears of anguish may arise when safety is threatened. Boys are no exception. Parents need early to instill a sense of security in their Pisces Sun child.

Emotional immaturity may be a problem when time for school comes, and Pisces Sun may fare best if not pushed out to pre-school but kept at home until development occurs. Never tease this child for being "babyish," for you will only exacerbate the situation and get more tears and clinging. Gradually acclimate Pisces to experiences of separation to provide a sense of security from fear of abandonment. Don't worry about "spoiling" Pisces or "giving in" to childish fears. Possessing a remarkable ability to understand the feelings of others, a secure Pisces is a delight, loving and sensitive, eager to help. Take care not to trample Piscean sensibilities.

Shy and retiring, Pisces may have trouble making friends, preferring to retreat into a private (and safe) world of fantasy. Out of this comes artistic creation and beautiful music. Nurture this perceptive imagination.

See page 41 for key concepts of Sun in Pisces.

MOON

Through the Signs

ARIES Moon babies will early show a need to excel at what they do, always wanting to be first. Because the Moon is the unconscious, Arians often do not realize they are being pushy. Naturally active and vital, Aries Moon children display leadership abilities and love to take chances. Easily bored, they need frequent changes in routine and are happiest when kept busy.

Aries Moon children quickly learn to take care of themselves and are unlikely to want to be babied. Aries Moon's mother isn't a traditional cookie-baking mom but a courageous, lively, and assertive woman with a fighting spirit. She passes on to her child these action-oriented qualities. As emotions are an obstacle to getting out and being active, Aries Moon is impatient with them and avoids discussing inner feelings. This child works out emotions on the playground and is attracted to rough-and-tumble sports.

Fiercely independent, Aries Moon children fight for their rights, especially when freedom is threatened. Anger is easily aroused, exacerbated when there is nothing that Aries Moon can *do* about a situation. Luckily, this anger is fast-burning and dissipates quickly as Aries Moon is eager to get on to the next activity. Prone to quick emotional outbursts, Aries Moon needs help to get in touch with feelings and express them positively.

When emotionally upset, Aries Moon can suffer headaches or incur head injuries from rash action, for this emotional nature is aggressive and impulsive and these children will rush headlong into anything without looking before leaping. They hate being sick, as illness interferes with their independence. It's vitally important to teach them to "take five." Fire Sign Aries' emotions are expressed vehemently and selfishly. "Me first," is their motto!

It's important for Aries Moon children to be active enough to ensure a sound sleep, for they are restless of nature and resist sleep. Their fast and furious energy exhausts itself suddenly and fatigue can bring on a bad temper or an argument. On outings, rest periods should be planned in advance. Arian need for self-sufficiency (you'll hear a lot of "I can do it myself, mother."), while being encouraged, may also have to be curtailed.

The best way to comfort this child is with activity or the promise of activity. A tired, grumpy child, told that tomorrow there will be a new game to play, is easier to put to bed. Or, a bedridden child, given action toys, will accept your assurance that independence will return with renewed health. With Aries, impatience is always a factor. The wise parent will recognize that this is an inherent part of the child's makeup and not impose unnecessary restrictions, for Aries Moon will fight demanding or controlling parents.

Aries Moon needs to learn that actions have consequences and that others may be much more sensitive than they are.

See page 12 for key concepts of Moon in Aries.

TAURUS Moon babies are serene. Their emotions function with a high degree of stability. Physical comfort is what they need the most, and this should be as luxurious as possible. Naturally sensual, Taurus Moon responds to experiences that involve the physical senses. Provide soft clothing, plush blankets, furry stuffed toys, soothing music, crooning sounds, pleasant smells (bathe your little Taurus Moon in scented soap!), warmth, indirect lighting, and ample food.

This is an extremely security-conscious Moon placement which does not readily tolerate change. Even very small Taurus Moons can be conservative and show a tendency to hang on to their possessions. They are not unwilling to share, but they want ownership recognized. "That's *mine*," is a statement you will hear frequently. Given material security, Taurus Moon is an equable child, mellow and serene, not given to tantrums nor easily upset.

Taurus Moon is likely to have a traditional mother, the real stay-at-home cookie-baking Earth Mother type. Even if she works outside the home, she will appreciate the joys of old-fashioned mothering. A practical sort, she is sensible and good with money management. A born nurturer, she gives her child the solid reassurance needed for proper development, unless there is an aspect conflict.

Your Taurus Moon child tends to shrug off little upsets, for this child is grounded. However, when unpleasant feelings do occur there can be a problem with overdoing — an upset Taurus Moon at any age tends to overeat (for the comfort of it) and older children may go on a shopping binge. This latter is mitigated by Taurus Moon's preference for what is of good quality and long-lasting. Money attracts Taurus Moon who will early evidence an ability to accumulate the stuff. A growing bank account will please this youngster more than anything.

Don't mistake your little flower-sniffing Bull for a wimp. If pushed beyond their considerable limits, they will dig in for the battle royale. Slow to anger, when changes are forced on them in a hurry, they can become extremely stubborn and unmovable. Taurus Moon is the "unmovable object" par excellence. And they don't cool off quickly. The Bull Moon in action is formidable, even if only a toddler. The first experience of this magnificent rage is an eye-opener for a parent. How could that sweet, loving, cuddly little child turn into Stonewall Jackson just because of getting, without any advance notice, a new room and all new furniture? And you thought your child would be tickled pink with the new arrangement! And that, my friend, is how you learn of Taurus Moon's resistance to change.

Fortunately, being innately a nurturer, Taureans instinctively know how to soothe themselves when upset. If you do have to transplant your little Taurus Moon, make sure to include familiar objects and give plenty of warning about what's to come.

See page 15 for key concepts of Moon in Taurus.

GEMINI Moon babies are bright, quick, witty, and may seem more Geminian than Gemini Sun. Moon governs mood changes and Gemini is changeable by nature, so Gemini Moon flips from mood to mood with astonishing rapidity. This Moon hates boredom — *emotional boredom* — and will do almost anything to liven up a situation. The key to the Gemini Moon baby is mental stimulation. Talk to them, even if they can't yet understand the words. Their curiosity is endless and precociousness likely. Think of the delightful charm of Shirley Temple and you'll have a good idea of the Gemini Moon child's ability to sparkle.

Gemini Moon's mother has many interests and likes to be on the move as much as possible. She's a kind of Peter Pan figure who is more likely to be like a big sister than a mother. Or there can be a real older sister who for some reason gets the role of the mother. Whichever, there is always a lot of communication between mother and child, especially of the verbal sort. Gemini Moons ask "Why?" about as often as they open their mouths, and the Gemini Moon's mother is likely to respond intellectually to questioning, giving the verbal explanations Gemini wants.

Emotions are interesting to Gemini Moon, as curiosities. They want to know about *your* emotions and will ask a zillion questions, but they like to keep their own emotions at bay, using mental activity as a technique. When confronted with an emotionally-laden situation, they will dive into rationalizing until they have talked the thing to death. Pre-verbal Gemini Moons need diversity and distraction to help them deal with unpleasant or unfamiliar situations. Because the need for verbal expression is so great, this child will talk early on.

The best way to handle upsets is with continual mental challenge. You might find your Gemini Moon toddler fiddling with the home computer in an effort to become more communicative. Remember, Mercury rules Gemini, and Gemini Moon is emotionally Mercurial, sliding up and down the scale of feelings with alacrity. Boredom is the enemy of the Gemini Moon child and consistency of routine may equal excruciating tedium. Variation will keep this mentally quick and agile child happy and playful.

As Gemini Moon gives an intellectual approach to emotions, this child will respond best to having any problem treated in a rational manner. Even quite small children will want to talk about their feelings and reactions to people and events, often at length. Gemini Moon loves to travel as a way of sopping up new experiences, the best antidote to ever-threatening boredom, so take little Gemini Moon with you on short trips — the market, the mall, the dry cleaner. A fussy Gemini Moon child will perk right up when taken for an outing. Feeding their innate curiosity provides as much nourishment as food. Don't be alarmed if your Gemini Moon turns into a nonstop talker, for this is an outlet for nervousness. Maintain a calm atmosphere and insist on proper rest.

See page 17 for key concepts of Moon in Gemini.

CANCER Moon babies are supersensitive emotionally, no matter how independent the Sun Sign. It's important for this child to receive nurturing and support early, for if misunderstood the emotional nature can go underground and hide away, like a Crab retreats into its shell. Mother is all-important to Cancer Moon, who does not like to be separated from her even for a moment. As the Moon rules Cancer, moon issues in general are paramount here, and Cancer Moon is more emotionally sensitive and easily wounded than is Cancer Sun.

Home and family are extremely important to Cancer Moon children, for this is where they find comfort and solace. It follows that if the home is disrupted, so will the child be upset. Cancer Moon is especially sensitive to the emotions of others in the environment, keenly feeling any negative vibrations. More than any other Moon placement, Cancer needs the nurturing of a stable family.

The Cancer Moon's mother usually has a special bond with her child, which will last a lifetime whether the tenor of it is positive or negative. Mothers of Cancer Moons need to guard against overprotectiveness, or smother love, or else Cancer Moon will never grow emotionally mature. This child is a natural "mother's little helper," so care should be taken not to impose adult roles of caregiving. Because the maternal feelings come easily to Cancer Moon children, they are in danger of being saddled with babysitting younger siblings. Boys as well as girls exhibit maternal traits and one way to help Cancer Moon reach emotional maturity is to provide plenty of "babies" in the form of pets, plants, and dolls.

All emotional issues affect Cancer Moons strongly, and tears are a common response even in boys, who should not be made to feel ashamed of their deep and heartfelt emotional natures. Quashing emotions in small Cancer Moons can have devastating effects later on. Never call a Cancer Moon "crybaby." A major trait is holding on to the past, and in the instance of divorce or other family disruption, take care to give extra attention and reassurance or Cancer Moon may carry the grief of the amputation for many years.

Security of the home is a prime issue for Cancer Moon. Family difficulties are hard to handle. Any trauma affecting the home, such as moving, can rock their sense of security and throw them totally off base for many months, depending on the age involved. Maintaining the family unit with emphasis on family gatherings can help, as can the building of a surrogate family in new surroundings. If loved ones move away from Cancer Moon, it is important to keep in touch by calling, writing, and visiting as often as possible. Lost contact with loved ones is extremely painful to Cancer Moon, especially with older relatives such as grandparents and aunts and uncles.

Stress may upset Cancer Moon's stomach and bland food along with reassurance and a return to calm is prescribed.

See page 20 for key concepts of Moon in Cancer.

LEO Moon babies are warm and strongly affectionate, so receiving plenty of affection makes them feel wanted and important. From day one they crave attention, and histrionics is a favored method of achieving this end. A born ham, this child is impossible to ignore. Leo Moon's arrival in the world seems to be a media event, even if it's only dad popping flash bulbs or recording the momentous event on video. The tiniest of Leo Moons are accomplished at grabbing the spotlight of adult attention and this marvelous ability only increases as they get older. They may display their innate regal natures right away by "lording it over" all and sundry. If you don't want to be a full-time applause clack for your Leo Moon youngster, sign him or her up for acting lessons as soon as possible. Performance is in this kid's blood and Leo Moon's sunny and warmly radiant nature makes charisma second nature.

Leo Moon's mom is herself a real Queen Bee, no stranger to the center stage, even if she is a frustrated actress and center stage is in her living room. Sometimes little Leo Moons find they are competing with their moms for attention, so mother needs to let her generous nature rule and share with her child. This is a talented placement and sometimes Leo Moon children are pushed into the spotlight by ambitious mothers, to the detriment of their childhood needs. This is all too easy to do, however, as Leo Moon craves that spotlight. A wise mother must balance her own and her child's need for attention with the requirements of healthy and normal development.

Emotional reactions are always full-blooded, but as Leo Moons like to keep up appearances, they shy away from public displays of negative emotions and may simply withdraw in regal grace from a scene of confrontation. Easily offended, pride is their Achilles' heel, but Leo Moon is not one to hold grudges, forgiving of transgressions and magnanimous toward offenders. Loving attention turns an angry lion back into a sweet pussycat.

Praise and positive feedback are vital to the Leo Moon child and the lack thereof will inhibit proper emotional development and bring on a bad case of poor self-esteem. In order to feel all is right with the world, Leo Moons need continual recognition and assurance that they are valued. Feeling special and important helps Leo Moon to build a strong ego.

As the prideful Leo Moon would rather be in the position of giving help than asking for it, dependence on others is usually not a problem with this placement. Nonetheless, their needs should not be ignored or given short-shrift, for Leo Moon children aren't very good at meeting their own emotional needs. Emotion-driven generosity is a primary trait and there is the risk Leo Moon will overdo the giving and need to have a large heart restrained. Always willing to help a younger child, Leo's protective nature fosters leadership.

Leo Moon's fondness for luxuriating in the finer things of life can appear to be laziness, especially in teenagers.

See page 22 for key concepts of Moon in Leo.

VIRGO Moon babies will show a need for cleanliness and orderliness immediately. Kept clean, dry, warm, and fed, Virgo Moon infants are peaceable and undemanding. So self-contained are these children, they seem to be miniature adults. As they get a bit older, Virgo Moons want activities that engage both the mind and the hands. Careful and meticulous, Virgo Moon hates disorder, and may be compulsively neat, taking pleasure in arranging possessions and keeping toys in a precise manner, becoming upset if that order is disrupted.

Virgo Moon sets high standards and expects no less of others. Such expectations lead first to self-criticism and then to criticism of others. Though not of itself bad, this striving for perfection can plunge the Virgo Moon child into self-doubt and a sense of defeat if the effort falls short of the desired result. Virgo Moons need to learn early that everyone makes mistakes, including themselves, and that perfection is not for this world.

Cleanliness is next to godliness in the view of Virgo Moon, which can result in compulsive behavior. They must be helped to realize that into each life some dirt must fall, which is not a fatal occurrence. Naturally helpful, Virgo Moon loves to be busy at some detail-oriented project and will relish being given small tasks and helping with chores around the house. Though by nature somewhat shy, they like to be useful in a practical way.

About the only time Virgo Moon wants to be taken care of is when sick. Then, they need to be babied and given extra-special attention. By nature rather detached, this placement expresses emotions, in a rational, mental way, making it a bit hard to comfort an upset Virgo Moon with the usual methods of cheering up. Reassurance that they do indeed measure up and being told it's okay to be who they are will help. Acknowledge the child's valid needs and try to meet them so that he or she doesn't grow up feeling undeserving and that no one's ever going to fulfill those needs.

Virgo Moon's mother is likely to be a working woman, perhaps a nurse or social worker, with full-time duties and responsibilities. Often there is a supercritical parent of either sex who values order over spontaneity. Virgo Moon needs to be allowed to play and to be messy at least once in a while. Encourage your Virgo Moon child to get outside, even if it's only to read a book in the backyard.

As Virgo Moon gets into the adolescent years, work becomes a hobby, and this youngster may well have a paying job after school, especially if there is any tension at home from which Virgo Moon needs to escape. Sensitive to psychosomatic illnesses, Virgo Moon may suffer from food allergies or internal upsets as a result of not dealing directly with emotional stress.

See page 25 for key concepts of Moon in Virgo.

LIBRA Moon babies are the soul of charm, with dimples and a winning smile. They need peace and quiet in calm, beautiful surroundings, for they hate strife of any kind and will shrink from loud voices and arguments. They like refinement and seek harmony and balance. Relationship is all to Libra Moon, and this child will reach out, seeking to unite with others. Early on, Libra Moon shows its sociable and gentle nature, enjoying interaction, even with strangers. Libra Moon children are affectionate and good-natured and make friends easily.

Being alone is difficult for Libra Moon, who craves the society of others and needs the continual presence of loving and caring persons in order to feel secure. Emotions that are ugly or negative are quickly pushed aside, buried, or denied. Libra Moon must learn that life is not always harmonious and that unpleasant feelings must be dealt with straightforwardly. It's never a good idea to let Libra Moon put bad feelings on hold for "tomorrow," for that tomorrow may be years down the line and the effects of emotional repression can be crippling.

Libra Moon's mother is usually a romantic, even if a closet-case one. She's prone to pamper her little darling or to reward Libra Moon for polite, socially pleasing behavior. It's in this way that Libra Moon learns the value of pleasing others. Conflict is threatening to Libra Moon's emotional stability, which makes for a peace-at-any-price attitude that can be detrimental to Libra's getting needs met. This is especially true in the case of family quarrels or divorce. Libra Moon children tend to become the go-betweens for warring parents, overstraining themselves to make everything right. Under such conditions, Libra Moon learns how to use charm in a manipulative way to influence others, so as to secure the love base.

The Libra Moon teen, boy or girl, is an incurable romantic and is likely to be interested in romance at an early age. Love comes first in the Libra Moon imagination and life isn't worth living without it. Thus, this highly romantic Moon Sign is prone to put the love connection above all other considerations, such as grades and achievement. To this end, Libra Moon subjugates the self to the "other," always striving to please a partner. This placement is prone to premature involvement in inappropriate love relationships, a tendency that needs to be guarded against. The problem is that Libra Moon is emotionally dependent on the idea of having a partner. Without one, they feel unloved and find the world is a scary place. Libra Moons, especially girls, need strong emotional support at home to overcome the notion that being in a romantic relationship is the only worthwhile thing in life. The dread of being alone makes them stick with a hurtful relationship until the bitter end. They must be taught not to put all their eggs in one relationship basket.

See page 27 for key concepts of Moon in Libra.

SCORPIO Moon babies are perhaps the hardest to understand because their emotions run deep and silent, like a submarine. Sadly, many Scorpio Moons suffer an early traumatic experience, such as separation from a parent, or some betrayal of trust, which sets the stage for a pattern of mistrust and refusal to share feelings. Scorpio Moons are intensely emotional children with a tendency to brood over past hurts, and they *never* forget who hurt them.

This brooding intensity is evident from the start, even if there has as yet been no trauma. It's as if little Scorpio Moon knows the hurt is coming and is gathering up inner strength by withdrawing into some deeply internal safe place. Understand that this tender being needs your love and compassion. Unable to express feelings, Scorpio Moon needs parents who are alert enough to observe the subtle signs and changes in their child in order to drive out the inner trouble.

Give all the love you can. Offer soothing words and comforting caresses frequently and watch carefully for signs of emotional distress. If your Scorpio Moon child isn't acknowledged for having deep feelings, emotional coldness may result.

Even in the best of circumstances, Scorpio Moon has great difficulty expressing deeply internalized feelings. Unless there is a facile Mercury in the chart, Scorpio Moon may not even be *able* to verbalize emotions. Encouragement provided by an attentive, caring adult who is there to really *listen* will succeed in freeing up Scorpio Moon's inhibitions about revealing inner secrets. But if subjected to impatience, inattention, or ridicule, Scorpio Moon will shut down the emotional centers against prying eyes.

There are no halfway measures for Scorpio Moon. Joy is unbounded, misery sends them into the pits. This intense all-or-nothing emotional ground results in strong feelings about everything, and the fixed nature of Scorpio makes it all but impossible to change their minds. Stubborn Scorpio's fixations can last a lifetime.

Experience is the best teacher, even if that means a lot of hard knocks along the way, for this Sign wants to fully savor intense feelings. Beware of extremes and curb them if possible. Though not an easy lesson to teach, Scorpio Moon needs to learn self-discipline and the value of moderation in all things.

Scorpio Moon's mother has had her own battles in life. This placement prefigures early trauma — abandonment, abuse, death, and betrayal are the scarmarks common to Scorpio. That is not to say that every Scorpio Moon child will suffer in this way. Sometimes the suffering is of what is *perceived* as much as of what actually happened. Perhaps the mother simply had to go out to work and the child perceived this necessity as abandonment. There are many scenarios in which the Scorpio Moon drama can be played out.

See page 30 for key concepts of Moon in Scorpio.

SAGITTARIUS Moon babies seem to be delighted with life from the first moment and give off an innate sense of optimism. They expect everything to go well and this joy is contagious. Moon in Sagittarius' emotions are right up front, nothing concealed. When happy, they smile, laugh, coo, and gurgle. When unhappy, they cry until picked up and dandled and then they smile again. It's easy to soothe the little hurts of the Sagittarius Moon, who already believes that things are going to get better soon.

Perpetually upbeat, these children may seem to live on a pink cloud of happiness. They do not welcome depressed fellows, or else they work to cheer them up. If Sagittarians have to deal with a difficult situation, they begin by looking for the silver lining. Like the child who, when presented with a horse box full of manure, gleefully chortled, "There must be a pony for me somewhere."

When your little Sagittarius Moon reaches the stage of learning, expect a lot of questions. Answer one, get another. Learning is the lifelong passion of Sagittarius, and the Moon placed here puts an emotional value on learning, not merely an intellectual one. There is a real *passion* for knowledge. It doesn't make much difference to Sagittarius Moon whether learning takes place in a formal setting or is self-taught, as long as horizons continue to expand.

The Sagittarius Moon's mom is most probably a person who loves knowledge for its own sake and has an interest in education. A natural philosopher, this mother gives her child an early sense of the quest to understand the meaning of life, and she never sneers at questions about profound subjects. Sagittarius Moon loves to travel, and ofttimes mother gets around a lot herself, either with child in tow or bringing back tales of far-off places and interesting people and experiences with which to entertain and teach.

An idealist, Sagittarius Moon wants the world to be better than it is, people to be brave and noble, and love to be pure and true. As that's not often the case, Sagittarius Moon comes in for a lot of disappointment and needs to learn to take people and the world as it is, not as it should be.

Independence is the watchword for Sagittarius Moon, who as soon as possible will leave the nest to go as far as possible in search of new experience. Always looking into the far distance, Sagittarius Moon youngsters can become armchair travellers, eagerly soaking up travel films and documentaries about foreign lands and people. *National Geographic* is a good birthday present for a Sagittarius Moon teen.

There's a strongly religious bent to the Sagittarius Moon, and a concern with religion and questions about God are common. Be honest about your beliefs and doubts, but rest assured that eventually this youngster will find the necessary spiritual way, for Sagittarius Moon safeguards emotional independence, knowing that freedom to feel is one of the great liberties.

See page 33 for key concepts of Moon in Sagittarius.

CAPRICORN Moon babies are solemn-eyed infants who seem like little adults even when newborn. Often they have an owl-eyed seriousness that is quite disturbing in a baby. When you "kitchy-coo" at the Capricorn Moon infant, you may get a look that clearly asks what's wrong with you. Can't you see that your behavior is unadult and rather silly? Don't be alarmed. The trouble is that the little one is uncomfortable with feelings, which are a source of difficulty, not pleasure. Despite being seemingly self-sufficient, this little being needs much love to thaw that natural Capricorn coldness. Parents especially are important because Capricorn Moon relates immediately to figures of authority and looks for role models.

Depression can attack Capricorn Moon children, and often this is the result of the mother's own anxiety or a postpartum depression on her part. Receptive as the Moon is to the mother's moods, Capricorn, being naturally pessimistic, soaks up negative feelings unconsciously. A Capricorn Moon child should be protected from such early trauma affecting the mother or any closely associated female.

Aside from the possibility of experiencing depression, Capricorn Moon's mother is usually a practical, no-nonsense type of woman with administrative talents and managerial capacities, whether or not she works outside the home. She often had stiff responsibilities herself when young and learned to manage the hard way, passing on this expedient to her offspring. Capricorn Moon's mom is not inclined to cuddle and cajole and may not have much patience with childish ways. She needs to relax more and give her child warmth and under-standing. A well-organized home is a pleasure, but it should not be gained at the sacrifice of a child's needs for love and companionship.

It's especially important for the Capricorn Moon child to be allowed to be a child, for this placement indicates premature assumption of adult responsibilities, often out of guilt. Resentment can follow. Though capable of sacrificing short-term satisfaction for long-term gains, Capricorn Moon needs the security of a solid emotional foundation of love, coupled with the knowledge that the material needs will be provided. Capricorn Moons are rarely dependent, forming self-reliance early, often as a response to having to take care of themselves.

The Sign of hard work, Capricorn affects the Moon by making this an emo-tional need as well as a practical necessity, so expect early interest in pursuing a career, for this placement sees success as an essential component of future security, and as a way to fulfill their own security needs. Fear of inadequacy also sends Capricorn Moon to work early and long. Ideally, Capricorn Moon children will have parents to whom they can look up to and respect and who will give them the love and reassuring praise they need so badly.

See page 36 for key concepts of Moon in Capricorn.

AQUARIUS Moon babies may seem to be out of this world as soon as they come into it! Anything but ordinary, your Aquarius Moon child is ready to experience all there is in this world — and beyond. Moon in Aquarius is almost a contradiction in terms, for Moon is concerned with feelings, family, and the past, while Aquarius is concerned with mind, the whole human race, and the future. Don't be surprised if your Aquarius Moon child early evidences an interest in UFOs and space travel, even claiming to have seen aliens or visited a spacecraft.

If Aquarius Moon at first doesn't seem to have the usual childish needs, don't be fooled. Like any other, this child needs mothering and understanding. It's just that Mother could be from another planet and Father a little green man and Aquarius Moon wouldn't care. In fact, Aquarius Moon's mother quite probably is a modern, liberated woman, in the vanguard of political and social advance. She's a forward-looking woman, with controversial ideas. Either that, or she's a kooky artist type, dripping fringes and beads, maybe a parent only accidentally. Mother is quite likely to be more of a friend than a traditional parent to the Aquarius Moon child. Or it could be her child just views her that way.

Aquarius Moon children seem even at an early age to want to stay far away from emotional expression and may seem extraordinarily detached from the usual infant demands. It's important that this child's unique personality be recognized and given its due, or else there's a propensity for an emotional detachment so complete that you may feel your child really is from another planet. Emotionally programmed to value freedom above all else, Aquarius Moon may fuss and fret when constrained. Clothing that gives freedom of movement is important. This child thrives on experimentation and thrives best in an unstructured environment.

Friends are quite important to Aquarius Moon and parents may feel left out when little Aquarius shows a preference for going off with a school group over staying home for a family birthday party. Born joiners, these people persons want to participate in clubs and activities where they can share ideas with others. Aquarius is a mental Sign, and it affects the Moon with excessive rationalizing of emotions. Even youngsters will intellectualize emotions to keep them at arm's length, because underneath Aquarius Moon fears the loss of control that results from being engulfed by emotional needs.

Sign of the rebel, this Moon placement expresses emotions radically and unconventionally, which can be offputting to conventionally minded parents. Patience is the solution. You are harboring an Earth-born E.T. who loves all fellow beings, alien or human. Give Aquarius Moon a lot of space and he or she will always find the way home.

See page 38 for key concepts of Moon in Aquarius.

PISCES Moon babies are the sweetest in the world. Totally trusting and as needful as any mother could want, this infant will steal your heart immediately. Like a nymph or sprite escaped from the woodland, Pisces Moon has an otherworldly ambience. Emotionally a little psychic sponge, your Pisces Moon child absorbs the moods of those around it. Sensitive to the nth degree, Pisces Moon needs a great deal of emotional support. This is the most emotional placement of the Moon, exaggerating both the Moon's receptivity and sensitivity. Pisces Moon takes *everything* personally, feeling the pain of others to the extent that it becomes internalized, feeling guilty and responsible if so much as a plant dies. Tears are frequent and boys especially must be allowed this natural outlet for their sensitive feelings.

Emotion is a potent force for Pisces Moon, providing a rich source of intuitive understanding of the pains of others and a deep connection to the creative realm. Neptune, Pisces' ruler, is emblematic of the watery depths where reside the psychic, spiritual, imaginative, dreamy, and poetic talents given to humankind. Some of the greatest creative geniuses had Pisces Moons — Leonardo da Vinci, Goethe, and Michelangelo to name a famous few.

There is also a latent mysticism in this Moon which is naturally attuned to worlds other than the one we see daily. If you are a practical type of parent, this may seem "spaced-out" or "weird," but take care not to trample on these very real perceptions in your Pisces Moon. If he or she suddenly announces that Aunt Mary is coming to dinner, just keep quiet and set an extra place. And don't be surprised when your unexpected relative knocks on the door, in the neighborhood because her car broke down.

Pisces Moon's mother is usually one of two kinds. A born rescuer of the world's strays, human and animal, she vibrates to the tune of compassion and spirituality and appears sainted to lesser folk. A sort of local Mother Theresa. The trouble with this mom is that she may be so caught up in her good works that she neglects her own children, just because they have a roof over their heads and food on the table. This mom inspires adulation in her offspring, but she is mysterious to them because of her inaccessibility. The second type of Pisces Moon mother is someone who herself needs to be taken care of. She may have problems with alcohol or drugs, be physically or emotionally ill, or waft in and out of her child's life like a ghost. This type of mother brings out the rescuer in the Pisces Moon child, who then becomes the caretaker of the parent, a bad situation. Those responsible should see to it that Pisces Moon receives proper nurturing.

Emotional maturity is a problem for Pisces Moon, whose emotions are often a confusing buzz. Learning to focus and having a spiritual outlet will allow this child to use the gifts of Pisces Moon constructively.

See page 41 for key concepts of Moon in Pisces.

MERCURY

Through the Signs

me

ARIES Mercury children communicate self-confidently, decisively, and force-fully. Their way of thinking is competitive and action-initiating. There is a fondness for debate and argument even at an early age and Aries Mercury often likes to start the argument. Fire Sign Aries projects into Mercury like a firecracker — there are sudden bouts of explosive talk.

At home, Aries Mercury is often hotheaded, impetuous, inconsiderate, and prone to temper outbursts. This is especially evident in the early years before speech is developed, as the inability to communicate frustrates Aries Mercury children so much they may even actually bang their heads on something. The key to keeping this frustration under control is to avoid delays and to present as little opposition as is congruent with safety.

In school, Aries Mercury is a competitor and will work hard to be first. With this placement, there is the ability to think rapidly, and Aries Mercury may produce original ideas of value. The problem is that Aries Mercury likes to start things (Aries is a cardinal Sign) but hates to have to finish them. Impulsiveness of thought is a trait, and Aries Mercury may jump around mentally.

Homework must be monitored carefully as there is little follow-through. However, Aries Mercury children usually make excellent students with the caveat that they must be allowed to follow an independent course of study. Learning by rote quickly bores them. They mentally spring ahead of the less aggressive Signs and become restless. While it's necessary to show appreciation for their natural mental agility, Aries Mercury must be required to complete one assignment before moving on to the next. Being positive and upbeat in your communications will smooth the way.

When faced with a difficult situation, Aries Mercury will often make a thought-less decision just to get on with things. The necessity of thinking things through before taking action is something that must be patiently taught. Aries Mercury children make good debaters for they enjoy the challenge of taking the opposite point of view.

Leaping to conclusions is another Aries Mercury trait. Often their decision-making is colored by viewing everything from a too personal vantage point. This can make Aries Mercury egotistical and self-centered. It's important to teach this youngster that rash decisions can cause problematic results and that other people have valid points of view, which must be taken into consideration.

As this is a very physical placement, the best way to communicate with Aries Mercury is with action — quick and to the point. Lengthy, detailed discussions will only bore them into a mental shutdown. Be dynamic and you will get their full attention. Also, talking things out before, during, and after physical exertion — walking, biking, a ball game — gets the flow going freely.

See page 13 for key concepts of Mercury in Aries.

TAURUS Mercury children communicate slowly, persistently, deliberately, and thoroughly. Taurus is a fixed Earth sign and not inclined either to physical movement or mental dashing about. Here, Mercury's natural quicksilver quality is slowed down to a crawl and Taurus Mercury children can be maddeningly painstaking to the faster-moving Signs. But do not sell Taurus Mercury short. Although not known for mental brilliance, this slow-but-sure placement has great common sense and is naturally adept at decision-making that has a practical aim in mind.

The fixed nature of Taurus gives Mercury great powers of concentration. Not easily distracted by external stimuli, this youngster works steadily to finish the task at hand, going over it a second time to make sure.

As Taurus is grounded in the material plane and attuned to the five senses, Mercury here responds well to being taught through the medium of the senses. If a Mercury Taurus can see, hear, touch, smell, or taste the experience, it will get through. Simple verbalizing often is not enough to penetrate Taurean need to learn experientially. For example, you want to teach the little one not to touch the hot stove. Rather than just verbalizing the warning, take the child's hand and hold it close enough to safely feel the heat and the message will register permanently.

Abstract concepts are difficult for Taurus Mercury who feels more comfortable with what is usable and concrete. If new information is presented thoroughly and slowly, so that the child can understand its relevance, it will be absorbed in time.

Problems in school tend to come from Taurus Mercury, inflexibility of mind, which can be perceived by a teacher as obstinence. Slowness need not indicate either lack of intelligence or deliberate refusal. This Mercury simply needs to be allowed to go along at its own pace. Persistent and reliable, children with this placement can be trusted with responsibilities of a mental nature.

Taurus loves physical comfort and the Taurus Mercury child will respond to a learning atmosphere that is cozy and comfortable. If you have something to teach or talk about to Taurus Mercury, set the stage with some soft music, a warm room, perhaps a bath and pajamas, and a plate of snacks. Touching, hugging, and stroking are all valuable adjuncts to learning for Taurus Mercury. A teenager struggling with a math problem will do better if a back rub is provided during the study hour.

Most importantly, to facilitate learning well, demonstrate to your Taurus Mercury the solid practicality and value of the lesson. If math's a problem, suggest that it's necessary for banking transactions! When Taurus Mercury sees the practical end, learning's a snap.

See page 15 for key concepts of Mercury in Taurus.

GEMINI Mercury children communicate quickly, adaptably, restlessly, and superficially. Their attention is easily distracted and the mental processes can be scattered due to the sheer agility of their minds. Mercury rules Gemini and is at home here where its quicksilver qualities are at their height. The mind of the Gemini Mercury child is very active, versatile, curious, and fond of change. Mental restlessness can become a problem and these children need constant diversion. A stimulus-starved baby may cry from the discomfort not of a wet diaper but of boredom.

What appears to be nervousness and instability in the Gemini Mercury child is actually a result of its ability to fast-process information coming in from the world around it. Little Gemini Mercury is quick-minded and alert and learns readily if kept interested. Intellectual stimulation at the earliest possible age — these children can learn to read at nine months — is a necessity to prepare the Gemini Mercury for a lifetime of learning.

Talkative and eager to communicate impressions of everything around, Gemini Mercury is variety-seeking, versatile, quick-witted, and inquisitive. The problem is not in lack of communication but in communication of substance. There is, with this easily distracted placement, a tendency for superficiality. Lack of follow-through is another trait, and young Gemini Mercury needs to learn to finish projects. Always eager for the next experience, youngsters with this placement have a difficult time staying with any one subject long enough to learn it in depth.

Though articulate and logical, there is propensity to babble simply for the sake of keeping the airwaves in motion. They need to learn the importance of having something to say, though often this talkativeness is a cover-up for unpleasant feelings, which Gemini Mercury finds difficult to express.

Gemini Mercury likes a complex, busy environment with lots going on — TV, radio, conversation, newspapers, and magazines — but is subject to mental fatigue and needs to retire periodically to a calm situation to restore a fragile mental constitution. With a highly sensitive nervous system that automatically registers all incoming external stimuli, Gemini Mercury must assimilate many and conflicting impressions at once, which can frazzle the nerves. As an overstimulated Gemini Mercury child becomes fatigued, confused, and irritable, parents recognizing this factor can provide appropriate conditions to restore the balance. For example, the tired child clamoring for just one more ride at the amusement park must be gently but firmly refused.

Gemini Mercury thrives on education, enjoys knowledge, and develops a wide vocabulary, which makes for impressive articulateness in both speech and writing. Although there can be mental originality, there is the risk of a "jack-of-all-trades and master of none" effect. Developing continuity of purpose and learning to finish projects without prematurely diverting attention is the solution.

See page 18 for key concepts of Mercury in Gemini.

CANCER Mercury children communicate sensitively, with feeling and emotion. This placement is indicative of a mind that is attached to and influenced by emotional factors. It's difficult for the Cancer Mercury child to distinguish between *feeling* and *thought*. Receptive, Moon-ruled Cancer's watery emotional nature makes Mercury's energies uncomfortable. Logic is his game! Still, Mercury does transit Cancer in his course through the heavens and Cancer Mercury children are not without mental virtue. For one thing, they have excellent memories because experience is recorded emotionally as well as mentally.

Learning often comes surprisingly easily to Cancer Mercury, who absorbs a lot of information by osmosis and knows without knowing how. This can be a great advantage where subtleties are important or where intuitive abilities count. Subjects dependent upon logic fare less well, for Cancer Mercury's thinking is always colored by emotion and detachment comes hard.

Cancer Mercury is especially susceptible to taking on the family thought patterns, accepting what is picked up in the home atmosphere without analysis or consideration. Thus, if mom says that too much reading will make you sick, the Cancer Mercury will never be a reader. So it's important to monitor the thoughts that are absorbed by Cancer Mercury as it is very difficult to change them once the information has been received and stored. Early learned incorrect ideas about the world or a limiting belief system can cause harm in later life, because these ideas embed themselves on the emotional plane.

When communicating with Cancer Mercury children, always refer to how they *feel* about the issue at hand, rather than asking what they think. This placement thinks emotionally, identifying feeling as thought and you will get better results by recognizing this factor. Hard, cold logic does not sway Cancer Mercury who, when thus assailed, may simply retreat into a closed shell. Appeal to their sympathies, which will draw them out.

Connection to family and family traditions is important to the Cancer Mercury child, who likes to learn about the family past from its older members. This rootedness in the past can help stabilize the ever-shifting mental moods of Cancer Mercury, who also needs to be taught *objectivity*, admittedly not an easy task. When emotionally distressed, the worldview of Cancer Mercury gets distorted and out of synch with reality. A little calmness and sympathy will help to restore the balance.

In school, Cancer Mercury will rely on instinct and intuition, absorbing information through listening and watching films, especially those with an emotional content. Unimpressed by fads, Cancer Mercury kids are traditional minded and are unlikely to get carried away by the current trendy idea, as there is a natural caution here.

See page 20 for key concepts of Mercury in Cancer.

LEO Mercury children communicate self-expressively, entertainingly, playfully, and dramatically. Leo is ruled by the Sun and here the Sun's influence bestows willpower and strength. Leo Mercury children display mental self-confidence early — the ability to focus and concentrate which can be seen even in small babies.

Leo Mercury children are confident of the rightness of their concepts and will bend every effort to make others agree. Leo is the Sign of pride and Mercury here means prideful thinking, which can lead to the mistaken belief that challenge or criticism of ideas means *personal* challenge or criticism. A stubborn refusal to change can result. Parents need to teach this youngster that there will *always* be other points of view, but that disagreement, need not mean disapproval. It takes patience, but the Lion can be swayed from defense of a wrong position by an appeal to the truth of the matter. Leo Mercury wants to be right, but not just because it's the easy way out.

As Fire Sign Leo gives Mercury tremendous energy while the fixed nature of the Sign bestows pertinacity and perseverance, learning is dynamic and solid. Although Leo Mercury children will put a great deal of energy into organizing, planning, and problem-solving, they need guidance to evaluate the relative importance of projects so as not to waste time and effort on unimportant tasks.

There is a tendency here for youthful arrogance and a know-it-all attitude, the result of mental pride. These youngsters must be taught that others' ideas also deserve consideration and that a difference of opinion does not make one right and the other wrong. Leo can be bossy and overbearing, and Mercury here displays these qualities intellectually. On the other hand, Leo Mercury has a playful mind, full of creative energy. It's a matter of accentuating the positive and eliminating the negative.

Leo Mercury needs recognition for its mental efforts and praise for accomplishment, which will spur it on to even greater efforts. Whenever there's a problem with communication or learning, use praise *first*, criticism last, and try the suggestion-box method. Discuss the problem and then ask Leo Mercury to suggest solutions. You may be surprised at how quickly and easily a creative answer can be found by your child. Whatever you do, do not destroy Leo Mercury's pride or the result will be a massive sulk of hurt feelings and a retreat into defensiveness. Warm and loving by nature, Leo will always respond to affectionate guidance when offered in a non-threatening manner.

Natural leaders, Leo Mercury children can direct others and when put in charge knows how to get the troops moving in the right direction. Praise and validation motivate Leo Mercury above all else, and if that is lacking a mental shutdown can occur. This placement needs appreciation and consistent feedback.

See page 22 for key concepts to Mercury in Leo.

VIRGO Mercury children communicate in an analytical, logical, intelligent, orderly, and detail-oriented way. The most mental of the Earth signs and Mercury-ruled, Virgo is a comfortable placement. Children with Virgo Mercury are quick and alert, their minds like darting birds. The ease with which they categorize can be amazing and they quickly develop sequential abilities, being able to put numbers and objects in proper order at an early age. Classifying things, such as shells or stamps, will interest young Virgo Mercury and can teach the rudiments of a later scholarship in a field requiring data compilation and sorting.

The child with Virgo Mercury has an analytical mind, with great practical reasoning ability, and is good in school, approaching the task of learning methodically, going from point A to point B to point C in meticulous sequence without missing a beat. The Virgo Mercury has a discriminating mind, one capable of seeing the precise order needed to reach the goal. They especially enjoy working on tasks or subjects with a practical end in mind, such as woodworking or model-building, and being health-conscious they like to learn about health, hygiene, and nutrition. This is a good mind that likes to pay attention to detail, which makes it easy for Virgo Mercury to learn subjects that require precise careful thought or complicated techniques.

Insistence on attention to detail may seem fussy and unnecessary to others, but nothing seems trivial to this placement, and studies that insist on minute precision and accuracy appeal to this child, who will never slouch in the finishing up of precise work. This is an excellent position for scientific and research activity or anything that requires careful and detailed study and reporting.

Concerned with acquiring information and ideas with a practical end result, Virgo Mercury is work-oriented and may make "play," such as hobbies or science projects, into what looks like real adult work. Virgo's seriousness of purpose pins down Mercury's fleet-of-mind to the achievement of something concrete.

There is usually an attraction to education as a means to later success. Often, there is interest and proficiency in writing and speaking, and with a ninth House emphasis, a gift for languages. In any case, this placement is eloquent in speech and writing, paying great attention to the niceties of grammar and style.

Self-criticism is the major flaw of the Virgo Mercury, a perfectionist at heart, who is never satisfied. This youngster needs to be reminded that everyone makes mistakes, most of which are correctable.

Somewhat shy and retiring, Virgo Mercury prefers not to waste time in idle talk or goalless activity and could be encouraged to relax more.

See page 25 for key concepts of Mercury in Virgo.

LIBRA Mercury children communicate diplomatically, sociably, impartially, fairly, and peacefully. As their minds are primarily concerned with human relations, school for them may be just another place to socialize. Even small Libra Mercury has a consuming need to know about the thinking and behaviors of others. Smooth communication and pleasant relationships are paramount to this placement.

Libra Mercury has a preference for mental partnerships, which makes communication easy. As impartiality is their byword, Libra Mercury children spend a lot of time examining all their options before coming to a conclusion. So adept are these kids at seeing both sides of a situation that indecisiveness becomes a real problem. Their vacillating mental process can prove irritating to those whose mental gears move decisively. The trouble is that Libra Mercury can see some good in every possible choice and so concerned are they to weigh merits out evenly, nothing gets done.

Conflict is abhorred by Libra Mercury who would rather take two opposing points of view and combine them into a compromise position than choose one over the other. Never extreme or radical, Libra Mercury thrives on moderation.

Balance is important to the mental stability of this placement, which likes ideas and objects to be neat and elegantly arranged in a harmonious pattern. Often there is a facility with music or art, or appreciation if not performing talent. This should be encouraged with trips to museums and concerts for hands-on experience of the arts.

When conversing, Libra Mercury is always polite and diplomatic, avoiding harsh criticism or ugly words, striving always to please. Strife or abrasive situations will either send Libra Mercury running for cover or oil to pour on troubled waters. Smoothing and soothing with kind words and a well-modulated tone of voice, Libra Mercury strives to make peace. In general, except for having its impulsiveness curbed by the need for judicial balancing, Mercury works well here.

Unless taught to stand up for their own views and rights, Libra Mercury can become a victim of the "peace at any price" syndrome. So eager are they to keep matters running on an even keel that they sacrifice their own interests, running the risk of becoming the doormat of more aggressive types. Young Libra Mercury can tune in to learning that it isn't possible always to have peace and harmony — that family disputes are unavoidable, that life is not a bowl of cherries — if the admonition is offered in a clear and rational manner without emotion.

In fact, emotion is a troublesome area for this rational and intellectualizing placement. Innately polite and well-mannered, Libra Mercury finds the rough-and-tumble of raw emotion freely expressed quite upsetting and not at all polite or well-mannered. Enlisting cooperation is the best course.

See page 28 for key concepts of Mercury in Libra.

SCORPIO Mercury children have a penetrating intelligence that is expressed intensely, forcefully, secretively, determinedly, and relentlessly. Little Scorpio Mercury can be intimidating, for it is evident that this child is already *thinking*. At an early age, Scorpio Mercury will ask disturbing questions about the nature of things, especially death. This is a mind that strives to get to the bottom of any and all mysteries and unanswered questions. If, for example, a relative committed suicide, don't try to fend off Scorpio Mercury with, "He just went away," because eventually this inquiring mind will uncover the truth.

Even the youngest Scorpio Mercury has a searching mind and works tirelessly to ferret out information about what is of interest, flinching from nothing in the quest for truth. There's really no point trying to keep secrets from them. Detective fiction is a favorite form of entertainment reading, but real-life mysteries are the prime attraction.

Water Sign Scorpio makes Mercury receptive, and there can be psychic powers with this placement. If your child shows indications of extrasensory abilities, don't back off in horror but allow the youngster to communicate to you what is being experienced. An emotionally upset Scorpio Mercury can confuse feelings with thinking and mix the two inextricably. It's important to guide them gently to where they feel safe in expressing their deepest thoughts, which may sometimes frighten and puzzle them.

School is rarely a problem for Scorpio Mercury children, who love getting answers to "Why?" Their intense, investigative minds learn readily and their well-developed intuition makes them great researchers. Often they will solve difficult school problems without quite knowing how they got the correct result. When you ask, the answer will likely be, "I just *knew*."

There is a deeply secretive side to Scorpio Mercury and, while they may seem to read your thoughts, penetrating theirs is no small task. It's best not to pry, however, for Scorpio Mercury guards privacy, and someone poking around in their affairs makes them suspicious of motives. To get the truth, be truthful in exchange. And never lie to a Scorpio Mercury, for you will eventually be found out and forfeit trust as a consequence.

Sexuality is another interest, and it may seem premature, but avoidance of the topic will only intensify Scorpio Mercury's fascination with it. Straightforward answers will engender belief in your integrity, which is vital to building trust. Take care not to betray that hard-won trust for they rarely forgive and never forget.

Mental discipline comes easily to Scorpio Mercury, who can produce profound insights when searching for solutions to problems. Perceptiveness which can seem startlingly like mind-reading is another characteristic.

See page 31 for key concepts of Mercury in Scorpio.

SAGITTARIUS Mercury children communicate openly, truthfully, honestly, enthusiastically, and perceptively. The truth-seeker of the Zodiac, Sagittarius imbues Mercury with idealism and a broad view. As soon as this child can talk, a very curious mind will want to know the answer to every question imaginable. Sagittarius Mercury soaks up learning and knowledge eagerly and loves to go to school. Books of knowledge, encyclopedias, and reference books are all magnetic attractions to this inquiring mind.

Subjects that examine the entire range of human experience and study the Universe as a whole fascinate Sagittarius Mercury, who can spend hours and hours in the library mentally travelling to faraway places. The only school problem likely to manifest is that, in the quest for the big picture, Sagittarius Mercury can forget the boring details. As a result there can be sloppy work done in a rush. Though homework won't be shirked, it should be checked for accuracy of detail.

Sagittarius is known for direct and blunt speaking and Mercury here makes speech particularly blunt. This placement doesn't care much for politese and the roundabout way of communication considered to be socially acceptable. If your dress looks awful on you, Sagittarius Mercury will come right out with it. Don't be offended, for no offense is meant. Sagittarius Mercury just tells it like it is. Honesty is very important to them, but they have to be taught that others may have sensitive feelings — that telling Aunt Millie her hat looks as if she got it at a yardsale won't win any Brownie points.

The main strength of Sagittarius Mercury is the ability to assimilate new ideas and concepts. Always forward thinking, this Mercury soars up to the heights of conceptual thought. No notion is too foreign to contemplate, every new idea is an opportunity to expand the horizon of knowledge. Unorthodox ideas are more intriguing than threatening to Sagittarius Mercury who always strives for broader knowledge. There can be a fascination with the study of religions and philosophy and interest in foreign languages.

Communicating with Sagittarius Mercury isn't usually any problem, especially if you are fairly direct. Although tact isn't a strong point, it can be taught by example. In reprimanding a youngster for blurting out hurtful truths, a parent can give examples of how honesty can be combined with consideration of another's feelings. It's not a lesson Sagittarius Mercury learns easily, but as this youngster has no wish to hurt or distress anyone, there is at least the willingness to change. Teach Sagittarius Mercury to think before speaking.

Don't deceive Sagittarius Mercury and don't break promises. Their idealism extends to you and can come crashing down if they are lied to or taken advantage of. Naturally good-natured, upbeat, and optimistic, Sagittarius Mercury is vulnerable and can be crushingly disappointed.

See page 33 for key concepts of Mercury in Sagittarius.

CAPRICORN Mercury children communicate carefully, hesitatingly, seriously, moodily, and humorously. Capricorn is ruled by Saturn, Planet of discipline and restriction, so there is with Capricorn Mercury a reluctance to commit to any course of action that hasn't been thoroughly planned in advance. The keynote of Capricorn Mercury is its *seriousness*. Above all, this is a serious mind, concerned with practical reality. No flights of abstract fancy for this placement.

Due to an excess of caution and a need to make sure of all the facts beforehand, children with this placement may seem like wise adults at a very early age. The mind does not work quickly, but it works in an organized and careful fashion that brings results in the long run. It's best not to try to rush these children through any learning tasks, for anxiety about performance is a major factor. Essentially a practical thinker, Capricorn Mercury learns best when there is a useful end to mental efforts. Administrative and business skills may be evidenced even in preteen Capricorn Mercury children, who like to be taught the concrete workings of things.

Capricorn Mercury is not interested in what is speculative, ideal, unrealistic, or imaginative but only in that which applies to the needs of daily life or the conditions which must be met for actual usefulness. What this means to the school-age child is that learning must be subservient to serviceability. Time spent in dreams and fantasy is considered a waste. The danger here is that the mind becomes too narrow and dogmatic. A little light needs to get in, and parents of a Capricorn Mercury can see to it that their offspring is at least introduced to the delights of idling by the river bank. Chances are, however, that young Capricorn Mercury, while watching the waters flow, will be mulling over how dams are constructed rather than thinking poetic thoughts about how water sounds.

A positive result of Capricorn Mercury's native caution and insistence on getting the facts straight is the ability to communicate diplomatically. Choosing words carefully comes naturally and thought is expressed in a disciplined manner, which they enjoy having complimented.

Capricorn Mercury's thoughts are of a very serious nature, and pessimism is a problem. When alone, there is a tendency to brood and see only the darker side of life. Care needs to be taken to offer this youngster some balance, an opportunity to see the brighter side. Sometimes, in an attempt to alleviate the inner darkness, this negativity is expressed in an ironic or satirical humor which can be quite funny. Many comedians known for wry, dry humor have this placement.

Good organizers, Capricorn Mercury children have a natural urge to live up to the maxim, "A place for everything and everything in its place." Messy rooms are as abhorrent to them as disorderly thinking.

See page 36 for key concepts of Mercury in Capricorn.

AQUARIUS Mercury children communicate in a friendly and forthright manner, but they can be opinionated and rebellious in their thinking. They like whatever is new and unique, going out of their way to find friends with unusual and innovative ideas.

Good at science and mathematics, Aquarius Mercury combines the qualities of air and fixity, which together give Mercury the ability to function well in the abstract realm and to persevere from concept to conclusion. This is an original mind, innovative and sometimes brilliant. Offbeat ideas are common and can be held onto with tenacity. It's very hard to change the mind of an Aquarius Mercury once it's been made up.

The best way to communicate is by using a rational approach. Naturally clear and objective, this mind refuses to permit any emotional interference with the thinking processes. The result is mental coldness, due to reliance on pure logic, as exemplified by Mr. Spock of **Star Trek** fame. If it's not logical, forget it! Displays of emotion are disturbing to the Aquarius Mercury's rarefied mental air.

As Mercury is exhalted in Aquarius, there is an awareness which comes early and intuitively of the fact that all thinking is patterned on the Universal Mind and that reason is a product of this process. It is this knowledge that gives Aquarius Mercury its impersonal objectivity, allowing the acceptance of ideas that would be incomprehensible or reprehensible to others. Aquarius Mercury, for example, has no trouble believing in UFOs, and, if an alien chanced to be in the neighborhood, would invite it home to dinner to have a jolly good conversation about life in outer space.

Communication with Aquarius Mercury children is easy if kept unemotional and direct. Allowances should be made for the unique character of this child's mental processes. There's no benefit to expressing shock and dismay at the "weird" ideas these children can come up with. Tolerance is the best tool for keeping the channels of communication wide open. If you as a parent are accepting of the new and startlingly unique, you will be amply rewarded by the results of allowing the brilliant mind of this unusual child free range of expression.

Taking up causes is a common manifestation of Aquarius Mercury, who loves to orate on behalf of justice. Idealistic when it comes to humanity in general, young Aquarius Mercury may get so caught up in the concept of humanitarianism that the actuality of individuals is overlooked. While organizing protests to help the downtrodden and minorities gain their rights, this youngster can lose sight of the very real needs of loved ones. Aquarius Mercury needs to be reminded (logically, of course) that charity begins at home, that saving the world or the whales must not take precedence over attending little sister's ballet performance or feeding the family dog.

See page 38 for key concepts of Mercury in Aquarius.

PISCES Mercury children communicate intuitively, imaginatively, psychically, sensitively, and emotionally. Neptune-ruled Pisces gives Mercury a vivid imagination and a photographic ability to visualize thoughts and memories. From birth, this child is gifted with intuitive faculties. Like a tender plant, Pisces Mercury requires much careful nurture. The ability to tune in to the thoughts and moods of those with whom it comes in contact on a daily basis influences the way this mind functions. There may be an early indication of telepathic capacity.

Pisces Mercury's thinking is emotionally based, which is to say that this child thinks through the medium of his or her feelings. The two are so intertwined that there is no way to separate them out. The Moon Sign placement will be a help or a hindrance depending on its compatibility to the Mercury. This child arrives at conclusions by a mysterious and diffuse process that frustrates more rational minds. The fact that they are uncannily correct is even more irritating to those who depend exclusively on the rational function of the mind. Pisces Mercury learns more by osmosis than through good study habits or applied thought. In fact, so potent is the photographic memory with this placement that a child may simply look at a book once and remember what's on every page, which causes some youngsters to be accused of memorizing rather than reading.

There is extreme mental sensitivity here, and as the mind is naturally poetic and imaginative, the Pisces Mercury child may well show artistic abilities. Musical talent is common. Pisces is a mutable Sign and it gives Mercury a flowing, diffuse coloration that often evidences in an empathetic perception of reality. As the emotions are never ruled out from the thinking process, there is danger that emotional upset will cause thinking disorders. This possibility needs to be recognized and guarded against. Make sure this youngster has an emotionally stable environment in which to learn and play.

Another problem here is that fluctuating emotions can cause vacillation in thinking and impede decision making. There is a tendency toward daydreaming and woolgathering that needs to be curbed without squashing the creativity implicit therein. Pisces Mercury children are often accused of inattention, and it may be a valid criticism, but this is a delicate mind that needs to be allowed to grow its own type of flowers. The educational system tries to force young Pisces Mercury into the standard learning format, which never works. It may be that this child needs the special ambience of a music or art academy rather than the usual curriculum.

Emotional trauma can cause a morbid imagination in this oversensitive child, who takes every criticism to heart. Even the chance overhearing of a negative remark will be painfully brooded over. When this happens, Pisces will retreat into a private fantasy world and spin dreams of glory for solace, escaping the cruel world of everyday life.

See page 41 for key concepts of Mercury in Pisces.

(handwritten margin notes: teenage years – HHS)

VENUS

Through the Signs

ARIES Venus expresses love *enthusiastically*. As Venus wants to reach out and incorporate others, and Aries is self-centered, Aries Venus expresses emotion assertively and is concerned with self-gratification above all else. Unless these children are taught the advantages of sharing, they may become hopelessly selfish, demanding that their wants take precedence over all others.

Quick to take the initiative, Aries Venus will pursue the object of desire relentlessly, persistently refusing to take no for an answer. At the dating age, the girls are upfront about what they want as the boys, even if social mores prevent them from chasing their quarry as obviously. This placement often makes for competition where love and sex are concerned, and a blunt and outspoken approach when sexual interest is aroused.

There's no appreciation of the waiting game for this Venus, which goes from feeling attraction to immediate pursuit. The upside of this is someone who knows what's wanted and is willing to go for it. The downside is an insistence on having one's own way, to the detriment of the partner, which makes for stormy, uneven relationships with both friends and lovers. There's no quick fix for this problem, but the child can be taught to respect the legitimate expectations of others in relationships and learn the give and take of compromise with family and friends.

See page 13 for key concepts of Venus in Taurus.

TAURUS Venus expresses itself *materialistically*. Venus rules Taurus and is well-placed here, but that famous Taurean stability can cause possessiveness. Attachment to the love object is total: *"Mine"* is a cry often heard when someone tries to take a toy or possession from a Taurus Venus. Being taught to share will help, but it's not really possible to eradicate this firm grip on the materialistic.

The innate sensuality of Venus in Taurus shows up early in both sexes. They love being hugged, petted, touched and enjoy the sensuality of bubble baths, soft fabrics, and sweet smells. Later, if too much indulged, this sensuality can become a preoccupation with the material world and its goods to the exclusion of spiritual pursuits. It's important that parents temper this tendency with some restrictions, not giving in to every demand for *things*.

Sexually, Taurus Venus has a sweet and placid nature which readily attracts but is lazy and reluctant to pursue, preferring to sit comfortably with something yummy to eat and wait for love to arrive. Frequently, there is a displacement onto the refrigerator or the pantry and excess weight results. Taurus Venus needs a push — both to get more exercise and to put forth some effort into getting into relationships, which, once made, are usually long-lasting.

Taurus Venus loves nature, especially flowers and gardens.

See page 15 for key concepts of Venus in Taurus.

GEMINI Venus expresses itself *superficially*. The desire for variety of experiences makes it difficult for Gemini Venus to settle on just one of anything. Here, in light, flighty Gemini, Venus has no desire for permanence. The term "planned obsolescence" was coined for this placement. This child is a born member of the throw-away generation and places little or no value on what is enduring. In smaller children, this will evidence as boredom with yesterday's toys and games and a continual demand for new things.

The Gemini Venus child has no trouble making friends, attracting them with charm and the sparkle of wit, and enjoys having as many as possible. Being on the go is also a trait of this placement, which will want to go to different places to meet and hang out with a myriad of friends. The reason for the numbers is that this placement wants to keep relationships light and easy, nothing heavy or too emotional. Gemini Venus isn't particularly interested in becoming *involved* in the lives of others, because that means commitment and responsibility, which Gemini Venus avoids. During the teen years, this placement will be a romantic gadabout, more interested in talking about the experience of love than in actually having it. The need for constant stimulation makes Gemini travel frequently in pursuit of new and different romantic adventures, which indicates a certain innate fickleness.

See page 18 for key concepts of Venus in Gemini.

CANCER Venus expresses itself *nurturingly*. Even quite small children like to take care of what they love — dolls, toys, pets, smaller children. Later, Cancer Venus will "mother" friends and loved ones as a way of showing love.

Deeply sensitive, Cancer Venus can be hurt so easily that it makes any relationship difficult. Self-knowledge and the development of objectivity, so as not to take everything to heart so much, are the antidote. Because they take everything so personally, Cancer Venus is moody and unpredictable. In smaller children, this can mean the rejection of something or someone that pleased them previously because of some small wound invisible to others.

Relationship for Cancer Venus children centers around the parents, with whom they want to be especially close and affectionate. Lack of this bond can cause tremendous difficulties with their sense of security, which is fragile. Children with this placement will attach fiercely to friends, preferring a few very close relationships that can be counted on for emotional support to many acquaintances.

Sibling rivalry is a possibility here because Cancer Venus often feels a need to compete for parental affection. Attachment to the mother is usually pronounced in both sexes and can become a problem later on if not addressed at the proper time. Teenage romances are often a result of the need for security, of having another person to depend on, rather than true affection.

See page 21 for key concepts of Venus in Cancer.

LEO Venus expresses itself *dramatically*. The most extravagant placement of Venus, Leo wants admiration and pursues love with great zest. This need for dramatics can be overblown, even in preschoolers who may want to dress up and act out at an early age. Leo Venus so craves the center of attention, that there can be outrageous demands upon parents and others if neglect is felt.

Leo Venus youngsters are likely to be quite popular and have a lot of friends, for they like people and are well liked in return. Leo is the sign of pride and Venus here means pride in love. This placement will stick by its friends loyally through thick and thin as long as there is no hint of dishonesty or deception, both of which wound Leo's pride most fearfully.

The Leo tendency to grab the spotlight may also make the choosing of friends a matter of what looks good to others, and in teens this can mean socializing with popular or especially good-looking boys and girls, those who dress well, drive fancy cars, or live in big houses. This is not obsequiousness but a love of the grandiose and magnificent. Leo Venus wants a palace to live in as befits royalty.

Basically warm and friendly, strong and honest, there is still a need to keep the romantic nature from going to excess and overdoing everything, from the sending of unwanted cards and gifts to the giving of praise so high it seems insincere.

See page 23 for key concepts of Venus in Leo.

VIRGO Venus expresses itself *discriminately*. Even small children delight in doing favors for the people they love, because serving is a major way that Virgo Venus shows love. The unselfishness of these children is charming, but there is a danger that Virgo Venus will choose only friends who need help, not those who genuinely care. Helpfulness is certainly a virtue to be encouraged, but the development of self-love is important to this placement who often is very self-critical. Try to get Virgo Venus to relax and indulge enjoyment in the non-rational side of life.

Venus, the Planet of love, in Virgo, the Sign of practicality, makes the love nature here realistic and disciplined. No foolish spending on luxuries, just what is utilitarian! Teenagers may criticize their more extravagant friends' spendthrift ways, especially if they are also less than neat. Virgo Venus puts high standards of perfection on personal habits and dress and turns a keen analytical ability toward relationships. This tendency to analyze romantic involvements and to criticize the love object makes the teen years a trial for the Virgo Venus, who just can't understand why people don't appreciate the intellectual approach to love. Virgo Venus has to learn that everyone has faults but it is the flaw in the diamond that gives it its unique value, that friendships are to be treasured for who the person is, not for what level of perfection has been reached.

See page 25 for key concepts of Venus in Virgo.

LIBRA Venus expresses itself *harmonizingly*. Friendly, and outgoing, Libra Venus likes to have fun with others. As Venus rules Libra, here her love nature is all about other people and one-on-one relationships. Libra Venus feels lonely very easily and seeks to assuage this by constantly being with companions. Libra rules marriage, and the Libra Venus will express a desire for marriage very early, even in childhood. As soon as they are old enough, these youngsters will bend every effort to reach that goal. Libra Venus children can be expected to marry young.

Though Venus is well-placed here, an aversion to discord and disagreements makes Libra hang on to a partner just to be in a relationship, at any cost. This can lead to trying to become what the other person wants rather than being true to one's self, what I call the "chameleon effect." This striving to adapt in order to gain approval by harmonizing with whoever is the current partner can produce much psychological and emotional strain.

Beautiful objects and fine clothing act like a magnet on Libra Venus, who will dress as tastefully and as fashionably, with as much elegance and grace, as the budget allows. There is excellent sense of proportion with this placement and possibly artistic talent.

Being in a harmonious relationship in beautiful surroundings is what Libra Venus strives for constantly, but any confrontation can make them nervous and upset.

See page 28 for key concepts of Venus in Libra.

SCORPIO Venus expresses love *intensely*. At an age when most children are still playing with toy trains or dolls, Scorpio Venus is already aware of sex. The internal level of emotion is so vivid for these children that the desire nature is of the all-or-nothing variety. If Scorpio Venus cannot have what is ardently desired, no substitute will be accepted.

The child with this placement has feelings about people that are vehement: either Scorpio Venus loves you or hates you. Possessiveness is a strong trait, and youngsters often do not want to be separated, even for a short time, from parents and others they love, which extends to pets and favorite possessions. This stems from the depths of the innate love nature, which cannot tolerate anything superficial or shallow. It is therefore difficult for Scorpio Venus to trust enough to become attached, but once attached the bond is permanent.

The problem this presents to the teen at the dating age is that this kind of possessiveness may drive the very ones who are wanted away by not giving them enough "space." Young Scorpio Venus needs to be taught that others, not as intense, need their freedom, and that there are valid relationships other than the inseparable kind. These youngsters are prone to form passionate attachment to a single friend with whom they want to spend all available time.

See page 31 for key concepts of Venus in Scorpio.

SAGITTARIUS Venus expresses love *objectively*. Idealism is the hallmark of Sagittarius, and Venus here can lead to an impractical image of the other person, whether parent, friend, or love object. In addition, with characteristic bluntness, Venus here can be insensitive to the feelings of others, even those very close. Because Sagittarius Venus wants everything to be on a high moral plane, especially its relationships, fairness is important, a trait that attracts many friends to this outgoing placement.

Young Sagittarius Venus is open about feelings, but, not wanting to be tied down, keeps romance somewhat at a distance. Possessive types seeking commitment send this teen running in the opposite direction. "Don't fence me in," could be the theme song for this placement. Friends are going to be those for whom friendship is a casual matter, with no strings attached. The tight one-on-one relationships of many teenagers do not appeal to Sagittarius Venus who likes to be free to choose friends without any one friendship getting in the way of another. Consequently, displays of jealousy can make them break off a relationship.

Sagittarius Venus teens avoid the going steady craze and may be well into adulthood before considering settling down. So strong is the desire for freedom that Sagittarius Venus accounts for many a lifelong single person. This is primarily a "good sport" placement.

See page 33 for key concepts of Venus in Sagittarius.

CAPRICORN Venus expresses love *cautiously*. Capricorn keeps feelings under control at all times, inhibiting Venus. Another factor is seriousness. Youthful Capricorn Venus will express feelings with more seriousness than others the same age, often leading to a preference for relationships with older people who have information about the world and how it works. Essentially a practical Sign, Capricorn gives Venus a certain coldness, for status and material possessions are considered of great importance. Sometimes friends are chosen for their wealth or other advantages they can bring to Capricorn Venus, and there can quite openly be marriage for gain. Young Capricorn Venus needs to learn that there are values in relationships beyond the practical. The tendency to use people and to choose friends for what they can do to promote materialistic ambitions should be curbed before it becomes a habit.

Sometimes the ordinary pleasures of life seem beyond the grasp of these youngsters, for whom enjoyment of simple, non-materialistic treats is hard. Their innate seriousness and concern for financial security drives them to concentrate on acquisition, not pleasure.

Displays of emotion are abhorrent to conservative Capricorn Venus teens who nevertheless need warmth and affection. Their seeming cold is a result of a deep natural shyness which can come across as snobbery and aloofness.

See page 36 for key concepts of Venus in Capricorn.

AQUARIUS Venus expresses love *detachedly*. Friendly with everyone, Aquarius Venus children have trouble forming close attachments because of their fear that emotional ties will lead to a curtailment of their freedom. Parents may feel rejected by their offspring, but an understanding of the inner dynamics of this child will help ease the pain. There is an impersonal quality to Aquarius Venus that goes against the nature of the Planet. Venus personalizes and relates; Aquarius distances and rationalizes. Venus thrives on intimacy; Aquarius loathes and fears it. The motivation for Aquarius Venus in making numerous friends is the excitement of variation and the reduction of the risks of intimacy. These kids collect the oddballs in the neighborhood and at school, and they are stout defender's of personal liberties.

As Aquarius Venus reaches the teen years of romantic involvement, they seek out free, nonbinding relationships with a variety of different people — those of another race, country, religion, or political orientation — often going far afield of their normal environment. There's little chance of Aquarius Venus forming a lasting romance in the school years, for at the first sign of ordinariness, Aquarius Venus moves on to greener pastures. Only later in life do these youngsters finally learn the value of intimacy and a tolerance for the messy side of an emotional encounter.

See page 39 for key concepts of Venus in Aquarius.

PISCES Venus expresses love *intuitively*. Dreamy and prone to fantasizing, Pisces gives Venus a spiritual quality. This child loves books of a romantic nature, stories of beautiful princesses held in castle fortresses by awful ogres and finally rescued by handsome heroes. The real world holds no charms for Pisces Venus, for this child has an inner fantasy world that is much more interesting and beautiful than ordinary reality. They may try to cover up their rich and sensitive inner life.

A child with this placement is unselfish, always giving, trying to help those less fortunate. The love nature here palpitates with empathy for everyone else, from those at home to waifs seen on TV. In fact, too much TV watching of "reality," or of violent cartoons can upset this child's inner stability. So sensitive is the heart, so full of love, that any display of insensitivity or cruelty is terribly upsetting, making it easy to manipulate these youngsters by appealing to their sympathetic natures.

In the teen years, Pisces Venus yearns for the ideal, fairytale relationship with the predictable result. Severe disappointments come in the wake of Pisces inability to discriminate the real from the unreal. The lesson of discrimination is important for Pisces Venus to learn, as early as possible, in order to avoid deep hurt later on in life. Help Pisces Venus child to be extremely careful when choosing friends and romantic relationships.

See page 42 for key concepts of Venus in Pisces.

MARS

Through the Signs

ARIES Mars children express action *self-assertively*. With abundant physical energy, they need hard play, preferably outdoors where they can run and shout. When they are cooped up for any length of time their active Mars energy turns restless and can become destructive. Mars rules Aries and is thoroughly at home here, but Aries Mars children hit, push, and shove as a response to any action from others they don't like. It's important to teach these children at an early age to take out excess energy, especially anger, in an alternatively nonviolent manner, such as hitting a punching bag instead of another child or the parent. Repressing this dynamic energy isn't a good idea, for it will go underground and emerge in an explosive way.

Motivated by challenge, the desire to be first, and a need to win, Aries Mars makes good leaders and can inspire others to greater heights than they might achieve alone.

This is a strong placement (unless aspected by Neptune) bestowing courage and force, strength and daring. The downside of Aries Mars is a headstrong, devil-may-care attitude which inclines the native to rush into any and all activity with little thought. Aries Mars must learn that action has consequences.

During the teen years, Aires Mars wants to drive soon and fast, is likely to take unnecessary risks for the sake of speed, and is prone to premature sexual activity.

See page 13 for key concepts of Mars in Aries.

TAURUS Mars children express action *slowly*. The earthy, stable nature of Taurus holds Mars back, with the result that physical energy is slow to ignite. This does not mean that Taurus Mars has less energy than other children, only that it burns at a different rate. There is tremendous stamina with this placement and Taurus Mars children will still be going when their quicker-burning companions have dropped by the wayside. Being naturally conservative, Taurus sees no need to waste energy (which can look like laziness but isn't). Side effects of this slow-burning energy are patience, persistence, and efficiency.

As Taurus gives Mars staying power, these youngsters persevere, never giving up until a task is finished, no matter how long it takes or how difficult the effort. However, this admirable trait also confers stubbornness, for Mars' power in Taurus is fixed and cannot be pushed or moved. Slow to anger, Taurus Mars is a formidable opponent when finally aroused. Often there is great physical strength, especially in the shoulders and neck.

Teen Bulls seek sensuous, including sexual, experience, and their earthy sensuality has a smouldering quality.

Possessiveness and an inability or unwillingness to communicate verbally can be problems, especially in the teen years. Teaching sharing and encouraging verbal communication will ameliorate the tendency to some extent, but it *is* built in.

See page 16 for key concepts of Mars in Taurus.

GEMINI Mars children express action *quickly*. A mental Sign, Gemini imbues Mars with quickness, talkativeness, and agility. Sports requiring agility and fast movement — tennis, fencing, ping-pong, or sprinting — are more likely to appeal to Gemini Mars than body-contact sports. Gemini Mars might prefer to report on these sports rather than actually playing them, for this placement often shows a talent for writing and favors journalists and critics.

Primarily motivated by intellectual stimulation, Gemini Mars children like to expend their energies in mental and social pursuits. Though they do have considerable nervous energy, there is rarely much physical stamina and they tire easily. Fatigue brings on irritability and susceptibility to respiratory ailments. Somewhat frail in childhood, they develop small, wiry physiques.

Being extremely agile verbally, Gemini Mars can be scathingly sarcastic when angered, but their ire burns out quickly. Like a fast-burning roman candle, there is a brilliant display, then it's over. And because they forget easily, they don't carry grudges. They will go to almost any length to enliven a situation they find tedious. Starting an argument for the sake of the argument, not because they care about the outcome, is a favorite diversionary tactic.

Sex is a matter of great interest for Gemini Mars teens — as a subject of conversation. They are accomplished flirts but don't take the subject too seriously.

See page 18 for key concepts of Mars in Gemini.

CANCER Mars children express action through *feelings*. Whatever they do is dependent on the mood of the moment. The Cancer Mars child who is feeling upbeat and positive, will act with confidence and self-possession, but when the tide turns and the mood changes this child will retreat into silence and inactivity. As the Moon rules Cancer, mood changes are to be expected.

As Water Sign Cancer dissolves the aggressive energy of Mars, softening its direct nature, it's hard for Cancer Mars to be forthright about anything, especially the expression of anger. Supersensitive, Cancer Mars is easily offended, becoming hurt and angry inside while repressing any outward show of feeling. So emotionally security-conscious are they that they hesitate to show displeasure for fear of losing love. Over time, this repression can make them sullen and hard to reach. This is especially true in the tumultuous teen years when emotions and hormones are interacting. To prevent a build-up of hostility, Cancer Mars needs to be given a firm sense of emotional security and a safe way to express negative feelings.

Attachment to home and family is strong and casual sex usually holds no appeal. Emotional dependency is a danger for Cancer Mars who may become involved in an unsuitable relationship out of a yearning for someone to lean on. Rarely, however, do these teens get into the kinds of difficulties of the more wandering types.

See page 20 for key concepts of Mars in Cancer.

Tim

LEO Mars children express action *dramatically*. There is always the grand gesture and the extravagant pose. Mars' energy combines with Leo's fixity to provide a tremendous vitality which also has staying power. This is a strong placement for Mars, which gives exceptional willpower and a natural authority. Motivated by pride, Leo Mars children prefer doing things on their own initiative, which makes them natural leaders. Drawn to physical activities of all kinds, Leo Mars enjoys individual over team sports.

Although Leo Mars angers slowly, usually as a result of wounded pride, temper displays can be quite melodramatic, for underneath the histrionic fireworks there lurks an injured lion whose dignity has been compromised. As the Lion hates losing face, restoration of dignity will set things right. Avoid using sarcasm with this child, and remember that praise will move mountains.

Enthusiasm and personal magnetism belong to Leo Mars, and this teen will be popular and sexually attractive. Leo's regal nature gives Mars a tendency toward arrogance and a domineering attitude, but underneath is a born protector.

The Leo Mars youth is attracted to the glamour of romance and the passion of sex, and love involvements will be of the soap opera type with many cliff-hanging episodes and dramatic entrances and exits. In love as in all else, Leo seeks the bold and full-blown experience and wants the partner to be a King or a Queen.

See page 23 for key concepts of Mars in Leo.

VIRGO Mars children express action *cautiously*. Temperate and reliable, modesty and moderation are natural to them. Because they approach any task in a careful and systematic manner, with an aim toward perfection, Virgo Mars children may be quite upset with themselves if a project doesn't come up to a preconceived standard. Self-criticism may make them throw the whole effort away in disgust. Though relatively impervious to praise, they need encouragement to accept that their efforts, even if they fall short, are still worthwhile. Virgo Mars children like to learn the use of tools or instruments and can be trusted to handle them with appropriate care.

Interest in activities that produce a practical, usable result, such as model-building, woodworking, beading, and sewing, usually takes precedence over sports. Intelligent and motivated by the desire to achieve perfection, Virgo tames Mars' energy into practical applications giving this placement an ability to excel in activities which require manual dexterity combined with precise detail, such as crafts and computers.

Virgo Mars' anger is expressed with deliberate logic. Rarely are there any fireworks of temperament. Likely is a scathingly detailed critique of the opponent's faults.

Under Virgo Mars careful ways lurks an appreciation for sexuality and outward appearances of primness and neatness can be deceptive. Virgo Mars teens are definitely interested in exploring their urges but will do so in a refined manner.

See page 26 for key concepts of Mars in Virgo.

LIBRA Mars children express action *diplomatically*. When self-oriented Mars confronts relationship-oriented Libra, the result is a state of confusion. This is resolved either as a strong sense of cooperation with others and a preference for partnership activities where compromise is part of the endeavor, or as a strong sense of competition. The former type knows that working in tandem is a better way of getting more done than working separately and is willing to forfeit self-gratification in order to get along with the group. With the second type, Mars' assertiveness overwhelms Libra's conciliatory nature. Frequently, Libra Mars switches back and forth between the two types of behavior.

Whichever mode is operating, Libra Mars will weigh both sides of the matter before taking action, which seems like procrastination but is in reality wavering between options.

Motivated by the need for relationships, Libra Mars has a low tolerance for acting alone, initiating and organizing social events, parties, and get-togethers of all kinds. In the teen years, Libra Mars expends much energy on partnerships, becoming the social butterfly. The Libran insistence on good manners, fair play, sophistication, beauty, and propriety can result in superficiality.

Gracious and charming, Libra Mars has much romantic appeal but finds "basic instinct" difficult to tolerate. Refinement and esthetics are what count to this teen for whom being in a relationship is of utmost importance.

See page 28 for key concepts of Mars in Libra.

SCORPIO Mars children express action *intensely*. They do nothing halfway or half-heartedly. This powerful Mars placement is combustible, determined, and persistent. There is a terrific willpower, even among the very young. Scorpio Mars children are the ones who will hold their breath until they turn blue or refuse food until malnutrition sets in. It's a mistake to think you can break the will of a Scorpio Mars, for here Mars energy combines with Scorpio power and can turn destructive if thwarted.

Although slow to anger, once provoked, Scorpio Mars' rage has both power and endurance. Pointed and biting sarcasm are one way the stinging Scorpion shows anger, and the emotional intensity behind such remarks can be intimidating. As a long build-up can result in physical illness or explosive destruction, young Scorpio Mars needs to be shown how to release anger safely. Heed warning signs, and understand that Scorpio Mars children, frightened of the intensity of their feelings, may need help to prevent being overwhelmed. Never take the feelings of a Scorpio Mars youngster lightly.

Because emotions are always involved, Scorpio Mars is physically forceful — persistent and enduring, continuing to the bitter end, and welcoming high risks to personal safety.

Scorpio Mars is drawn to the darker side of sexuality, seeking to test self-discipline and personal mettle. Secrecy about sexual interests and activities is likely.

See page 31 for key concepts of Mars in Scorpio.

SAGITTARIUS Mars children express action *uninhibitedly*. The effect of freewheeling Sagittarius on Mars is to scatter its energy to the four winds. Like the wild mustang, Sagittarius Mars is all speed and no endurance. This child needs to learn self-discipline and energy rationing. Without it, that impetuous burst of energy fizzles in exhaustion. Sports like horseback riding are especially appealing to Sagittarius Mars, who likes to fly like the wind. Sagittarius Mars may express a desire for skydiving or hang gliding — for these sports give a sense of freedom.

Sagittarius Mars children like to be outdoors in the fresh air with the wind in their hair. This energy just naturally rebels against restriction. Give Sagittarius Mars the room to express freedom and spontaneity. Fortunately, so strongly motivated are they by the need for freedom that they willingly assume responsibility for it, being reliable and not inclined to unnecessary risk-taking. Reward a teen Sagittarius Mars with an adventure trip.

Idealistic Sagittarius Mars is roused to anger by injustice and will fight for any good cause. They chafe at curtailment of personal liberty and this affects their romantic inclinations which are of a spiritual as well as a carnal nature. Sagittarius Mars is looking for the ideal love and may seek it for many years.

See page 34 for key concepts of Mars in Sagittarius.

CAPRICORN Mars children express action *seriously*. Nothing is considered to be just a lark to this child who likes every activity to be as well-planned as a military campaign. As Capricorn imbues Mars with discipline and organizational abilities, even the young are ambitious and willing to work hard for results. The preteen Capricorn Mars may go out and collect soda bottles for the refund money, cut a neighbor's lawn, or get a paper route. And the money earned will go into a savings account, not be frittered away on childish pursuits.

Career-minded Capricorn Mars will be perusing college catalogs while in junior high school, and by high school will know exactly where to apply. Because tangible results are what motivate Capricorn Mars, responsibility is no problem for this youngster, who can be trusted to be reliable and prompt. Doing battle does not appeal to Capricorn Mars, but efficiently organizing the troops does. This placement favors generals, politicians, and CEOs.

Capricorn Mars gets angry in a controlled but powerful way, not fire but ice is what you see. Sometimes anger is colored by contempt for idleness, sloppiness, or incompetence — all of which annoy ambitious Capricorn.

Though possessed of an earthy sensuality, Capricorn Mars is controlled about sex, willing to wait for the right partner who will contribute to the climb up the ladder of social and financial success.

See page 36 for key concepts of Mars in Capricorn.

AQUARIUS Mars children express action *unconventionally*. Whatever the usual or traditional way of doing things, Aquarius Mars will want to find another way. Never mind grandma's tried and tested recipe, the budding cook will throw together whatever comes to mind, pop it in the oven, and, voilà! — a new creation.

Motivated by the need to be different, Aquarius Mars chooses friends whom parents may classify as "weird." Extreme modes of dress, hairstyle, or makeup are a hallmark. Rather than getting upset about this expressionistic behavior, parents need to remain calm and give Aquarius Mars permission to express individuality. Criticism or demands to revise the way they dress, the music they listen to, or the friends they see, will only result in rebellion and eventually alienation. Resisting authority is natural to Aquarius Mars, but it will respond to suggestions made on an intellectual, rational level.

Aquarius Mars anger is of the cool, logical type, very intellectual and remote. Emotional displays make this placement extremely uncomfortable.

Drawn to humanitarian causes, Aquarius Mars works well with groups but avoids the restrictions implicit in romantic relationships. As emotional involvement makes Aquarius Mars queasy, these teens usually prefer the safety of the group to romantic entanglement.

See page 39 for key concepts of Mars in Aquarius.

Pisces Mars children express action *sensitively*. Watery, idealistic Pisces takes the wind out of Mars' fiery, independent sails. Here, Mars retreats from his usual aggressive role and sulks under the sea, waterlogged and uneasy. Low physical energy is the norm, and these children often need extra sleep, which should not be misconstrued as laziness. Pisces must make frequent contact with dreamland where it can restore depleted energies. Pisces finds Mars' ordinary world of action anathema. The only wars that interest are the ones King Arthur and his knights fought.

Motivated by feelings and imagination, the way to ignite Pisces Mars is to provide tools for inspiration — music, books, or art. Give Pisces Mars its due and one day this fertile imagination may create a masterpiece! With plenty of sleep and private time, young Pisces Mars is sweet-natured, loving and giving. If they are not good at physical activities, don't push or make fun of them. Let them watch tapes of *The Neverending Story* instead. Encourage them to express their feelings in stories, poems, and drawings, and work to build up their self-confidence. Ridicule will only drive Pisces Mars further into the depths of fantasy.

In love with love, Pisces Mars teens are likely to moon over far-distant or unattainable ideals. When they do get romantically involved, it is in an old-fashioned moonlight-and-roses way.

See page 42 for key concepts of Mars in Pisces.

THE INTERMEDIATE PLANETS

The Cycles of Jupiter and Saturn

CHAPTER IV

JUPITER

The Universal Principle

With Jupiter, we move from the realm of the strictly *personal* toward the *external* world and *society* at large. Ruled by idealistic Sagittarius, this "greater benefic" serves as the interface between the individual and the institutions upon which the social order rests — schools and universities, churches, the legal system, banking, charitable organizations, government, and the like. According to esoteric tradition, where Jupiter is placed is where we have already earned "karmic" benefit and protection from the Universe.

Whereas Mars is the slowest of the faster moving personal Planets, taking two years to transit the entire Zodiac, Jupiter is the fastest of the slower moving "outer" Planets, taking twelve years to make an entire transit of the Zodiac. This timing factor means that Jupiter stands squarely between the two sets of Planets and, along with Saturn and its 28-year cycle, serves an intermediary between the inner and outer realms of being.

Thus it is that Jupiter's influence partakes somewhat of both spheres but does not entirely belong to either. The twelve-year cycle means that he spends a year in each Sign, making his influence much less personal than that of the Sun, Moon, Mercury, Venus, and Mars.

Therefore, unless Jupiter makes direct connection to one or more of the personal Planets, his effect on the individual chart is somewhat impersonal.

Known as the "second sun," Jupiter has generally been thought to symbolize positive energies such as prosperity, success, good luck, honor, and accomplishment, but as with every planetary energy, there is always a downside. This giant among the Planets is credited with being the representative of the principles of *expansion* and *growth*, and whereas ordinarily these things are beneficial, there is always the danger of *overexpansion* and *too much growth*. The primary worldwide example of this is the ecological destruction caused by overpopulation. In an individual life, excess expansion can mean overeating, overspending, overworking, and other excessive behaviors.

Through association with learning and religion, Jupiter is representative of the Higher Mind and, consequently, of the development of higher mental and spiritual attributes. He goes beyond the purely rational level of Mercury to seek an understanding of universal principles on which thought is based. This desire of the mind for the grand overview is exemplar of Jupiter's *integrative* function.

As Jupiter is the ideological basis for systems of thought, be they philosophical or religious, orthodox or unorthodox, his Sign and House position give information about our ethical, religious, and philosophic attitudes and show how we are interested in philosophy and higher education. So, we look to Jupiter for *spiritual* as well as social development.

Jupiter key characteristics:

Expansiveness	Overexpansion
Optimism	Foolhardiness
Abundance	Exaggeration
Ethical	Judgemental
Enthusiasm	Unrealistic
Principles	Dogmatic
Society	Hypocritical

Jupiter rules Sagittarius where he is especially well-placed in a good match between Sign and ruler.

Jupiter's *exhaltation* is in Cancer, which rules the home, and as parents are the child's first teachers, the principle of learning is established at home. As Jupiter also rules social conduct, and as the family is the basic unit of society, Jupiter in Cancer is powerfully placed and produces emotionally sympathetic people who understand that all of humankind is a family.

Jupiter represents *how we grow beyond the personal sphere* and *how we integrate things.*

KEY CONCEPTS FOR JUPITER THROUGH THE SIGNS
How we grow beyond the personal sphere with Jupiter:

In *ARIES* by taking chances and trying new things.

In *TAURUS* by conserving resources, loving nature, and determining values.

In *GEMINI* by expanding our information base and communicating about it.

In *CANCER* by mothering, caring, and empathic responses.

In *LEO* by expressing creativity and assuming leadership responsibilities.

In *VIRGO* by paying attention to small things and doing service work.

In *LIBRA* by being involved in relationships, beauty, and ideas of justice.

In *SCORPIO* by sensing what is beneath the surface and going through changes.

In *SAGITTARIUS* by learning, philosophical study, and the expansion of horizons, especially by travel.

In *CAPRICORN* by being goal-oriented, dealing with reality, and being alert to practical opportunities.

In *AQUARIUS* by developing friendships, abstract thinking, and living humanitarian ideals.

In *PISCES* by helping others, creative endeavors, and spiritual pursuits.

How we integrate things with Jupiter:

In *ARIES*, quickly, immediately, rashly.
In *TAURUS*, slowly, deliberately, resistantly.
In *GEMINI*, logically, mentally, scatteredly.
In *CANCER*, emotionally, personally, worriedly.
In *LEO*, playfully, grandly, self-referentially.
In *VIRGO*, carefully, practically, compulsively.
In *LIBRA*, cooperatively, aesthetically, indecisively.
In *SCORPIO*, secretively, perceptively, suspiciously.
In *SAGITTARIUS*, openly, philosophically, carelessly.
In *CAPRICORN*, conservatively, efficiently, unimaginatively.
In *AQUARIUS*, analytically, originally, impersonally.
In *PISCES*, imaginatively, idealistically, ambiguously.

In children, Jupiter expresses the desire to expand and grow and to integrate knowledge into the Self and the Self into the larger world. This process, of course, requires a certain amount of maturity prior to attaining expression. Therefore, when relating Jupiter to children, it is necessary to be aware of the 12-year Jupiter cycle.

Before reaching maturity, a child will experience two full Jupiter cycles: birth to age 12 and age 12 to 24. The Jupiter cycle can be likened to an ascending spiral: each turn repeats the one before on a higher level of development. Thus, there are repetitions of growth patterns evident at each stage along the cycle. What happens at age 12 will be mirrored at age 24, and so on.

Though the Jupiter function lies dormant in the early years — as a child must have developed some cognitive skills before the Jupiterian energy can be brought forth consciously — even small children are imbued with a sense of wonder. They can experience faith, accept the idea of a higher power, be open to grace, possess optimism, and grow spiritually.

THE FIRST CYCLE

What precipitates the Jupiterian urge is the dawning of awareness of being separate beings in a larger world, which usually occurs at about age three. At this time, Jupiter is three signs forward from its natal position, making the first aspect by square. Children become conscious of themselves as separate entities with limited control over their environments, which leads to the urge to expand out into the world.

Next, at about age six, when Jupiter opposes the natal position, comes the phase of actually going out into the world, which is usually concurrent with beginning school.

As both physical and psychological growth progresses, increasing the scope of the child's action and experience, Jupiter becomes more evident, and by age nine, when Jupiter makes the second square to the natal position, the child is beginning to assert a new sense of self and is testing independence and social relations beyond the family.

By age 12, when Jupiter returns to his natal position, a measure of independence has been reached and with it conscious awareness of a desire to learn, travel, be free, and make moral decisions.

During this first cycle, it is imperative that the parents give the child encouragement and support in the effort to grow and expand into the larger world. New challenges, especially in education, arise daily, and for each challenge there should be a corresponding encouragement to give the child sufficient faith and self-confidence, thus preparing the ground for the second cycle.

THE SECOND CYCLE

At age 12, a new phase of development of individuality begins with the new Jupiter cycle, and the child now uses Jupiter energies in an increasingly conscious and individualized manner.

During the second cycle, the integrative side of Jupiter comes to the fore. Jupiter, known in the Greek pantheon as Zeus, was the *father god*, and it is during the second Jupiter cycle that the relationship to the father in terms of the world comes into play. Whether he is the actual biological parent or not, during this time it is the function of the father figure to aid in the child's growth beyond the personal by providing constant challenges and the emotional, physical, and educational help needed to meet those challenges. It is during this cycle that the child must find a place in the world, determine a role to play, a sphere in which to be effective.

For the next three years, ages 12-15, the Jupiter function develops new facets of the personality in a subjective, interiorized manner. The child may express an interest in religion, or rebel against the family religion, asking many questions, attempting to integrate what is felt internally with what is given externally. The same is true of learning and school. Nothing much of this inner process may show up in the outward life, but, like a seed planted deep within the Earth, the Jupiter energy is preparing to burst forth.

In the opposition phase, ages 15-18, the child begins to integrate the Jupiter energies. The Jupiter function becomes more observable as something begins to happen, like green shoots protruding above the dark soil. This germination of the Jupiter influence carries much potential. During this time the child should be aided to build ties to the community and to expand areas of competence.

The third quarter, ages 18-21, will generally coincide either with the college years and the acquisition of higher education or entry into the work force. At this time it will be evident how well the person is able to function within a social context. The potential glimpsed in the second quarter will now show whether it will bear fruit or die on the vine. During this period, the young adult must decide whether to grow spiritually or stagnate in the materialistic sphere. By now the developing person should have the use of sufficient "tools," whether of a mental or physical nature, to take into adult life. This is possibly the most important phase of this cycle, for during this period the young person will be able to use conscious awareness to reach beyond the self and meet others as equals. This is the time, too, for asserting an individual vision of life and the ideals upon which it will be based, of assimilating new experiences, previously unknown or considered alien, and of blending one's unique vision with the social reality in a cooperation of values.

The last quarter of the second cycle, ages 21-24, brings the opportunity to test Jupiter values in real life. By now, a social context should have been established in which to do this, producing concrete results, such as getting a job or going on to graduate school. It is now that the person is challenged, once again, to grow. As this cycle ends with the second Jupiter return at age 24, the seed of the new cycle is already forming, which will take the individual another spiral up the ladder of Jupiterian growth and integration.

SATURN

The Great Teacher

Saturn is the planet of discipline and structure, time and ambition, and represents where we are tested by the Universe, bringing tasks and trials to the person from whatever area is indicated by the Sign and House he occupies. He also brings stability, permanence, responsibility, and a capacity for self-sacrifice as well as dependability and endurance. A hard worker, Saturn rules Capricorn, the natural executive of the Zodiac. Once his often harsh lessons are learned, he grants wisdom and an understanding of practical reality. During the approximately 28 years he takes to transit all the Signs of the Zodiac, he points to the necessary ways a person must develop in order to achieve maturity.

A major factor in career choice and development, Saturn's position can give vital clues about what type of profession or what kind of work will suit or attract a person. Where Saturn is strongly placed, the person may be not only a hard worker but a workaholic, but if Saturn is weak or indifferent there may be many false starts and lack of strong career development. Nevertheless, whatever position he occupies, he indicates the kinds of responsibilities and tasks that each must face in this journey through life. Saturn's is the serious face of the planetary influences, and where he is placed shows what we take most seriously, as well as where we must face obstacles. However, by overcoming the tests he sets for us, we learn, sometimes with many trials and tribulations, what we need to know to develop spiritually, for in the end this is the purpose of any of life's trials, no matter how hard it may be to accept that idea when we are in the throes of coping with them.

It is through this process of growth — or trial by fire — that we eventually find order and security and understand that Saturn is the king of the manifest world, which is to say that he stabilizes and brings forth into Time what is otherwise ephemeral and only mental. The person using Saturn correctly can build castles in the air and then construct them on the ground so people can live in them.

Saturn is much concerned with status and recognition, and where he is placed by House is the area in which he tries to produce something of long-lasting value, permanent if possible (probably the Egyptian pyramid builders were a Saturnian lot!). The eyes of the world are important to Saturn — he demands respect, even at the cost of love. Yet his love is sturdy, when it has been earned, and you can depend on him in a pinch. The road may be long and hard where he leads, but he carries his share and more along the way.

On the negative side, where Saturn is found is where one has a feeling of disappointment, insecurities breed, and overcompensation often takes place to overcome painful feelings of inadequacy.

Saturn represents the law of limitation — necessary limitation — and that of conservation of energy and resources.

If adults, who presumably are used to and accept that there are limitations in life, find the structured energy of Saturn difficult to cope with — and most of us do — then this restrictive energy can have a strangulating effect on children. Saturn in a child's life is first encountered through the parents saying, "No, you can't do this. No, you can't have that." And though it is necessary for parents to place restraints on children, *the manner in which this is done* will dramatically effect the child's ability to later incorporate Saturnian limitations into the psyche, thus using the energy corrrectly and productively. Saturn is the planetary representative of the archetypal Authority Figure, and parents are the first authority figures. How children learn to relate to parental authority will bear fruit — sweet or bitter — in adult life.

If parents provide arbitrary authority that makes no sense to the child, enforce rules erratically or provisionally, do not themselves deal well with restraints and responsibilities, or follow a course of "Do as I say, not as I do," then the pattern is set for the child's negative use of Saturnian energies, which eventually will evidence as either fear of authority or disregard of it.

In order to give the child a positive experience of the Saturn energy, parents must provide a consistent and logical framework (remember, Saturn is a mental planet) that the child can trust, learning that rules are for protection and safety. When necessary discipline is given with abundant love, the child can respect the parents through knowing they truly care. On the other hand, when discipline is capricious or merely an acting-out of the parent's frustration or unresolved personal problems, the child quickly sees what is really going on and learns to distrust all adult authority.

Teachers are second in line as authority figures, and it is important for the parent who understands the child's Saturnian challenge to communicate with the teachers on a level that will enable them to provide a positive and beneficial authority role for the child. If this is done, the child should have no trouble coping with later authority figures such as police, civic officials, examiners, and future employers.

What ultimately is needed is for the child to be able to incorporate a positive authority figure into the psyche rather than to rely on an external one. One problem is when a parent's natal Saturn falls on the child's Sun. This is a difficult placement between charts, especially when the father is the parent with the Saturn on the child's Sun. When this conjunction occurs, the father is often experienced as menacing in some way, whether real or imagined. The parent can take care to ameliorate the situation, but projection of the child's fears onto the parent is another matter entirely. If not dealt with properly, this projection can extend itself to teachers and society as a whole. Counseling may be advised.

When a parent's Saturn contacts a child's Moon, a sense of loss or sadness may ensue, quite often from a real cause. In these cases, extra love and attention to the child's Moon needs is prescribed.

Sun/Saturn and Moon/Saturn contacts in the chart of the child are reflections of the same difficult life lessons (see Chapter X, The Aspects).

In the long run, Saturn teaches the child about reality. The world is not an easy place for anyone, but the person who has a firm sense of inner structure and discipline is better equipped to deal with life's unpredictable vagaries than the one who must always look outside for authoritative guidance.

Saturn exhaltation in Libra, the Planet of harmony and balance, may seem odd, for Venus-ruled Libra's nature is sweet, but Libra rules marriage, which is perhaps the most exquisite balancing act in human life. And nowhere is there more need for *voluntary* restriction and restraint than in marriage where the happiness of both parties depends on the cooperation of each with the other. In the final analysis, Saturn teaches us how to live in harmony with ourselves, balancing emotional needs with worldly realities, using inner discipline to take responsibility for our actions, acting not for our own benefit but for that of those we love and, by extension, for all of society.

Saturn key characteristics:

Disciplined	Restricted
Practical	Limited
Structured	Rigid
Time-conscious	Fearful
Conservative	Confined
Mature	Cautious
Wise	Restrained

Saturn's *exhaltation* is in Libra, which rules marriage and one-on-one relationships, and deals with the interaction of the self with the other. As the bringer of stability, Saturn favors Libra and here best expresses the idea of partnership, not only with a spouse but with the rest of humanity. Saturn here teaches the lesson of cooperation with others in the real sphere of time and space.

KEY CONCEPTS FOR SATURN THROUGH THE SIGNS

Saturn represents *how the greatest lessons are learned, what we are afraid of*, and *what we need to change.*

The greatest lessons are learned with Saturn:

In *ARIES* by assuming leadership positions and dealing with aggression, self-assertion, or the lack thereof.

In *TAURUS* by developing personal resources and value systems and dealing with acquisitiveness.

In *GEMINI* by socializing, teaching, and having a variety of experiences.

In *CANCER* by emotional attachments, nurturing, and feeling deprived.

In *LEO* by dealing with pride, power, and self-expression.

In *VIRGO* by dealing with regular schedules, details, and health.

In *LIBRA* by making judgements, having relationships, and romantic encounters.

In *SCORPIO* by dealing with sexuality, deep feelings, and sharing resources.

In *SAGITTARIUS* by overdoing things, studying ideas, and exploring foreign cultures and lands.

In *CAPRICORN* by being dutiful, ambitious, and materialistic.

In *AQUARIUS* by group associations, friendships, and mental experimentation.

In *PISCES* by creative discipline, surrendering to a higher principle, and showing love.

The greatest fears are with Saturn:

In *ARIES* of appearing weak or being at someone's mercy.

In *TAURUS* of physical discomfort, hunger, privation.

In *GEMINI* of being confined, unable to communicate.

In *CANCER* of loneliness, starvation.

In *LEO* of appearing foolish.

In *VIRGO* of not being perfect.

In *SCORPIO* of being found out.

In *SAGITTARIUS* of not knowing.

In *CAPRICORN* of being improper.

In *AQUARIUS* of not understanding.

In *PISCES* of lack of direction.

The greatest need to change is with Saturn:

In *ARIES* to stop pushing so hard.

In *TAURUS* to loosen up.

In *GEMINI* to lighten up mentally.

In *CANCER* to stop worrying so much.
In *LEO* to let myself love.
In *VIRGO* to relax my overactive conscience.
In *LIBRA* to develop discipline.
In *SCORPIO* to admit to being wrong.
In *SAGITTARIUS* to avoid self-righteousness.
In *CAPRICORN* to have fun.
In *AQUARIUS* to warm up to others.
In *PISCES* to be free of guilt feelings.

THE FIRST SATURN CYCLE

With its cycle more that twice the length of Jupiter's, Saturn remains approximately two-and-one-half years in each Sign, making it the second of the generational Planets and the last of the intermediate Planets. Whereas Jupiter stands closest to the personal Planets, Saturn stands closest to the outer, or trans-Saturnian, Planets. He is therefore the gateway to the outer realm of the collective unconscious, that which is least personal to the individual and most common to the whole.

But Saturn's cycle, unlike Jupiter's, covers the entire process of childhood development from birth to the threshold of full maturity. Thus, this Planet is the *timer* of the Zodiac. Often called Father Time, Saturn, with his restrictions and limitations, is concerned with both time and timing. His cycle of approximately 28 years is divided into four sections of seven years each, coinciding with other seven-year cycles in the astrological system, which allows us to predict with some reliability the major *crises* of an individual's development which punctuate the cycle of 28 years.

In *Cycles of Becoming* (p. 8)

Astrologer Alexander Ruperti describes a crisis as follows, "Cycles are measurements of change. In order for any purpose to be realized, change must take place, and change necessarily involves crises. Many have difficulty with the word *crisis*, confusing it with "catastrophe." [However] . . . it derives from the Greek word *krino*, "to decide," and means simply a *time for decision*. A crisis is a turning point — that which precedes CHANGE."

So, even though Saturn is a generational planet with its Sign placement describing whole groups of people, it is valuable as a marker of the stages of development.

THE FIRST QUARTER: THE "ORGANIC LEVEL"

The first quarter of the first Saturn cycle, from birth to age seven, corresponds with the "Organic Level" of development. During this period, the physical body and the organs, with their inherent psychic energies, are growing. Equally important to the child's continuing development is the possibility of missing factors in the growth equation. Just as a lack of calcium or Vitamin D can cause bone deficiency during the first seven years, so a lack of love can cause psychic stunting and damage the child's later ability to love and be loved.

Saturn is about separation, and the infant's first conscious experience of separation from the mother comes at about the time Saturn moves into the next Sign from where it was placed at birth, at approximately age two.

Saturn is also about the past. In this organic phase, the child is expressing the genetic heredity and also inheriting the existing family structure with its traditions, prejudices, points of view, and so on. Family dynamics begin here.

As Saturn moves farther from its natal position into the third sign forward (age five), the child is becoming progressively more independent and more interested in separating from the parents. Small rebellions are characteristic of this age.

By age seven, the end of the first quarter, known as a square aspect, the child has reached the "age of reason," and is usually attending school and has adjusted to the idea of daily separation from home and parents. This is the first important step in the process of growth from undifferentiated infancy to individuality.

The first Saturn crisis occurs at ages 7 to 8 when the child's fledgling attempts to assert volition begin. This can be a time of great stress, as the child wants to make choices — what food to eat, what clothes to wear, what time to sleep and wake up — and may rebel. This questioning of the absolute authority of parents is a necessary step in the growing-up process, but one fraught with danger for the young psyche.

If this initial crisis is met with understanding and love, the child will weather it and earn a measure of self-confidence. If, on the other hand, parental authority comes down on the child like the proverbial ton of bricks, preventing a stretching out to meet the world and squashing the nascent urge toward self-responsibility, the crisis will deepen. One result of the unresolved crisis with authority is that the youngster may become a bully and, in the quest to become an authority figure, lord it over younger siblings or smaller classmates.

Should the crisis occur while Saturn is transiting a personal planet, especially the Sun or the Moon, the situation will be exacerbated. If the Sun, there will be difficulties with the father; if the Moon, with the mother. This could mean a divorce, or separation from one or both parents, a move to another location where the child would feel inadequate and deprived of familiar surroundings, or a death in the family. If a contact is made with Mercury, there could be trouble with school and learning; if with Venus, problems with relations with others; if with Mars, unwonted aggressiveness brought on by some traumatic event.

This is a very vulnerable time in the development of the Self and extra care and attention from those responsible for the child's well-being is needed.

THE SECOND QUARTER: THE "POWER LEVEL"

The second quarter of the Saturn cycle, ages 7 to 14, corresponds to what has been called "The Power Level," or the time that the child is building *consciousness* of the world and becoming aware of ego, or the "I am," factor. This period is a time of proving personal powers by testing in the fields of experience. Interestingly, the beginning of this phase is when permanent teeth begin to emerge! By now the child is fully aware of being separate from mother and all others.

It is during this quarter of the Saturn cycle that the child's efforts at self-expression begin to operate in an autonomous way. Now, instead of "Me wants," the child says, "I want," with the emphasis on *I*. The world which up to now was mother-centric now becomes ego-centric. This new "I" which is developing takes over and fascinates the owner. This is a time of posturing and assuming attitudes, trying on as it were different personalities to see which one fits "I" better. Often this trying on of personalities is accompanied by a literal trying on — of clothes, friends, music, hairstyles, jewelry — first borrowed from adults, later purchased at the mall.

The purpose of all this trying on is creative self-expression and self-assertion. The new Self, having discovered its existence, wants everyone to know about that existence. Visibility is prized. As in the previous stage, how parents handle this trying period is vital to the child's later development. Allowing as much self-expression as is consistent with safety, basic courtesy, and home rules will move the child up the ladder of successful Saturnian development. Efforts to crush this attempt at making Self visible will result in both immediate and later difficulties.

At this time the challenge for the developing ego is to realize itself and then communicate that Self to others. One way is through games and activities where there is an opportunity to show leadership, prowess, and power. Another is through artistic creativity and the showing of a product. Still another, through rebellion against what is perceived to be the adversaries to such expression. This latter comes along as Saturn moves one more Sign along, at about ages 9½ to 10½.

Once again, parental handling of these attempts at individuation will influence the success of the next period.

The second crisis overlaps the end of the first quarter and the beginning of the second quarter of the cycle, when Saturn reaches the point opposite of its natal position, at ages 14 to 15. Signaling the burst of both physical and psychic growth that is adolescence; it coincides with or follows the physical/emotional state of puberty. For the next seven years, hormonal development is the primary factor. With it comes all the confusion we associate with that period between childhood and adulthood. Already physically mature (in that sex and procreation are possible now), the budding adult must realize that maturity is more than sexual activity. If the route of early sexual activity is chosen, the individual learns, usually to his or her sorrow, that being grown-up is a lot more than having sex and babies. Saturn teaches this lesson ruthlessly.

Given proper parental supervision and guidance, the teenager coping with oncoming sexual maturity need not lose the way. Saturn, in the form of parents and other authority figures, teaches that with freedom comes responsibility, and that without responsibility freedom is often taken away — as in being incarcerated or tied down by a newborn. Though the onslaught of sexuality and its possible negative consequences seems paramount at this stage, there is more to the crisis.

What is of equal or greater importance now is the growth of the *mind*, the rational faculty. Schoolwork is intensifying, plans for a career or college are in the making, and if the development of objectivity about the world and the ability to critically evaluate experience is not solid during this phase, then adulthood will be both delayed and impaired. During this crisis period there is usually some sort of confrontation with society having either positive or negative results. It is at this time that the still-developing ego structure must incorporate into itself an authority figure to guide and direct from within.

For some, the peer group becomes the new authority — replacing parents, teachers, and even society's laws. For those teenagers heavily dependent on group approval, this is a difficult time, fraught with dangers. The important thing for both parent and child to realize is that giving in to "peer pressure" is merely another form of submitting to an authority *outside one's self*. This point cannot be emphasized enough. Whether the uniform is a buzz haircut and a single earring worn with ripped jeans and a T-shirt, or the neatly pressed khaki suit of the uniformed soldier, it is still regulation and does not represent individual expression nor freedom of the Self.

Parents who have helped their child to successfully pass the first crisis and who have provided firm and stable guidance during the intervening period will reap the rewards of their attitudes and actions during the second period and their teenage offspring will weather the second crisis and take another giant step into maturity. Those parents who either repressed the need for self-expression or who took the course of least resistance and simply provided unlimited latitude will now reap the fruits of their earlier parenting mistakes. During this crisis the adolescent needs authority *against which to rebel*. If the authority stands firm and strong, the youngster is able to test strength without destroying the needed support. If the authority fails to withstand the onslaught, or simply isn't there, trouble results.

Though the adolescent may appear grown-up, this is an extremely vulnerable time. The child needs the security of knowing that parental attention is available while still being respected as an emerging adult.

THE THIRD QUARTER: THE "PSYCHOLOGICAL LEVEL"

The third quarter of the Saturn cycle, ages 14 to 21, begins with the crisis described above and corresponds to the "Psychological Level" of development.

Now, emotional and mental spheres are to the fore as a result of the rise of the I-sense. Having found a way to express Self (if things have gone right), the teen is now concerned with *relationships* of all kinds, both personal and institutional.

At this time, most everything in the child's life is emotionally centered and self-oriented. Saturn's lesson now — the central challenge of adolescence — is to become *aware of others' needs* in intimate and public relationships.

Prior to now, all sorts of self-absorbed experimentations were tried out in order to discover the fascinating range of inner possibilities available to outward expression. In this third quarter, however, Saturn will teach the child through the process of relating to others.

As the newly forming adolescent's urge toward relationship becomes primary, like a butterfly emerging from its chrysalis of self-absorbtion, the teen is now ready to visit and feed on the nectar of many relationship flowers.

Following this emergence, the adolescent is griped by the need to fulfill two separate and sometimes conflicting urges. The one, clamoring from within under the stimulation of biological and glandular changes, is for *love*, for an intimate relationship of singular significance. The other, stemming from a different inner need — the drive to become a functioning part of the larger whole, the society into which the child was born and of whose continuity he or she is an expression — is for *education*.

Depending on the balance of the chart — and here is where the energies of Venus and Mars come in most strongly on the side of the sexual/romantic craving — the teenager will often seek to concentrate on one over the other. In the case of the more romantic, *feeling* chart (strong Venus/Mars, Water or Libra emphasis) the urge to merge will be dominant. This type of adolescent will be prone to crushes and bouts of puppy love, given to mooning about, yearning for a love that will provide completion. Grades may suffer under the impact of this search for the ideal love. At this juncture, parental guidance is vital and Saturn's placement will indicate where the trials will occur and where discipline is needed.

The larger purpose of this love-orientation is to reflect the young person in the mirror of love and romantic attachment. This phase is an extension of the search after Self, only now the Self is seen in the eyes of the Other. In psychological terms, this is the first *identity crisis* and it is resolved by having a partner. *I am* because I am *with someone* is the emotional equation, exemplified by the words of a popular song, "You're nobody until somebody loves you."

What is happening here is that the teen is projecting out to the world at large an image of a concept of the ideal love partner. This image is usually derived from the media, which blitzkriegs the young at every stage of their development. Movies, TV, and romance novels all contribute to the formation of this ideal image. Most of the time the imaginary picture is based on purely physical attributes — a certain hair and eye color, height, weight, body measurements, muscle proportion, athletic ability, etc. Rarely does this image go beyond the merely physical to include such things as character, mental power, ethical principles, moral values, and the like. However, when, under the pressure of the yearning for love, the teen chooses an actual real person to carry the image being projected, Saturn steps in to shatter the illusion, forcing the teen to undergo the experience of *reality*, warts and all. At this point, one of three things can happen. The adolescent may jettison the relationship to continue in the search for the idealized image, or continue in the relationship while attempting to mold the partner to the image, or, if lucky, will learn from the experience and modify the romantic illusions to better fit reality.

During this process, which is likely to last several years, the child's chart can be most helpful to the parent. Used as a guide to the romantic/sexual nature and proclivities, it can provide significant information which will allow the parents to offer sensitive guidance to their teenage child. And guidance is vital, for if this identity crisis is not met properly, the young person can go into adulthood with romantic illusions that can never be fulfilled, leading to broken marriages and an eternal seeking for a love that does not exist and therefore cannot be found. The love vision is necessary, for without it there is no quest, but the teenager must be made to understand that love can only serve its purpose of nourishing the highest aspirations of the Self when a consciousness of reality replaces the projected image. This is a lesson that teenagers desperately need to learn and one which many of today's adults have not learned yet.

The second type, which chooses education over the pursuit of the idealized love, usually has a chart with an preponderance of mental and practical placements, such as Venus in Capricorn or Mercury in Virgo, to name two possibilities. This type recognizes that this period of life has a greater purpose and there is a natural expansion into the awareness of social responsibility. Higher education is the goal of this youngster. Whereas the former type may need active persuasion to remain in school, this type thinks of school as a primary goal which will lead to a later successful life. These teens take responsibility seriously and are eager to make the first step into the assumption of full adulthood. Often there is overt interest in social issues, politics, and the choosing of a profession. The parents can help this young person by encouraging the desire to remain in school and seek higher education. Even if funds are short, emotional support and parental belief in the child's ability to surmount obstacles and reach the envisioned goal can work miracles. Without family support, the most talented individual may achieve little, whereas the youngster with family support will seize upon every opportunity to get ahead.

It must be said that most young people are a combination of the two types, for even the most dedicated college student needs and seeks love and sex and the most romantic dreamer is faced with the necessity of earning a living. It is the balance between the two that is important and helping a child to achieve that balance is one of the most essential tasks of the parents.

THE FOURTH QUARTER: THE "SOCIAL-CULTURAL LEVEL"

The fourth and last quarter of the Saturn cycle, ages 21 to 28 approximately, corresponds to the "Social-Cultural Level" of development.

The young person, legally an adult, who can vote and drink alcohol, sign legal contracts, open a bank account, or marry without a parental signature, is now approaching graduation from college, if that route was chosen, or entering the work force from some other portal.

Now, two challenges await. The first is forward-moving — venturing into the workaday and community life to become a full participant in adult society. The second, backward-oriented, to break away from the bonds and restrictions of the past, usually the result of parental and social conditioning.

The ensuing crisis, at ages 21 to 22, has been called the "crisis of consciousness." It is a time of calling into question those beliefs, ideas, ideals, and attitudes that comprise the mental furniture which has sustained the youth up until now. Seen to be worn and shabby, it requires reexamination in the light of present-day realities. For more rebellious youth, who may already be in full cry against the values of their traditional past, the crisis may be a joyful catapult into the freedom of being at last on their own. For most, however, this is a difficult and strenuous time. The ideas and ideals of aspiring youth, which generally sees itself as the generation that will finally change the world, now must meet the grim Saturnian visage of adult necessity. Many student-held attitudes, never having been tested, must be shorn away and many young people, wishing to cling to the carefree unrealities of school, acting only upon their own personal aims and wishes, experience this as a time of real anguish. Decisions about what is real and valuable are agonized over until, gradually, like a bird molting in order to grow another season, the vestiges of youthful dependence are finally shed in the wake of this last of the first-cycle Saturn crises.

At this time there is a changeover from being outwardly pointed into the field of action to being inwardly pointed into the field of inner growth. It is a time of soul-searching, of assessing the past to determine those things which now must be left behind, like a sports letter jacket, on the passage into maturity. The task is to relinquish childish things while retaining what is of value from the past and past associations. It is a time of choosing associates and determining how one is to participate in the larger society. If rebellion did not occur in the teen years, chances are it will appear now. Parental authority may be seen as not only unnecessary but ridiculous and, especially to the college student, the parents now seem intolerably stupid. The fruits of this crisis, if it is handled well will be the ability to act in a responsible manner toward all relationships, private and social. However, if this crisis fails of resolution, the young adult will remain psychically in the parental womb, fixed in past patterns that eventually will suffocate and strangulate growth. It is a time for the parents to, metaphorically speaking, kick the fledgling out of the nest. This nest-leaving time is without doubt one of the most difficult for the parents who must help the youngster to sever the bonds that have been so carefully nurtured for the past 21 or so years. But until the young person has broken past the emotional and intellectual accumulation of the growing-up years, which form barriers to the true Self's coming into being, there can be no real individuality, no permanent growth into healthy maturity.

An additional task is the breaking away from the peer group which has been a buttress for the teen. Not only must parent-child bonds be dismantled, but dependence upon the group must be left behind as well. It is a tumultuous time. Young people with strong placements of natural independence in their charts, such as Aries and Scorpio, may temporarily become "loners," spending much time in isolation in order to grapple with the severance from the past. Others, more dependent, such as Cancer and Libra, may rush into early marriage to avoid the necessary task of individuation, replacing dependence on parents with dependence on a spouse. If this happens, the youth may marry a mother or father figure instead of becoming an independent adult capable of choosing another independent adult as a life partner. Failure to separate from the influence of the peer group will result in someone who is always looking for collegiate type approval from "the gang."

As the Saturn cycle winds to its close at ages 28 to 29, the youth will be faced with more and more choices and given more and more options. Choices made and options taken or refused will determine the life path of the following cycle. Whatever is done during these years will set the tone for the next 28 to 30 years. If the Saturn crises are successfully passed, the youth will have emerged from the family pattern and the social matrix fully fledged, independent, self-reliant, spirited, and confident — ready to fully assume the mantle of adult responsibility.

On the other hand, if the crises are not fully met the youth will remain caught in what Joseph Campbell has called "the nursery triangle," of dependence on the established family and social patterns, unable to realize the Self and, embedded in the patterns of the past, passively content to repeat the parental life.

This is not to say that failure is doom. There is always another chance with Saturn. If these early crises are not met, a second opportunity will come round with the next cycle. What it does mean is that a person will be coping at 45 with what should have been resolved at 17. And it's no fun and a great deal of work to face an adolescent crisis when one is also facing a mid-life crisis!

Clearly, then, to reprise, all of the crises of the first Saturn cycle are major turning-points, and all need parental help and guidance to come to a successful conclusion. With astrology's help and the understanding to be derived from a knowledge of this crucial cycle, parents can give their child the great gift of a realized Self!

Saturn rules Capricorn where he is especially well-placed in a good match between Sign and ruler.

THE
TRANSPERSONAL
PLANETS

Uranus
Neptune
Pluto

CHAPTER V

Beyond Saturn are the outer, or *transpersonal*, Planets — Uranus, Neptune, and Pluto — the realm of the great collective of humankind. Astrologers call these Planets "of the higher octave." The outer Planets are of particular importance to the raising and understanding of children, for they show us the *generational patterns* which will impact today's parents, for the nature of these planetary energies is expressed by entire generations of people due to their long orbits. Uranus, for example, takes 84 years, an average lifetime, to transit the Zodiac, spending approximately seven years in a single Sign (the length of a Saturn quarter-cycle). Neptune spends about 12 years in a Sign, and Pluto from 13 to 32, owing to its erratic orbit.

Although the Sign position of the outer Planets is not irrelevant, it is less specific than that of the other Planets. While the previously discussed Planets deal specifically with the physical, emotional, and character development of the *individual*, the transpersonal Planets are concerned with both spiritual and generic evolution. The energies of these trans-Saturnian Planets are not easily personalized. The way we contact them most directly is through aspects to one or more of the personal Planets, which act as transformers to funnel the higher octave energies into our lives. The House position as well as the aspects furnish more specific information about how the Planet will affect an individual.

URANUS

The Higher Mind

Destroyer of old ideologies, concepts, and structures, Uranus is the antithesis of Saturn and represents not only the advanced thinker, modern scientist, and esoteric occultist but also the bohemian, the beatnik, the hippie — nonconformists of all stripes including revolutionaries, anarchists, and those radical humanitarians who believe and preach that all of humanity is but one family.

Uranus was discovered in 1781, just 29 years (a complete Saturn cycle!) after Benjamin Franklin made his famous kite experiment. Thus, its discovery coincided with that of electricity and the subsequent development of electronics and telecommunications. Uranus produces sudden change of all sorts, and, like a thunderstorm, often serves to clear the psychic air.

It is the opinion of esoteric astrologers that Uranus has to do with the unique task of each person in this particular incarnation, that he is a clue to the soul's reason for making this journey. In a sense, where Uranus is found the soul is most free of restrictions, for old karma has already been dissolved and there you can be truly yourself — unique and individual. The well-known astrologer Alan Oken has this to say of Uranus,

> Uranus symbolizes Man's liberation from the bondage of the personality and signifies the power which may be achieved through the collected energies of truly individualized souls working toward a conscious connection with the Source of Life. (*Complete Astrology*, p. 216)

Where Uranus is placed in the chart is where we tend to behave in a free-spirited way — be unconventional, knock over tradition, be an iconoclast, do the unusual thing, or produce the far-out idea.

Saturn symbolizes restrictions and obstacles while Uranus is the urge for freedom from all restrictions, physical or mental. Ruler of Aquarius, an Air Sign, he is decidedly mental in nature. It is where Uranus operates in the chart that ideas are born, and through which individuality is expressed. Where he is by Sign and House is where you will find the most need for self-expression and freedom from restriction. It is where you will kick up your heels (or at least want to) and it is where you have the opportunity to make direct contact with the Universal Mind, through the faculty of intuition. Uranus holds out to us the link between our own mental efforts and the laws of the Universe that bring things into being. With Uranus, we soar into the realms of originality and innovation and there find new ways to solve life's problems. Uranus is the force for the awakening of our higher consciousness.

Uranus, the higher octave of Mercury, is the mind's pattern-maker and he tries out everything mentally and then sets goals based on mental preoccupation. The action of Uranus, the "cosmic magician," who rules magic and invention as well as electricity and electronics, is sudden and unexpected.

He shows us where we hope and dream and wish. Uranus is the "what if?" or "why not?" attitude of the inventor who says, "Let's see what happens if we do this," or the experimenter who isn't afraid of putting two unknowns together to find out what will happen. It is where we are least afraid and most spontaneous, where we get most excited, where we express our creativity and the intuitive, or sixth sense, faculties.

Probably everyone at one time or another has had a "flash" of intuition, sensing with subtle antennae that an event is about to take place, that Aunt Jane is at that very moment on the way over and the doorbell rings and there stands Aunt Jane. This "psychic" ability is in us all but we are seldom aware of it except in rare instances, and when it does flash out, we distrust it. So we were right about Aunt Jane, and maybe a few other things, but. . . ? We don't think it safe to rely on this rather erratic source of information, even if we have had it proven to us that the information can be correct. With proper attention, it *is* possible to hook into this so-called "sixth sense" and harness it for our personal use. Those of us who have done so are usually called "psychic," a catch-all term for anyone who is tuned into the powers of intuition.

In the past, such people were variously venerated or burned at the stake, depending on the time and culture, but today there is a renewed interest in psychic powers for the good of all humanity. When everyone is aware of this intuitive ability, which resides in us all, then we will truly have our Aquarian Age, a revolution properly presided over by Uranus, Planet of the Higher Mind.

Uranus represents the expression of *brilliance* and *freedom*.

Uranus key characteristics:

Intuitive	Undisciplined
Innovator	Iconoclast
Unexpected	Explosive
Awakener	Destroyer
Liberator	Rash
Humanitarian	Anarchist
Revolutionary	Rebel

Uranus rules Aquarius and when found in this Sign his characteristics are all emphasized.

Uranus is *exhalted* in Scorpio and gains power there. The current generation of people with Uranus in Scorpio will show unusual courage and daring, some staking life itself on adventures into the unknown — probably advanced space exploration — and will seek out new forms of mental power which are connected to the hidden forces in nature.

URANUS FUNCTIONS THROUGH THE SIGNS

As Uranus remains so long in one Sign, we will cover only those Signs applicable to the current and forthcoming generations.

Uranus in Scorpio (1974–1981). The Scorpio generation is an unusual one that may seem moody and puzzling with a good deal of obsessive/compulsive behavior. Feelings for these children can be quite difficult to handle and even more difficult to express openly and verbally. There is a tendency toward silent preoccupation, even sullenness or moroseness coupled with deep insight, which in itself can be frightening for there are no roadmaps or role models available to the traveller on uncharted inner paths. This is an important generation, the first to come to adulthood in the wake of the momentous changes in the former Soviet Union territory, the first not to live under the constant, unrelenting possibility of nuclear attack. As they mature, these children will want to work for changes of great magnitude in the world. Scorpio is the Sign of the healer, and as adults they may invent and/or discover new ways of healing, for they will understand intuitively that mind and body are one.

Uranus in Sagittarius (1981–1988). The Sagittarius generation will begin to come of age just as the new millennium — the year 2000 heralding the Age of Aquarius — arrives. These children will want to devote their energies to achieving a spiritual regeneration of humankind. They will propose and actuate new philosophies, questioning all previously accepted tenets of established religion and society. Building on the work of the Scorpio generation, which will have cleared away many obstacles to necessary change, these children will be attracted to new and innovative *ideas* and they will brook no restraints on their right to think as they please. In fact, they may be quite eccentric and the generation may produce a large number of freedom-loving and free-thinking innovators who will implement their ideas with action.

Uranus in Capricorn (1988–1996). The Capricorn generation is another that will question established authority and want to make changes in the social institutions. However, they will be extremely practical and down-to-earth about the *how* of making these changes. As inheritors of the previous generation's innovative thinking, they will be the builders of the so-called "New World Order," laying down firm foundations for tomorrow. Prior to their coming of age, there will be tensions with adult authority figures who will react negatively to their far-reaching plans for social change.

Uranus in Aquarius (1996–2004). When Uranus reaches his own Sign, he will produce a generation of children who will be extremely gifted in the realm of humanitarian effort, able to effect change and to evaluate that change objectively. This will be a mental generation, given to lofty thoughts about humanity and its role on the Planet. Many of them will develop their intuitive powers easily, understanding that the sixth sense is a powerful tool for the further development of humanity. This may be a generation which produces many inventors and innovators whose ideas and products will be aimed at bettering the lot of all humans everywhere. The negative side of all this Aquarian energy is that they are so involved with ideas of humanity *en masse* that they lose sight of the personal, not considering individual humans to be of much consequence. As a result, they will need help to establish good one-on-one relationships from an early age. They will need to be schooled in the importance of emotions and will need to learn to accept their own emotions as an essential and valuable part of being human.

Uranus in Pisces (2004–2012). The Piscean generation, having received the benefits of previous efforts, will not be very interested in the practical day-to-day realities of existence. Looking to their own spiritual development, the nitty-gritty of the here and now won't have much appeal. Instead of worrying about the physical realities — such as hunger (which may well have been eradicated by the time they come of age) — they will concentrate on the spiritual concerns of humankind. These children may well express interest in religious and mystical thought at an early age and they should be given the opportunity to explore religious mysticism. However, as they will be inclined to dreams and ideals, with the result of being impractical and ineffective in the real world, they also will need to be given solid grounding, taught the lessons of Saturn as a basis for their spiritual quest.

NEPTUNE:

The Creative Impulse

Neptune is a Planet difficult to define. Symbolizing all that is unreal, ethereal, mystical, otherworldly, invisible, and inspirational — in a word, creative — this Planet's discovery perhaps tells a better tale of its elusive nature than any description.

Located on September 23, 1846, during the reign of Queen Victoria, Neptune's unknown presence had been suspected by two astronomers as the only logical explanation for the then unexplained erratic orbit of Uranus, which would arrive either before or after it was supposed to. As each Planet in the solar system affects the others due to gravitational forces, Uranus's peculiarities could not be accounted for by what was already known. Neptune itself is so far from Earth that it can only be seen with the aid of a very powerful telescope, and then it is only a pale greenish globe with little visible detail. It is interesting to contemplate that Uranus, the Planet of eccentricity, was directly responsible for the discovery of Neptune because of its curious orbital behavior! And that Neptune was the mysterious force behind the odd orbit of its neighbor.

Only two years after Neptune's sighting, Mme. Blavatsky, the founder of Theosophy (a new religious movement based on ancient wisdom), journeyed to Tibet and India in search of spiritual enlightenment. Afterwards, the nineteenth century set off a wave of spiritualistic, psychic, mediumistic, and table-tapping experiences all over Britain and the United States. Is it only coincidence, one wonders, that Neptune is identified with the dreamer, the artist, the musician, the filmmaker, psychic powers, mysticism, and spiritualism?

It is also identified — and here's the rub — with escapism, use of drugs and alcohol, avoidance of life's responsibilities, excuse-making, destructive self-indulgence, deception, fraud, delusions of all sorts, not the least of which is the self-delusion that one is the embodiment of God, or personally hears the word of God (e.g., Charles Manson, Jim Jones, David Koresh). The self-deluded followers of these and other self-appointed spiritual charlatans are firmly in the grip of negative Neptune, which fosters glamorization of all kinds from fascination with celebrities' lives to involvement in religious cults which promise to create another, better world in which to live.

At its highest, Neptune, which is primarily involved with the emotions, being the higher octave of Venus, becomes the "celestial musician," in us who thrills to the rhythm of the Universe, unheard by physical ears but known to the dreamer and poet. This "cosmic dancer" is the progenitor of the seven Muses, those spinners of artistic inspiration. Not only patron of the creative arts, Neptune is the inspirer of prophecy and visions, which bring understanding of Universal Truth impenetrable by the power of reason alone. Through his energies, we can contact the Universal Guides, or "master souls," who govern our Planet's evolution. Edgar Cayce, known as the "sleeping prophet," was a Piscean Sun who received his visions while in a state of deep altered consciousness where he tapped the vibrations of Neptune.

Venus is exhalted in Pisces, the Sign which Neptune rules, and while she deals with human love, he is concerned with the transpersonal in the expression of universal love. This often means self-sacrifice. Many mediums, psychics, and others who are tuned into the "other world," have a powerfully placed Neptune. These people have learned to love at large, as it were — they do their work for humankind as a whole, for the true Neptunian personality loves for the sake of love itself, and many of the saintly and historically religious have belonged to this category. Where Neptune is, we are filled with sympathy and compassion, learn about universal love, and may be entirely too sensitive and escape into drugs and alcohol or other negative behavior.

Neptune is like a marvelous singer of songs and teller of stories who simply *flows out*. He doesn't particularly care whether his vision is made manifest in the "real" world. He needs a lyricist and a composer to get them down on paper and properly orchestrated for the general public to enjoy and appreciate. And he needs a manager and marketing director to sell his work and bring in an income. That's where Uranus and Saturn come into the overall picture.

In the charts of children, look to Neptune for creative potential and spiritual leanings. Also, for susceptibility to delusion and substance abuse potential.

Neptune key characteristics:

Transcendental	Escapist
Spiritual	Deluded
Mystical	Unrealistic
Creative	Undisciplined
Compassionate	Self-pitying
Dreamer	Self-delusional
Inspired	Addictive

Neptune rules Pisces and when found in this Sign his characteristics are exaggerated.

Neptune is *exalted* in Cancer, a sign that deals with emotions, which find their highest expression in the form of universal love. The last Neptune in Cancer (1938-1958) generation brought forth the concept of human rights and freedom for all and was responsible for the establishment of the United Nations.

Neptune represents *the flow into life* and *illusions*.

NEPTUNE FUNCTIONS THROUGH THE SIGNS

As Neptune remains so long in one Sign, we will cover only those Signs applicable to the current and forthcoming generations.

Neptune in Sagittarius (1970–1984). The first wave of this generation has already reached maturity, while the last of them will come of age after the 2000 year mark has passed. Social factors affecting the different ages must be taken into account (and, again, House position and aspects will show how the energy is personalized), but in general this generation has brought into being young persons who need to find positive expression for their higher religious and spiritual values. Witness the revival of fundamentalism all over the world and a new acceptance of psychic guidance (now widely available via TV marketing). When these children reach adulthood, they will explore the mysteries and powers of the mind and mystical experiences will become commonplace. Instead of looking for the God without (the one up in heaven with a long white beard), they will realize the God within. It is interesting to note that the great mythologist, Joseph Campbell, who taught that true spiritual realization is to be found within, not "out there," did some of his most important work during this period. His beautiful illustrated volume *The Mythic Image* was published in 1974, after which he began to be recognized for the visionary he was. Then came the PBS TV series with Bill Moyer, and the subsequent publication of the interviews in book form. His work inspired George Lucas's *Star Wars* which in turn inspired the Sagittarius generation of kids! Even as I write, the Campbell programs are being repeated on PBS and he will continue to inspire the young of the Sagittarius generation for years to come.

Neptune in Capricorn (1984–2000). This period ushered in the collapse of the former Soviet Union with resultant chaos in economic and political structures, a process which will continue until the end of the decade. The children born during this time will express Neptune's creative energies in a practical way, for it will be their future job to put back together what has been rent asunder, to bring order out of chaos, to discipline the spiritual impulse. This generation will be required to incorporate its spiritual values into the practical realities of life in the coming era when new forms of government and political concepts will be born out of necessity. The end of this period will mark the onset of true world government.

As children, this generation will face a future in which work, economic restraint, practicality, and social responsibility will be inescapable. They are the unfortunate inheritors of lax and irresponsible fiscal policies of past governments and it will be up to them to right these errors and rebuild what has been torn down. The problem here is that their idealization of these values may not be very effective unless they are taught early on how to actualize and manifest them in their daily lives.

Neptune in Aquarius (2000-2014). The entrance of Neptune into the Sign of Aquarius will signal the real beginning of the long-awaited Aquarian Age. This generation will have the opportunity to create a new civilization in the wake of dissolution of social and political forms during the Capricorn period. The last children of this period will not reach their full maturity until the middle of the twenty-first century. On their shoulders will fall the tasks of creating a new world order based on enlightened humanitarianism, as yet unanticipated forms of energy, and super-advanced technologies, with their potential for human engineering through genetics. The Book of Revelation speaks of this period as beginning a thousand years of peace, but peace must first be made and then kept. These children are the true bearers of the principle of universal brotherhood. They quite probably will come into the world already equipped with intuitive and clairvoyant faculties which will surface at an early age.

PLUTO

The Transformer

This most recent discovery of the inhabitants of our solar system was found in 1930 and symbolizes the transformative processes of both the inner psyche and outer form. Another word for transformation is *regeneration*, which essentially breaks down the previous form and turns it into something else. Vegetation rots and becomes mulch, from which arises new vegetation. The individual sperm and ovum both "die" to be transformed into the embryo.

Pluto is not totally understood. Astronomers are even unsure of its true size. Some speculate that it is small and dense; others that the central sphere which can be seen is merely the light-reflecting center of a much larger orb. Though not much is known absolutely, there seems to be no question that power resides there, power of a most potent sort. Perturbations in the orbits of both Uranus and Neptune are a result of Pluto's as yet undetermined physical characteristics. It is interesting to note that just five years after Pluto's discovery the daughter of Marie Curie, Irene, with her husband, won the Nobel Prize for synthesis of the new radioactive elements. It would not be too much to say that the resulting Plutonium, the trigger of the atom bomb, transformed the entire world forever after.

Astrologers associate this most compelling of the Planets with the transformative process that goes on in the dark underworld of the psyche, sending up its aromas via dreams and, sometimes, compulsive behaviors. Here, we are in the realm of the ancient Hades, as Pluto was known to the Greeks, who had great respect for the powers of the Underworld.

As Pluto takes some 244 years to circle the Zodiac, none of us will ever experience more than a small slice of his influence. But that fragment can be powerful indeed, especially if he is in close aspect to one or more of the personal planets. Ruler of Scorpio, the Great Transformer causes whatever he touches to become something else. King Midas evoked Plutonian energies — to his sorrow — when he wished for everything he touched to turn to gold. Great wealth — and the transformation of dross into gold — also belongs to Pluto's realm. He is the bottom-line fundamental in our lives, and where he is by House and aspect says a lot about how we deal with the hidden aspects of our own psyches and lives. He symbolizes death and rebirth on the spiritual plane, as well as power struggles of all sorts — those we have with others, those with ourselves.

Because of his long, erratic orbit, he symbolizes the Great Collective, the point where we connect, for good or for ill, with the rest of our society — not just our local environment, but the totality of humanity, which somewhere shares a single psyche. Everywhere the forms of the psyche are the same, though they manifest differently in different cultures and at different times. Known as "Mr. Moneybags," because power begets money, and the great riches of our century have come from deep within the Earth's dark interior — oil, gold, gems, and minerals. As ruler of the underworld, he is a subterranean force to be reckoned with, and his House position shows which department of life favors regeneration for the individual. Individual karma is always in the end linked to the karma of the society into which we are born.

In children, Pluto is rarely an active force, although Plutonian inferences can be indicative of certain negative conditions, such as abuse, an encounter with death, or severe losses. Crime and incarceration are also indicated by certain afflictions involving Pluto. Close aspects to the Sun, Moon, and Venus are the most likely to cause trouble and need to be given special attention and consideration. Pluto contacting *any* Planet closely will give that Planet a definite Scorpionic coloration.

A well-aspected Pluto gives ambition and the desire to change world conditions for the better, and it endows the individual with persistence and the ability to overcome the harshest of obstacles. The Plutonian type is likely to be at one extreme or the other — a natural healer/psychologist who gives out energy unstintingly for the good of all, or a ruthless, willful tyrant who crushes opposition without compunction. Children should be watched for the latter trait, and, if it appears, steps should promptly be taken to prune the tendency before it takes root. Power struggles are another problem for these children, who may experience a distressing lack of powerlessness prior to growing into their own strength and power.

Pluto represents where we *experience power* and the *ability to transform ourselves*.

Pluto key characteristics:

Transformer	Compulsive
Powerful	Dictatorial
Regenerator	Obsessive
Revitalizer	Annihilator

Renewer	Fanatic
Metamorphosis	Ruthless
Redeemer	Eliminator

Pluto rules Scorpio and when found in that Sign his characteristics are emphasized.

Pluto is *exhalted* in Leo, which is a Sign of self-awareness. The generation born with Pluto in Leo (1938-1958) has the power to bring about regenerative changes through increasing self-awareness, which leads to awareness of all. They have the task of spiritually regenerating themselves in order to save the Planet from destruction due to overpopulation and the resulting pollution. From their ranks come the leaders who will take the world into the twenty-first century.

PLUTO FUNCTIONS THROUGH THE SIGNS

As Pluto remains so long in one Sign, we will cover only those Signs applicable to the current and forthcoming generations.

Pluto in Scorpio (1984–1995). This generation will come of age after a period of worldwide conflict and will be responsible as adults for the transformation of society in the wake of the dissolution of the Piscean Age. With such a task ahead of them, they will be concerned with the breakdown of old forms. Their intensity is unmatched in our experience and may even be somewhat frightening to their Pluto in Libra parents. Look to the House position for where the child needs help.

Pluto in Sagittarius. This generation, to be born after 1995, will herald the New Age, and their iconoclasm will be intense. They will look for new ways of attaining freedom, bringing in a period of spiritual transformation. Religions as they exist today will be swept away in this transformative maelstrom and these children will be the ones to usher in a deep and fundamental understanding of the values common to all peoples. They will become powerful teachers of the new religion, which will combine the great philosophies of the past with modern scientific knowledge of the underlying energies that support physical life.

Look to the House position to see where the child's Pluto energies will be expressed.

THE ASCENDANT

The Gateway to Life

CHAPTER VI

Astrology connects us to the universal energy of the cosmos, both in *time* and in *space*. Therefore, an accurate horoscope is mathematically plotted for both the exact time and the exact place (geographical location) of birth. This calculation identifies the *Ascendant*, or rising Sign, which refers to the Sign appearing on the eastern horizon at the moment of birth. Prior to birth, the gestating embryo contains all the energies of the Planets in as yet undifferentiated relationships. At birth, the Ascendant is fixed, along with the planetary relationships (aspects) that constitute the horoscope.

The twelve Signs of the Zodiac are like an ever-turning starwheel containing all 24 hours of our Earth clock. Each of the Signs has within it 30 degrees and as the great celestial clock turns, a new Sign appears on the horizon every two hours, and a different degree of the same Sign arrives every four minutes. The Sign and the degree depend on both *when* and *where* you are on Planet Earth. Just knowing the Ascendant Sign will provide another important perspective.

The Ascendant is of equal importance to the Sun Sign, and can even overshadow it. The child may seem more like the Ascendant than like the Sun Sign, because the Ascendant represents how we react to the immediate environment and to new stimuli constantly coming from it. The Ascendant also shows how the world views us. This point (the Ascendant is not a Planet but a point in time/space) governs the impression we make on the outer world and the action we take in response to it. It is related to the formation of the personality, what C.G. Jung has termed the *persona*, and what astrologer Robert Hand has termed "the outermost aspect of one's inner being."

To understand the significance of the Ascendant, imagine that you are behind a color-tinted glass, like the filter in a camera, and that you must *always* view the world from behind this perception-altering screen. In return, the world has no choice but to view you *through* your perception-altering screen.

When at birth the child receives the lifelong imprint of the Ascendant, it becomes a deeply internal part of the evolving individual who will always be marked by the portal through which life was entered. The Ascendant is therefore the most *personal* point on the entire chart. The qualities it symbolizes permeate the entire being, just as a single drop of dye colors a whole container of water.

Esoteric astrologers believe that the "soul" chooses the Ascendant, which controls the chart by dividing it into the Houses, or fields of experience, through which the energies of the Planets, focused through the medium of the Signs, are expressed. I do not know about this, but it is interesting to note that a

Czechoslovakian psychiatrist and gynecologist, Dr. Eugen Jonas, discovered that the baby, when ready to be born, releases adrenalin into it's mother's bloodstream, thus, in effect, causing the birth. Dr. Jonas believed that each infant possesses an "inherent personality," and that the time of birth reflects "a basic impulse from the universe, a sort of vibrational range that will be more or less permanent with respect to the organism." [Reported in *Astrological Birth Control* by Sheila Ostrander and Lynn Schroeder (Englewood Cliffs, N.J.: Prentice-Hall, 1972, p. 127).] According to Ostrander and Schroeder, Jonas "suggests that the configurations in the cosmos are part of the imprint forming the frequency pattern of a human at the beginning of life."

The Ascendant represents our innately natural response to any social situation or first encounter of experience. It is the most *visible* part of the complex human entity. Ascendant behavior can be predominant in the early years, and it's important that it not be misconstrued as the totality of the child. Though a vital part, it is only a part.

Psychologically speaking, the Ascendant serves as the first line of defense against the realities of life and its difficulties. If, for example, Moon needs go unmet, a child learns to rely on the Ascendant to take up the slack. The resultant overemphasis on the part can put the whole into disequilibrium, for being forced to use the Ascendant as a coping mechanism causes the child to become internally out of balance, using the Ascendant as a shield.

The Ascendant represents *the manner in which you project yourself.*

Ascendant key characteristics:

Personality	Self-observation
Physical body	Self-consciousness
Personal vitality	Self-awareness
Facial structure	Self-image
Personal outlook	Self-expression
Personal appearance	Self-acceptance
Conscious focus	Self-analysis

ASCENDANT FUNCTIONS THROUGH THE SIGNS

ARIES Ascendant is a free spirit whose first response to a new situation is *action*. Basically restless, Aries favors the direct approach, like Mars, its ruler. Aries Ascendant children are extroverted and headstrong. Rarely do they show physical fear. They will exhibit ambitious competitiveness, even when it isn't appropriate. Aries fights readily in response to the need to be in control, making aggressiveness a problem, while courageousness and dynamism are positive expressions. Aries Ascendant needs to learn to cooperate, to accept losing, and to develop true self-confidence, which does not depend on winning. Learning to think before taking action is necessary for this child.

TAURUS Ascendant is a placid spirit whose first response to a new situation is *waiting*. Naturally calm and serene, this peaceful child will quietly wait for attention but will not like to be moved about quickly or jostled roughly, and needs time to absorb new impressions. The child will move slowly and deliberately but show stubbornness when under pressure. It is best not to hurry these children. Gentle persuasion, delivered with affection, works wonders. Stabile and grounded, Taurus Ascendant rarely gets upset and works to calm down those who do. Warm and friendly, with an earthy charm that makes for lovability, Taurus Ascendant may cover up painful feelings, so Moon needs must be carefully considered and used as a window to what may be troublesome.

GEMINI Ascendant is a blythe spirit whose first response to a new situation is *communicating*. Flexible as a wand, changeable as the winds, this child has all the qualities of a sprite. The pre-verbal infant will coo and gurgle winningly, and the child will crawl and walk early, out of eagerness to explore the environment. Restlessness is a trait, and these children hate to be confined. It's hard for them to stay with one activity for very long. Lots of brightly colored toys of the throw-away type are indicated, because this child bores easily. The urge to communicate makes staying quiet difficult, and outings which demand stillness and silence are trying for both child and adults. The Gemini Ascendant youth will seem younger than classmates, a veritable Peter Pan.

CANCER Ascendant is a caring spirit whose first response to a new situation is *nurturing*. Basically timid, these children are very attached to home and mother and don't accept environmental changes readily, retreating from unpleasantness. Extremely sensitive, this child can quickly withdraw into a tightly-closed shell when upset, often becoming moody and remote. Harsh words and loud voices frighten them and tears are frequent. These children will want to take care of dolls, pets, and smaller children, and when made to feel secure are charming and gracious. A stable, loving, secure homelife helps to establish self-confidence, which can be a problem. Security-seeking, Cancer Ascendant needs protection both emotionally and physically in order to cope with new experiences.

LEO Ascendant is a dramatic spirit whose first response to a new situation is to get *attention*. Whatever will call attention to them is what they will do. They especially like dramatics — singing, dancing, posturing, acting, and dressing up. Motivated by pride, Leo Ascendant likes to appear strong and confident and may try to dominate other children. Pride extends to appearances, and Leo likes to have rich and elegant, even flamboyant, things with which to impress others, valuing good looks and taking pride in personal appearance, which brings popularity. Leo Ascendant displays generosity and style in an attempt to win approval and attention. It's important for Leo Ascendant to learn the difference between appearance and substance. This strong personality has good leadership qualities.

VIRGO Ascendant is a practical spirit whose first response to a new situation is *analyzing*. Orderly and organized, with common sense, there is a tendency to fuss over unimportant details. Babies like to be kept clean and neat and older children may be picky about food and the environment. Shy and lacking self-assertiveness, Virgo Ascendant is likeable and helpful but suffers from self-criticism which extends to the criticism of others. Learning tact is important. Possessed of an incisive mind, Virgo Ascendant likes to see the point to any activity, and wants an end purpose, even to recreational activities. A perfectionist, this child needs to be encouraged to relax and be less self-demanding. Virgo Ascendant is happiest when engaged in some useful project.

LIBRA Ascendant is a cooperative spirit whose first response to a new situation is *socializing*. Even tiny babies will make eye contact and smile. These children are pretty with winning ways, eager to please and be liked by others. Popular because they take the trouble to get along with their peers, they are peacemakers, unable to bear strife and argument. "People pleasers," they need to learn self-assertiveness to risk angry feelings. Despising ugliness, Libra Ascendant will either turn away from or try to hide unpleasantness, and, liking to be surrounded by beautiful things, may collect items just for their esthetic qualities. Niceness, good manners, politeness, and intellectual conversation are predominant qualities.

SCORPIO Ascendant is an intense spirit whose first response to a new situation is thinking. Even tiny children will have a penetrating stare and look wise. Quiet and reserved, this child experiences deep emotions and may say little. Fearful of being misunderstood, Scorpio Ascendant needs encouragement to express feelings in a safe and receptive environment. Though not easily angered, this youngster will fight fiercely when necessary. Strong-willed and determined, they never give in. Scorpio Ascendant often concurs with childhood trauma. There is a totality about Scorpio Ascendant, a kind of devil-may-care, go-for broke attitude that enables this youngster to plunge into any life experience unhesitatingly. Sensitive to the feelings of others, Scorpio Ascendant is a natural psychologist who divines the inner selves of others, like X-ray vision.

SAGITTARIUS Ascendant is an expansive spirit whose first response to a new situation is *enjoyment*. A sunny, happy baby who expects the best, this open and outgoing child will be frank and honest, expressing opinions forthrightly. Although young Sagittarius Ascendant must be taught that others have more sensitive feelings and that brutal honesty is not always the best policy, there is a freshness about this child that is invigorating. And no harm is ever meant. Freedom of thought, speech, and action are important to Sagittarius Ascendant who can easily feel trapped and restless. Activities connected with nature are best. Sagittarius Ascendant is playful and high-spirited, full of optimism and the joy of living, friendly and good humored.

CAPRICORN Ascendant is a serious spirit whose response to a new situation is *reticence*. Tiny Capricorn Ascendant may be delicate and childhood is never easy. This Ascendant never seems really young, never the carefree child, never a giggly teen, always solemn. You are raising a practical natured child who will want to achieve something of value in life. While the other kids are messing up the playroom, the Capricorn Ascendant will be busily organizing the crayons according to color and size, putting them in *order*, which is important, as is competence. This child is serious, a hard worker who seems to feel that nothing comes without earnest effort. Encourage play and goal-less activities. Disruption of the parental relationship can bring on a sense of isolation and loneliness.

AQUARIUS Ascendant is an individualistic spirit whose first response to a new situation is *gregariousness*. Time-honored methods and traditional attitudes are not for this youngster who wants to experience whatever is different and foreign to the home environment. Expect your Aquarius Ascendant to bring home all sorts of odd and quirky friends, to want to keep unusual pets from exotic climes. Aquarius Ascendant feels that everyone should be equal and may early evidence an interest in social reform, taking up causes that relate to injustice or the importance of the rights of others. This egalitarian nature may find it difficult to accept parents and other adults as authorities unless convinced they are absolutely impartial. Aquarius Ascendant isn't prone to emotional display, being rather detached.

PISCES Ascendant is a sensitive spirit whose first response to a new situation is *feeling* the way. Pisces flows, knows no boundaries, and the Pisces Ascendant child can perceive others' feelings almost immediately. A veritable psychic sponge, this child, when in a negative environment, will respond to the atmosphere by becoming it. Like a chameleon, the Pisces Ascendant child tunes in to the vibrations around it and then can't tell the feelings are someone else's. It's necessary to protect this child from excessively negative situations for psychosomatic health problems can result from the imbibing of others' psychic poison. A Pisces Ascendant child needs a private place, if not a room then at least a protected corner, in which to retreat and hide away and dream.

THE HOUSES

The Field of
Encounter

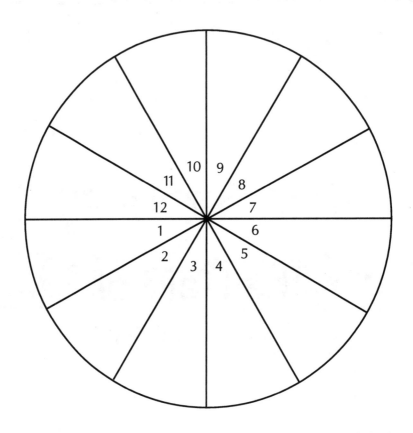

ASTROPOINTS
☉ SUN

☽ MOON

♀ VENUS

♂ MARS

THE NATURAL ORDER OF THE SIGNS

♈ ARIES   ♎ LIBRA

♉ TAURUS   ♏ SCORPIO

♊ GEMINI   ♐ SAGITTARIUS

♋ CANCER   ♑ CAPRICORN

♌ LEO   ♒ AQUARIUS

♍ VIRGO   ♓ PISCES

CHAPTER VII

The "Houses" are twelve pie-shaped slices of the chart wheel which represent the various areas of life's activities and needs, what might be described as "stage settings," where the Planets act out their energies. The Houses tell us where each planetary energy is highlighted. The Ascendant always falls on the "cusp," or beginning point, of the first House. See chart. Thus, the Ascendant organizes the chart into the Houses, following the "natural" order of the Zodiac, shown below.

Aries
Taurus
Gemini
Cancer
Leo
Virgo
Libra
Scorpio
Sagittarius
Capricorn
Aquarius
Pisces

To determine the House placements of the various Planets, draw a circle and divide it into twelve equal-sized sections, numbering them 1 to 12, as shown in the illustration. After determining in which Sign the Ascendant falls, place that Sign in the first House. Then place succeeding Signs of the Zodiac, following the natural order shown above, around the outside of the wheel, one on each cusp, or division line.

For example, a Cancer Ascendant would put Leo on the cusp of the second House, Virgo on the third, and so on.

Now, having determined which Signs govern which Houses, look up the Planets in the Signs, and put each into its corresponding House. Using the preceding example of a Cancer Ascendant, a Cancer Sun is a first House Sun, a Virgo Moon would belong in the third House, and so on.

When working with the Houses, remember that the Sign tells *how* the basic energy of the Planet operates, and that the House tells *where* the energy will be expressed.

If a House has more than one Planet in it, the House is emphasized in the chart. Several Planets in one House are an indication of over-emphasis requiring balancing.

The Houses also can give vocational information.

Function of The Planets Through the Houses

The First House: The Self
(Natural Affinity: Aries)

The first House is the quintessential "I." It is one's personality or self-projection, the physical body and appearance. The House of ego — which in this sense means that core within each of us that makes life choices — and ego-development, the first House in the chart of a child tells of developing self-awareness, of how the child feels about the body and how it appears to others, or *consciousness of the Self*. Basic physical vitality is also the domain of this House.

Planets in the first House exemplify energies that are self-related. Several Planets in the first House will emphasize this self regard, which is involved in what others think of one as well as what one thinks of one's self. Planets here extend their energies *outward*.

Sun	**A strong, energetic personality, "Me first."**
Moon	**Emotionally impulsive, impressionable, likeable.**
Mercury	**Alert, lively, curious, a talker, jokester.**
Venus	**Attractive, charming, agreeable, tactful.**
Mars	**Assertive, high-energy level, combative, rash.**
Jupiter	**Expansive, generous, helpful, eats too much.**
Saturn	**Pessimistic, unchildlike, tense, responsible.**
Uranus	**Unconventional, innovative, hates restriction.**
Neptune	**Assumes different roles, impressionable, spacey.**
Pluto	**Intense, self-aware, powerful, willful, strong.**

The Second House: Personal Resources
(Natural Affinity: Taurus)

The second House has to do with what is considered valuable. This includes money, personal possessions, and attitudes toward them, but it also suggests valuing as a means of identity. *I am what I value* can be extended to *I am what I own*. The process of identification with material possessions makes them a part of oneself. For example, when one's home is burglarized, one feels personally violated. We own our home, what's in it is ours, and there is a personal sense of attachment that goes beyond the price paid for our real estate. We use the term "valuables," and refer to "sentimental value" as being of more importance than mere economic value. Our mother's stolen brooch is valued not for its diamonds and pearls alone but for the fact that it attaches us to her memory.

In the child's chart, the second House refers to self-worth, beliefs (what the child values as a result of parental and societal influence), personal money, such as an allowance or gifts, and personal property, such as toys, clothes, instruments, and tools.

Planets in the second House are possession-related and, depending on their basic natures, will tend to increase or disregard possessions. A number of Planets in the second House will indicate possessiveness and overconcern with the materialistic.

Sun	**Financial consciousness of money and costs.**
Moon	**Emotional attachment to possessions and security.**
Mercury	**Values ideas, books, learning; witty, thrifty.**
Venus	**Likes beautiful possessions, may be spendthrift.**
Mars	**Controlling, strong sense of property, frugal.**
Jupiter	**Likes to spend, collect material possessions.**
Saturn	**Cautious about money, thrifty, values work.**
Uranus	**Careless about possessions, impulsive about money.**
Neptune	**Feels money unimportant; unrealistic, generous.**
Pluto	**Uses money/resources to get what is wanted: power.**

THE THIRD HOUSE: THE ENVIRONMENT
(NATURAL RULER: GEMINI)

The third House covers three areas of life which at first may not seem related, but taken together represent normal daily life, what astrologers call the "near environment." The first has to do with *communications* related to the routine of everyday life — the myriad of daily telephone calls, conversations, letters faxes, bills, paperwork, small talk, involvement with friends, neighbors and the community at large — as we go about our accustomed round. It is the mind operating on its customary level when performing routine tasks. This House also relates to *short-distance travel* such as commuting, business trips, weekends away, and whatever moving about we do that does not take us into unfamiliar territory but is a part of our usual routine. *Siblings and relatives* (except parents) are also the province of this House, insofar as we are concerned with routine interactions with them.

In the child's chart, the primary concerns of the third House will be brothers and sisters, aunts and uncles, cousins, school, neighbors, community, and information-gathering events such as trips to the library or museums.

Planets in the third House give energy to daily life and its plethora of small communications. A concentration of Planets here will indicate much busyness, mental energy, talkativeness, and a pressing need to communicate about details, whether or not they have any relevance. Gossiping is a form of this. Physical as well as mental restlessness can be indicated, as with the person who simply cannot sit still. Emphasis here would be Mercurial in nature.

Sun	**Active, quick, curious; talks, asks questions.**
Moon	**Talks about feelings, attached to siblings.**
Mercury	**Mentally gregarious, restless, impatient.**
Venus	**Writing ability, verbally charming, artistic.**
Mars	**Intellectually aggressive, much mental stamina.**
Jupiter	**Good learner, intellectually curious, reads.**
Saturn	**Slow to speak, thinks things through, planner.**
Uranus	**Quick, original mind, full of creative ideas.**
Neptune	**Vivid imagination, can believe own fantasies.**
Pluto	**Deep mental involvement in whatever is studied.**

THE FOURTH HOUSE: ROOTS
(NATURAL AFFINITY: CANCER)

The fourth House is the basic foundation of one's life — home, family, parenting (especially the mother), tradition, the past, one's homeland. In short, roots. The cusp of the fourth House is at the bottom of the chart, what might be called the "Earth point." It follows that the fourth House has a deeper meaning than one's immediate family. This is the sense of support we derive from Earth itself, which is the basis of our life here. It is the House of the Great Mother Goddess, as well as that of the personal mother. Cancerian images and symbolism imbue this House — nurturing, emotional support, belonging, the maternal, forebears, the ancestral land. The Moon, symbolic of the unconscious, rules Cancer, and so the fourth House also refers to humanity's collective unconscious and the symbols that link together the human *family*.

In the chart of a child, this House deals with the home life and the basic support system derived from it — emotional security, nurturance, parents, especially the mother (or mothering), and grandparents (as representatives of the traditional past). This House is extremely important in the lives of children, for if they are not nurtured sufficiently they can grow up to be insecure, withdrawn, emotionally possessive. On the other hand, good parenting in this area of life gives a grounding upon which the developing child can stand.

Planets in the fourth House will be influenced by the nurturing, mothering quality it possesses. Those already related to such qualities will have them enhanced. Those not related naturally will be "softened." Many Planets here indicate much subjectivity in personal matters and an unreasoning attachment to the past. Attention to this House is crucial, for negative energies here will have to be balanced elsewhere.

Sun	**Home-oriented, needs family, quiet, personal.**
Moon	**Very emotionally attached to home, family, mother.**
Mercury	**Introverted, likes to learn about the past.**

Venus	**Craves parental love, beautiful home, tradition.**
Mars	**Wants to dominate domestic scene, energizes home.**
Jupiter	**Indicates a happy home life, self-confidence.**
Saturn	**Needs more parental warmth and affection, insecure.**
Uranus	**Home life inconsistent and unpredictably erratic.**
Neptune	**Deeply emotional about family, feels unnurtured.**
Pluto	**Heavy parental shadow, lack of self-confidence.**

THE FIFTH HOUSE: SELF-EXPRESSION
(NATURAL AFFINITY: LEO)

The fifth House is where we play and amuse ourselves, are creative and self-expressive, encounter romance, and have children. The fifth House is where we do what we want, not what we must. As all people know, "All work and no play makes Jack a dull boy," but the relevance of play to our growth has been overlooked. For the child, play is work. The child's work is to play and through play to learn to work. Amusements do not only foster relaxation, taking us away from our ordinary chore-filled life, they release the mind and spirit to engage in creativity and self-expression.

In the child's chart, the fifth House is best represented as having fun, learning what gives pleasure, and the process of creative self-expression, which is a learning process along the way to developing a Self.

Planets in the fifth House are energized by the firey characteristic of the House. What falls here is uplifted and outgoing. Naturally playful planets do well here while stricter ones limit the release of natural energy.

Sun	**Fun-loving creative, energetic, childish.**
Moon	**Strong feelings, open, loves a good time, eager.**
Mercury	**Loves games, amusement, learning through fun.**
Venus	**Fun-loving, artistic, sensual, appreciative.**
Mars	**Self-expressive, open, abundant lively energy.**
Jupiter	**Optimistic, cheerful giving, hates restriction.**
Saturn	**Reserved, poor self-expression, can't have fun.**
Uranus	**Likes unusual forms of fun, spontaneous, sudden.**
Neptune	**Dreamy, creative, artistic, fantasizes, imagines.**
Pluto	**Makes play a power struggle, always wants to win.**

THE SIXTH HOUSE: HEALTH
(NATURAL AFFINITY: VIRGO)

The sixth House involves one's health and health-promoting routines, nutrition in the form of eating preferences and habits, daily work or chores, service to others, and the capacity for self-sacrifice. This House is often emphasized in the charts of nurses, social workers, and the service professions and trades generally. Propensity to illness can be found here as well as concern for health. It represents what is *necessary* as opposed to what one chooses to do for its own, or one's own, sake, our day-to-day duties and responsibilities. It is relationships based on duty rather than pleasure.

In the chart of a child, the sixth House is concerned with forming good health habits and establishing hygiene routines, with undertaking chores and taking responsibility, doing homework instead of watching TV, understanding that sometimes we must forgo our own pleasure to attend to the needs of others, such as an ill person. It also shows where the child may be inclined to illness. Traditionally, this House also covers small animals, and the care of a pet is a good way to teach children responsibility for something other than themselves.

Planets in the sixth House are funneled into a somewhat narrow expression. In contrast to the fun-loving nature of the fifth House, the sixth House is work-oriented, tends to worry about health, and can produce psychosomatic illnesses. A concentration of Planets here can stifle the Self through excessive concern for health and hygiene, which makes for fussy, picky eaters and fear of anything being dirty. Self-sacrifice can become a way of life, an ego-trip all its own.

Sun	**Quiet, hardworking, high standards, likes to help.**
Moon	**Moods affect health, fussy about food, routines**.
Mercury	**Mentally orderly, good with tools, likes hobbies.**
Venus	**Healthy, unselfish, likes creative projects.**
Mars	**Hard worker but wants control, a know-it-all.**
Jupiter	**Learns through hands-on experience, likes work.**
Saturn	**Weak health, poor digestion, serious, worries.**
Uranus	**Restless in school, chafes at restrictive rules.**
Neptune	**Allergies, psychosomatic illnesses, empathetic.**
Pluto	**Total involvement in whatever task is at hand.**

THE SEVENTH HOUSE: ONE-ON-ONE RELATIONSHIPS
(NATURAL AFFINITY: LIBRA)

Traditionally the House of marriage and partnerships, the seventh House has to do with all of our one-on-one relationships, including those with enemies. In the seventh House one engages in chosen relationships, such as marriage, as opposed to those which are given, such as family. There is here a sense of mutuality, which can be extended to include those with whom we compete.

In the charts of children, who obviously are not married or in business partnerships, the seventh House is concerned with partnerships such as the best friend or the other child assigned as a co-project worker. Sometimes children form very tight bonds of the "blood brother" type during the preteen years. This is seventh House business. Also included are competitors, whether in sports or in academic efforts. Later on, as the youth approaches the teen years, the seventh House indicate relations with the opposite sex.

Planets in the seventh House are seeking relationship and partnership. The more Planets in the seventh House the more the person will dislike doing anything alone. Such people will be happier and do well when interacting with another person, the closer the better. The child with a seventh House emphasis will complete homework quicker when studying with a chum rather than alone.

Sun	**Relationship-oriented, social, conciliatory.**
Moon	**Relates through emotion, needs intimacy, closeness.**
Mercury	**Conversational, lively, intelligent, debater.**
Venus	**Boy- or girl-crazy, a peacemaker, graceful.**
Mars	**Fighter, wants own way, lots of physical stamina.**
Jupiter	**Open, benevolent, friendly, many relationships.**
Saturn	**Afraid of partnerships, prefers to be alone.**
Uranus	**Relationships erratic, fast-changing, unusual.**
Neptune	**Easily affected by moods and feelings of others.**
Pluto	**Transformed by relations with strong-willed others.**

THE EIGHTH HOUSE: THE PAST
(NATURAL AFFINITY: PLUTO)

The eighth House is the House of the past, transformative change, death, inheritance, and other people's money. In this case, death may mean actual death, but also it can mean a death of the old so that the new can be given life in rebirth.

In the charts of children, the eighth House represents their personal past, including older relatives who may indeed die during their childhood years, giving the possibility of inheritance of other people's money. Most seriously traumatic events are eighth House business, such as a death in the family or sexual abuse.

Planets in the eighth House signify the way a person will undergo changes, whether easily or with difficulty. They are also involved with the deep past, the unknown part of one's history and antecedents. It is in the eighth House that we are separated from our attachments. The eighth House can be related to the organic process of growth, decay, death, and regrowth, or rebirth, through a series of crises which may be internal or brought on by external events.

Sun	**Serious attracted to the mysterious, intense.**
Moon	**Changeable, intensely emotional, secretive.**
Mercury	**Mystery-oriented, deep thinker, quiet, firm.**
Venus	**Intense, possessive, controlling, magnetic.**
Mars	**Strong-willed, determined, difficult to deter.**
Jupiter	**Sharing, attracts helpful adults' resources.**
Saturn	**Fear of change, death, the unknown, losses.**
Uranus	**Interested in the hidden aspects of life.**
Neptune	**Psychic tendencies, fascinated by supernatural.**
Pluto	**Serious, investigative, noncompromising, deep.**

THE NINTH HOUSE: LEARNING
(NATURAL AFFINITY: JUPITER)

The ninth House represents the higher mind, philosophy, religion, the law and legal matters, and long-distance travel. This House, in contradistinction to the third House, is concerned with what is highly conscious in our thinking. It is the level of mind necessary for serious study and learning, for striving to relate the parts to the whole, and seeking meaning in life's experiences. Jupiter is a social planet and the ninth House is concerned with the institutions that underpin the social order. The reason long journeys are covered here is that they, especially when destined to foreign lands, take us out of our ordinary, everyday world and expand our horizons. Travel is indeed a great way to learn.

In the chart of a child, the ninth House has to do with aspiration, a sense of God, country, and the larger world. It also indicates a place where freedom is ardently desired and where there is a reaching out for the new and different. Children with a strong ninth House make good exchange students and usually evidence early on a desire for things foreign — food, friends, travel. Planets in the ninth House will indicate what sort of higher education the child will desire.

Planets in the ninth House will influence the person's way of thinking about the world, of integrating new experiences. The more Planets in this House, the more the person will be unwilling to accept the restrictions imposed by church, school, tradition, or society, reaching out to other cultures, the more foreign the better, to take more and more of the world into consciousness. Children will first do this through books and TV documentaries, and later through actual travel.

Sun	**Questioning, seeking, restless, likes travel.**
Moon	**Craves new experiences for the emotional "high."**
Mercury	**Desires to learn through travel, eclectic mentally.**
Venus	**Harmony-oriented, poetic, beauty-seeking, fair.**
Mars	**Adventure-seeker, likes outdoor sports, causes.**
Jupiter	**Love of philosophy, religion, higher education.**
Saturn	**Conservative, wary of the new, diligent worker.**
Uranus	**Rejects traditional ideal for the new and radical.**
Neptune	**Attracted to spiritual concepts, can be religious.**
Pluto	**Probes, questions deeply, seeks serious knowledge.**

THE TENTH HOUSE: LIFE TASK
(NATURAL AFFINITY: CAPRICORN)

The tenth House represents social or professional status, career, life work, and parents (the father especially). This is a House of being out in the world, acting, doing. It might be likened to the process of initiation that turns a child into an adult. Whereas the fourth House is the intimate home, the tenth House is the life task that one must perform in the larger world. The parental energy here is the father-energy (whether or not that role is played by the actual father), or the figure of masculine authority. It is also the experience of being fathered and of difficulties with the father or father figures. What is experienced here in youth will color the relationship with authority figures in later life, for good or for ill. In the tenth House, we must take on a social role and achieve, becoming in turn authority figures for others. Honor and reputation are tenth House matters.

In the chart of a child, who clearly has no profession, the tenth House answers the question, "What do you want to be when you grow up?" and indicates what the child feels confers status among its peers. The tenth House area of development usually begins with the school years, and the study habits acquired during these years. At this time, the child will deal with questions of "honor," and become aware of having a reputation to uphold. Planets here will be good indicators of future career choices. A strong tenth House can indicate a youth who takes on a father-role.

Planets in the tenth House indicate a need to achieve in the outside world, to be recognized as an individual with some worth, to become the father by supporting dependents, to put effort into the control of one's own destiny. Many Planets here can indicate a father figure who is the typical workaholic, duty-driven personality who gives all for the family but is perceived by the child as being cold and neglectful.

Sun	**Achiever, status-seeking, practical, sensible.**
Moon	**Emotionally involved with career and status.**
Mercury	**Education and career-oriented with logical mind.**
Venus	**Wants social status, emotionally serious, artistic.**
Mars	**Career-oriented, dislikes authority figures.**
Jupiter	**Honest, reliable, grows through learning, travel.**
Saturn	**Wants to make a mark, plans early for a career.**
Uranus	**Seeks unusual career, individualistic, original.**
Neptune	**Can be difficulty in finding a career or direction.**
Pluto	**Pushes against the rules, encounters opposition.**

THE ELEVENTH HOUSE: FRIENDSHIPS
(NATURAL AFFINITY: AQUARIUS)

The eleventh House refers to one's friends, groups with which one is affiliated, goals, and hopes and wishes. This House is the area of life in which one must get along with large numbers of other people through becoming involved in group efforts, which in turn support the individual.

In the chart of a child, the eleventh House is primarily concerned with those groups and friendships formed at school, at church, or in some other general social context. This House indicates what the child seeks in friends and response to being part of a group. The area of self-development here is that of formulating goals through which to achieve one's aspirations. This is a humanitarian House, concerned with the welfare and benefit of the whole, not the individual alone.

Planets in the eleventh House (or lack of them) will indicate whether or not the person is a "joiner." Many Planets will show someone whose energies are devoted to group activities, who has many friends (though not necessarily close ones). A lack of Planets here will indicate someone who prefers to act alone.

Sun	**Friendship-oriented, cooperative, unselfish.**
Moon	**Needs many friends but blows hot and cold on them.**
Mercury	**Seeks clever, interesting friends to share with.**
Venus	**Sociable, likes fun, company, good times, people.**
Mars	**Active, vigorous, independent when with friends.**
Jupiter	**Collects many acquaintances, loves group activity.**
Saturn	**Loner, likes older people, has few friendships.**
Uranus	**Very unconventional friends, offbeat associates.**
Neptune	**Unrealistic about friends, confusion, deception.**
Pluto	**Intense about friends, seeks powerful friends.**

THE TWELFTH HOUSE: THE HIDDEN
(NATURAL AFFINITY: NEPTUNE)

The twelfth House has been given a bad rap by traditional astrologers who saw nothing here but mental illness, incarceration, "self-undoing," and the like. Astrologer Bob Hand makes a very good case for the twelfth House being a place where things are just coming into being, nascent, vulnerable, still forming. This is based on the fact that Planets in the twelfth House are *rising* and therefore, at dawn, coming into the light. It makes me think of the phrase "It dawned on me." So, let us look at this House as that which is hidden, including our dreams and fantasies. True, fears — usually of the unknown — reside here, but so does spirituality. In the twelfth House we are deeply connected on an intuitive level with the powers of the Universe, themselves unseen.

In a child's chart, the twelfth House represents the inner life — dreams, fantasies, fears, nightmares, and feelings of inadequacy or guilt. Here is where the child puts what is felt needs to be hidden away, either for protection or because of shame. This is probably why the House is connected to mental illness. Neptune rules here, and his is the realm of the watery deep where many strange and wonderful creatures abide, as well as some that are dark and frightening. Look to the twelfth House in your child's chart for where the fairies live!

Planets in the twelfth House, according to Hand, are "in a critical stage." They need to be carefully assessed and tended, because children are not equipped to handle crises. Hand says further that twelfth House Planets can "work for, not against, an individual's ego expression so long as they have not been the *subject of a major ego defeat early in life* (italics mine)."

Sun	**Shy, retiring, introverted, compassionate.**
Moon	**Daydreamer, fantasizes, hides feelings, empathetic.**
Mercury	**Secretive, hides thoughts, works behind the scenes.**
Venus	**Fears emotional rejection, reserved, ethereal.**

Mars	**Easily discouraged, lacks self-confidence, quiet.**
Jupiter	**Introspective, intuitive, kind, gentle, sweet.**
Saturn	**Lacks self-esteem, pessimistic, can be depressed.**
Uranus	**Indicates clairvoyance, intuitive abilities.**
Neptune	**Sympathetic, helpful, religious, spiritual, fey.**
Pluto	**Telepathic sensitivity to other's feelings.**

A NOTE ON EMPTY HOUSES

Not all Houses in the chart will be tenanted. This does not mean that the House plays no role or that its area of life doesn't matter. It only means that there is no particular emphasis on the area (in this life). Many Planets in one House indicate both an emphasis and an imbalance which needs correction. Look always to the House *opposite* for clues about how to handle the energies of the full House. In a mathematically precise chart, the Sign on the cusp of the House may be different from one or more of the Planets in the House, but for the purposes of this book we are using a system in which the Planets in the Houses and the cusps are the same Sign.

THE ELEMENTS

Our Personal Weather

CHAPTER VIII

The *Elements* — **Fire**, **Earth**, **Air**, and **Water** — refer to the most basic energies within us, essential dynamic life forces. The elemental makeup of the chart is the energy pattern of the individual. A grasp of these life principles and how they operate is a major step toward understanding one's self or another.

Every person relates variously to the four energies symbolized by the elements, depending on how they are distributed in the chart. One person may be a "natural" swimmer, preferring to exercise in the water, while another is a "natural" runner. Thus, we each express the Elements inherently in us in a way that complements our individual nature. And it's important that the Elements be allowed expression.

In the charts of children, especially in the early years, the interplay of the Elements provides information about inner states of being and about patterns of reaction to the environment. A child's elemental balance provides important clues to the maintenance of health, best learning methods, proper recreation, and ways and means of resolving conflicts in the family.

Each Sign of the Zodiac is represented by an Element. Signs in the *same* Element are considered to be most compatible. Fire and Air get along well and Earth and Water have similar vibrations. When a parent (or both parents) is elementally quite different from a child, the result can be both conflict and misunderstanding. For example, an intellectually-minded Air parent can find a Water child to be exasperatingly emotional and immune to the logical approach, while a practical-minded Earth parent can find a Fire child exhaustingly energetic and self-centered. Once again, understanding is the key, especially when dealing with small children — though it is also of a great help when conflict arises with schoolage and teenage children. Allowing the child to "be in his Element" will go a long way toward resolving differences. The first step is to admit that there *are* differences and not to place any judgement on that fact. After all, if we were all the same it would be a boring world indeed!

Function of the Elements Through the Signs

FIRE: THE LIFE FORCE
(ARIES, LEO, SAGITTARIUS)

Aries is the most obviously fiery of the Fire signs — quick, impulsive, impatient, driven to action.

In Leo, the energy of Fire is more stable — creative, given to the grand gesture, dramatic, ardent.

At Sagittarius, Fire becomes more mental and objective — seeking learning and avid to disseminate what it knows.

The energy of *Fire* is radiant. It is excitable and enthusiastic. Fire people are spontaneous, quick, full of flowing energy. They can appear to be self-centered or too objective. High-spirited, they have self-esteem and strength that comes in spurts, a strong desire to express themselves, and a need for freedom. They tend toward impatience, especially with Earth and Water Signs, fearing that Water will drench their Fire and Earth will smother their enthusiastic energy with practicality. Fire people are most compatible with other Fire people or with Air, which fans the flames of Fire's leaping, diffuse energy, as well as inspiring Fire with new ideas for their active natures and minds. But Fire can quickly tire of Air's endless intellectual speculations, unless they can be translated into action without delay.

Fire children hate to be cooped up and need vigorous physical activity *during the daytime*, preferably out in the sunshine. Winter (in cold climates) is hard on these children, but sufficient outdoor activity during the hot summer months will allow them to store up the energy of their Element against the indoor winter months. Fire children need as much contact with the sun as possible (with care taken, of course, against sunburn) and are best sent to bed early, after an active day, as their energy peters out when the sun goes down.

EARTH: The Physical Plane
(Taurus, Virgo, Capricorn)

Taurus is the earthiest of the Earth signs — strongly materialistic, possessive, stolid, stubborn, immovable.

At Virgo, Earth becomes more mental and less oppressive — still practical and no dreamer, it is however, a thinker.

In Capricorn, Earth reaches its epitome as the Sign of the leader, general, CEO — a mover and a shaker in the world.

The energy of *Earth* is solid, related closely to the physical plane and senses. Known for hard-headed practicality, Earth Signs want results and are patient and willing to discipline themselves to get them. They have an innate understanding of the world and its many forms and the stamina to persist until the goal is reached. Slow to start, they rarely give up no matter how hard the road or tiresome the journey. Earth finds Water easy and Fire difficult but attractive, but Air seems to be from another planet entirely. Earth and Air rarely understand each other.

Earth children need to get their hands and feet in the mud, at least occasionally, and making mud-pies is an excellent activity for them. By the sea, they can build sand-castles while their Water siblings swim. The Earth child needs contact with growing things and should be given a small garden to plant and tend. A rock collection is a good hobby for the Earth child, as is building and constructing toys and games. Physical activity needs to be encouraged, for Earth children aren't prone to running around unless there is a Fire Sign Ascendant. Inclined to be slugabeds, they need time to wake up in the morning. Being rushed unduly can make them balky.

AIR: The Realm of the Mind
(Gemini, Libra, Aquarius)

Gemini is the airiest of the Air Signs — the most abstractly intellectual, feeding on information of all kinds like a bird feeds on insects, berries, and seeds.

At Libra, Air energy is translated into balancing relationships of all kinds — weighing, pondering, relating.

In Aquarius, Air reaches its most stable point — building ideas, turning ideas into real projects.

The energy of *Air* is ephemeral, constantly shifting, like the blowing of the winds. The realm of Air is the realm of the mind freed of all physical restrictions (imagine if you could fly). It is the non-material, where form does not yet exist and is only "in the mind," but it is compelling nonetheless. Ideas must precede manifestation. Every building on earth was once nothing more than an idea in the mind of the architect, mere drawings on perishable paper prior to being translated into the hard reality of stone, bricks, and mortar. Air Signs emphasize theory and concepts, which leads to their expressing themselves in words, usually through abstract reasoning. Air likes to keep detached from the "messy" human emotions, preferring to talk about them rather than dealing with them. Air likes other Air best, but together they get nothing done. Fire is easy for Air, and Water is difficult but attractive. Earth is a bore to Air, which tends to lack empathy.

Air children need relationships with other Air people and social activities that give them an opportunity to talk and exchange ideas. When of school age, they thrive on studies that give them intellectual freedom and stimulate abstract thinking. In a humid climate, they should have a dehumidifier in their room as wet air tends to make them feel poorly. Emotional heaviness is also detrimental to Air children who cannot take much emotional display. Weeping and outbursts of temperament cause them to flee in exhaustion. Discipline should be delivered in a rational no-nonsense way that appeals to the rational mind and doesn't drain the emotional tank. Air children have lots of nervous energy and need to work it off with mental activities in order to get a good night's sleep. However, they should be allowed ample time to wind down from the excitement of conversation, visitors, and such before bedtime.

WATER: The Intangible World
(Cancer, Scorpio, Pisces)

Cancer is the Mother of us all — maternal, yielding, caring, guarding, nurturing — the very bosom of the sea of life itself.

In Scorpio, Water runs deep and fathomless — mysterious and filled with the unknown. Out of its murky depths come strange creatures of the unconscious psyche.

At Pisces, Water becomes the most watery of the Water Signs. Ruled by the Sea King, Neptune, Pisces is at home in the world of feelings, that never-ceasing ebb and flow of inner life.

The energy of *Water* is flowing and various intangibles play a large part in the lives of Water-inclined people. Intuitive, psychic, and imaginative, they are exquisitely tuned in to feelings — their own and other people's. Water signs express deep emotion, and their feeling responses can go from extreme compassion to total self-pity. They are very aware of their unconscious processes, even if these seem dim and weird to others. *They know*. Whence their knowledge comes, they may not know — but they trust their inner promptings and act on them, sometimes willy-nilly, flying in the face of ordinary reality. Mystics and dreamers, they are in touch with the deeper dimensions of life even if they cannot prove this contact. They flow as water flows — into and out of minute crevices in their own and others' psyches. Deeply internal, they are buffeted by invisible currents which sway them this way and that. Water flows with Water but too much Water tends toward insularity. Water finds Earth easy and Air difficult but attractive. Fire boils Water, uncomfortably, and Water can smother Fire with its insecurity.

Water children flow with feeling and when their feelings are stopped up or repressed (as in telling the child to stop crying) they can become psychosomatically ill. The Water child needs to be allowed to express feelings freely, and boys especially should not be told that "little boys don't cry," for the tears will stay inside and solidify into resentment and a bad temper. An upset Water child can be soothed by being given a warm bath until feelings have settled back down to normal. All Water children are feeling-oriented and their inner landscape, like the tides, is forever changing. Internal waves of feeling wash over them constantly, taking them out to sea, so to speak, and if they are not allowed expression for these undulant feelings, trouble results. Calling a Water child a "crybaby" is counterproductive. Permitting the child to express feelings in a nonjudgemental atmosphere will right matters much more quickly. Water children need time and space to themselves, a private nook to where they can escape to deal with inner stress. If the child does not have a private room, a sheet draped over a table makes a great, secure-feeling cave!

Finding the Element Theme

To find the Element theme in a chart, simply count the number of Planets in each Element, giving two points to the Sun and Moon, one point to the others. Add in the Element of the Ascendant, giving it two points. If there is *one* highest number, there is a single Element dominance. If there is no *one* highest number then there is a mixed theme. When considering mixed themes, the Elements of the personal Planets are likely to be the ones that most affect children, but the placements of Jupiter and Saturn need to be considered as well. The outer Planets, being generational in nature, will have less elemental impact but are useful as a balance. If, for example, a chart is lacking one Element, such as Air, but an outer Planet is found in an Air Sign, then the chart still contains the Element Air, even if in a nonpersonal way.

A missing Element means that there is an imbalance as ideally all four Elements would be represented. When this occurs (and it is not uncommon) the missing Element can be "added" by consciously seeking to tune in to it. For example if Earth is missing, then earth-grounding can be added by planting a garden, working with the hands, or just sitting on the ground and tuning into Nature.

Parents seeking more understanding of their children can tally their own Element theme and compare it to that of the child. For example, if you are Fire/Earth and want to know how to get along better with an Air child, you would read Fire and the description of how Fire relates to Air. Then, read the discussion of Earth to see how Earth relates to Air, combining the two to understand how a Fire/Earth person would relate to an Air person.

The Element Mixtures

Fire/Earth mixes practicality with impracticality, impulsiveness with patience. One day the most reliable person, next off on a tangent. Fire/Earth can make visions into reality, mixing strength and courage. The negative side of this combination is insensitivity, self-centeredness, and a tendency to bulldoze others.

Fire/Air puts idea into action and joins vision to logic. Warm, yet objective, Fire/Air combinations are knowledgeable, fun, exciting, inspired, and idealistic with the ability to make things happen. The negative side of this combination is restlessness, being unfocused, getting into a tizzy, and following one unrealistic venture after another.

Fire/Water is the most intuitive of all combinations. It can have amazing hunches. Impressionable and sensitive, this combination can be shockingly blunt, extremely patient, and impulsive by turns. The negative side to this combination is selfishness, a tendency to hysteria, and being totally absorbed in one's own little world.

Earth/Air is one of the most efficient people around, combining objectivity with practicality. In this combination, the ideal and the real meet. This person can go off on flights of fancy and then return and get solidly to work. The negative side to this combination is skepticism, lack of empathy, and cynicism.

Earth/Water is a productive combination, being simultaneously sensitive and grounded, both intuitive and practical. With a talent for accepting life as it is found and making it work, this combination is able to give compassion and feeling form in the real world. The negative side to this combination is self-satisfaction and tunnel vision.

Air/Water is an extremely sensitive combination, with compassionate feeling mixed with objectivity. There is the ability to experience sympathy and display kindness and then to detach and analyze the emotional experience. Mental conceptual ability is humanized by the ability to feel. The negative side to this combination is being high-strung, nervous, and impractical.

What the Elements in the chart reveal is how a person will tend to use energies, which ones he or she is most attuned to consciously, and what he or she is most in touch with naturally. The dominant Element will show where in life you or your child feel most at ease, what you experience comfortably, and how you can participate spontaneously (or cautiously, as the case may be) in which areas of life.

Knowing your child's elemental picture (and your own as well) will help when any physical illness or psychological upset needs attention.

Fire people recuperate best out in the sun and with lots of physical activity.

Earth people gain rejuvenation from contact with the earth itself, being around plants, gardens, trees, playing with clay or mud.

Air people recover from stress best in the thin, clear air found in mountainous regions—humidity depresses them.

Water people reenergize themselves at the seaside or by a lake or near a waterfall where they can immerse themselves in their element figuratively and literally.

A great advantage to knowing your child's and your own elemental makeup is that you can learn a great deal about your natural inner attunement, or lack of it, to the physical world. Often, this can clear up misunderstandings between people who feel somehow "alien" to another's personality, but don't realize it's and elemental problem, one susceptible of solution.

THE MODES
Astrological Weather

CHAPTER IX

"To everything there is a season," we are advised in Ecclesiastes, and this fundamental truth is reflected astrologically by the *Modes.*

There are three *Modes* — **Cardinal, Fixed,** and **Mutable** — and these tie us to the seasons of the year, to which we humans respond with internal rhythms.

Each Sign of the Zodiac is represented by a Mode. Three Modes and twelve Signs equals four Signs in each Mode. These are called the "quadruplicities." Unlike same-Sign Elements, which are compatible, the same-Sign Modes require the overcoming of obstacles and difficulties.

Each of the three months of a season corresponds to a Mode: the first, **Cardinal;** the second, **Fixed,** the third, **Mutable.**

Cardinal Signs *initiate*. Fixed Signs *conserve*. Mutable Signs *change*.

The cycle of Earth's seasons in the Northern hemisphere shows a correspondence between the Modes and the turning of our planet in relation to our Sun, giving us Spring, Summer. Fall, and Winter.

Just as the Elements do, the Modes follow a regular order around the Zodiac, with the consequence that there is in each Mode one Fire Sign, one Earth Sign, one Air Sign, and one Water Sign.

CARDINAL Fire **(Aries)**	FIXED Fire **(Leo)**	MUTABLE Fire **(Sagittarius)**
CARDINAL Earth **(Capicorn)**	FIXED Earth **(Taurus)**	MUTABLE Earth **(Virgo)**
CARDINAL Air **(Libra)**	FIXED Air **(Aquarius)**	MUTABLE Air **(Gemini)**
CARDINAL Water **(Cancer)**	FIXED Water **(Scorpio)**	MUTABLE Water **(Pisces)**

The Function of the Modes Through the Signs

THE CARDINAL SIGNS: THE INITIATORS
(ARIES, CANCER, LIBRA, CAPRICORN)

The cardinal Signs are the *initiators*. Active and self-confident, they are usually ambitious and self-motivated. As each represents the first manifestation of its Element, cardinals are fond of beginnings of all kinds. They like to start projects but don't care much about the detail-oriented drudgery of finishing what they start. When the more aggressive planets, like the Sun and Mars, are in Cardinal Signs, they are likely to leave a trail of unfinished business. The Moon and Venus will tend toward open-ended emotional situations.

Aries is the primary initiator of the Zodiac, famous for spreading himself too thin and starting more than he finishes. It is his spring-like nature to thrust forth his self-expression into the environment, to hold up his experience to view. An "idea man," he is ever searching out new pathways for his vitality and expressive fiery nature.

Cancer seeks to satisfy her watery moods and deep emotional needs by initiating feelings. Though somewhat shy in other areas of life, Cancer does not hesitate to make emotional contact in order to get feelings flowing freely. Cancer isn't daunted by precedence when dealing in the ever evocative realm of feeling, instinct, and emotion.

Libra, being Air, is social and wants to inspire human interactions of all kinds, ranging from those of an intimate personal nature to those of a public or community nature. The initiator of relationships, Libra wishes to unite, to create balance and harmony, to get things going, and to keep them going smoothly.

If Cardinal Signs are dominant in a chart, there can be restlessness and an overactive nature. In children, this can, at an extreme, become hyperactivity. An imbalance of Cardinals produces a person who generates new ideas and projects like popping corn, throwing them out in all directions, too many for any practical results. Pairing this type with a Fixed Sign can help to channel the Cardinal's energy and will give the Fixed inspiration. Cardinals stimulate each other but increase the level of competition. Mutables easily adjust to the flow of ideas from Cardinals but may slither away when the crux arrives.

THE FIXED SIGNS: THE CONSERVERS
(TAURUS, LEO, SCORPIO, AQUARIUS)

The Fixed Signs *concentrate* energy. They are the conservationists of the Zodiac. Though this can result in conservatism, basically its function is to keep things afloat on a daily basis in a reliable and consistent manner. As can be implied by the word, the fixed Signs are stubborn and resist change. Extremely strong-willed, they are nearly impossible to move against their will. (This quality can be observed even in infants and small children who become truculent and recalcitrant when pushed where they don't want to go.) Blessed with almost inexhaustible endurance, patience, and persistence, they rarely give up, and, in a test of wills, the opposer, unless equally fixed, is sure to be the loser in the end. Unfortunately, the fixed Signs sometimes hold on long past the time to let go, which results in extreme possessiveness to the point of obsession.

Taurus, being Earth, is the most fixed of the fixed Signs, representing the time when spring is fully manifested and there is great activity in the material realm. Taurus has a great appreciation for Nature and all living, growing things — plants, animals, and babies. He is Nature's banker and financial planner, bringing fruition and enabling Her to concentrate Her riches for later use. Taurus wants to hold on to material possessions, both conserving and increasing them.

Leo, being Fire, gives us the hottest of temperatures — he is that fixed, glaring eye of the Sun, unrelenting, merciless in its intensity, which tells us a lot about Leo's strength of purpose. The Sun rules Leo and he likes to concentrate authority in rulership of some sort. Just as the Sun rules during the long hot summer, Leo seeks to rule whatever is around him. Even small Leo children will create a miniature fiefdom with themselves as regent. As summer is a time for children, play, and family, so is Leo a lover of and protector of these things.

Scorpio, represents the concentration of Nature's power in the season of autumn, when the trees shed their leaves so that they can be regenerated the following Spring. The sign of death and regeneration, Scorpio's water nature relates him to the instinctual and unconscious powers. While all of the fixed Signs are of great intensity, Scorpio is the most intense of them all, seeking to make feelings and perceptions permanent.

Aquarius as the Fixed Air Sign may seem a contradiction in terms. Yet, think of how one can be immobilized in the cold air as it bites into the flesh and the lungs! This Fixed Air is not to be taken lightly. The fixity of Air is in the mind, and, although open to new — even radical — ideas, Aquarius mental concentration is such that once he has made up his mind getting him to change it is an extremely difficult, if not impossible, task.

When Fixed Signs dominate a chart, there is danger of so much resistance to change that nothing ever gets done. Pairing an overabundance of fixed with a mutable person can alleviate this condition by bringing change to the fixed while benefiting the mutable with needed stability. The cardinals excite fixed but their speed and start-up pace intimidates and strong wills may clash. Fixed Signs feel good together but there is the danger of rigidity and stodginess.

THE MUTABLE SIGNS: THE VARIABLES
(GEMINI, VIRGO, SAGITTARIUS, PISCES)

The mutable Signs are flexible. What is most characteristic of them is that they can do many things at once and switch easily from one activity or one topic of conversation to another without missing a beat. This shifting about can drive the logical thinking types mad with frustration, but though mutables seldom stick to the point they can always return to it with ease. The mutable Signs don't get into ruts because they thrive on variety and are tremendously versatile, sometimes to the point of being scattered. Nonetheless, their versatility allows them to change with the prevailing winds without getting blown off course. They can be manipulative and sometimes they resort to double-talk to get their way.

Gemini, being Air, is the most mutable of the mutables. Endlessly variable, Gemini is extremely flexible and thrives on change and being many-sided. His changeability is mirrored in his season, the transitional time between spring and summer. Diversity is his watchword, and this mutable Sign revels in his protean quality of shape-shifting. Gemini is ordinary, everyday thought, taking in whatever information presents itself without any concern for what he will do with it. He loves information for its own sake.

Virgo is the most mental of the Mutable Signs. Usually multi-talented, he seeks to find the right occupation so that he can use his skills in the service of others and see results from his meticulous efforts. Though as changeable and flexible as the other mutables, Virgo does not seek change for its own sake (like his Gemini cousin), but for the practical applications he can envision. Virgo has knowledge of the physical world, which he strives to use efficiently and effectively.

Sagittarius signals the period of change from autumn to winter. A Fire Sign, Sagittarius is a seeker, looking for life adventures that will give him ample opportunity to express his quick-moving mind, sensual nature, and spiritual side. Sagittarius likes to be on the move constantly, looking for new experiences that will enhance his broad overview of the world and allow him to see how to fit every part into the Whole. This mutable is always questioning life. His appetite for intellectual speculation knows no bounds. Trying to find the answers to questions that have no answers is the goal that keeps him going.

Pisces, a Water Sign, is the most difficult to define. Signifying the time when winter changes to spring, when melting snow cascades down the mountains into rivers and streams, Pisces has a flowing, formless quality. Ever-changing, unstable, inconstant, Pisces relies on shifting moods, feelings, and intuitions to guide him along his watery way. Like a leaf drifting on a current, he goes where his inner life directs. Pisces has the otherworldly air of one who converses with elves and faeries, who glimpses wonders the rest of us cannot imagine, let alone see.

Many mutable Signs in a chart is an indication of energy that is scattered. Gemini especially needs direction to keep from going off in all directions at once. Virgo can usually handle details well, but tends to get fixated on doing the same thing over a dozen different ways, trying for perfection. Sagittarius is so busy with the big picture that he misses the target half the time, while Pisces simply isn't there at all.

Mutables do well with one another, reveling in each other's changeability, but it's not the best way to get anything done. Together, they just keep shifting around the problem. Cardinal types are good for mutables in that they provide needed direction, but they may be too aggressive. Fixed types can provide stability to mutables, but they can cause frustration because of their inability to change.

THE MODE THEME

To find the Mode theme, follow the same procedure as outlined on pages 158–159.

The Mode Mixtures

Cardinal/Fixed is a dynamic combination — a person with strong opinions and a force to be reckoned with. This combo switches back and forth between being a creative starter who is full of new ideas to one who is continually getting stuck in a rut. Flexibility is what's needed here and a mutable pal may be the answer.

Cardinal/Mutable is an interesting combination, a person who is full of new ideas and a myriad of projects. There's never a dull moment around this combo because of the flux of inspiration and lightning-like changes. What's needed here is a fixed friend with staying power to help make positive use of both the ideas and the flexibility.

Fixed/Mutable is a curious contradiction, sometimes the most flexible of people, sometimes the most stubborn, alternating between the two or being inwardly consistent and outwardly changeable, or vice versa. Getting started is the problem here and a cardinal pal may provide the outer energy needed to get this combo's staying power and flexibility in gear and on a roll.

THE ASPECTS

The Blend of Individuality

CHAPTER X

Aspects represent the mathematical relationship between Planets, which are fixed in the horoscope at birth. The Planets all rotate at different speeds around the Sun, as observed from Earth, and these planetary motions result in angular relationships. In geometry, an angle is that part of a circle between two straight lines that intersect at the center of the circle.

As the astrology chart is a circle containing 360 degrees, aspects can be envisioned as pie-shaped slices of the circle. Certain aspects are very important to interpreting a birth chart—0°, 60°, 90°, 120°, 180°, are the *major* aspects. These are known as the *conjunction*, the *sextile*, the *square*, the *trine*, and the *opposition*.

As space is limited and interpretation of aspects complicated, we will deal only with the conjunction, square, opposition, and trine. For those wanting to delver deeper into the subject of aspects, we recommend the *Astrologer's Handbook* (see Appendix II).

THE CONJUNCTION — 0°

The easiest Aspect to understand is that of the *conjunction*, which occurs when two or more planets are lined up in the same Sign. Conjunct planets combine energies, creating a very dynamic aspect which marks a strong point of focus along with a tendency for direct action. More than two Planets in a Sign/House place a heavy emphasis on that field of endeavor.

CONJUNCTION KEY WORDS:

Joins, touches, blends with, connects, energizes, activates, complements, intensifies, unites, colors, strengthens, binds.

Compatible planets in conjunction carry positive energies, while incompatible planets in conjunction can cause difficulties. However, the resolution of these difficulties can be used as a source of strength.

For example, Venus, the Planet of love and harmony, conjunct Saturn, the Planet of limitation and restriction, can cause the natural flow of the love nature to be tight and constricted, resulting in lack of confidence in love. But learning to use Saturn's energies to restrain Venus's natural overflowing proclivity can bring stability to love. It's important also to consider both the Sign and the House in which the conjunction falls. If the Venus/Saturn conjunction occurs in the first House, it will affect the person at a very personal level; in the eleventh House, it would have an effect on friendships and group associations. In Taurus,

Venus's own Sign, Venus would be strengthened and Saturn could serve to restrain her abundance and put it to use in the material realm; in Capricorn, where Venus is not happy and where Saturn rules, the Venus energy would be subservient to Saturn's stern hand and be put to use in a materialistic fashion, perhaps marrying for money.

THE SQUARE — 90°

Planets in square aspect are three signs apart and indicate both dynamism and obstacles. Known as a "hard" aspect, squares represent areas in life where much effort must be expended in order to realize gains. Often the person with square aspects is unaware of the source of inner or outer conflict and therefore has difficulty resolving it. This is a prime area where astrological understanding can help. The square always creates ongoing change, which can mean progress or change made simply for the sake of relieving the tension of the conflict.

The energies of the squares are expressed subjectively, or seen to be coming from inner tensions. Although they are the most difficult of the aspects, squares are called "dynamic," because the effort at resolution causes growth beyond limitations. The person with a chart full of squares is usually driven to succeed.

SQUARE KEY WORDS:

Challenges, tests, activates, contrasts with, intensifies, requires decision, inhibits, confines, makes demands, disciplines, pressures, stresses, blocks, impedes, frustrates, obstructs, manifests, realizes, enforces.

Which Planets ae involved in a square will indicate the type and quality of the conflict and the Houses will tell which areas of life are affected.

THE OPPOSITION — 180°

The *opposition* aspect is, like the square, a "hard" aspect. It's very name indicates conflict. Yet, opposites are reconcilable and can be complementary. The energies linked by the opposition produce instability and require change in order to effect balance. Rather like a seesaw, the opposition causes a person alternatively to favor one side or the other until balance is achieved.

As well as indicating polarity, strife, and conflict, the opposition implies partnership. Opposites attract as well as repel.

OPPOSITION KEY WORDS:

Balances, opposes, confronts, makes conscious, mirrors, tests, stresses, frustrates, need for cooperation, pulls in different directions, conflicts, bridges, stresses, stretches, fatigues, makes aware, separates, defines.

Again, the Signs and Houses in which opposing Planets occur affects the interpretation of the aspect.

HOW TO DETERMINE SQUARES AND OPPOSITIONS BY SIGNS

The *opposition* and the *square* are both derived from the crosses created by the Modes, or quadruplicities, with the result that Signs in the *same* Mode will be either opposite or square to one another. Each pair of opposite Planets crosses with another pair, and the second pair form the squares.

Aries	*square*	**Cancer/Capricorn**
	opposite	**Libra**
Taurus	*square*	**Leo/Aquarius**
	opposite	**Scorpio**
Gemini	*square*	**Virgo/Pisces**
	opposite	**Sagittarius**
Cancer	*square*	**Aries/Libra**
	opposite	**Capricorn**
Leo	*square*	**Taurus/Scorpio**
	opposite	**Aquarius**
Virgo	*square*	**Gemini/Sagittarius**
	opposite	**Pisces**
Libra	*square*	**Cancer/Capricorn**
	opposite	**Aries**
Scorpio	*square*	**Leo/Aquarius**
	opposite	**Taurus**
Sagittarius	*square*	**Virgo/Pisces**
	opposite	**Gemini**
Capricorn	*square*	**Aries/Libra**
	opposite	**Cancer**
Aquarius	*square*	**Taurus/Scorpio**
	opposite	**Leo**
Pisces	*square*	**Gemini/Sagittarius**
	opposite	**Virgo**

The Trine — 120°

The *trine* is created by Signs in the same Element, which come in threes. Thus, Fire Signs are in trine to each other (Aries, Leo, Sagittarius), Earth to Earth (Taurus, Virgo, Capricorn), Air/Air (Gemini, Libra, Aquarius), and Water/Water (Cancer, Scorpio, Pisces).

The trine is a "soft" or nonchallenging aspect. It usually brings ease but because it is easy it is also passive. The trine simply *is*. It makes no demands and lacks the dynamism of the hard aspects. An excess of trines can mean a life of always choosing the safest path of least resistance. A lack of trines can indicate a person who has much difficulty finding balance in life.

The trine tends to have the same effect as homeostasis. Just as the human body attempts to keep itself in a state of equilibrium by canceling out one process with another (you get tired, you rest, you are no longer tired), so the trine tends to maintain a state of being even while going through change.

Trine key words:

Flows with, harmonizes with, works easily with, brings benefits, cheers, eases, helps, comforts, aids, entertains, rewarding, enjoying, encouraging, easing, increasing, rejuvenating, inspiring, comforting, broadening, giving, indulging, going to excess.

The energies of Planets in trine flow smoothly, practically without effort. A trine between Venus/Mars would mean that the love/lust worked together, each knowing when it was appropriate to bring forth the energy, being assertive or receptive in turn.

Interpreting the Aspects

SUN ASPECTS

Aspects to the Sun affect the basic "I am" of the person, for the Sun is representative of our life's fundamental purpose, the identity of who "I am." These aspects involve ego, power, and identity issues, affecting the masculine energy field of both men and women. As a "masculine" energy, the Sun indicates males in one's life, and Sun aspects comment on the relationships involved. In the charts of children, Sun aspects usually involve the relationship to the father, as well as to the child's own concept of the masculine within. Girls with strong Sun aspects may well identify more with their fathers than with their mothers, or be tomboys, or like boys for playmates and pals. Restrictive Sun aspects (such as Sun/Saturn in square or opposition) can indicate a problem with the father, or father figure, or authority in general.

MOON ASPECTS

Aspects to the Moon deal with the unconscious mind, the past, and our automatic reactions. Moon aspects involve our needs, feelings, and emotional responses and give clues to the feminine side of both males and females. In the life of a boy, the Moon usually has to do with his relationship to his mother, or mother substitute. Positive Moon aspects strengthen a boy's relationship to his mother while negative Moon aspects (such as Moon square Saturn) can indicate difficulties. In the chart of a girl, the Moon will tell of her inner feelings about motherhood and the maternal feminine role expected of her.

MERCURY ASPECTS

Mercury represents the rational mind. Thus, aspects with Mercury will always have to do with how we think and what energies are affecting our thinking process. Mercury aspects indicate how we communicate and express our thoughts. Hard aspects may indicate difficulty of expression, especially with Saturn, whereas a Jupiter trine would indicate an overflow of easy communication.

In the charts of children, Mercury aspects tell about how they learn and communicate and give clues as to the best methods of teaching and communicating.

VENUS ASPECTS

Aspects to Venus show where there is a desire for love and loving, the personal, how we are good to ourselves, aesthetics, and harmony. Venus aspects are ordinarily benign, although hard aspects can indicate conflict about love, the need for approval, or self-indulgent behaviors.

In the charts of children, Venus aspects tell us about what the child enjoys doing (or where there is difficulty attaining enjoyment), what likes and dislikes are in terms of clothing, personal effects, room decor, music, artwork, toys, and, later, romantic partners.

MARS ASPECTS

Mars aspects indicate where strong emotions are involved, the need for self-expression, fields of action. Hard aspects can mean destructive behavior, especially with Saturn and Pluto, while trines are usually indicative of a positive flow and use of energy.

In the charts of children, Mars aspects tell us what factors affect the child's urge to action. Mars/Pluto, for example, can indicate destructive or overly aggressive tendencies while Mars/Saturn can mean restricted, inhibited action. Mars aspects also tell what makes a child angry and how best to appease anger, or sublimate it, or divert it to constructive use. A chart with many Mars aspects indicates a child who is extremely active and self-assertive, and the Sign and House positions of the aspects will indicate how the Mars energy is expressed and in what area of life. Lack of Mars aspects may mean lack of energy or passiveness.

JUPITER ASPECTS

Known as the "greater benefic," Jupiter is an energy that ordinarily feels good and behaves expansively. Jupiter aspects give optimism, enthusiasm, and uplift but have a tendency to overspill in excess and overblow in spirits. Made of hot gases, the planet Jupiter is glorious but not solid. Hard aspects to Jupiter, especially Saturn, can keep him within bounds but don't usually present any special difficulties. Venus square Jupiter, for example, can be someone who is simply overgenerous, who gives expansively without thinking of whether the giving is appropriate or not. Jupiter trines are totally beneficial in nature but may not produce anything concrete without effort.

Jupiter aspects in a child's chart will indicate how the child wants to share self and creative output. Strong Jupiter aspects bring protection and faith in a higher power while weak or no Jupiter aspects can indicate a lack of trust in life itself.

SATURN ASPECTS

Saturn brings structure and authority into our lives, and his aspects, even the trines, are often difficult. Where there are Saturn aspects is where the need for self-discipline arises, where reality lessons will be taught. Saturn aspects aren't fun, but they are useful for they stabilize otherwise flighty energies (such as Mercury) and feed ambition to achieve.

In the charts of children, Saturn aspects indicate where the child will have difficulties coping. The square and opposition are the most difficult, respectively, but the trine also slows down the other Planet contacted. Mercury trine Saturn, for example, indicates a mind that works slowly though with good results. Mercury square Saturn might indicate a mind that becomes so frustrated with the difficulties of expression that the person quits altogether. Saturn teaches patience by trial and error and will continue with the lessons over and over again until they are learned.

URANUS ASPECTS

Uranus, the Planet of the unexpected and erratic, can bring turmoil, but it also brings liveliness and idiosyncrasies, the yearning for freedom and the unusual in persons and lifestyle. Uranus aspects are not personal in nature unless with the personal Planets – Sun, Moon, Mercury, Venus, Mars. The trine enlivens the energy of the aspected Planet, the hard aspects can disrupt it.

In the charts of children, Uranus aspects to the personal planets indicate where there is excitement, or overexcitement, what is unusual, or rebellion. The House placement is the main factor for it will show the area of life affected.

NEPTUNE ASPECTS

Where Neptune is aspected we are prone to dreaminess and creativity; sometimes to psychic ability. Neptune aspects involve the other planet(s) in transcendental experiences, which can cause confusion and uncertainty to what the aspected planet really represents. Neptune is like a fog — diffuse and hard to grab hold of, enveloping and obscuring.

In the charts of children, Neptune aspects are where there is confusion, uncertainty, lack of confidence, spaciness, artistic inclination, inward-turning, and the propensity to alcohol and drugs. Many Neptune aspects can indicate extreme sensitivity to substances, which can produce allergies or allergic reactions to prescription or doctor-administered drugs. House position is the key.

PLUTO ASPECTS

Pluto is the planet of transformation, and whatever planet he aspects will be transformed over the course of the entire lifetime. His aspects are regenerative and concerned with the uses (and misuses) of power. Whatever he touches acquires a Scorpionic cast.

In the charts of children, aspects to the Sun, Moon, Mercury, Venus and Mars will tint the personal planets with the energy of Scorpio. Where Pluto aspects fall by House position will show the area of life that will manifest the energy. Pluto tells us where the child experiences power (or powerlessness) and can indicate where abuse is likely to occur — whether given or received.

ASCENDANT ASPECTS

As the most personal point on the chart, that which makes your chart yours alone, aspects to the Ascendant are of vital importance. Any planet making a close aspect to the Ascendant will color how the Ascendant operates.

With the conjunction, the aspecting planet can occur in either the first House or the twelfth House. The House that the aspecting planet occupies will indicate how it affects the Ascendant.

Planets in the first House will be involved with the manner in which the Self is projected, the personality, the physical body. For example, a first House Jupiter conjuncting the Ascendant will indicate self-projection that is open and optimistic, an expansive personality, and a body that tends to be large (overweight can be a problem here). If, on the other hand, Jupiter is conjuncting the Ascendant from the twelfth House side, then there would be an interest in learning about the hidden or esoteric aspects of life.

Oppositions to the Ascendant occur in the seventh House of one-to-one relationships and any opposition to the Ascendant will affect seventh House matters for good or for ill depending on the Planet involved. Study the section on the seventh House for interpreting this aspect.

Squares to the Ascendant occur in the fourth and/or the tenth Houses and usually indicate conflict between the personal sphere and the home or emotional life (fourth House) and/or conflict between the personal sphere and the career area.

This square will also affect the Descendant (cusp of the seventh House). For example, Mercury square the Ascendant/Descendant axis would indicate difficulties in self-expression (first House) and with partners (seventh House). The person with this aspect would project Self, by means of thoughts, learning, speech, and writing, awkwardly or self-consciously which in turn could lead to being misunderstood by a partner or the public.

THE BLEND OF ASPECTS

To understand how an aspect works, combine the Planets/Ascendant function(s) with the Sign(s) and the House(s) involved.

Moon in .... **Taurus** in the .... **Seventh House**

Needs .... Stable .... One-to-one relationships

Emotions .... Practical, Sensuous

OPPOSITE

Jupiter in .... **Scorpio** in the .... **First House**

Expansion .... Intense .... Personality

Generosity .... Powerful .... The Body

Optimism .... Passionate .... Self-projection

---

Using the keywords given throughout this book for the Signs, Planets, Ascendant, and Houses, make *sentences* to create a blending.

In the above example, we could say that My NEED (Moon) for STABILITY (Taurus) in a RELATIONSHIP (seventh House) STRESSES (opposition) my INTENSE (Scorpio) GENEROUS (Jupiter) PERSONAL WAY OF EXPRESSING MYSELF (first House).

With this aspect, the problem would be balancing (or coming to terms with) the emotional need for conservation and stability with the urge to distribute largesse to all and sundry as a means of ego identification. The relationship might suffer because the person would tend to promise more than could be delivered and would lack discrimination in bestowing generosity. Personal extravagance often causes problems in relationships and this in turn is usually caused by unresolved emotional issues.

In the above example, if the aspect were a trine rather than an opposition, the Moon would flow freely with the Jupiterian expansion, causing no trouble, only operating differently with a Fire trine, Air trine, or Earth trine.

When interpreting aspects for the charts of children, use the same formula shown above but take into consideration both the age and development level of the child. The above opposition aspect could mean a child who routinely promises more than he or she can deliver because it feels good to be thought of as generous. Unless curbed, this tendency could lead to a repeated problem of spreading one's self too thin with the resultant loss of friendships due to broken promises. The child with this aspect would need to be taught that promises should not be made casually or under emotional pressure, and that they are not to be broken without good and sufficient cause. In this case, the parents can set a good example by themselves making and keeping promises carefully.

This process also applies to aspects *between* charts. For example, suppose there is a Sun *opposite* Saturn between the child and the father. This would be an indication of the child's ego identity (Sun) being in conflict with the father's authority (Saturn) which might be too severely disciplinary with the result that the child would swing back and forth in relation to authority and discipline.

HOW ASPECTS ARE CALCULATED

In a mathematically precise chart, aspects, or the angular relationships between Planets and points on the chart, such as the Ascendant/Descendant horizontal axis and the Midheaven/IC vertical axis, are calculated using what is called an *orb*. As explained, each Sign of the Zodiac spans 30 degrees of orb, the twelve together adding up to the 360 degrees of the full circle.

As this book is intended for a general audience and does not presume or require any previous knowledge of astrology, the fine points of aspect tuning are not covered. Therefore, the aspects chartable with the tables in this book are *by Sign only*. In order to fully understand a chart, however, it is necessary to know the *exact degree* of the aspects. Planets forming the major aspects discussed above are usually calculated to be within an orb of 10 degrees or less. The other aspects (sextile, semisextile, semisquare, quintile, sesquiquad, inconjunct) are usually figured within only a few degrees of orb (2–7).

Anyone wanting to go further with understanding the aspects will need a professionally computed chart. For information about how to order a computer-calculated chart, see Appendix III: Computer Services.

A Word About Transits

Transits are aspects formed by the *daily movement* of the Planets to the fixed pattern of the birth chart.

In other words, if on the day you were born the Planet Venus were in 10 degrees of Sagittarius and if today the Planet Uranus were in 10 degrees of Sagittarius, we would say that Uranus is transiting your Venus by conjunction.

Although transits provide valuable information in terms of understanding growing children and the crises and turning-points in their lives, the subject is beyond the scope of this book.

However, since the transits — especially those of the intermediate and transpersonal Planets — are important and can shed real light on both inner and outer phases of a child's development, we do recommend a computer-accurate chart as a means of tracking them. The reason for a professionally prepared, mathematically correct chart is for the degree of orb, as mentioned above. If, for example, a child is having a transit of Saturn to a personal Planet, such as the Sun or Moon, it could signify a rough patch, a time of restrictions and frustrations, but without the exact degree of the planetary placements it is not possible to predict the timing, that is to say how long the effect will last. But, with specific transit data you can predict that the difficulty will last only a couple of months — or a couple of years as the case may be. Armed with this information, you are better prepared to help the child weather the crisis and understand what is happening.

Concomitantly, if a parent (or the parents' relationship) is going through a major transit, this can affect the child's environment. Knowledge of what is going on astrologically is an enormous help to maintaining psychological balance and can be a great comfort. Not all transits bring difficulties. There are beneficial transits as well. Planetary transits of the Houses also affect our lives, even when there are no natal Planets in the Houses being transited.

In addition to calculating birth charts, our computer can calculate the transits charts. (See Appendix III: Computer Services.)

FAMILY DYNAMICS

Chart Comparisons

CHAPTER XI

Human relations are the most difficult part of life for most people, and their basis is formed in the matrix of childhood. The list of what damages us in childhood is long, and the issues we confront as adults as a result of that early damage (even if not overtly traumatic) can occupy much of our time and energy as we move into the area of voluntary relationships. Psychologists tell us what most of us already know from our own personal experience — that our relationship with our parents is the basis for all later relating with others, for good or for ill.

Psychology (and I include psychiatry in this category), having been originally formulated and codified during the early part of this century, makes many assumptions based upon the prevailing, or traditional, family structure in place at the time, much of which is simply no longer applicable in today's fast-changing world of single parenthood, multiple divorces, significant others instead of spouses, and same-sex partnerships.

Astrology, too, has been mired in the expectations of what was "normal" a century ago, or up until recently — what has been termed the "nuclear family." The patterns or relationships which traditional astrology and conventional psychology describe may or may not be relevant to any particular case today and so our interpretations must take these factors into account.

Early psychology assumed that every child had a mother who played a conventional mother role, and the majority of the current literature is based on that assumption. However, in today's world it is possible that a father will play the "mother role," or that a mother will play the "father role," or even that strangers, in the form of foster parents, will inherit these roles. For some children, there will be no one to play one role or the other, and in some cases the roles become reversed, with the child in the role of mother or father.

That being said, the astrological chart still functions remarkably well in defining the child's relationship to the actual parents, or substitute parents, or no parents at all. We need only look at it from a different angle when the usual pattern has been disrupted by divorce, death, or some other circumstance.

The reason that the chart continues to work is that there is a mythological basis to the Planets and Signs, which remains applicable even in drastically altered situations. Additionally, the chart as here interpreted is not to be used as a predictive tool but as a means for inner exploration of a human being. Everything that becomes outer is first derived from the inner, and the chart tells us about that inner plane. Thus, the concept of "mother" is embedded in the human psyche whether or not there is an actual mother to whom to relate. Likewise, there is an inner feminine and an inner masculine in each of us, male or female. As we grow, no matter what our experience of having been parented, we gradually replace (or fail to replace) our actual parents with inner ones which may or may not be an improvement over the originals.

How Family Dynamics Are Determined by Astrology

In determining family dynamics through astrology, there are *two* areas of information.

The first has to do with the child's *perception* of the parents, which is seen through the chart of the child.

The second has do with the relationship between child and parent, which is revealed by *comparing the two charts*, a technique known as *synastry*.

THE MOON AND THE MOTHER

Much of the child's experience of the parents is through the child's *perception* of the parents. It is precisely here that much of the misunderstanding between parents and children is seeded, and if left untended, will grow into poisonous weeds.

There is much debate among astrologers about whether the fourth House is the "mother" and the tenth House, the "father." As the fourth House is ruled by Cancer, the quintessential Mother and the tenth House is ruled by old Saturn, the stern Father, the fourth is usually assigned to the mother and the tenth to the father. Some, however, feel the reverse is true. One theory is that the tenth House represents the legacy of the mother.

Without entering the debate, for I believe there is a certain amount of latitude available here, let me say that it is generally agreed that the fourth/tenth House axis does in some way represent the parents, or the experience of being parented.

The Moon unquestionably represents the Universal Mother and, by extension, the personal mother, both as concrete fact and as perceived experience. The Moon also indicates how we *internalize* mother energy.

Already in the section on the Moon through the Signs I have indicated how the various Moon placements beget certain perceptions of the mother. This is not an absolutely foolproof system, but it works as a rule of thumb. There is a positive and a negative side to each placement.

Let me give an example of a mother with three children. The first, eagerly desired by both parents, was born with the Moon in Cancer, and his first experience of his mother was of someone who was totally nurturing, even over-protective. She was quite young and returned to her parents' house after the baby's birth so that *her* mother could continue to mother the new mother.

After returning to her own home, she continued as a stay-home mom who devoted much care and attention to her new infant. This boy, now a man, is not only deeply attached to his mother, but, true to Moon in Cancer, he is a very nurturing, sensitive, family-oriented man with several children.

The second son, an unexpected and unwanted pregnancy, arrived only a year later — with the Moon in Scorpio. His perception of his mother, who resented having another baby so soon and who, since it was inevitable, would have preferred a daughter, was and is quite different from that of his older brother. This boy went deeply inside himself, keeping his feelings closely guarded against a sense of rejection, formed relationships with women who had difficulty with commitment, and remains a confirmed bachelor.

The third child, a girl, five years younger, was a planned event, arriving when the Moon was in Pisces. Her mother suffered a severe post-partum depression and had to be hosptitalized frequently. When she was at home, she loved and pampered her only daughter — but would then disappear (from the child's point of view) into the shrouded world of a mental hospital. As her debility persisted for some time, she faded in and out of the child's perception — a shadowy figure who was much revered but never reliable. This daughter perceived her mother as a vague figure, both fragile and spiritual, and eventually began to take care of her, becoming in time a psychiatric nurse herself.

In the above example, we have three different children from the same parents whose perceptions of the mother are entirely different from one another, and whose adult lives can be seen reflected in the Moon Sign.

Aspects to the Moon in the child's chart will affect the child's perception of the Mother as will the Moon's Sign and House position.

Remembering that there are "hard" and "soft," or easy and challenging aspects, read the Moon's aspects for more information in specific areas indicated by the Planet aspecting the Moon, paying particular attention to Saturn and the transpersonal Planets. A Moon/Saturn conjunction, for example, would indicate that the child perceives the mother as rigid and limiting, overdemanding, or alienating, whereas a Moon/Uranus conjunction would mean that the mother is perceived as being erratic and giving inconsistent nurturing, as being "different" from other moms.

It is important to note that the Moon in the chart of a female and in the chart of a male connote different things in terms of the person's inner, and later adult, life because the Moon-as-mother affects men and women differently. The Moon in a man's chart will indicate how he perceives both the experience of being mothered and the experience of the maternal in the women in his life. Every male/female relationship carries within it the germ of the paternal/maternal axis with the result that every person in an adult relationship experiences the opposite-sex partner both as a lover and as a parent. The many complexities of the male/female relationship and the inner masculine/feminine components within all of us are far beyond the scope of this book (indeed, a thorough treatment of the Moon alone would fill a thick volume), but an understanding of the

Moon-as-mother *and* as the inner feminine is basic to an understanding of the dynamics of human relationships. Not only is the mother the child's first experience of a human relationship, the basis upon which all else is founded, but the internalization of fundamental mother energy in both men and women deeply affects how they will function both as spouses and as parents.

THE FATHER IMAGE

Whereas we can indisputably say that the Moon and the mother are connected, the father connection is somewhat harder to pin down. Perhaps this is because the relationship with the mother (if not disrupted) is a primal one, while the relationship with the father must be built. The child shares the mother's body — in the most intimate of all relationships — for nine months and beyond, through the nursing stage, and is literally a part of the mother. But the father is "out there," external to both child and mother and he must be incorporated into the child slowly and deliberately. The mother simply *is* while the father *becomes*, a crucial difference.

Astrology and psychology both look upon the mother role as that of giving unconditional love and nurturance, but the role of the father (at least traditionally) is to prepare the child for the trials of adult life, to separate the growing being from adhesion to the world of the mother, which is soft and supportive, and thrust the child out of the nest. In primitive societies, there are ritual rites of passage for this experience, some of which are both awesome and frightening. The theory here is that as long as the child is clinging to the mother's protection the duties and responsibilities of adulthood cannot be assumed.

THE SUN AND THE FATHER

In defining the father, the Sun is one component. Where the Sun lies in the birth chart tells something of the child's perception of the father, or in the case of an absent father, whoever is filling in the role, even if it is the child's mother.

An example of this: a Sun in Capricorn daughter is born to a single mother. This mother has to be both mother and father, and, as she works full-time, she relies on strict discipline to keep the household running smoothly. The child perceives the mother — in the father role — as restrictive and limiting. Due to the duality of her parenting roles, this mother has no time to be softly nurturing, and there is a lack of balance. Yet, and this is where things can get very complicated, the child also has a perception of her mother in the mother role, seen by her Moon Sign. The child is forced to integrate these two conflicting images of her single parent.

The strength or weakness of the Sun in the chart, by Sign and House position and by how it is aspected are all indicators of the father energy.

Aspects from the intermediate and transpersonal Planets will reveal the child's perception of the father. With Sun/Jupiter contacts, for example, there will be a sense of the father as expansive — perhaps giving much material support. Sun/

Saturn aspects are usually considered to indicate a negative experience of the father, though this is not inevitable. Saturn has to do with separation, and the child with a Sun/Saturn aspect may feel that the father is not there, whether in fact he is not due to death or divorce, or metaphorically, by the demands of his job or lack of emotional support for the child. Sun/Uranus can make the father seem erratic, unconventional, aloof, or undependable. Sun/Neptune can give great difficulties, making the father seem like an illusion. Sometimes there is a problem with alcohol or drugs. Sun/Pluto can indicate power struggles between father and child, and abuse can occur.

SATURN AND THE FATHER

The next component of the father picture is Saturn. Where he is placed by Sign and by House will indicate much about the child's perception of the father.

As Saturn represents the material world with its structures, forms, and concreteness, the energy of this important Planet often feels restrictive to the growing child, especially those with the Sun in a freedom-loving Sign. Saturn's energy, however, must be dealt with and it is in this forum that the father perception plays such a vital role, for it will color the child's later attitudes toward all authority, and often toward all men.

Too much Saturnian restriction can create a rebelliousness, while not enough can result in irresponsibility and immaturity. The lessons of Saturn *must be learned* and it is immensely easier for the child if they are learned at the proper time — not at a later stage in life. Ideally, the lessons of Saturn — discipline and responsibility — will be learned from a responsible and disciplined source, which will result in a positive perception of the father.

SIBLING RELATIONS

The child's general pattern of sibling relations can be seen in the third House, by Planets found there and by the aspects formed to them. Further information will be shown by chart comparisons (synastry) between the charts of individual children.

FAMILY DYNAMICS AS SHOWN THROUGH SYNASTRY

Synastry is the technique of chart comparison and is used to understand interpersonal human dynamics. Unfortunately, it is beyond the scope of this book to present a full treatment of this immensely valuable, interesting, and complex subject. There are already excellent books available on synastry, including my own *Love Planets*, (see Appendix II), though these are not specifically directed to comparison of charts between children and parents. Relationship astrology is well worth studying, and family dynamics can be seen to stretch over generations (if and when the data are available). There are patterns to these things, documented in psychological literature (for example, we know that abusers tend to have been abused as children), and these patterns can be seen in the charts of entire families.

Nonetheless, it is possible for you as a parent to come to an understanding of how your own chart connects with that of your child, and thereby to understand the daily interpersonal dynamics that affect your relationship and the decisions you must make about childrearing.

In synastry there are three areas of interest:

1. SIGN POSITIONS OF PLANETS AND THE ASCENDANT.

By reading your own Planetary placements and those of your child, keeping in mind the function of the Planet being considered, you can readily see where the compatibilities and the possible disharmonies exist. For example, a parent with a Taurus Sun and a child with a Taurus Moon will be compatible at a mental/emotional level, while a child with a Scorpio Moon will be difficult for the Taurus Sun parent to understand emotionally. However, if the Scorpio Moon child also has a Taurus Venus, there will be an easy affection between parent and child that will help to overcome the difficulty.

2. ELEMENTAL AND MODAL CORRESPONDENCES.

By determining your own elemental and modal dominances, as well as your child's, you can understand how these react to each other. Also, the Element and Mode of each individual Planet will indicate how well these same energies get along. Like Elements are compatible; like Modes are at loggerheads (see Chapters VIII and IX).

Difficulties in relationships between parents and children, and between siblings, can often be traced to dissimilar Elements and Modes between the charts. A person involved in such a relationship may love, but not truly like the other. Inharmonious Elements and Modes need not always cause trouble, however, if they are understood for what they are — the expression of personal energies in different ways. And if allowances are made for these basic differences, the tides of family life can flow more smoothly.

For example, if a child does not find a particular form of recreation "fun," it may just be that there is an *elemental* factor involved. A Fire child will be happiest out in the bright sunshine; an Earth child will like to be around rocks, trees, mud; an Air child will respond to the mountains; a Water child will thrive near the sea or a lake. Fire children become restless cooped up in an automobile on a long drive, but frequent run-around stops will let them burn off excess energy. Earth children will be content to sit still if they are made physically comfortable and have plenty of snacks. Air children can be kept occupied with mind games and verbal play and an assortment of toys, books, and magazines to stave off boredom. Water children should be encouraged to talk abut how they feel or keep a picture-book diary in which to record feelings. Planning to take each child's elemental makeup into consideration is the best way of maintaining harmony among differing temperaments. It's never fair to make the child do all the compromising.

When conflict arises, Fire children will try to overpower the obstacle and conquer it with sheer force. The Earth child will simply absorb the problem stolidly while taking time to sort it out. The Air child will immediately respond verbally, often arguing rationally and at length. The Water child will usually flow into the situation while waiting for its feeling nature to guide its response.

Parental response will be similar, depending on the parent's dominant Element. It's easy to see that Fire with Fire can bring on a lot of noisy, hard-to-resolve conflicts — that old saw about the child being too much like the parent for the parent to like the child. Earth with Earth can be a Mexican standoff, for when Earth is pushed too hard it digs its heels in and can go from stonewalling to using fists with surprising strength and determination. Air with Air will get into a talkathon that can last hours and go nowhere. Water with Water will be an emotional flood that will either end in understanding and reconciliation or bitter withdrawal.

Understanding *both* your own and your child's elemental makeup can be of enormous help in conflict resolution. For example, an Air parent with a Water child might use rational argument, while the child will respond only to having feelings acknowledged, if not understood.

Careful study of the four Elements will provide you, the parent, with knowledge of your child's basic makeup and of how you and your child interact elementally.

The dominant Element will show where in life you and your child feel most at ease, what you experience comfortably, and how you can participate spontaneously (or cautiously, as the case may be) in which areas of life.

When considering the Mode themes of both child and parents, remember that the Cardinal, Fixed, and Mutable Signs either oppose or square each other. Thus, a parent with a predominantly Cardinal Mode will not necessarily get along well with a child with a Cardinal Mode. Cardinals tend to fight over who gets to go first, make the decisions, initiate projects, and run the show. If both child and parent have Fixed Mode themes, titanic conflict can arise because of immobility and stubbornness on both parts. The fixed Mode hates to give in and can dig in its heels for a long battle. No doubt "Stonewall" Jackson was a Fixed Mode theme. Two people with Mutable Mode themes are less likely to be in conflict, because both are easy to change and there is more room to maneuver. However, mutual mutability between parents and children can create discipline problems as the children learn they can manipulate the parents.

For additional information on how the Modes interact, see the section on Mode themes and calculate the themes for both the parent's and the child's chart. Then read about the theme for each person to understand how they interact.

3. ASPECTS BETWEEN CHARTS.

These operate in a similar manner as aspects within the individual chart, with the exception that the energy is an *exchange* between two people (see Chapter

X, The Aspects).

Aspects in a child's chart are often echoed by the aspects between the child and the parent. For example, a child with a Moon square Saturn aspect may well have the same aspect with the mother. In such a case, the child's perception of the mother is backed up by actual experience. In aspects *between* charts, it is important to pay attention to what Planets are involved, which are in the child's chart and which in the parent's. In the example just cited, if the Saturn is in the child's chart and the Moon in the mother's chart, the child will experience the energy differently than if the Moon is in the child's chart and the Saturn in the mother's chart. To learn more about synastry, see Appendix II, Recommended Reading.

To get a computerized "Relationship Profile" between yourself and your child, or between yourself and your spouse, see Appendix III, Computer Services.

RETROGRADES

When Planets
Go Backward

CHAPTER XII

Most people with only a passing interest in astrology have heard of "Mercury retrograde," generally in a negative sense. And, in fact, during the periods when the Planet Mercury is retrograde by its daily transiting motion, it does appear that communications snarls are more common than when Mercury is in direct motion.

What does *retrograde* mean? What is the difference between a regular Planet (in direct motion) and a Planet in retrograde motion in the interpretation of that Planet in a chart? (The Sun and the Moon are *never* retrograde.)

First off, retrograde literally means "to go backward," but, as we know a Planet cannot do that, what does it actually signify?

As mentioned in Chapter I, THE BASICS, astrology is *geocentric*, or *as seen from Earth*. Thus, when Planets *appear to us to be moving backward*, we say that they are retrograde. What actually happens in physical reality is that there is a point in the Planet's orbit when the relative speeds between Earth and the Planet alter, so that it appears from our point of view that the Planet first stops and then moves backward.

When a Planet is retrograde, its energies manifest in the chart differently — more internally — than when the same Planet is in direct motion. Like everything else in astrology, there is a positive and a negative aspect to retrograde Planets in the birth chart.

On the positive side, retrograde Planets convey a sense of introspection, a heightened inner life. Several retrogrades can indicate someone who is much more inwardly oriented than usual, where life is lived somewhat hidden away, on the interior plane.

Negatively, retrograde Planets can delay development and cause frustration, making dealings with the outside world more difficult than usual. A person with many retrogrades can be misperceived by the outer world.

The average chart has two Planets retrograde, and the chart with no retrogrades at all is that of someone who is absolutely direct and with no subterfuge, a "what you see is what you get" kind of person.

With children, it is important to pay attention to retrograde Mercury, Venus, and Mars, as these are the Planets most active during early development. The planetary tables in Appendix I indicate retrograde times for Mercury with this symbol, (R). In addition, we have given, previous to the planetary tables for Venus and Mars, tables of those two Planets's retrograde periods. Space does not permit the interpretation of retrograde Planets beyond Mars, but if you want this information you can order a computer correct chart (see Appendix III).

UNDERSTANDING RETROGRADE PLANETS IN THE BIRTH CHART

MERCURY RETROGRADE

Mercury, our fastest moving Planet, retrogrades about three times each year in its orbit about the Sun. Children born during these times, no matter which Sign Mercury occupies, will tend to think more deeply and inwardly and may express themselves less easily than children born with Mercury direct.

With Mercury retrograde at birth, the mind is sensitized and feelings color the mental and rational processes. The child born with Mercury retrograde (even in an outgoing sign) may appear to be slower than others, but this is only because the thinking process is more deliberate. It is important that this child be shown patience lest he or she come to believe that his or her *natural* thinking apparatus is somehow at fault. These children should not be pressed to express themselves verbally if they feel awkward or shy about it. It is notable that many fine and well-known writers were born when Mercury was retrograde. The position seems to favor writers, perhaps because they overcome their own communications difficulties by working in silence.

Children with Mercury retrograde should be given the opportunity to communicate in their own way, at their own pace, and should be encouraged to keep a diary as a means of self-communication and to write letters — perhaps have a pen pal — as a method of communicating with others.

VENUS RETROGRADE

Venus, representing social activity, affection, and what is valued, when turned inward by retrograde motion often indicates a difficulty in expressing the affections, which are deeply felt but somehow inarticulate. There may be a sense of shyness and holding back. It's important not to *force* the Venus retrograde child to show affection overtly just for the sake of the gesture. If little Susie doesn't want to kiss Aunt Jane, then let it be. Allowed to express affection in her own way, Susie may later pick a bunch of wildflowers and shyly present them to Aunt Jane.

With Venus retrograde it is also possible that the love nature may need a longer maturation period, and teenagers who delay dating should not be teased for their reluctance to become emotionally involved. Each in its own time is the best approach to Venus retrograde.

MARS RETROGRADE

When Mars is retrograde, the outgoing, assertive, competitive energy of this fiery Planet is subdued and turned inward, sometimes producing a competitive urge that wants to compete with the self instead of with others. A youngster with Mars retrograde may push to outdo yesterday's performance, swimming more laps or running more miles.

With Mars retrograde the expression of physical energy is slowed, sometimes actually blocked, by a lack of self-confidence in the physical side of life. This youngster needs to be given ways to build both physical strength and personal confidence. Drive may seem lacking, but it will manifest in due time, once the deliberations which must be done internally are complete. Patience is needed, and this young person should not be pushed into physical activity when reluctant to undertake it. Hard sports may be avoided by the child with Mars retrograde, but those which benefit from visualization and derive their power from grace rather than brawn, such as tennis and golf, may be appealing.

PLANETARY TABLES

APPENDIX I

How to Find The Sun Sign

ARIES	March 22–April 21
TAURUS	April 22–May 22
GEMINI	May 23–June 22
CANCER	June 23–July 23
LEO	July 24–August 23
VIRGO	August 24–September 23
LIBRA	September 24–October 22
SCORPIO	October 23–November 22
SAGITTARIUS	November 23–December 2
CAPRICORN	December 23–January 20
AQUARIUS	January 21–February 20
PISCES	February 21–March 21

If birth occurred on the first or last day of a given time period, it is possible that the Sun is in the former or latter Sign, depending on the exact time of birth. If in any doubt (though most people know their Sun Sign), a computer chart will clarify the question (see Appendix III.)

Many people mistakenly believe that if born on the day that the Sun is changing Signs they are "on the cusp," but actually most people are clearly either one Sign or the other. The true cusp occurs at the exact moment the Sun changes Signs; only the person born exactly when the Sun is within a fraction of a degree from the next Sign is considered to be on the cusp. When this rare instance does occur, the person partakes somewhat of both Signs.

MOON EPHEMERIS: HOW TO FIND YOUR MOON SIGN

Find the year of birth in the tables provided. Then find the birth month at the top of the tables. Find date of birth in the column below it. If it is not listed, then the sign listed for the earlier date is the Moon sign. For instance, if you were born on February 3, 1950, you would see that for February 2, the sign listed is Leo, meaning the moon was in the sign Leo. For February 5, Virgo is listed. This means that the moon is in the sign Leo until February 5 and your Moon is in the sign Leo.

If you are born on a day that starts a new sign (February 5 in this example), your Moon may be in the preceding sign. The only way to be absolutely sure is to have your chart done professionally or by a computer service. In lieu of this, read the text for both signs, and see which seems more like you.

1950

JAN	FEB	MAR	APR	MAY	JUN	JUL	AUG	SEP	OCT	NOV	DEC
1 GEM	1 CAN	1 CAN	1 VIR	1 LIB	1 SAG	1 CAP	1 PIS	1 ARI	1 GEM	1 CAN	1 LEO
4 CAN	2 LEO	2 LEO	3 LIB	2 SCO	2 CAP	2 AQU	3 ARI	2 TAU	4 CAN	3 LEO	2 VIR
6 LEO	5 VIR	4 VIR	5 SCO	4 SAG	4 AQU	4 PIS	5 TAU	4 GEM	6 LEO	5 VIR	5 LIB
8 VIR	7 LIB	6 LIB	7 SAG	6 CAP	7 PIS	6 ARI	8 GEM	7 CAN	9 VIR	7 LIB	7 SCO
10 LIB	9 SCO	8 SCO	9 CAP	8 AQU	9 ARI	9 TAU	10 CAN	9 LEO	11 LIB	9 SCO	9 SAG
13 SCO	11 SAG	10 SAG	11 AQU	10 PIS	12 TAU	11 GEM	13 LEO	11 VIR	13 SCO	11 SAG	11 CAP
15 SAG	13 CAP	12 CAP	13 PIS	13 ARI	14 GEM	14 CAN	15 VIR	13 LIB	15 SAG	13 CAP	13 AQU
17 CAP	15 AQU	15 AQU	16 ARI	15 TAU	17 CAN	16 LEO	17 LIB	16 SCO	17 CAP	15 AQU	15 PIS
19 AQU	18 PIS	17 PIS	18 TAU	18 GEM	19 LEO	19 VIR	19 SCO	18 SAG	19 AQU	18 PIS	17 ARI
21 PIS	20 ARI	19 ARI	21 GEM	20 CAN	21 VIR	21 LIB	21 SAG	20 CAP	21 PIS	20 ARI	20 TAU
24 ARI	23 TAU	22 TAU	23 CAN	23 LEO	24 LIB	23 SCO	23 CAP	22 AQU	24 ARI	22 TAU	22 GEM
26 TAU	25 GEM	24 GEM	26 LEO	25 VIR	26 SCO	25 SAG	26 AQU	24 PIS	26 TAU	25 GEM	25 CAN
29 GEM	28 CAN	27 CAN	28 VIR	27 LIB	28 SAG	27 CAP	28 PIS	26 ARI	29 GEM	28 CAN	27 LEO
31 CAN		29 LEO	30 LIB	29 SCO	30 CAP	29 AQU	30 ARI	29 TAU	31 CAN	30 LEO	30 VIR
		31 VIR		31 SAG		31 PIS	31 ARI	30 TAU			31 VIR

1951

JAN	FEB	MAR	APR	MAY	JUN	JUL	AUG	SEP	OCT	NOV	DEC
1 LIB	1 SCO	1 SAG	1 AQU	1 ARI	1 ARI	1 GEM	1 CAN	1 VIR	1 LIB	1 SCO	1 CAP
3 SCO	2 SAG	3 CAP	3 PIS	3 ARI	2 TAU	4 CAN	3 LEO	4 LIB	3 SCO	2 SAG	3 AQU
5 SAG	4 CAP	5 AQU	6 ARI	5 TAU	4 GEM	6 LEO	5 VIR	6 SCO	5 SAG	4 CAP	5 PIS
7 CAP	6 AQU	7 PIS	8 TAU	8 GEM	7 CAN	9 VIR	7 LIB	8 SAG	8 CAP	6 AQU	7 ARI
9 AQU	8 PIS	9 ARI	11 GEM	10 CAN	9 LEO	11 LIB	10 SCO	10 CAP	10 AQU	8 PIS	10 TAU
11 PIS	10 ARI	12 TAU	13 CAN	13 LEO	12 VIR	14 SCO	12 SAG	12 AQU	12 PIS	10 ARI	12 GEM
14 ARI	12 TAU	14 GEM	16 LEO	15 VIR	14 LIB	16 SAG	14 CAP	14 PIS	14 ARI	13 TAU	15 CAN
16 TAU	14 GEM	17 CAN	18 VIR	18 LIB	16 SCO	18 CAP	16 AQU	17 ARI	16 TAU	15 GEM	17 LEO
19 GEM	17 CAN	19 LEO	20 LIB	20 SCO	18 SAG	20 AQU	18 PIS	19 TAU	19 GEM	17 CAN	20 VIR
21 CAN	20 LEO	22 VIR	22 SCO	22 SAG	20 CAP	22 PIS	20 ARI	21 GEM	21 CAN	20 LEO	22 LIB
24 LEO	22 VIR	24 LIB	24 SAG	24 CAP	22 AQU	24 ARI	22 TAU	24 CAN	24 LEO	22 VIR	24 SCO
26 VIR	24 LIB	26 SCO	26 CAP	26 AQU	24 PIS	26 TAU	25 GEM	26 LEO	26 VIR	25 LIB	27 SAG
28 LIB	27 SCO	28 SAG	28 AQU	28 PIS	26 ARI	29 GEM	27 CAN	29 VIR	28 LIB	27 SCO	29 CAP
30 SCO	28 SCO	30 CAP	30 AQU	30 ARI	29 TAU	31 CAN	30 LEO	30 VIR	31 SCO	29 SAG	31 AQU
31 SCO		31 CAP		31 ARI	30 TAU		31 LEO			30 SAG	

1952

JAN	FEB	MAR	APR	MAY	JUN	JUL	AUG	SEP	OCT	NOV	DEC
1 AQU	1 ARI	1 TAU	1 GEM	1 CAN	1 VIR	1 LIB	1 SAG	1 CAP	1 PIS	1 ARI	1 GEM
2 PIS	2 TAU	3 GEM	2 CAN	2 LEO	3 LIB	3 SCO	3 CAP	2 AQU	3 ARI	2 TAU	4 CAN
4 ARI	5 GEM	5 CAN	5 LEO	4 VIR	5 SCO	5 SAG	5 AQU	4 PIS	5 TAU	4 GEM	6 LEO
6 TAU	7 CAN	8 LEO	7 VIR	7 LIB	8 SAG	7 CAP	7 PIS	6 ARI	8 GEM	6 CAN	8 VIR
8 GEM	10 LEO	11 VIR	9 LIB	9 SCO	10 CAP	9 AQU	9 ARI	8 TAU	10 CAN	9 LEO	11 LIB
11 CAN	12 VIR	13 LIB	12 SCO	11 SAG	12 AQU	11 PIS	12 TAU	10 GEM	12 LEO	11 VIR	14 SCO
13 LEO	15 LIB	15 SCO	14 SAG	13 CAP	14 PIS	13 ARI	14 GEM	13 CAN	15 VIR	14 LIB	16 SAG
16 VIR	17 SCO	18 SAG	16 CAP	15 AQU	16 ARI	15 TAU	16 CAN	15 LEO	17 LIB	16 SCO	18 CAP
18 LIB	19 SAG	20 CAP	18 AQU	17 PIS	18 TAU	18 GEM	19 LEO	18 VIR	20 SCO	18 SAG	20 AQU
21 SCO	21 CAP	22 AQU	20 PIS	19 ARI	20 GEM	20 CAN	21 VIR	20 LIB	22 SAG	21 CAP	22 PIS
23 SAG	23 AQU	24 PIS	22 ARI	22 TAU	23 CAN	23 LEO	24 LIB	23 SCO	24 CAP	23 AQU	24 ARI
25 CAP	26 PIS	26 ARI	25 TAU	24 GEM	25 LEO	25 VIR	26 SCO	25 SAG	26 AQU	25 PIS	26 TAU
27 AQU	28 ARI	28 TAU	27 GEM	27 CAN	28 VIR	28 LIB	29 SAG	27 CAP	29 PIS	27 ARI	29 GEM
29 PIS	29 ARI	30 GEM	29 CAN	29 LEO	30 LIB	30 SCO	31 CAP	29 AQU	31 ARI	29 TAU	31 CAN
31 ARI		31 GEM	30 CAN	31 VIR		31 SCO		30 AQU		30 TAU	

1953

JAN	FEB	MAR	APR	MAY	JUN	JUL	AUG	SEP	OCT	NOV	DEC
1 CAN	1 VIR	1 VIR	1 LIB	1 SAG	1 CAP	1 AQU	1 ARI	1 GEM	1 CAN	1 VIR	1 LIB
2 LEO	4 LIB	3 LIB	2 SCO	4 CAP	2 AQU	2 PIS	2 TAU	3 CAN	2 LEO	4 LIB	3 SCO
5 VIR	6 SCO	5 SCO	4 SAG	6 AQU	4 PIS	4 ARI	4 GEM	5 LEO	5 VIR	6 SCO	6 SAG
7 LIB	9 SAG	8 SAG	6 CAP	8 PIS	6 ARI	6 TAU	6 CAN	8 VIR	7 LIB	9 SAG	8 CAP
10 SCO	11 CAP	10 CAP	9 AQU	10 ARI	8 TAU	8 GEM	9 LEO	10 LIB	10 SCO	11 CAP	10 AQU
12 SAG	13 AQU	12 AQU	11 PIS	12 TAU	11 GEM	10 CAN	11 VIR	13 SCO	12 SAG	13 AQU	13 PIS
14 CAP	15 PIS	14 PIS	13 ARI	14 GEM	13 CAN	13 LEO	14 LIB	15 SAG	14 CAP	15 PIS	15 ARI
15 AQU	17 ARI	16 ARI	15 TAU	16 CAN	15 LEO	15 VIR	16 SCO	17 CAP	17 AQU	18 ARI	17 TAU
18 PIS	19 TAU	18 TAU	17 GEM	19 LEO	18 VIR	18 LIB	19 SAG	20 AQU	19 PIS	20 TAU	19 GEM
20 ARI	21 GEM	20 GEM	19 CAN	21 VIR	20 LIB	20 SCO	21 CAP	22 PIS	21 ARI	22 GEM	21 CAN
23 TAU	23 CAN	23 CAN	21 LEO	24 LIB	23 SCO	22 SAG	23 AQU	24 ARI	23 TAU	24 CAN	23 LEO
25 GEM	26 LEO	25 LEO	24 VIR	26 SCO	25 SAG	25 CAP	25 PIS	26 TAU	25 GEM	26 LEO	26 VIR
27 CAN	28 VIR	28 VIR	27 LIB	29 SAG	27 CAP	27 AQU	27 ARI	28 GEM	27 CAN	28 VIR	28 LIB
30 LEO		30 LIB	29 SCO	31 CAP	29 AQU	29 PIS	29 TAU	30 CAN	30 LEO	30 VIR	31 SCO
31 LEO		31 LIB	30 SCO		30 ARI	31 GEM	31 GEM		31 LEO		

1954

JAN	FEB	MAR	APR	MAY	JUN	JUL	AUG	SEP	OCT	NOV	DEC
1 SCO	1 CAP	1 CAP	1 PIS	1 ARI	1 GEM	1 CAN	1 VIR	1 LIB	1 SCO	1 CAP	1 AQU
2 SAG	3 AQU	3 AQU	3 ARI	3 TAU	3 CAN	3 LEO	2 SCO	2 SAG	2 SAG	3 PIS	3 PIS
5 CAP	5 PIS	5 PIS	5 TAU	5 GEM	5 LEO	5 VIR	6 SCO	5 CAP	5 CAP	6 PIS	5 ARI
7 AQU	7 ARI	7 ARI	7 GEM	7 CAN	7 VIR	7 LIB	9 SAG	7 CAP	7 AQU	8 ARI	7 TAU
9 PIS	9 TAU	9 TAU	9 CAN	9 LEO	10 LIB	10 SCO	11 CAP	10 AQU	9 PIS	10 TAU	9 GEM
11 ARI	11 GEM	11 GEM	11 LEO	11 VIR	12 SCO	12 SAG	13 AQU	12 PIS	11 ARI	12 GEM	11 CAN
13 TAU	14 CAN	13 CAN	14 VIR	14 LIB	15 SAG	15 CAP	15 PIS	14 ARI	13 TAU	14 CAN	13 LEO
15 GEM	16 LEO	15 LEO	16 LIB	16 SCO	17 CAP	17 AQU	18 ARI	16 TAU	15 GEM	16 LEO	16 VIR
17 CAN	18 VIR	18 VIR	19 SCO	19 SAG	19 AQU	19 PIS	20 TAU	18 GEM	18 CAN	18 VIR	18 LIB
20 LEO	21 LIB	20 LIB	21 SAG	21 CAP	22 PIS	21 ARI	22 GEM	20 CAN	20 LEO	21 LIB	21 SCO
22 VIR	23 SCO	23 SCO	24 CAP	24 AQU	24 ARI	24 TAU	24 CAN	23 VIR	22 VIR	23 SCO	23 SAG
25 LIB	26 SAG	25 SAG	26 AQU	26 PIS	26 TAU	26 GEM	26 LEO	25 LIB	25 LIB	26 SAG	26 CAP
27 SCO	28 CAP	28 CAP	29 PIS	28 ARI	28 GEM	28 CAN	29 VIR	27 SCO	27 SCO	28 CAP	28 AQU
30 SAG		30 AQU	30 PIS	30 TAU	30 CAN	30 LEO	31 LIB	30 SCO	30 SAG	30 CAP	30 PIS
31 SAG				31 TAU		31 LEO			31 SAG		31 PIS

1955

JAN	FEB	MAR	APR	MAY	JUN	JUL	AUG	SEP	OCT	NOV	DEC
1 PIS	1 TAU	1 GEM	1 CAN	1 VIR	1 LIB	1 SCO	1 CAP	1 AQU	1 PIS	1 TAU	1 GEM
2 ARI	2 GEM	3 CAN	2 LEO	4 LIB	2 SCO	2 SAG	2 PIS	2 PIS	2 ARI	2 GEM	2 CAN
4 TAU	4 CAN	6 LEO	4 VIR	6 SCO	5 SAG	5 CAP	4 AQU	4 ARI	4 TAU	4 CAN	4 LEO
6 GEM	6 LEO	8 VIR	6 LIB	9 SAG	7 CAP	7 AQU	6 PIS	6 TAU	6 GEM	6 LEO	6 VIR
8 CAN	8 VIR	10 LIB	9 SCO	11 CAP	10 AQU	10 PIS	8 ARI	8 CAN	8 CAN	9 VIR	8 LIB
10 LEO	11 LIB	13 SCO	11 SAG	14 AQU	12 PIS	12 ARI	11 TAU	11 CAN	10 LEO	11 LIB	10 SCO
12 VIR	13 SCO	15 SAG	14 CAP	16 PIS	15 ARI	14 TAU	13 GEM	13 LEO	13 VIR	13 SCO	13 SAG
14 LIB	16 SAG	18 CAP	16 AQU	18 ARI	17 TAU	16 GEM	15 CAN	15 VIR	15 LIB	16 SAG	16 CAP
17 SCO	18 CAP	20 AQU	19 PIS	20 TAU	19 GEM	18 CAN	17 LEO	17 LIB	17 SCO	18 CAP	18 AQU
19 SAG	21 AQU	22 PIS	21 ARI	22 GEM	21 CAN	20 LEO	19 VIR	19 SAG	19 SAG	21 AQU	21 PIS
22 CAP	23 PIS	24 ARI	23 TAU	24 CAN	23 LEO	22 VIR	21 LIB	22 CAP	22 CAP	23 PIS	23 ARI
24 AQU	25 ARI	27 TAU	25 GEM	26 LEO	25 VIR	25 LIB	23 SCO	24 AQU	24 AQU	26 ARI	25 TAU
27 PIS	27 TAU	29 GEM	27 CAN	29 VIR	27 LIB	27 SCO	26 SAG	27 PIS	27 PIS	28 TAU	27 GEM
29 ARI	28 TAU	31 CAN	29 LEO	31 LIB	30 SCO	29 SAG	28 CAP	29 ARI	29 ARI	30 GEM	29 CAN
31 TAU			30 LEO			31 SAG	31 AQU	30 PIS	31 TAU		31 LEO

1956

JAN	FEB	MAR	APR	MAY	JUN	JUL	AUG	SEP	OCT	NOV	DEC
1 LEO	1 LIB	1 SCO	1 SAG	1 CAP	1 PIS	1 ARI	1 TAU	1 CAN	1 LEO	1 LIB	1 SCO
2 VIR	3 SCO	4 SAG	3 CAP	3 AQU	4 ARI	3 TAU	2 GEM	2 LEO	2 VIR	2 SCO	2 SAG
4 LIB	6 SAG	6 CAP	5 AQU	5 PIS	6 TAU	6 GEM	4 CAN	4 VIR	4 LIB	5 SAG	4 CAP
7 SCO	8 CAP	9 AQU	8 PIS	7 ARI	8 GEM	8 CAN	6 LEO	6 LIB	6 SCO	7 CAP	7 AQU
9 SAG	11 AQU	11 PIS	10 ARI	10 TAU	10 CAN	10 LEO	8 VIR	9 SCO	8 SAG	10 AQU	9 PIS
12 CAP	13 PIS	14 ARI	12 TAU	12 GEM	12 LEO	12 VIR	10 LIB	11 SAG	11 CAP	12 PIS	12 ARI
14 AQU	15 ARI	16 TAU	14 GEM	14 CAN	14 VIR	14 LIB	12 SCO	13 CAP	13 AQU	15 ARI	14 TAU
17 PIS	18 TAU	18 GEM	17 CAN	16 LEO	16 LIB	16 SCO	15 SAG	16 AQU	16 PIS	17 TAU	17 GEM
19 ARI	20 GEM	20 CAN	19 LEO	18 VIR	18 SCO	18 SAG	17 CAP	18 PIS	18 ARI	19 GEM	19 CAN
21 TAU	22 CAN	22 LEO	21 VIR	20 LIB	21 SAG	21 CAP	20 AQU	21 ARI	21 TAU	21 CAN	21 LEO
24 GEM	24 LEO	24 VIR	23 LIB	22 SCO	24 CAP	23 AQU	22 PIS	23 TAU	23 GEM	23 LEO	23 VIR
26 CAN	26 VIR	27 LIB	25 SCO	25 SAG	26 AQU	26 PIS	25 ARI	25 GEM	25 CAN	25 VIR	25 LIB
28 LEO	28 LIB	29 SCO	28 SAG	27 CAP	29 PIS	28 ARI	27 TAU	27 CAN	27 LEO	28 LIB	27 SCO
30 VIR	29 LIB	31 SAG	30 CAP	30 AQU	30 PIS	31 TAU	29 GEM	30 LEO	29 VIR	30 SCO	29 SAG
31 VIR				31 AQU			31 CAN		31 LIB		31 SAG

1957

JAN	FEB	MAR	APR	MAY	JUN	JUL	AUG	SEP	OCT	NOV	DEC
1 CAP	1 AQU	1 PIS	1 ARI	1 TAU	1 CAN	1 LEO	1 LIB	1 SAG	1 CAP	1 AQU	1 PIS
3 AQU	2 PIS	4 ARI	2 TAU	2 GEM	3 LEO	2 VIR	3 SCO	3 CAP	3 AQU	2 PIS	2 ARI
6 PIS	5 ARI	6 TAU	5 GEM	4 CAN	5 VIR	4 LIB	5 SAG	6 AQU	6 PIS	4 ARI	4 TAU
8 ARI	7 TAU	9 GEM	7 CAN	6 LEO	7 LIB	6 SCO	7 CAP	8 PIS	8 ARI	7 TAU	7 GEM
11 TAU	9 GEM	11 CAN	9 LEO	9 VIR	9 SCO	9 SAG	10 AQU	11 ARI	11 TAU	9 GEM	9 CAN
13 GEM	11 CAN	13 LEO	11 VIR	11 LIB	11 SAG	11 CAP	12 PIS	13 TAU	13 GEM	12 CAN	11 LEO
15 CAN	14 LEO	15 VIR	13 LIB	13 SCO	14 CAP	13 AQU	15 ARI	15 CAN	15 CAN	14 LEO	13 VIR
17 LEO	15 VIR	17 LIB	15 SCO	15 SAG	16 AQU	16 PIS	17 TAU	18 CAN	16 LEO	16 VIR	15 LIB
19 VIR	17 LIB	19 SCO	18 SAG	17 CAP	19 PIS	18 ARI	20 GEM	20 LEO	20 VIR	18 LIB	17 SCO
21 LIB	20 SCO	21 SAG	20 CAP	20 AQU	21 ARI	21 TAU	22 CAN	22 VIR	22 LIB	20 SCO	20 SAG
23 SCO	22 SAG	24 CAP	22 AQU	22 PIS	23 TAU	23 GEM	24 LEO	24 LIB	24 SCO	22 SAG	22 CAP
26 SAG	24 CAP	26 AQU	25 PIS	25 ARI	26 GEM	25 CAN	26 VIR	26 SCO	26 SAG	24 CAP	24 AQU
28 CAP	27 AQU	29 PIS	27 ARI	27 TAU	28 CAN	27 LEO	28 LIB	28 SAG	29 CAP	27 AQU	27 PIS
30 AQU	28 AQU	31 ARI	30 TAU	29 GEM	30 LEO	29 VIR	30 SCO	30 AQU	30 AQU	29 PIS	29 ARI
31 AQU				31 GEM		31 LIB	31 SCO		31 AQU	30 PIS	31 ARI

1958

	JAN	FEB	MAR	APR	MAY	JUN	JUL	AUG	SEP	OCT	NOV	DEC
	1 TAU	1 GEM	1 CAN	1 LEO	1 LIB	1 SCO	1 CAP	1 AQU	1 ARI	1 TAU	1 GEM	1 LEO
	3 GEM	2 CAN	3 LEO	2 VIR	3 SCO	2 SAG	3 AQU	2 PIS	3 TAU	3 GEM	2 CAN	4 VIR
	5 CAN	4 LEO	5 VIR	4 LIB	5 SAG	4 CAP	6 PIS	4 ARI	6 GEM	6 CAN	4 LEO	6 LIB
	7 LEO	6 VIR	7 LIB	6 SCO	7 CAP	6 AQU	8 ARI	7 TAU	8 CAN	8 LEO	6 VIR	8 SCO
	9 VIR	8 LIB	9 SCO	8 SAG	10 AQU	8 PIS	11 TAU	10 GEM	11 LEO	10 VIR	9 LIB	10 SAG
	12 LIB	10 SCO	11 SAG	10 CAP	12 PIS	11 ARI	13 GEM	12 CAN	13 VIR	12 LIB	11 SCO	12 CAP
	14 SCO	12 SAG	14 CAP	12 AQU	14 ARI	13 TAU	16 CAN	14 LEO	15 LIB	14 SCO	13 SAG	14 AQU
	16 SAG	14 CAP	16 AQU	15 PIS	17 TAU	16 GEM	18 LEO	16 VIR	17 SCO	16 SAG	15 CAP	16 PIS
	18 CAP	17 AQU	18 PIS	17 ARI	20 GEM	18 CAN	20 VIR	18 LIB	19 SAG	18 CAP	17 AQU	19 ARI
	20 AQU	19 PIS	21 ARI	20 GEM	22 CAN	20 LEO	22 LIB	20 SCO	21 CAP	20 AQU	19 PIS	21 TAU
	23 PIS	22 ARI	24 TAU	22 GEM	24 LEO	23 VIR	24 SCO	22 SAG	23 AQU	23 PIS	22 ARI	24 CAN
	25 ARI	24 TAU	26 GEM	24 LEO	26 VIR	26 LIB	26 SAG	25 CAP	26 PIS	25 ARI	24 TAU	26 CAN
	28 TAU	27 GEM	28 CAN	26 VIR	28 LIB	27 SCO	28 CAP	27 AQU	28 ARI	28 TAU	27 GEM	29 LEO
	30 GEM	28 GEM	31 LEO	28 LIB	31 SCO	29 SAG	31 AQU	29 PIS	30 ARI	30 GEM	29 CAN	31 VIR
	31 GEM			29 VIR		30 SAG		31 PIS		31 GEM	30 CAN	
				30 VIR								

1959

	JAN	FEB	MAR	APR	MAY	JUN	JUL	AUG	SEP	OCT	NOV	DEC
	1 VIR	1 SCO	1 SCO	1 CAP	1 AQU	1 ARI	1 TAU	1 GEM	1 LEO	1 VIR	1 SCO	1 SAG
	2 LIB	3 SAG	2 SAG	2 PIS	2 PIS	3 TAU	3 GEM	2 CAN	2 LIB	2 LIB	3 SAG	2 CAP
	4 SCO	5 CAP	4 CAP	5 PIS	4 ARI	6 GEM	6 CAN	4 LEO	4 SCO	4 SCO	5 CAP	4 AQU
	6 SAG	7 AQU	6 AQU	7 ARI	7 TAU	8 CAN	8 LEO	7 VIR	7 SCO	7 SAG	7 AQU	7 PIS
	8 CAP	9 PIS	9 PIS	10 TAU	9 GEM	10 LEO	10 VIR	9 LIB	9 SAG	9 CAP	9 PIS	9 ARI
	11 AQU	12 ARI	11 ARI	12 GEM	12 CAN	13 VIR	13 LIB	11 SCO	11 CAP	11 AQU	12 ARI	11 TAU
	13 PIS	14 TAU	13 TAU	15 CAN	14 LEO	15 LIB	15 SCO	13 SAG	13 AQU	13 PIS	14 TAU	14 GEM
	15 ARI	17 GEM	16 GEM	17 LEO	17 VIR	17 SCO	17 SAG	15 CAP	15 PIS	15 ARI	17 GEM	16 CAN
	18 TAU	19 CAN	18 CAN	19 VIR	19 LIB	19 SAG	19 CAP	17 AQU	18 ARI	18 TAU	19 CAN	19 LEO
	20 GEM	21 LEO	21 LEO	22 LIB	21 SCO	21 CAP	21 AQU	20 PIS	20 TAU	20 GEM	22 LEO	21 VIR
	23 CAN	24 VIR	23 VIR	24 SCO	23 SAG	23 AQU	23 PIS	22 ARI	23 GEM	23 CAN	24 VIR	24 LIB
	25 LEO	26 LIB	25 LIB	26 SAG	25 CAP	26 PIS	25 ARI	24 TAU	25 CAN	25 LEO	26 LIB	26 SCO
	27 VIR	28 SCO	27 SCO	28 CAP	27 AQU	28 ARI	28 TAU	27 GEM	28 LEO	28 VIR	28 SCO	28 SAG
	29 LIB		29 SAG	30 AQU	29 PIS	30 TAU	30 GEM	29 CAN	30 VIR	30 LIB	30 SAG	30 CAP
	31 LIB		31 CAP		31 PIS		31 CAN	31 CAN		31 LIB		31 CAP

1960

	JAN	FEB	MAR	APR	MAY	JUN	JUL	AUG	SEP	OCT	NOV	DEC
	1 AQU	1 PIS	1 ARI	1 GEM	1 CAN	1 LEO	1 VIR	1 SCO	1 CAP	1 AQU	1 ARI	1 TAU
	3 PIS	2 ARI	2 TAU	3 LEO	3 LEO	2 VIR	2 LIB	3 SAG	3 AQU	2 PIS	3 TAU	3 GEM
	5 ARI	4 TAU	5 GEM	6 LEO	6 VIR	4 SCO	4 SCO	5 CAP	5 PIS	5 ARI	5 GEM	5 CAN
	8 TAU	6 GEM	7 CAN	8 LIB	8 LIB	7 SCO	6 SAG	7 AQU	7 ARI	7 TAU	8 CAN	8 LEO
	10 GEM	9 CAN	10 LEO	11 LIB	10 SCO	9 SAG	8 CAP	9 PIS	9 TAU	9 GEM	10 LEO	10 VIR
	13 CAN	11 LEO	12 VIR	13 SCO	12 SAG	11 CAP	10 AQU	11 ARI	12 GEM	12 CAN	13 VIR	13 LIB
	15 LEO	14 VIR	14 LIB	15 SCO	14 CAP	12 PIS	12 PIS	13 TAU	14 CAN	14 LEO	15 LIB	15 SCO
	18 VIR	16 LIB	17 SCO	17 CAP	16 AQU	15 PIS	14 ARI	15 GEM	17 LEO	17 VIR	18 SCO	17 SAG
	20 LIB	18 SCO	19 SAG	19 PIS	19 PIS	17 ARI	17 TAU	18 CAN	19 VIR	19 LIB	20 SAG	19 CAP
	22 SCO	20 SAG	21 CAP	21 PIS	21 ARI	19 TAU	19 GEM	20 LEO	22 LIB	21 SCO	22 CAP	21 AQU
	24 SAG	23 CAP	23 AQU	24 ARI	23 TAU	22 GEM	22 CAN	23 VIR	24 SCO	23 SAG	25 CAP	23 PIS
	26 CAP	25 AQU	25 PIS	26 TAU	26 GEM	24 CAN	24 LEO	25 LIB	26 SAG	25 CAP	26 PIS	25 ARI
	28 AQU	27 PIS	27 ARI	28 GEM	28 CAN	27 LEO	27 VIR	28 SCO	28 CAP	28 AQU	28 ARI	28 TAU
	30 PIS	29 ARI	30 TAU	30 GEM	31 LEO	29 VIR	29 LIB	30 SAG	30 AQU	30 PIS	30 TAU	30 GEM
	31 PIS		31 TAU			30 VIR	31 SCO	31 SAG		31 PIS		31 GEM

1961

	JAN	FEB	MAR	APR	MAY	JUN	JUL	AUG	SEP	OCT	NOV	DEC
	1 GEM	1 LEO	1 LEO	1 LIB	1 SCO	1 CAP	1 AQU	1 AQI	1 TAU	1 CAN	1 LEO	1 VIR
	2 CAN	3 VIR	2 VIR	3 SCO	3 SAG	3 AQU	3 P15	3 TAU	2 GEM	4 LEO	3 VIR	3 LIB
	4 LEO	5 LIB	5 LIB	5 SAG	5 CAP	5 PIS	5 ARI	5 GEM	4 CAN	6 VIR	5 LIB	5 SCO
	7 VIR	7 SCO	7 SCO	7 CAP	7 AQU	7 ARI	7 TAU	8 CAN	7 LEO	9 LIB	8 SCO	7 SAG
	9 LIB	10 SAG	9 SAG	10 AQU	9 PIS	10 TAU	9 GEM	10 LEO	9 VIR	11 SCO	10 SAG	10 CAP
	11 SCO	12 CAP	11 CAP	12 PIS	11 ARI	12 GEM	12 CAN	13 VIR	12 LIB	14 SAG	12 CAP	12 AQU
	14 SAG	14 AQU	13 AQU	14 ARI	13 TAU	14 CAN	14 LEO	15 LIB	14 SCO	16 CAP	14 AQU	14 PIS
	16 CAP	16 PIS	16 PIS	16 TAU	16 GEM	17 LEO	17 VIR	18 SCO	16 SAG	18 AQU	17 PIS	16 ARI
	18 AQU	18 ARI	18 ARI	18 GEM	18 CAN	19 VIR	19 LIB	20 SAG	18 CAP	20 PIS	19 ARI	18 TAU
	20 PIS	20 TAU	20 TAU	21 CAN	21 LEO	22 LIB	22 SCO	22 CAP	20 PIS	22 ARI	21 TAU	20 GEM
	22 ARI	23 GEM	22 GEM	23 LEO	23 VIR	24 SCO	24 SAG	24 AQU	22 ARI	24 TAU	23 GEM	23 CAN
	24 TAU	25 CAN	24 CAN	26 VIR	26 LIB	26 SAG	26 CAP	26 PIS	25 ARI	27 GEM	25 CAN	25 LEO
	26 GEM	28 LEO	27 LEO	28 LIB	28 SCO	29 CAP	28 AQU	28 ARI	27 TAU	29 CAN	28 LEO	27 VIR
	29 CAN		29 VIR	30 LIB	30 SAG	30 CAP	30 PIS	31 TAU	29 GEM	31 LEO	30 VIR	30 LIB
	31 LEO		31 VIR		31 SAG		31 PIS		30 GEM			31 LIB

1962

	JAN	FEB	MAR	APR	MAY	JUN	JUL	AUG	SEP	OCT	NOV	DEC
	1 SCO	1 SAG	1 SAG	1 AQU	1 PIS	1 TAU	1 GEM	1 LEO	1 VIR	1 SCO	1 SAG	1 CAP
	4 SAG	2 CAP	2 CAP	2 PIS	2 AQU	2 GEM	2 CAN	3 VIR	2 LIB	4 SAG	3 CAP	2 AQU
	6 CAP	4 AQU	4 AQU	4 ARI	4 TAU	4 CAN	4 LEO	5 LIB	4 SCO	6 CAP	5 AQU	4 PIS
	8 AQU	6 PIS	6 PIS	6 TAU	6 GEM	7 VIR	7 VIR	8 SCO	7 SAG	9 AQU	7 PIS	6 AQU
	10 PIS	8 ARI	8 ARI	8 GEM	8 CAN	9 VIR	9 LIB	10 SAG	9 CAP	11 PIS	9 ARI	9 TAU
	12 ARI	11 TAU	10 TAU	11 CAN	10 LEO	12 LIB	12 SCO	13 CAP	13 PIS	13 ARI	11 TAU	11 GEM
	14 TAU	12 GEM	12 GEM	13 LEO	13 VIR	14 SCO	14 SAG	15 AQU	13 PIS	15 TAU	13 GEM	13 CAN
	16 GEM	15 CAN	14 CAN	16 VIQ	15 LIB	17 SAG	17 CAP	17 PIS	15 ARI	17 GEM	15 CAN	15 LEO
	19 CAN	18 LEO	17 LEO	18 LIB	18 SCO	19 CAP	18 AQU	19 ARI	17 TAU	19 CAN	17 LEO	17 VIR
	21 LEO	20 VIR	19 VIR	21 SCO	20 SAG	21 AQU	20 PIS	21 TAU	19 GEM	21 LEO	20 VIR	20 LIB
	24 VIR	23 LIB	22 LIB	23 SAG	22 CAP	23 PIS	21 ARI	23 GEM	22 CAN	24 VIR	22 LIB	22 SCO
	26 LIB	25 SCO	24 SCO	25 CAP	25 AQU	25 ARI	25 TAU	25 CAN	24 LEO	26 LIB	25 SCO	25 SAG
	29 SCO	27 SAG	27 SAG	28 AQU	27 PIS	27 TAU	28 GEM	28 LEO	26 VIR	29 SCO	27 SAG	27 CAP
	31 SAG	28 SAG	29 CAP	30 PIS	29 ARI	30 GEM	29 CAN	30 VIR	29 LIB	31 SAG	30 CAP	29 AQU
			31 AQU		31 TAU		31 LEO	31 VIR	30 LIB			31 AQU

1963

JAN	FEB	MAR	APR	MAY	JUN	JUL	AUG	SEP	OCT	NOV	DEC
1 PIS	1 TAU	1 TAU	1 CAN	1 LEO	1 VIR	1 SCO	1 SAG	1 AQU	1 PIS	1 ARI	1 GEM
2 ARI	3 GEM	2 GEM	3 LEO	3 VIR	2 LIB	4 SAG	3 CAP	4 PIS	2 ARI	2 TAU	3 CAN
5 TAU	5 CAN	5 CAN	6 VIR	5 LIB	4 SCO	6 CAP	5 AQU	6 ARI	5 TAU	3 GEM	5 LEO
7 GEM	7 LEO	7 LEO	8 LIB	8 SCO	7 SAG	9 AQU	7 PIS	8 TAU	7 GEM	6 CAN	7 VIR
9 CAN	10 VIR	9 VIR	11 SCO	10 SAG	9 CAP	11 PIS	9 ARI	10 GEM	9 CAN	8 LEO	10 LIB
11 LEO	12 LIB	11 LIB	13 SAG	13 CAP	11 AQU	13 ARI	11 TAU	12 CAN	11 LEO	10 VIR	12 SCO
14 VIR	15 SCO	14 SCO	16 CAP	15 AQU	14 PIS	15 TAU	14 GEM	14 LEO	14 VIR	12 LIB	15 SAG
16 LIB	17 SAG	17 SAG	18 AQU	17 PIS	16 ARI	17 GEM	16 CAN	16 VIR	16 LIB	15 SCO	17 CAP
19 SCO	20 CAP	19 CAP	20 PIS	20 ARI	18 TAU	19 CAN	18 LEO	19 LIB	19 SCO	17 SAG	20 AQU
21 SAG	22 AQU	22 AQU	22 ARI	22 TAU	20 GEM	22 LEO	20 VIR	21 SCO	21 SAG	20 CAP	22 PIS
23 CAP	24 PIS	24 PIS	24 TAU	24 GEM	22 CAN	24 VIR	23 LIB	24 SAG	24 CAP	22 AQU	24 ARI
26 AQU	26 ARI	26 ARI	26 GEM	26 CAN	24 LEO	26 LIB	25 SCO	26 CAP	26 AQU	25 PIS	26 TAU
28 PIS	28 TAU	28 TAU	28 CAN	28 LEO	26 VIR	29 SCO	28 SAG	29 AQU	28 PIS	27 ARI	28 GEM
30 ARI		30 GEM	30 LEO	30 VIR	29 LIB	31 SAG	30 CAP	30 AQU	31 ARI	29 TAU	30 CAN
31 ARI		31 GEM		31 VIR	30 LIB		31 CAP			30 TAU	31 CAN

1964

JAN	FEB	MAR	APR	MAY	JUN	JUL	AUG	SEP	OCT	NOV	DEC
1 LEO	1 VIR	1 LIB	1 SCO	1 SAG	1 AQU	1 PIS	1 TAU	1 GEM	1 LEO	1 VIR	1 SCO
4 VIR	2 LIB	3 SCO	2 SAG	2 CAP	3 PIS	3 ARI	3 GEM	2 CAN	3 VIR	2 LIB	4 SAG
6 LIB	5 SCO	5 SAG	4 CAP	4 AQU	5 ARI	5 TAU	5 CAN	4 LEO	5 LIB	4 SCO	6 CAP
8 SCO	7 SAG	8 CAP	7 AQU	7 PIS	7 TAU	7 GEM	7 LEO	6 VIR	8 SCO	6 SAG	9 AQU
11 SAG	10 CAP	11 AQU	9 PIS	9 ARI	9 GEM	9 CAN	9 VIR	8 LIB	10 SAG	9 CAP	11 PIS
13 CAP	12 AQU	13 PIS	11 ARI	11 TAU	11 CAN	11 LEO	11 LIB	10 SCO	12 CAP	11 AQU	14 ARI
16 AQU	15 PIS	15 ARI	14 TAU	13 GEM	13 LEO	13 VIR	14 SCO	13 SAG	15 AQU	14 PIS	16 TAU
18 PIS	17 ARI	17 TAU	16 GEM	15 CAN	16 VIR	15 LIB	16 SAG	15 CAP	17 PIS	16 ARI	18 GEM
20 ARI	19 TAU	19 GEM	18 CAN	17 LEO	18 LIB	17 SCO	19 CAP	18 AQU	20 ARI	18 TAU	20 CAN
23 TAU	21 GEM	21 CAN	20 LEO	19 VIR	20 SCO	20 SAG	21 AQU	20 PIS	22 TAU	20 GEM	22 LEO
25 GEM	23 CAN	24 LEO	22 VIR	22 LIB	23 SAG	23 CAP	24 PIS	22 ARI	24 GEM	22 CAN	24 VIR
27 CAN	25 LEO	26 VIR	24 LIB	24 SCO	25 CAP	25 AQU	26 ARI	24 TAU	26 CAN	24 LEO	26 LIB
29 LEO	27 VIR	28 LIB	27 SCO	26 SAG	28 AQU	27 PIS	28 TAU	26 GEM	28 LEO	27 VIR	28 SCO
31 VIR	29 VIR	30 SCO	29 SAG	29 CAP	30 PIS	30 ARI	30 GEM	28 CAN	30 VIR	29 LIB	31 SAG
		31 SCO	30 SAG	31 CAP		31 ARI	31 GEM	30 CAN	31 VIR	30 LIB	

1965

JAN	FEB	MAR	APR	MAY	JUN	JUL	AUG	SEP	OCT	NOV	DEC
1 SAG	1 AQU	1 AQU	1 PIS	1 TAU	1 GEM	1 LEO	1 VIR	1 LEO	1 SAG	1 AQU	1 PIS
2 CAP	4 PIS	3 PIS	2 ARI	3 GEM	2 CAN	3 VIR	2 LIB	2 SAG	2 CAP	4 PIS	3 ARI
5 AQU	6 ARI	5 ARI	4 TAU	5 CAN	4 LEO	5 LIB	4 SCO	5 CAP	5 AQU	6 ARI	6 TAU
7 PIS	8 TAU	8 TAU	6 GEM	8 LEO	6 VIR	8 SCO	6 SAG	7 AQU	8 TAU	9 TAU	8 GEM
10 ARI	11 GEM	10 GEM	8 CAN	10 VIR	8 LIB	10 SAG	9 CAP	10 PIS	10 ARI	11 GEM	10 CAN
12 TAU	13 CAN	12 CAN	10 LEO	12 LIB	10 SCO	12 CAP	11 AQU	12 ARI	12 TAU	13 CAN	12 LEO
14 GEM	15 LEO	14 LEO	12 VIR	14 SCO	13 SAG	15 AQU	14 PIS	15 TAU	14 GEM	15 LEO	14 VIR
16 CAN	17 VIR	16 VIR	15 LIB	16 SAG	15 CAP	17 PIS	16 ARI	17 GEM	17 CAN	17 VIR	16 LIB
18 LEO	19 LIB	18 LIB	17 SCO	19 CAP	18 AQU	20 ARI	19 TAU	19 CAN	19 LEO	19 LIB	19 SCO
20 VIR	21 SCO	20 SCO	19 SAG	21 AQU	20 PIS	22 TAU	21 GEM	21 LEO	21 VIR	21 SCO	21 SAG
22 LIB	23 SAG	23 SAG	22 CAP	24 PIS	23 ARI	25 GEM	23 CAN	23 VIR	23 LIB	24 SAG	23 CAP
25 SCO	26 CAP	25 CAP	24 AQU	26 ARI	25 TAU	27 CAN	25 LEO	26 LIB	25 SCO	26 CAP	26 AQU
27 SAG	28 AQU	28 AQU	27 PIS	29 TAU	27 GEM	29 LEO	27 VIR	28 SCO	28 SAG	28 AQU	28 PIS
30 CAP		30 PIS	29 ARI	31 GEM	29 CAN	31 VIR	29 LIB	30 SAG	30 CAP	30 AQU	31 ARI
31 CAP		31 PIS	30 ARI		30 CAN		31 SCO		31 CAP		

1966

JAN	FEB	MAR	APR	MAY	JUN	JUL	AUG	SEP	OCT	NOV	DEC
1 ARI	1 GEM	1 GEM	1 LEO	1 VIR	1 SCO	1 SAG	1 AQU	1 PIS	1 ARI	1 GEM	1 CAN
2 TAU	3 CAN	2 CAN	3 VIR	2 LIB	3 SAG	2 CAP	4 PIS	2 ARI	2 TAU	3 CAN	3 LEO
5 GEM	5 LEO	5 LEO	5 LIB	4 SCO	5 CAP	5 AQU	6 ARI	5 TAU	5 GEM	5 LEO	5 VIR
7 CAN	7 VIR	7 VIR	7 SCO	7 SAG	8 AQU	7 PIS	9 TAU	7 GEM	7 CAN	8 VIR	7 LIB
9 LEO	9 LIB	9 LIB	9 SAG	9 CAP	10 PIS	10 ARI	11 GEM	9 CAN	10 LEO	10 LIB	9 SCO
11 VIR	11 SCO	11 SCO	11 CAP	11 AQU	13 ARI	12 TAU	13 CAN	12 LEO	11 VIR	12 SCO	11 SAG
13 LIB	13 SAG	13 SAG	14 AQU	14 PIS	15 TAU	15 GEM	15 LEO	14 VIR	13 LIB	14 SAG	13 CAP
15 SCO	16 CAP	15 CAP	16 PIS	16 ARI	17 GEM	17 CAN	17 VIR	16 LIB	15 SCO	16 CAP	16 AQU
17 SAG	18 AQU	18 AQU	19 ARI	19 TAU	20 CAN	19 LEO	19 LIB	18 SCO	17 SAG	18 AQU	18 PIS
20 CAP	21 PIS	20 PIS	21 TAU	21 GEM	22 LEO	21 VIR	21 SCO	20 SAG	20 CAP	21 PIS	21 ARI
22 AQU	23 ARI	23 ARI	24 GEM	23 CAN	24 VIR	23 LIB	24 SAG	22 CAP	22 AQU	23 ARI	23 TAU
25 PIS	26 TAU	25 TAU	26 CAN	25 LEO	26 LIB	25 SCO	26 CAP	25 AQU	24 PIS	26 TAU	26 GEM
27 ARI	28 GEM	27 GEM	28 LEO	27 VIR	28 SCO	27 SAG	28 AQU	27 PIS	27 ARI	28 GEM	28 CAN
30 TAU		30 CAN	30 VIR	30 LIB	30 SAG	30 CAP	31 PIS	30 ARI	29 TAU	30 CAN	30 LEO
31 TAU		31 CAN		31 LIB		31 CAP			31 TAU		31 LEO

1967

JAN	FEB	MAR	APR	MAY	JUN	JUL	AUG	SEP	OCT	NOV	DEC
1 VIR	1 LIB	1 SCO	1 SAG	1 AQU	1 PIS	1 ARI	1 GEM	1 CAN	1 LEO	1 LIB	1 SCO
3 LIB	2 SCO	3 SAG	2 CAP	4 PIS	2 ARI	2 TAU	3 CAN	2 LEO	2 VIR	2 SCO	2 SAG
5 SCO	4 SAG	5 CAP	4 AQU	6 ARI	5 TAU	5 GEM	6 LEO	4 VIR	4 LIB	4 SAG	4 CAP
8 SAG	6 CAP	8 AQU	6 PIS	9 TAU	7 GEM	7 CAN	8 VIR	6 LIB	6 SCO	6 CAP	6 AQU
10 CAP	8 AQU	10 PIS	9 ARI	11 GEM	10 CAN	9 LEO	10 LIB	8 SCO	8 SAG	8 AQU	8 PIS
12 AQU	11 PIS	13 ARI	11 TAU	14 CAN	12 LEO	12 VIR	12 SCO	10 SAG	10 CAP	11 PIS	10 ARI
14 PIS	13 ARI	15 TAU	14 GEM	16 LEO	14 VIR	14 LIB	14 SAG	12 CAP	12 AQU	13 ARI	13 TAU
17 ARI	16 TAU	18 GEM	16 CAN	18 VIR	16 LIB	16 SCO	16 CAP	15 AQU	14 PIS	16 TAU	15 GEM
19 TAU	18 GEM	20 CAN	19 LEO	20 LIB	18 SCO	18 SAG	19 AQU	17 PIS	17 ARI	18 GEM	18 CAN
22 GEM	21 CAN	22 LEO	21 VIR	22 SCO	21 SAG	20 CAP	21 PIS	20 ARI	19 TAU	21 CAN	20 VIR
24 CAN	23 LEO	24 VIR	23 LIB	24 SAG	23 CAP	22 AQU	23 ARI	22 TAU	22 GEM	23 LEO	23 VIR
26 LEO	25 VIR	26 LIB	25 SCO	26 CAP	25 AQU	25 PIS	26 TAU	25 GEM	24 CAN	25 VIR	25 LIB
28 VIR	27 LIB	28 SCO	27 SAG	28 AQU	27 PIS	27 ARI	28 GEM	27 CAN	27 LEO	28 LIB	27 SCO
30 LIB	28 LIB	30 SAG	29 CAP	31 PIS	30 ARI	30 TAU	31 CAN	29 LEO	29 VIR	30 SCO	29 SAG
31 LIB		31 SAG	30 CAP			31 TAU		30 LEO	31 LIB		31 CAP

1968

JAN	FEB	MAR	APR	MAY	JUN	JUL	AUG	SEP	OCT	NOV	DEC
1 CAP	1 PIS	1 ARI	1 TAU	1 GEM	1 LEO	1 VIR	1 LIB	1 SAG	1 AQU	1 PIS	1 ARI
2 AQU	3 ARI	4 TAU	3 GEM	3 CAN	4 VIR	3 LIB	2 SCO	2 CAP	4 PIS	2 ARI	2 TAU
4 PIS	6 TAU	6 GEM	5 CAN	5 LEO	6 LIB	5 SCO	4 SAG	4 AQU	6 ARI	5 TAU	4 GEM
7 ARI	8 GEM	9 CAN	8 LEO	7 VIR	8 SCO	7 SAG	6 CAP	6 PIS	8 TAU	7 GEM	7 CAN
9 TAU	11 CAN	11 LEO	10 VIR	10 LIB	10 SAG	9 CAP	8 AQU	9 ARI	11 GEM	10 CAN	9 LEO
12 GEM	13 LEO	14 VIR	12 LIB	12 SCO	12 CAP	11 AQU	11 PIS	11 TAU	13 CAN	12 LEO	12 VIR
14 CAN	15 VIR	16 LIB	14 SCO	14 SAG	14 AQU	14 PIS	13 ARI	13 GEM	16 LEO	15 VIR	14 LIB
17 LEO	17 LIB	18 SCO	16 SAG	16 CAP	16 PIS	16 ARI	15 TAU	16 CAN	18 VIR	17 LIB	16 SCO
19 VIR	19 SCO	20 SAG	18 SCO	18 AQU	19 ARI	18 TAU	17 GEM	18 LEO	20 LIB	19 SCO	18 SAG
21 LIB	22 SAG	22 CAP	20 AQU	20 PIS	21 TAU	21 GEM	20 CAN	20 VIR	23 SCO	21 SAG	20 CAP
23 SCO	24 CAP	24 AQU	22 ARI	22 ARI	24 GEM	23 CAN	22 LEO	23 LIB	25 SAG	23 CAP	22 AQU
25 SAG	26 AQU	26 PIS	23 PIS	25 TAU	26 CAN	26 LEO	24 VIR	25 SCO	27 CAP	25 AQU	24 PIS
27 CAP	28 PIS	29 ARI	25 ARI	27 GEM	28 LEO	28 VIR	27 LIB	27 SAG	29 AQU	27 PIS	27 ARI
30 AQU	29 PIS	31 TAU	28 TAU	30 CAN	30 LEO	30 LIB	29 SCO	29 CAP	31 PIS	29 ARI	29 TAU
31 AQU			30 GEM	31 CAN		31 LIB	31 SAG			30 ARI	31 TAU

1969

JAN	FEB	MAR	APR	MAY	JUN	JUL	AUG	SEP	OCT	NOV	DEC
1 GEM	1 CAN	1 LEO	1 VIR	1 LIB	1 SAG	1 CAP	1 PIS	1 TAU	1 GEM	1 CAN	1 LEO
3 CAN	2 LEO	4 VIR	2 LIB	2 SCO	2 CAP	2 AQU	2 ARI	3 GEM	3 CAN	2 LEO	2 VIR
6 LEO	4 VIR	6 LIB	5 SCO	4 SAG	4 AQU	4 PIS	4 TAU	5 CAN	6 LEO	5 VIR	4 LIB
8 VIR	7 LIB	8 SCO	7 SAG	6 CAP	6 PIS	6 ARI	6 GEM	8 LEO	8 VIR	7 LIB	7 SCO
10 LIB	9 SCO	10 SAG	9 CAP	8 AQU	9 ARI	8 TAU	9 CAN	11 VIR	11 LIB	9 SCO	9 SAG
13 SCO	11 SAG	12 CAP	11 AQU	10 PIS	11 TAU	11 GEM	12 LEO	13 LIB	13 SCO	11 SAG	11 CAP
15 SAG	13 CAP	15 AQU	13 PIS	12 ARI	13 GEM	13 CAN	15 VIR	16 SCO	15 SAG	13 CAP	13 AQU
17 CAP	15 AQU	17 PIS	15 ARI	15 TAU	16 CAN	16 LEO	17 LIB	18 SAG	17 CAP	15 AQU	15 PIS
19 AQU	17 PIS	19 ARI	18 TAU	17 GEM	19 LEO	18 VIR	19 SCO	20 CAP	20 AQU	18 PIS	17 ARI
21 PIS	19 ARI	21 TAU	20 GEM	20 CAN	21 VIR	21 LIB	22 SAG	22 AQU	22 PIS	20 ARI	19 TAU
23 ARI	22 TAU	24 GEM	22 CAN	22 LEO	23 LIB	23 SCO	24 CAP	24 PIS	24 ARI	22 TAU	22 GEM
25 TAU	24 GEM	26 CAN	25 LEO	25 VIR	26 SCO	25 SAG	26 AQU	26 ARI	26 TAU	24 GEM	24 CAN
28 GEM	27 CAN	29 LEO	27 VIR	27 LIB	28 SAG	27 CAP	28 PIS	28 TAU	28 GEM	27 CAN	27 LEO
30 CAN	28 CAN	31 VIR	30 LIB	29 SCO	30 CAP	29 AQU	30 ARI	30 TAU	30 CAN	29 LEO	29 VIR
31 CAN				31 SAG		31 PIS	31 ARI		31 CAN	30 LEO	31 VIR

1970

JAN	FEB	MAR	APR	MAY	JUN	JUL	AUG	SEP	OCT	NOV	DEC
1 LIB	1 SCO	1 SAG	1 AQU	1 PIS	1 TAU	1 GEM	1 CAN	1 VIR	1 LIB	1 SCO	1 CAP
3 SCO	2 SAG	3 CAP	4 PIS	3 ARI	4 GEM	3 CAN	2 LEO	3 LIB	3 SCO	2 SAG	3 AQU
5 SAG	4 CAP	5 AQU	6 ARI	5 TAU	6 CAN	6 LEO	4 VIR	5 SCO	5 SAG	4 CAP	5 PIS
7 CAP	6 AQU	7 PIS	8 TAU	7 GEM	8 LEO	8 VIR	6 LIB	8 SAG	8 CAP	6 AQU	8 ARI
9 AQU	8 PIS	9 ARI	10 GEM	10 CAN	11 VIR	11 LIB	9 SCO	10 CAP	10 AQU	8 PIS	10 TAU
11 PIS	10 ARI	11 TAU	12 CAN	12 LEO	13 LIB	13 SCO	12 SAG	12 AQU	12 PIS	10 ARI	12 GEM
13 ARI	12 TAU	13 GEM	15 LEO	15 VIR	16 SCO	15 SAG	14 CAP	14 PIS	14 ARI	12 TAU	14 CAN
16 TAU	14 GEM	16 CAN	17 VIR	17 LIB	18 SAG	18 CAP	16 AQU	16 ARI	16 TAU	14 GEM	16 LEO
18 GEM	17 CAN	18 LEO	20 LIB	19 SCO	20 CAP	20 AQU	18 PIS	19 TAU	18 GEM	17 CAN	19 VIR
20 CAN	19 LEO	21 VIR	22 SCO	22 SAG	22 AQU	22 PIS	20 ARI	21 GEM	20 CAN	19 LEO	22 LIB
23 LEO	22 VIR	23 LIB	24 SAG	24 CAP	24 PIS	24 ARI	22 TAU	23 CAN	23 LEO	22 VIR	24 SCO
25 VIR	24 LIB	26 SCO	27 CAP	26 AQU	26 ARI	26 TAU	24 GEM	25 LEO	25 VIR	24 LIB	26 SAG
28 LIB	27 SCO	28 SAG	29 AQU	28 PIS	28 TAU	28 GEM	27 CAN	28 VIR	27 LIB	26 SCO	29 CAP
30 SCO	28 SCO	30 CAP	31 PIS	30 ARI	30 TAU	30 CAN	29 LEO	30 VIR	30 SCO	29 SAG	31 AQU
31 SCO		31 CAP		31 ARI		31 CAN	31 LEO		31 SCO	30 SAG	

1971

JAN	FEB	MAR	APR	MAY	JUN	JUL	AUG	SEP	OCT	NOV	DEC
1 AQU	1 ARI	1 TAU	1 GEM	1 CAN	1 VIR	1 LIB	1 SCO	1 CAP	1 AQU	1 ARI	1 TAU
2 PIS	2 TAU	4 GEM	2 CAN	2 LEO	3 LIB	3 SCO	2 SAG	3 AQU	2 PIS	3 TAU	2 GEM
4 ARI	4 GEM	6 CAN	5 LEO	4 VIR	6 SCO	5 SAG	4 CAP	5 PIS	4 ARI	5 GEM	4 CAN
6 TAU	7 CAN	8 LEO	7 VIR	7 LIB	8 SAG	8 CAP	6 AQU	7 ARI	6 TAU	7 CAN	6 LEO
8 GEM	9 LEO	11 VIR	9 LIB	9 SCO	11 CAP	10 AQU	8 PIS	9 TAU	8 GEM	9 LEO	9 VIR
10 CAN	12 VIR	13 LIB	12 SCO	12 SAG	13 AQU	12 PIS	10 ARI	11 GEM	10 CAN	11 VIR	11 LIB
13 LEO	14 LIB	16 SCO	15 SAG	14 CAP	15 PIS	14 ARI	13 TAU	13 CAN	13 LEO	14 LIB	14 SCO
16 VIR	17 SCO	18 SAG	17 CAP	16 AQU	17 ARI	16 TAU	15 GEM	15 LEO	15 VIR	16 SCO	16 SAG
18 LIB	19 SAG	21 CAP	19 AQU	19 PIS	19 TAU	18 GEM	17 CAN	18 VIR	18 LIB	19 SAG	19 CAP
20 SCO	21 CAP	23 AQU	21 PIS	21 ARI	21 GEM	21 CAN	19 LEO	20 LIB	20 SCO	21 CAP	21 AQU
23 SAG	23 AQU	25 PIS	23 ARI	23 TAU	23 CAN	23 LEO	22 VIR	23 SCO	23 SAG	24 AQU	23 PIS
25 CAP	25 PIS	27 ARI	25 TAU	25 GEM	26 LEO	25 VIR	24 LIB	25 SAG	25 CAP	26 PIS	25 ARI
27 AQU	27 ARI	29 TAU	27 GEM	27 CAN	28 VIR	28 LIB	27 SCO	28 CAP	28 AQU	28 ARI	27 TAU
29 PIS	28 ARI	31 GEM	30 CAN	29 LEO	30 VIR	30 SCO	29 SAG	30 AQU	30 PIS	30 TAU	30 GEM
31 ARI				31 LEO		31 SCO	31 SAG		31 PIS		31 GEM

1972

JAN	FEB	MAR	APR	MAY	JUN	JUL	AUG	SEP	OCT	NOV	DEC
1 CAN	1 LEO	1 VIR	1 SCO	1 SAG	1 CAP	1 AQU	1 ARI	1 GEM	1 CAN	1 VIR	1 LIB
3 LEO	2 VIR	2 LIB	4 SAG	3 CAP	2 AQU	2 PIS	2 TAU	3 CAN	2 LEO	3 LIB	3 SCO
5 VIR	4 LIB	4 SCO	6 CAP	6 AQU	4 PIS	4 ARI	4 GEM	5 LEO	4 VIR	5 SCO	5 SAG
8 LIB	6 SCO	7 SAG	8 AQU	8 PIS	7 ARI	6 TAU	6 CAN	7 VIR	7 LIB	8 SAG	8 CAP
10 SCO	9 SAG	10 CAP	11 PIS	10 ARI	9 TAU	8 GEM	8 LEO	9 LIB	9 SCO	10 CAP	10 AQU
13 SAG	11 CAP	12 AQU	13 ARI	12 TAU	11 GEM	10 CAN	11 VIR	12 SCO	12 SAG	13 AQU	13 PIS
15 CAP	14 AQU	14 PIS	15 TAU	14 GEM	13 CAN	12 LEO	13 LIB	15 SAG	14 CAP	15 PIS	15 ARI
17 AQU	16 PIS	16 ARI	17 GEM	16 CAN	15 LEO	14 VIR	16 SCO	17 CAP	17 AQU	18 ARI	17 TAU
19 PIS	18 ARI	18 TAU	19 CAN	18 LEO	17 VIR	17 LIB	18 SAG	19 AQU	19 PIS	20 TAU	19 GEM
22 ARI	20 TAU	20 GEM	21 LEO	21 VIR	19 LIB	19 SCO	21 CAP	22 PIS	21 ARI	22 GEM	21 CAN
24 TAU	22 GEM	22 CAN	23 VIR	23 LIB	22 SCO	22 SAG	23 AQU	24 ARI	23 TAU	24 CAN	23 LEO
26 GEM	24 CAN	25 LEO	26 LIB	25 SCO	24 SAG	24 CAP	25 PIS	26 TAU	25 GEM	26 LEO	25 VIR
28 CAN	27 LEO	27 VIR	28 SCO	28 SAG	27 CAP	27 AQU	27 ARI	28 GEM	27 CAN	28 VIR	27 LIB
30 LEO	29 VIR	29 LIB	30 SCO	31 CAP	29 AQU	29 PIS	29 TAU	30 CAN	29 LEO	30 LIB	30 SCO
31 LEO		31 LIB			30 AQU	31 ARI	31 GEM		31 LEO		31 SCO

1973

JAN	FEB	MAR	APR	MAY	JUN	JUL	AUG	SEP	OCT	NOV	DEC
1 SAG	1 CAP	1 CAP	1 PIS	1 ARI	1 GEM	1 CAN	1 VIR	1 LIB	1 SAG	1 CAP	1 AQU
4 CAP	3 AQU	2 AQU	3 ARI	3 TAU	3 CAN	2 LEO	3 LIB	2 SCO	4 CAP	3 AQU	3 PIS
6 AQU	5 PIS	4 PIS	5 TAU	5 GEM	5 LEO	4 VIR	5 SCO	4 SAG	7 AQU	5 PIS	5 ARI
9 PIS	7 ARI	7 ARI	7 GEM	7 CAN	7 VIR	7 LIB	8 SAG	7 CAP	9 PIS	8 ARI	7 TAU
11 ARI	10 TAU	9 TAU	9 CAN	9 LEO	9 LIB	9 SCO	10 CAP	9 AQU	11 ARI	10 TAU	9 GEM
13 TAU	12 GEM	11 GEM	11 LEO	11 VIR	12 SCO	12 SAG	13 AQU	12 PIS	13 TAU	12 GEM	11 CAN
15 GEM	14 CAN	13 CAN	14 VIR	13 LIB	14 SAG	14 CAP	15 PIS	14 ARI	16 GEM	14 CAN	13 LEO
17 CAN	16 LEO	15 LEO	16 LIB	16 SCO	17 CAP	17 AQU	18 ARI	16 TAU	18 CAN	16 LEO	15 VIR
19 LEO	18 VIR	17 VIR	18 SCO	18 SAG	19 AQU	19 PIS	20 TAU	18 GEM	20 LEO	18 VIR	18 LIB
22 VIR	20 LIB	20 LIB	21 SAG	21 W	22 PIS	21 ARI	22 GEM	20 CAN	22 VIR	20 LIB	20 SCO
24 LIB	23 SCO	22 SCO	23 CAP	23 AQU	24 ARI	24 TAU	24 CAN	21 LEO	24 LIB	23 SCO	22 SAG
26 SCO	25 SAG	24 SAG	26 AQU	26 PIS	26 TAU	26 GEM	26 LEO	24 VIR	26 SCO	25 SAG	25 CAP
29 SAG	28 CAP	27 CAP	28 PIS	28 ARI	28 GEM	28 CAN	28 VIR	27 LIB	29 SAG	28 CAP	27 AQU
31 CAP		29 AQU	30 ARI	30 TAU	30 CAN	30 LEO	30 LIB	29 SCO	3I CAP	30 AQU	30 PIS
		31 AQU		31 TAU		31 LEO	31 LIB	30 SCO			31 PIS

1974

JAN	FEB	MAR	APR	MAY	JUN	JUL	AUG	SEP	OCT	NOV	DEC
1 ARI	1 TAU	1 GEM	1 CAN	1 VIR	1 LIB	1 CAP	1 CAP	1 AQU	1 ARI	1 TAU	1 GEM
4 TAU	2 GEM	4 CAN	2 LEO	3 LIB	3 SCO	2 SAG	3 AQU	2 PIS	4 TAU	2 GEM	2 CAN
6 GEM	4 CAN	6 LEO	4 VIR	5 SCO	5 SAG	4 CAP	5 PIS	4 ARI	6 GEM	4 CAN	4 LEO
8 CAN	6 LEO	8 VIR	6 LIB	7 SAG	7 CAP	7 AQU	8 ARI	6 TAU	8 CAN	7 LEO	6 VIR
10 LEO	8 VIR	10 LIB	8 SCO	9 CAP	9 AQU	9 PIS	10 TAU	9 GEM	10 LEO	9 VIR	8 LIB
12 VIR	10 LIB	12 SCO	10 SAG	13 AQU	12 PIS	12 ARI	13 GEM	11 CAN	12 VIR	11 LIB	10 SCO
14 LIB	13 SCO	14 SAG	13 CAP	15 PIS	14 ARI	14 TAU	15 CAN	13 LEO	15 LIB	13 SCO	13 SAG
16 SCO	15 SAG	17 CAP	16 AQU	18 ARI	17 TAU	16 GEM	17 LEO	15 VIR	17 SCO	15 SAG	15 CAP
19 SAG	17 CAP	19 AQU	18 PIS	20 TAU	19 GEM	18 CAN	19 VIR	17 LIB	19 SAG	17 CAP	17 AQU
21 CAP	20 AQU	22 PIS	21 ARI	22 GEM	21 CAN	20 LEO	21 LIB	19 SCO	21 CAP	20 AQU	20 PIS
24 AQU	22 PIS	24 ARI	23 TAU	24 CAN	23 LEO	22 VIR	23 SCO	21 SAG	24 AQU	23 PIS	22 ARI
26 PIS	25 ARI	26 TAU	26 GEM	26 LEO	25 VIR	24 LIB	25 SAG	24 CAP	26 PIS	25 ARI	25 TAU
29 ARI	27 TAU	29 GEM	27 CAN	27 VIR	27 LIB	26 SCO	28 CAP	26 AQU	29 ARI	27 TAU	27 GEM
31 TAU	28 TAU	31 CAN	29 LEO	29 VIR	29 SCO	29 SAG	30 AQU	29 PIS	31 TAU	30 GEM	29 CAN
			30 LEO	31 LIB	30 SCO	31 CAP	31 AQU	30 PIS			30 LEO

1975

JAN	FEB	MAR	APR	MAY	JUN	JUL	AUG	SEP	OCT	NOV	DEC
1 LEO	1 LIB	1 LIB	1 SAG	1 CAP	1 AQU	1 ARI	1 TAU	1 CAN	1 LEO	1 LIB	1 SCO
2 VIR	3 SCO	2 SCO	3 CAP	3 AQU	2 PIS	4 TAU	3 GEM	3 LEO	3 VIR	3 SCO	3 SAG
4 LIB	5 SAG	4 SAG	5 AQU	5 PIS	4 ARI	6 GEM	5 CAN	5 VIR	5 LIB	5 SAG	5 CAP
6 SCO	7 CAP	7 CAP	8 PIS	8 ARI	6 GEM	9 CAN	7 LEO	7 LIB	7 SCO	8 CAP	7 AQU
9 SAG	10 AQU	9 AQU	10 ARI	10 GEM	9 CAN	11 LEO	9 VIR	9 SCO	9 SAG	10 AQU	10 PIS
11 CAP	12 PIS	12 PIS	13 TAU	13 CAN	11 LEO	13 VIR	11 LIB	12 SAG	11 CAP	12 PIS	12 ARI
14 AQU	15 ARI	14 ARI	15 GEM	15 LEO	14 VIR	15 LIB	13 SCO	14 CAP	14 AQU	15 ARI	15 TAU
16 PIS	17 TAU	17 TAU	18 CAN	17 VIR	15 VIR	17 SCO	15 SAG	16 AQU	16 PIS	17 TAU	17 GEM
19 ARI	20 GEM	19 GEM	20 LEO	19 LIB	17 LIB	19 SAG	18 CAP	19 PIS	19 ARI	20 GEM	19 CAN
21 TAU	22 CAN	21 CAN	22 VIR	21 SCO	19 SCO	21 CAP	20 AQU	21 ARI	21 TAU	22 CAN	22 LEO
23 GEM	24 LEO	24 LEO	24 LIB	23 SAG	21 SAG	24 AQU	22 PIS	24 TAU	23 GEM	24 LEO	24 VIR
26 CAN	26 VIR	26 VIR	26 SCO	25 CAP	22 SAG	26 PIS	25 ARI	26 GEM	26 CAN	27 VIR	26 LIB
28 LEO	28 LIB	28 LIB	28 SAG	28 AQU	24 CAP	29 ARI	28 TAU	29 CAN	28 LEO	29 LIB	2B SCO
30 VIR		30 SCO	30 CAP	30 AQU	26 AQU	31 TAU	30 GEM	30 CAN	30 VIR	30 LIB	30 SAG
31 VIR		31 SCO		31 AQU	29 PIS		31 GEM		31 VIR		31 SAG
					30 PIS						

1976

JAN	FEB	MAR	APR	MAY	JUN	JUL	AUG	SEP	OCT	NOV	DEC
1 CAP	1 AQU	1 PIS	1 ARI	1 TAU	1 CAN	1 LEO	1 LIB	1 SAG	1 CAP	1 PIS	1 ARI
4 AQU	2 PIS	3 ARI	2 TAU	2 GEM	3 LEO	2 VIR	3 SCO	3 CAP	3 AQU	4 ARI	3 TAU
6 PIS	5 ARI	6 TAU	4 GEM	4 CAN	5 VIR	4 LIB	5 SAG	5 AQU	5 PIS	6 TAU	6 GEM
8 ARI	7 TAU	8 GEM	7 CAN	6 LEO	7 LIB	6 SCO	7 CAP	8 PIS	7 ARI	9 GEM	9 CAN
11 TAU	10 GEM	11 CAN	9 LEO	9 VIR	9 SCO	9 SAG	9 AQU	10 ARI	10 TAU	11 CAN	11 LEO
13 GEM	12 CAN	13 LEO	11 VIR	11 LIB	11 SAG	11 CAP	11 PIS	13 TAU	12 GEM	14 LEO	13 VIR
16 CAN	14 LEO	15 VIR	13 LIB	13 SCO	13 CAP	13 AQU	14 ARI	15 GEM	15 CAN	16 VIR	15 LIB
18 LEO	16 VIR	17 LIB	15 SCO	15 SAG	15 AQU	15 PIS	16 TAU	18 CAN	17 LEO	18 LIB	18 SCO
20 VIR	18 LIB	19 SCO	17 SAG	17 CAP	18 PIS	18 ARI	19 GEM	20 LEO	20 VIR	20 SCO	20 SAG
22 LIB	21 SCO	21 SAG	19 CAP	19 AQU	20 ARI	20 TAU	21 CAN	22 VIR	22 LIB	22 SAG	22 CAP
24 SCO	23 SAG	23 CAP	22 AQU	21 PIS	23 TAU	23 GEM	24 LEO	24 LIB	24 SCO	24 CAP	24 AQU
26 SAG	25 CAP	25 AQU	24 PIS	24 ARI	25 GEM	25 CAN	26 VIR	26 SCO	26 SAG	26 AQU	26 PIS
29 CAP	27 AQU	28 PIS	27 ARI	26 TAU	28 CAN	27 LEO	28 LIB	28 SAG	28 CAP	29 PIS	28 ARI
31 AQU	29 AQU	30 ARI	29 TAU	29 GEM	30 LEO	29 VIR	30 SCO	30 CAP	30 AQU	30 PIS	31 TAU
		31 ARI	30 TAU	31 CAN		31 VIR	31 SCO		31 AQU		

1977

JAN	FEB	MAR	APR	MAY	JUN	JUL	AUG	SEP	OCT	NOV	DEC
1 TAU	1 CAN	1 CAN	1 LEO	1 LIB	1 SCO	1 CAP	1 AQU	1 ARI	1 TAU	1 CAN	1 LEO
2 GEM	4 LEO	3 LEO	2 VIR	3 SCO	2 SAG	3 AQU	2 PIS	3 TAU	2 GEM	4 LEO	3 VIR
5 CAN	6 VIR	5 VIR	4 LIB	5 SAG	4 CAP	5 PIS	4 ARI	5 GEM	5 CAN	6 VIR	6 LIB
7 LEO	8 LIB	7 LIB	6 SCO	7 CAP	6 AQU	7 ARI	6 TAU	8 CAN	7 LEO	8 LIB	8 SCO
9 VIR	10 SCO	9 SCO	8 SAG	9 AQU	8 PIS	10 TAU	9 GEM	10 LEO	10 VIR	11 SCO	10 SAG
12 LIB	12 SAG	11 SAG	10 CAP	11 PIS	10 ARI	13 GEM	11 CAN	12 VIR	12 LIB	13 SAG	12 CAP
14 SCO	14 CAP	14 CAP	12 AQU	14 ARI	13 TAU	15 CAN	14 LEO	15 LIB	14 SCO	15 CAP	14 AQU
16 SAG	16 AQU	16 AQU	14 PIS	16 TAU	15 GEM	17 LEO	16 VIR	17 SCO	16 SAG	17 AQU	16 PIS
18 CAP	19 PIS	18 PIS	17 ARI	19 GEM	18 CAN	20 VIR	18 LIB	19 SAG	18 CAP	19 PIS	18 ARI
20 AQU	21 ARI	20 ARI	19 TAU	21 CAN	20 LEO	22 LIB	20 SCO	21 CAP	20 AQU	21 ARI	21 TAU
22 PIS	23 TAU	23 TAU	21 GEM	24 LEO	23 VIR	24 SCO	23 SAG	23 AQU	23 PIS	23 TAU	23 GEM
25 ARI	26 GEM	25 GEM	24 CAN	26 VIR	25 LIB	26 SAG	25 CAP	25 PIS	25 ARI	26 GEM	26 CAN
27 TAU	28 GEM	28 CAN	27 LEO	29 LIB	27 SCO	28 CAP	27 AQU	28 ARI	27 TAU	28 CAN	28 LEO
30 GEM		30 LEO	29 VIR	31 SCO	29 SAG	30 AQU	29 PIS	30 TAU	30 GEM	30 CAN	31 VIR
31 GEM		31 LEO	30 VIR		30 SAG	31 AQU	31 ARI		31 GEM		

1978

JAN	FEB	MAR	APR	MAY	JUN	JUL	AUG	SEP	OCT	NOV	DEC
1 VIR	1 SCO	1 SCO	1 CAP	1 AQU	1 ARI	1 TAU	1 CAN	1 LEO	1 VIR	1 SCO	1 SAG
2 LIB	3 SAG	2 SAG	3 AQU	2 PIS	3 TAU	2 GEM	4 LEO	2 VIR	2 LIB	3 SAG	2 CAP
4 SCO	5 CAP	4 CAP	5 PIS	4 ARI	5 GEM	5 CAN	6 VIR	5 LIB	4 SCO	5 CAP	4 AQU
6 SAG	7 AQU	6 AQU	7 ARI	6 TAU	8 CAN	7 LEO	9 LIB	7 SCO	7 SAG	7 AQU	6 PIS
8 CAP	9 PIS	8 PIS	9 TAU	9 GEM	10 LEO	10 VIR	11 SCO	9 SAG	9 CAP	9 PIS	9 ARI
10 AQU	11 ARI	10 ARI	11 GEM	11 CAN	13 VIR	12 LIB	13 SAG	12 CAP	11 AQU	11 ARI	11 TAU
12 PIS	13 TAU	13 TAU	14 CAN	14 LEO	16 LIB	15 SCO	15 CAP	14 AQU	13 PIS	14 TAU	13 GEM
15 ARI	16 GEM	15 GEM	16 LEO	16 VIR	17 SCO	17 SAG	17 AQU	16 PIS	15 ARI	16 GEM	16 CAN
17 TAU	18 CAN	18 CAN	19 VIR	19 LIB	19 SAG	19 CAP	19 PIS	18 ARI	17 TAU	18 CAN	18 LEO
19 GEM	21 LEO	20 LEO	21 LIB	21 SCO	21 CAP	21 AQU	21 ARI	20 TAU	20 GEM	21 LEO	21 VIR
22 CAN	23 VIR	23 VIR	23 SCO	23 SAG	23 AQU	23 PIS	24 TAU	22 GEM	22 CAN	23 VIR	23 LIB
25 LEO	26 LIB	25 LIB	26 SAG	25 CAP	25 PIS	25 ARI	26 GEM	25 CAN	25 LEO	26 LIB	25 SCO
27 VIR	28 SCO	27 SCO	28 CAP	27 AQU	28 ARI	27 TAU	28 CAN	27 LEO	27 VIR	28 SCO	28 SAG
29 LIB		29 SAG	30 AQU	29 PIS	30 TAU	30 GEM	31 LEO	30 VIR	29 LIB	30 SAG	30 CAP
31 LIB		31 CAP				31 GEM			31 LIB		31 CAP

1979

JAN	FEB	MAR	APR	MAY	JUN	JUL	AUG	SEP	OCT	NOV	DEC
1 AQU	1 ARI	1 ARI	1 GEM	1 CAN	1 LEO	1 VIR	1 SCO	1 SAG	1 AQU	1 PIS	1 TAU
3 PIS	3 TAU	4 CAN	4 LEO	2 VIR	2 LIB	3 SAG	2 CAP	2 CAP	4 PIS	2 ARI	3 GEM
5 ARI	6 GEM	5 GEM	6 LEO	6 VIR	5 LIB	5 SCO	5 CAP	4 AQU	6 ARI	4 TAU	6 CAN
7 TAU	8 CAN	7 CAN	9 VIR	9 LIB	7 SCO	7 SAG	8 AQU	6 PIS	8 TAU	6 GEM	8 LEO
9 GEM	11 LEO	10 LEO	11 LIB	11 SCO	10 SAG	9 CAP	10 PIS	8 ARI	10 GEM	8 CAN	10 VIR
12 CAN	13 VIR	12 VIR	14 SCO	13 SAG	12 CAP	11 AQU	12 ARI	10 TAU	12 CAN	11 LEO	13 LIB
14 LEO	16 LIB	15 LIB	16 SAG	15 CAP	14 AQU	13 PIS	14 TAU	12 GEM	14 LEO	13 VIR	16 SCO
17 VIR	18 SCO	17 SCO	18 CAP	17 AQU	16 PIS	15 ARI	16 GEM	15 CAN	17 VIR	16 LIB	18 SAG
19 LIB	20 SAG	20 SAG	20 AQU	20 PIS	18 ARI	17 TAU	18 CAN	17 LEO	19 LIB	18 SCO	20 CAP
22 SCO	23 CAP	22 CAP	22 PIS	22 ARI	20 TAU	20 GEM	21 LEO	20 VIR	22 SCO	20 SAG	22 AQU
24 SAG	25 AQU	24 AQU	25 ARI	24 TAU	22 VIR	22 CAN	23 VIR	22 LIB	24 SAG	23 CAP	24 PIS
26 CAP	27 PIS	26 PIS	27 TAU	26 GEM	25 LIB	25 LEO	26 LIB	25 SCO	27 CAP	25 AQU	26 ARI
28 AQU	28 PIS	28 ARI	29 GEM	28 CAN	27 SCO	27 VIR	28 SCO	27 SAG	29 AQU	27 PIS	29 TAU
30 PIS		30 TAU	30 GEM	31 LEO	30 SAG	30 LIB	31 SAG	29 CAP	31 PIS	29 ARI	31 GEM
31 PIS		31 TAU				31 LIB		30 CAP		30 ARI	

1980

JAN	FEB	MAR	APR	MAY	JUN	JUL	AUG	SEP	OCT	NOV	DEC
1 GEM	1 LEO	1 VIR	1 LIB	1 SCO	1 CAP	1 AQU	1 ARI	1 TAU	1 CAN	1 LEO	1 LIB
2 CAN	3 VIR	4 LIB	3 SCO	2 SAG	3 AQU	3 PIS	3 TAU	2 GEM	3 LEO	2 VIR	2 LIB
4 LEO	6 LIB	6 SCO	5 SAG	5 CAP	6 PIS	5 ARI	5 GEM	4 CAN	6 VIR	5 LIB	4 SCO
7 VIR	8 SCO	9 SAG	8 CAP	7 AQU	8 ARI	7 TAU	8 CAN	6 LEO	8 LIB	7 SCO	7 SAG
9 LIB	11 SAG	11 CAP	10 AQU	9 PIS	10 TAU	9 GEM	10 LEO	9 VIR	11 SCO	10 SAG	9 CAP
12 SCO	13 CAP	13 AQU	12 PIS	11 ARI	12 GEM	11 CAN	11 LIB	11 SCO	13 SAG	12 CAP	12 AQU
14 SAG	15 AQU	16 PIS	14 ARI	13 TAU	14 CAN	14 LEO	15 LIB	14 SCO	16 CAP	14 AQU	14 PIS
16 CAP	17 PIS	18 ARI	16 TAU	15 GEM	16 LEO	16 VIR	17 SCO	16 SAG	18 AQU	17 PIS	16 ARI
19 AQU	19 ARI	20 TAU	18 GEM	18 CAN	19 VIR	18 LIB	20 SAG	18 CAP	20 PIS	19 ARI	18 TAU
21 PIS	21 TAU	22 GEM	20 CAN	20 LEO	21 LIB	21 SCO	22 CAP	21 AQU	22 ARI	21 TAU	20 GEM
23 ARI	23 GEM	24 CAN	22 LEO	22 VIR	24 SCO	23 SAG	24 AQU	23 PIS	24 TAU	23 GEM	22 CAN
25 TAU	26 CAN	26 LEO	25 VIR	25 LIB	26 SAG	26 CAP	26 PIS	25 ARI	26 GEM	25 CAN	24 LEO
27 GEM	28 LEO	29 VIR	27 LIB	27 SCO	28 CAP	28 AQU	28 ARI	27 TAU	28 CAN	27 LEO	27 VIR
29 CAN	29 LEO	31 LIB	30 SCO	30 SAG	30 CAP	30 PIS	30 TAU	29 GEM	31 LEO	29 VIR	29 LIB
31 CAN				31 SAG		31 PIS	31 TAU	30 GEM		30 VIR	31 LIB

1981

JAN	FEB	MAR	APR	MAY	JUN	JUL	AUG	SEP	OCT	NOV	DEC
1 SCO	1 SAG	1 CAP	1 AQU	1 PIS	1 TAU	1 GEM	1 LEO	1 LIB	1 SCO	1 SAG	1 AQU
3 SAG	2 CAP	4 AQU	2 PIS	2 ARI	2 GEM	2 CAN	2 VIR	3 SCO	3 SAG	2 CAP	3 AQU
6 CAP	4 AQU	6 PIS	4 ARI	4 TAU	4 CAN	4 LEO	5 LIB	6 SAG	6 CAP	5 AQU	4 PIS
8 AQU	6 PIS	8 ARI	6 TAU	6 GEM	6 LEO	6 VIR	7 SCO	8 CAP	8 AQU	7 PIS	6 ARI
10 PIS	9 ARI	10 TAU	8 GEM	9 CAN	9 VIR	8 LIB	10 SAG	11 AQU	11 PIS	9 ARI	9 TAU
12 ARI	11 TAU	12 GEM	10 CAN	10 LEO	11 LIB	11 SCO	12 CAP	13 PIS	13 ARI	11 TAU	11 GEM
14 TAU	13 GEM	14 CAN	13 LEO	12 VIR	13 SCO	13 SAG	14 AQU	15 ARI	15 TAU	13 GEM	13 CAN
17 GEM	15 CAN	16 LEO	15 VIR	15 LIB	16 SCO	16 CAP	17 PIS	17 TAU	17 GEM	15 CAN	15 LEO
19 CAN	17 LEO	19 VIR	17 LIB	17 SCO	18 SAG	18 AQU	19 ARI	19 GEM	19 CAN	17 LEO	17 VIR
21 LEO	19 VIR	21 LIB	20 SCO	20 SAG	21 CAP	20 PIS	21 TAU	21 CAN	21 LEO	19 VIR	19 LIB
23 VIR	22 LIB	24 SCO	22 SAG	22 CAP	23 AQU	23 ARI	23 GEM	24 LEO	23 VIR	22 LIB	21 SCO
25 LIB	24 SCO	26 SAG	25 CAP	25 AQU	25 PIS	25 TAU	25 CAN	26 VIR	26 LIB	24 SCO	24 SAG
28 SCO	27 SAG	29 CAP	27 AQU	27 PIS	28 TAU	27 GEM	27 LEO	28 LIB	28 SCO	27 SAG	27 CAP
31 SAG	28 SAG	31 AQU	30 PIS	29 ARI	30 GEM	29 CAN	30 VIR	30 LIB	30 SAG	29 CAP	29 AQU
				31 TAU		31 LEO	31 VIR		31 SAG	30 CAP	31 PIS

1982

JAN	FEB	MAR	APR	MAY	JUN	JUL	AUG	SEP	OCT	NOV	DEC
1 PIS	1 TAU	1 TAU	1 CAN	1 LEO	1 LIB	1 SCO	1 SAG	1 AQU	1 PIS	1 TAU	1 GEM
3 ARI	3 GEM	3 GEM	3 LEO	2 VIR	3 SCO	3 SAG	2 CAP	3 PIS	3 ARI	4 GEM	3 CAN
5 TAU	5 CAN	5 CAN	5 VIR	5 LIB	5 SAG	6 CAP	4 AQU	6 ARI	5 TAU	6 CAN	5 LEO
7 GEM	7 LEO	7 LEO	8 LIB	7 SCO	8 CAP	8 AQU	7 PIS	8 TAU	7 GEM	8 LEO	7 VIR
9 CAN	10 VIR	9 VIR	10 SCO	10 SAG	10 AQU	11 PIS	9 ARI	10 GEM	9 CAN	10 VIR	9 LIB
11 LEO	12 LIB	11 LIB	12 SAG	12 CAP	13 PIS	13 ARI	12 TAU	12 CAN	11 LEO	12 LIB	12 SCO
13 VIR	14 SCO	14 SCO	15 CAP	15 AQU	15 ARI	15 TAU	14 GEM	14 LEO	14 VIR	14 SCO	14 SAG
15 LIB	17 SAG	16 SAG	17 AQU	17 PIS	18 TAU	17 GEM	16 CAN	16 VIR	16 LIB	17 SAG	16 CAP
18 SCO	19 CAP	18 CAP	20 PIS	19 ARI	20 GEM	19 CAN	18 LEO	18 LIB	18 SCO	19 CAP	19 AQU
20 SAG	22 AQU	21 AQU	22 ARI	22 TAU	22 CAN	21 LEO	20 VIR	20 SCO	21 SAG	22 AQU	22 PIS
23 CAP	24 PIS	23 PIS	24 TAU	24 GEM	24 LEO	23 VIR	22 LIB	23 SAG	23 CAP	24 PIS	24 ARI
25 AQU	26 ARI	26 ARI	26 GEM	26 CAN	26 VIR	26 LIB	24 SCO	25 CAP	25 AQU	27 ARI	26 TAU
28 PIS	28 TAU	28 TAU	28 CAN	28 LEO	28 LIB	28 SCO	27 SAG	28 AQU	28 PIS	29 TAU	28 GEM
30 ARI		30 GEM	30 LEO	30 VIR	30 LIB	30 SAG	29 CAP	30 AQU	30 ARI	30 TAU	30 CAN
31 ARI		31 GEM		31 VIR		31 SAG	31 CAP		31 ARI		31 CAN

1983

JAN	FEB	MAR	APR	MAY	JUN	JUL	AUG	SEP	OCT	NOV	DEC
2 VIR	1 LIB	2 SCO	1 SAG	1 CAP	2 PIS	2 ARI	1 TAU	1 CAN	1 LEO	1 LIB	1 SCO
4 LIB	3 SCO	5 SAG	3 CAP	3 AQU	5 ARI	4 TAU	3 GEM	3 LEO	3 VIR	3 SCO	3 SAG
7 SCO	5 SAG	7 CAP	6 AQU	6 PIS	7 TAU	7 GEM	5 CAN	5 VIR	5 LIB	6 SAG	5 CAP
9 SAG	8 CAP	10 AQU	8 PIS	8 ARI	9 GEM	9 CAN	7 LEO	7 LIB	7 SCO	8 CAP	8 AQU
12 CAP	10 AQU	12 PIS	11 ARI	11 TAU	11 CAN	11 LEO	9 VIR	10 SCO	9 SAG	10 AQU	10 PIS
14 AQU	12 PIS	15 ARI	13 TAU	13 GEM	13 LEO	13 VIR	11 LIB	12 SAG	12 CAP	13 PIS	13 ARI
17 PIS	15 ARI	17 TAU	15 GEM	15 CAN	15 VIR	15 LIB	13 SCO	14 CAP	14 AQU	15 ARI	15 TAU
19 ARI	17 TAU	19 GEM	17 CAN	17 LEO	17 LIB	17 SCO	15 SAG	17 AQU	16 PIS	18 TAU	17 GEM
21 TAU	19 GEM	21 CAN	20 LEO	19 VIR	20 SCO	19 SAG	18 CAP	19 PIS	19 ARI	20 GEM	20 CAN
24 GEM	22 CAN	23 LEO	22 VIR	21 LIB	22 SAG	22 CAP	20 AQU	22 ARI	21 TAU	22 CAN	22 LEO
26 CAN	24 LEO	26 VIR	24 LIB	23 SCO	24 CAP	24 AQU	23 PIS	24 TAU	24 GEM	24 LEO	24 VIR
28 LEO	26 VIR	28 LIB	26 SCO	26 SAG	27 AQU	27 PIS	25 ARI	26 GEM	26 CAN	26 VIR	26 LIB
30 VIR	28 LIB	30 SCO	28 SAG	28 CAP	29 PIS	29 ARI	28 TAU	29 CAN	28 LEO	29 LIB	28 SCO
				31 AQU			30 GEM		30 VIR		30 SAG

1984

JAN	FEB	MAR	APR	MAY	JUN	JUL	AUG	SEP	OCT	NOV	DEC
2 CAP	3 PIS	1 PIS	2 TAU	2 GEM	1 CAN	2 VIR	3 SCO	1 SAG	1 CAP	2 PIS	1 ARI
4 AQU	5 ARI	4 ARI	5 GEM	4 CAN	3 LEO	4 LIB	5 SAG	3 CAP	3 AQU	4 ARI	4 TAU
6 PIS	8 TAU	6 TAU	7 CAN	6 LEO	5 VIR	6 SCO	7 CAP	6 AQU	5 PIS	7 TAU	6 GEM
9 ARI	10 GEM	8 GEM	9 LEO	9 VIR	7 LIB	9 SAG	9 AQU	8 PIS	8 ARI	9 GEM	9 CAN
11 TAU	12 CAN	11 CAN	11 VIR	11 LIB	9 SCO	11 CAP	12 PIS	11 ARI	10 TAU	12 CAN	11 LEO
14 GEM	15 LEO	13 LEO	13 LIB	13 SCO	11 SAG	13 AQU	14 ARI	13 TAU	13 GEM	14 LEO	13 VIR
16 CAN	17 VIR	15 VIR	15 SCO	15 SAG	13 CAP	16 PIS	17 TAU	16 GEM	15 CAN	16 VIR	15 LIB
18 LEO	19 LIB	17 LIB	17 SAG	17 CAP	16 AQU	18 ARI	19 GEM	18 CAN	18 LEO	18 LIB	17 SCO
20 VIR	21 SCO	19 SCO	20 CAP	19 AQU	18 PIS	21 TAU	22 CAN	20 LEO	20 VIR	20 SCO	20 SAG
22 LIB	23 SAG	21 SAG	22 AQU	22 PIS	21 ARI	23 GEM	24 LEO	22 VIR	22 LIB	22 SAG	22 CAP
24 SCO	25 CAP	23 CAP	25 PIS	24 ARI	23 TAU	25 CAN	26 VIR	24 LIB	24 SCO	24 CAP	24 AQU
26 SAG	28 AQU	26 AQU	27 ARI	27 TAU	26 GEM	27 LEO	28 LIB	26 SCO	26 SAG	27 AQU	26 PIS
29 CAP		28 PIS	30 TAU	29 GEM	28 CAN	29 VIR	30 SCO	28 SAG	28 CAP	29 PIS	29 ARI
31 AQU		31 ARI			30 LEO	31 LIB			30 AQU		31 TAU

1985

JAN	FEB	MAR	APR	MAY	JUN	JUL	AUG	SEP	OCT	NOV	DEC
3 GEM	2 CAN	1 CAN	2 VIR	1 LIB	2 SAG	1 CAP	2 PIS	1 ARI	3 GEM	2 CAN	1 LEO
5 CAN	4 LEO	3 LEO	4 LIB	3 SCO	4 CAP	3 AQU	4 ARI	3 TAU	5 CAN	4 LEO	4 VIR
7 LEO	6 VIR	5 VIR	6 SCO	5 SAG	6 AQU	6 PIS	7 TAU	6 GEM	8 LEO	6 VIR	6 LIB
9 VIR	8 LIB	7 LIB	8 SAG	7 CAP	8 PIS	8 ARI	9 GEM	8 CAN	10 VIR	9 LIB	8 SCO
12 LIB	10 SCO	9 SCO	10 CAP	9 AQU	11 ARI	10 TAU	12 CAN	10 LEO	12 LIB	11 SCO	10 SAG
14 SCO	12 SAG	11 SAG	12 AQU	12 PIS	13 TAU	13 GEM	14 LEO	13 VIR	14 SCO	13 SAG	12 CAP
16 SAG	14 CAP	14 CAP	14 PIS	14 ARI	16 GEM	15 CAN	16 VIR	15 LIB	16 SAG	15 CAP	14 AQU
18 CAP	17 AQU	16 AQU	17 ARI	17 TAU	18 CAN	18 LEO	18 LIB	17 SCO	18 CAP	17 AQU	16 PIS
20 AQU	19 PIS	18 PIS	20 TAU	19 GEM	20 LEO	20 VIR	20 SCO	19 SAG	20 AQU	19 PIS	19 ARI
23 PIS	21 ARI	21 ARI	22 GEM	22 CAN	23 VIR	22 LIB	22 SAG	21 CAP	23 PIS	21 ARI	21 TAU
25 ARI	24 TAU	23 TAU	25 CAN	24 LEO	25 LIB	24 SCO	25 CAP	23 AQU	25 ARI	24 TAU	24 GEM
28 TAU	27 GEM	26 GEM	27 LEO	26 VIR	27 SCO	26 SAG	27 AQU	25 PIS	28 TAU	26 GEM	26 CAN
30 GEM		28 CAN	29 VIR	29 LIB	29 SAG	28 CAP	29 PIS	28 ARI	30 GEM	29 CAN	29 LEO
		31 LEO		31 SCO		31 AQU		30 TAU			31 VIR

1986

JAN	FEB	MAR	APR	MAY	JUN	JUL	AUG	SEP	OCT	NOV	DEC
2 LIB	1 SCO	2 SAG	2 AQU	2 PIS	3 TAU	3 GEM	2 CAN	3 VIR	2 LIB	1 SCO	2 CAP
4 SCO	3 SAG	4 CAP	5 PIS	4 ARI	5 GEM	5 CAN	4 LEO	5 LIB	4 SCO	3 SAG	4 AQU
6 SAG	5 CAP	6 AQU	7 ARI	7 TAU	8 CAN	8 LEO	6 VIR	7 SCO	7 SAG	5 CAP	6 PIS
8 CAP	7 AQU	8 PIS	9 TAU	9 GEM	11 LEO	10 VIR	9 LIB	9 SAG	9 CAP	7 AQU	9 ARI
11 AQU	9 PIS	11 ARI	12 GEM	12 CAN	13 VIR	12 LIB	11 SCO	11 CAP	11 AQU	9 PIS	11 TAU
13 PIS	11 ARI	13 TAU	14 CAN	14 LEO	15 LIB	15 SCO	13 SAG	14 AQU	13 PIS	11 ARI	14 GEM
15 ARI	13 TAU	16 GEM	17 LEO	17 VIR	17 SCO	17 SAG	15 CAP	16 PIS	15 ARI	14 TAU	16 CAN
17 TAU	16 GEM	18 CAN	19 VIR	19 LIB	19 SAG	19 CAP	17 AQU	18 ARI	18 TAU	16 GEM	19 LEO
20 GEM	19 CAN	21 LEO	21 LIB	21 SCO	21 CAP	21 AQU	19 PIS	20 TAU	20 GEM	19 CAN	21 VIR
22 CAN	21 LEO	23 VIR	24 SCO	23 SAG	23 AQU	23 PIS	22 ARI	23 GEM	23 CAN	21 LEO	24 LIB
25 LEO	24 VIR	25 LIB	26 SAG	25 CAP	26 PIS	25 ARI	24 TAU	25 CAN	25 LEO	24 VIR	26 SCO
27 VIR	26 LIB	27 SCO	28 CAP	27 AQU	28 ARI	28 TAU	26 GEM	28 LEO	27 VIR	26 LIB	28 SAG
29 LIB	28 SCO	29 SAG	30 AQU	29 PIS	30 TAU	30 GEM	29 CAN	30 VIR	30 LIB	28 SCO	30 CAP
		31 CAP		31 ARI			31 LEO			30 SAG	

1987

JAN	FEB	MAR	APR	MAY	JUN	JUL	AUG	SEP	OCT	NOV	DEC
1 AQU	1 ARI	1 ARI	2 GEM	2 CAN	3 VIR	3 LIB	1 SCO	2 CAP	1 AQU	2 ARI	1 TAU
3 PIS	4 TAU	3 TAU	4 CAN	4 LEO	5 LIB	5 SCO	4 SAG	4 AQU	3 PIS	4 TAU	4 GEM
5 ARI	6 GEM	5 GEM	7 LEO	7 VIR	8 SCO	7 SAG	6 CAP	6 PIS	6 ARI	6 GEM	6 CAN
7 TAU	9 CAN	8 CAN	9 VIR	9 LIB	10 SAG	9 CAP	8 AQU	8 ARI	8 TAU	9 CAN	8 LEO
10 GEM	11 LEO	10 LEO	12 LIB	11 SCO	12 CAP	11 AQU	10 PIS	10 TAU	10 GEM	11 LEO	11 VIR
12 CAN	14 VIR	13 VIR	14 SCO	13 SAG	14 AQU	13 PIS	12 ARI	13 GEM	12 CAN	14 VIR	14 LIB
15 LEO	16 LIB	15 LIB	16 SAG	15 CAP	16 PIS	15 ARI	14 TAU	15 CAN	15 LEO	16 LIB	16 SCO
17 VIR	18 SCO	18 SCO	18 CAP	17 AQU	18 ARI	18 TAU	16 GEM	17 LEO	17 VIR	18 SCO	18 SAG
20 LIB	21 SAG	20 SAG	20 AQU	20 PIS	20 TAU	20 GEM	19 CAN	20 VIR	20 LIB	21 SAG	20 CAP
22 SCO	23 CAP	22 CAP	22 PIS	22 ARI	23 GEM	22 CAN	21 LEO	22 LIB	22 SCO	23 CAP	22 AQU
24 SAG	25 AQU	24 AQU	25 ARI	24 TAU	25 CAN	25 LEO	24 VIR	25 SCO	24 SAG	25 AQU	24 PIS
26 CAP	27 PIS	26 PIS	27 TAU	26 GEM	28 LEO	27 VIR	26 LIB	27 SAG	26 CAP	27 PIS	26 ARI
28 AQU		28 ARI	29 GEM	29 CAN	30 VIR	30 LIB	29 SCO	29 CAP	29 AQU	29 ARI	29 TAU
30 PIS		30 TAU		31 LEO			31 SAG		31 PIS		31 GEM

1988

JAN	FEB	MAR	APR	MAY	JUN	JUL	AUG	SEP	OCT	NOV	DEC
2 CAN	1 LEO	2 VIR	1 LIB	3 SAG	1 CAP	1 AQU	1 ARI	2 GEM	1 CAN	2 VIR	2 LIB
5 LEO	4 VIR	4 LIB	3 SCO	5 CAP	3 AQU	3 PIS	3 TAU	4 CAN	4 LEO	5 LIB	5 SCO
7 VIR	6 LIB	7 SCO	5 SAG	7 AQU	5 PIS	5 ARI	5 GEM	6 LEO	6 VIR	7 SCO	7 SAG
10 LIB	9 SCO	9 SAG	8 CAP	9 PIS	8 ARI	7 TAU	8 CAN	9 VIR	9 LIB	10 SAG	9 CAP
12 SCO	11 SAG	11 CAP	10 AQU	11 ARI	10 TAU	9 GEM	10 LEO	11 LIB	11 SCO	12 CAP	12 AQU
15 SAG	13 CAP	14 AQU	12 PIS	13 TAU	12 GEM	11 CAN	13 VIR	14 SCO	14 SAG	14 AQU	14 PIS
17 CAP	15 AQU	16 PIS	14 ARI	16 GEM	14 CAN	13 LEO	15 LIB	16 SAG	16 CAP	16 PIS	16 ARI
19 AQU	17 PIS	18 ARI	16 TAU	18 CAN	17 LEO	16 VIR	18 SCO	19 CAP	18 AQU	19 ARI	18 TAU
21 PIS	19 ARI	20 TAU	18 GEM	20 LEO	19 VIR	19 LIB	20 SAG	21 AQU	20 PIS	21 TAU	20 GEM
23 ARI	21 TAU	22 GEM	20 CAN	23 VIR	22 LIB	21 SCO	22 CAP	23 PIS	22 ARI	23 GEM	22 CAN
25 TAU	23 GEM	24 CAN	23 LEO	25 LIB	24 SCO	24 SAG	24 AQU	25 ARI	24 TAU	25 CAN	25 LEO
27 GEM	26 CAN	27 LEO	25 VIR	28 SCO	26 SAG	26 CAP	26 PIS	27 TAU	26 GEM	27 LEO	27 VIR
30 CAN	28 LEO	29 VIR	28 LIB	30 SAG	29 CAP	28 AQU	28 ARI	29 GEM	29 CAN	30 VIR	30 LIB
			30 SCO			30 PIS	30 TAU		31 LEO		

1989

JAN	FEB	MAR	APR	MAY	JUN	JUL	AUG	SEP	OCT	NOV	DEC
1 SCO	2 CAP	2 CAP	2 PIS	2 ARI	2 GEM	2 CAN	3 VIR	1 LIB	1 SCO	2 CAP	2 AQU
4 SAG	4 AQU	4 AQU	4 ARI	4 TAU	4 CAN	4 LEO	5 LIB	4 SCO	4 SAG	5 AQU	4 PIS
6 CAP	6 PIS	6 PIS	6 TAU	6 GEM	7 LEO	6 VIR	8 SCO	6 SAG	6 CAP	7 PIS	7 ARI
8 AQU	8 ARI	8 ARI	8 GEM	8 CAN	9 VIR	9 LIB	10 SAG	9 CAP	9 AQU	9 ARI	9 TAU
10 PIS	11 TAU	10 TAU	11 CAN	10 LEO	11 LIB	11 SCO	13 CAP	11 AQU	11 PIS	11 TAU	11 GEM
12 ARI	13 GEM	12 GEM	13 LEO	13 VIR	14 SCO	14 SAG	15 AQU	13 PIS	13 ARI	13 GEM	13 CAN
14 TAU	15 CAN	14 CAN	16 VIR	15 LIB	16 SAG	16 CAP	17 PIS	15 ARI	15 TAU	15 CAN	15 LEO
16 GEM	17 LEO	17 LEO	18 LIB	18 SCO	19 CAP	19 AQU	19 ARI	17 TAU	17 GEM	17 LEO	17 VIR
19 CAN	20 VIR	19 VIR	20 SCO	20 SAG	21 AQU	21 PIS	21 TAU	19 GEM	19 CAN	20 VIR	19 LIB
21 LEO	22 LIB	21 LIB	23 SAG	22 CAP	23 PIS	23 ARI	23 GEM	21 CAN	22 LEO	22 LIB	22 SCO
23 VIR	25 SCO	24 SCO	25 CAP	25 AQU	25 ARI	25 TAU	25 CAN	24 LEO	24 VIR	25 SCO	24 SAG
26 LIB	27 SAG	27 SAG	28 AQU	27 PIS	27 TAU	27 GEM	28 LEO	26 VIR	26 LIB	27 SAG	27 CAP
29 SCO		29 CAP	30 PIS	29 ARI	30 GEM	29 CAN	30 VIR	29 LIB	28 SCO	30 CAP	29 AQU
31 SAG		31 AQU		31 TAU		31 LEO			31 SAG		

1990

JAN	FEB	MAR	APR	MAY	JUN	JUL	AUG	SEP	OCT	NOV	DEC
1 PIS	1 TAU	2 GEM	1 CAN	3 VIR	1 LIB	1 SCO	2 CAP	1 AQU	1 PIS	2 TAU	1 GEM
3 ARI	3 GEM	5 CAN	3 LEO	5 LIB	4 SCO	4 SAG	5 AQU	3 PIS	3 ARI	4 GEM	3 CAN
5 TAU	5 CAN	7 LEO	6 VIR	8 SCO	6 SAG	6 CAP	7 PIS	6 ARI	5 TAU	6 CAN	5 LEO
7 GEM	8 LEO	9 VIR	8 LIB	10 SAG	9 CAP	9 AQU	9 ARI	8 TAU	7 GEM	8 LEO	7 VIR
9 CAN	10 VIR	12 LIB	10 SCO	13 CAP	11 AQU	11 PIS	12 TAU	10 GEM	9 CAN	10 VIR	9 LIB
11 LEO	12 LIB	14 SCO	13 SAG	15 AQU	14 PIS	13 ARI	14 GEM	12 CAN	11 LEO	12 LIB	12 SCO
13 VIR	15 SCO	16 SAG	15 CAP	17 PIS	16 ARI	15 TAU	16 CAN	14 LEO	14 VIR	15 SCO	14 SAG
16 LIB	17 SAG	19 CAP	18 AQU	20 ARI	18 TAU	17 GEM	18 LEO	16 VIR	16 LIB	17 SAG	17 CAP
18 SCO	20 CAP	21 AQU	20 PIS	22 TAU	20 GEM	19 CAN	20 VIR	19 LIB	18 SCO	20 CAP	19 AQU
21 SAG	22 AQU	24 PIS	22 ARI	24 GEM	22 CAN	21 LEO	22 LIB	21 SCO	21 SAG	22 AQU	22 PIS
23 CAP	24 PIS	26 ARI	24 TAU	26 CAN	24 LEO	24 VIR	25 SCO	24 SAG	23 CAP	25 PIS	24 ARI
26 AQU	26 ARI	28 TAU	26 GEM	28 LEO	26 VIR	26 LIB	27 SAG	26 CAP	26 AQU	27 ARI	26 TAU
28 PIS	28 TAU	30 GEM	28 CAN	30 VIR	29 LIB	28 SCO	30 CAP	29 AQU	28 PIS	29 TAU	28 GEM
30 ARI			30 LEO			31 SAG			30 ARI		30 CAN

1991

JAN	FEB	MAR	APR	MAY	JUN	JUL	AUG	SEP	OCT	NOV	DEC
1 LEO	2 LIB	2 LIB	3 SAG	2 CAP	1 AQU	1 PIS	2 TAU	3 CAN	2 LEO	2 LIB	2 SCO
4 VIR	4 SCO	4 SCO	5 CAP	5 AQU	4 PIS	3 ARI	4 GEM	5 LEO	4 VIR	5 SCO	4 SAG
6 LIB	7 SAG	6 SAG	8 AQU	7 PIS	6 ARI	6 TAU	6 CAN	7 VIR	6 LIB	7 SAG	7 CAP
8 SCO	9 CAP	9 CAP	10 PIS	10 ARI	8 TAU	8 GEM	8 LEO	9 LIB	8 SCO	10 CAP	9 AQU
11 SAG	12 AQU	11 AQU	12 ARI	12 TAU	10 GEM	10 CAN	10 VIR	11 SCO	11 SAG	12 AQU	12 PIS
13 CAP	14 PIS	14 PIS	15 TAU	14 GEM	12 CAN	12 LEO	12 LIB	13 SAG	13 CAP	15 PIS	14 ARI
16 AQU	17 ARI	16 ARI	17 GEM	16 CAN	14 LEO	14 VIR	15 SCO	16 CAP	15 AQU	17 ARI	17 TAU
18 PIS	19 TAU	18 TAU	19 CAN	18 LEO	16 VIR	17 LIB	17 SAG	18 AQU	17 PIS	19 TAU	19 GEM
20 ARI	21 GEM	20 GEM	21 LEO	20 VIR	19 LIB	19 SCO	20 CAP	21 PIS	19 ARI	21 GEM	21 CAN
23 TAU	23 CAN	22 CAN	23 VIR	22 LIB	21 SCO	21 SAG	22 AQU	23 ARI	21 TAU	23 CAN	23 LEO
25 GEM	25 LEO	25 LEO	25 LIB	25 SCO	23 SAG	23 CAP	25 PIS	25 TAU	23 GEM	25 LEO	25 VIR
27 CAN	27 VIR	27 VIR	28 SCO	27 SAG	26 CAP	26 AQU	27 ARI	28 GEM	25 CAN	28 VIR	27 LIB
29 LEO		29 LIB	30 SAG	30 CAP	29 AQU	28 PIS	29 TAU	30 CAN	28 LEO	30 LIB	29 SCO
31 VIR		31 SCO				31 ARI	31 GEM		31 VIR		

1992

JAN	FEB	MAR	APR	MAY	JUN	JUL	AUG	SEP	OCT	NOV	DEC
1 SAG	2 AQU	3 PIS	1 ARI	1 TAU	2 CAN	1 LEO	2 LIB	2 SAG	2 CAP	1 AQU	1 PIS
3 CAP	4 PIS	5 ARI	4 TAU	3 GEM	4 LEO	3 VIR	4 SCO	5 CAP	5 AQU	3 PIS	3 ARI
6 AQU	7 ARI	8 TAU	6 GEM	5 CAN	6 VIR	5 LIB	6 SAG	7 AQU	7 PIS	6 ARI	6 TAU
8 PIS	9 TAU	10 GEM	8 CAN	8 LEO	8 LIB	7 SCO	9 CAP	10 PIS	10 ARI	8 TAU	8 GEM
11 ARI	12 GEM	14 LEO	10 LEO	10 VIR	10 SCO	10 SAG	11 AQU	12 ARI	12 TAU	11 GEM	10 CAN
13 TAU	14 CAN	16 VIR	12 VIR	12 LIB	13 SAG	12 CAP	14 PIS	15 TAU	14 GEM	13 CAN	12 LEO
15 GEM	16 LEO	18 LIB	15 LIB	14 SCO	15 CAP	15 AQU	16 ARI	17 GEM	17 CAN	15 LEO	14 VIR
17 CAN	18 VIR	20 SCO	17 SCO	16 SAG	17 AQU	17 PIS	18 TAU	19 CAN	19 LEO	17 VIR	16 LIB
19 LEO	20 LIB	23 SAG	19 SAG	19 CAP	20 PIS	20 ARI	21 GEM	21 LEO	21 VIR	19 LIB	19 SCO
21 VIR	22 SCO	25 CAP	21 CAP	21 AQU	22 ARI	22 TAU	23 CAN	24 VIR	23 LIB	21 SCO	21 SAG
23 LIB	24 SAG	27 AQU	24 AQU	24 PIS	25 TAU	24 GEM	25 LEO	26 LIB	25 SCO	24 SAG	23 CAP
25 SCO	27 CAP	30 PIS	26 PIS	26 ARI	27 GEM	27 CAN	27 VIR	28 SCO	27 SAG	26 CAP	26 AQU
28 CAP	29 AQU		29 ARI	28 TAU	29 CAN	29 LEO	29 LIB	30 SAG	29 CAP	28 AQU	28 PIS
30 CAP				31 GEM		31 VIR	31 SCO				31 ARI

1993

JAN	FEB	MAR	APR	MAY	JUN	JUL	AUG	SEP	OCT	NOV	DEC
2 TAU	1 GEM	2 CAN	1 LEO	2 LIB	1 SCO	2 CAP	1 AQU	2 ARI	2 TAU	1 GEM	3 LEO
4 GEM	3 CAN	5 LEO	3 VIR	4 SCO	3 SAG	5 AQU	3 PIS	5 TAU	4 GEM	3 CAN	5 VIR
7 CAN	5 LEO	7 VIR	5 LIB	6 SAG	5 CAP	7 PIS	6 ARI	7 GEM	7 CAN	5 LEO	7 LIB
9 LEO	7 VIR	9 LIB	7 SCO	9 CAP	7 AQU	10 ARI	8 TAU	10 CAN	9 LEO	8 VIR	9 SCO
11 VIR	9 LIB	11 SCO	9 SAG	11 AQU	10 PIS	12 TAU	11 GEM	12 LEO	11 VIR	10 LIB	11 SAG
13 LIB	11 SCO	13 SAG	11 CAP	13 PIS	12 ARI	15 GEM	13 CAN	14 VIR	13 LIB	12 SCO	13 CAP
15 SCO	13 SAG	15 CAP	14 AQU	16 ARI	15 TAU	17 CAN	15 LEO	16 LIB	15 SCO	14 SAG	15 AQU
17 SAG	16 CAP	17 AQU	16 PIS	18 TAU	17 GEM	19 LEO	17 VIR	18 SCO	17 SAG	16 CAP	18 PIS
19 CAP	18 AQU	20 PIS	19 ARI	21 GEM	19 CAN	21 VIR	19 LIB	20 SAG	19 CAP	18 AQU	20 ARI
22 AQU	21 PIS	22 ARI	21 TAU	23 CAN	22 LEO	23 LIB	21 SCO	22 CAP	22 AQU	20 PIS	23 TAU
24 PIS	23 ARI	25 TAU	24 GEM	25 LEO	24 VIR	25 SCO	24 SAG	24 AQU	24 PIS	23 ARI	25 GEM
27 ARI	26 TAU	27 GEM	26 CAN	28 VIR	26 LIB	27 SAG	26 CAP	27 PIS	27 ARI	26 TAU	28 CAN
29 TAU	28 GEM	30 CAN	28 LEO	30 LIB	28 SCO	30 CAP	28 AQU	29 ARI	29 TAU	28 GEM	30 LEO
			30 VIR		30 SAG		31 PIS			30 CAN	

1994

JAN	FEB	MAR	APR	MAY	JUN	JUL	AUG	SEP	OCT	NOV	DEC
1 VIR	2 SCO	1 SCO	1 CAP	1 AQU	2 ARI	2 TAU	1 GEM	2 LEO	2 VIR	2 SCO	2 SAG
3 LIB	4 SAG	3 SAG	4 AQU	3 PIS	5 TAU	4 GEM	3 CAN	4 VIR	4 LIB	4 SAG	4 CAP
5 SCO	6 CAP	5 CAP	6 PIS	6 ARI	7 GEM	7 CAN	6 LEO	6 LIB	6 SCO	6 CAP	6 AQU
8 SAG	8 AQU	7 AQU	9 ARI	8 TAU	10 CAN	9 LEO	8 VIR	8 SCO	8 SAG	8 AQU	8 PIS
10 CAP	11 PIS	10 PIS	11 TAU	11 GEM	12 LEO	11 VIR	10 LIB	10 SAG	11 CAP	11 PIS	10 ARI
12 AQU	13 ARI	12 ARI	14 GEM	13 CAN	14 VIR	14 LIB	12 SCO	13 CAP	13 AQU	13 ARI	13 TAU
14 PIS	16 TAU	15 TAU	16 CAN	16 LEO	16 LIB	16 SCO	15 SAG	15 AQU	15 PIS	15 TAU	15 GEM
17 ARI	18 GEM	17 GEM	18 LEO	18 VIR	19 SCO	18 SAG	17 CAP	17 PIS	17 ARI	18 GEM	18 CAN
19 TAU	20 CAN	20 CAN	21 VIR	20 LIB	21 SAG	20 CAP	19 AQU	19 ARI	19 TAU	20 CAN	20 LEO
22 GEM	23 LEO	22 LEO	23 LIB	22 SCO	23 CAP	22 AQU	21 PIS	22 TAU	22 GEM	23 LEO	23 VIR
24 CAN	25 VIR	24 VIR	25 SCO	24 SAG	25 AQU	24 PIS	23 ARI	24 GEM	24 CAN	25 VIR	25 LIB
26 LEO	27 LIB	26 LIB	27 SAG	26 CAP	27 PIS	27 ARI	26 TAU	27 CAN	27 LEO	28 LIB	27 SCO
28 VIR		28 SCO	29 CAP	28 AQU	29 ARI	29 TAU	28 GEM	29 LEO	29 VIR	30 SCO	29 SAG
31 LIB		30 SAG		31 PIS			31 CAN		31 LIB		31 CAP

1995

JAN	FEB	MAR	APR	MAY	JUN	JUL	AUG	SEP	OCT	NOV	DEC
2 AQU	1 PIS	2 ARI	1 TAU	1 GEM	2 LEO	2 VIR	3 SCO	1 SAG	2 AQU	1 PIS	3 TAU
4 PIS	3 ARI	5 TAU	3 GEM	3 CAN	5 VIR	4 LIB	5 SAG	3 CAP	5 PIS	3 ARI	5 GEM
7 ARI	5 TAU	7 GEM	6 CAN	6 LEO	7 LIB	6 SCO	7 CAP	5 AQU	7 ARI	5 TAU	8 CAN
9 TAU	8 GEM	10 CAN	9 LEO	8 VIR	9 SCO	8 SAG	9 AQU	7 PIS	9 TAU	8 GEM	10 LEO
12 GEM	10 CAN	12 LEO	11 VIR	10 LIB	11 SAG	10 CAP	11 PIS	9 ARI	12 GEM	10 CAN	13 VIR
14 CAN	13 LEO	15 VIR	13 LIB	13 SCO	13 CAP	12 AQU	13 ARI	12 TAU	14 CAN	13 LEO	15 LIB
16 LEO	15 VIR	17 LIB	15 SCO	15 SAG	15 AQU	14 PIS	15 TAU	14 GEM	17 LEO	15 VIR	17 SCO
19 VIR	17 LIB	19 SCO	17 SAG	17 CAP	17 PIS	17 ARI	18 GEM	17 CAN	19 VIR	18 LIB	19 SAG
21 LIB	19 SCO	21 SAG	19 CAP	19 AQU	19 ARI	19 TAU	20 CAN	19 LEO	21 LIB	20 SCO	21 CAP
23 SCO	22 SAG	23 CAP	21 AQU	21 PIS	22 TAU	22 GEM	23 LEO	21 VIR	23 SCO	22 SAG	23 AQU
25 SAG	24 CAP	25 AQU	24 PIS	23 ARI	24 GEM	24 CAN	25 VIR	24 LIB	26 SAG	24 CAP	25 PIS
27 CAP	26 AQU	27 PIS	26 ARI	26 TAU	27 CAN	27 LEO	28 LIB	26 SCO	28 CAP	26 AQU	28 ARI
30 AQU	28 PIS	30 ARI	28 TAU	28 GEM	29 LEO	29 VIR	30 SCO	28 SAG	30 AQU	28 PIS	30 TAU
				31 CAN		31 LIB		30 CAP		30 ARI	

1996

JAN	FEB	MAR	APR	MAY	JUN	JUL	AUG	SEP	OCT	NOV	DEC
1 GEM	3 LEO	1 LEO	2 LIB	2 SCO	2 CAP	2 AQU	2 ARI	1 TAU	3 CAN	2 LEO	2 VIR
4 CAN	5 VIR	3 VIR	4 SCO	4 SAG	4 AQU	4 PIS	4 TAU	3 GEM	5 LEO	4 VIR	4 LIB
6 LEO	8 LIB	6 LIB	7 SAG	6 CAP	6 PIS	6 ARI	7 GEM	6 CAN	8 VIR	7 LIB	6 SCO
9 VIR	10 SCO	8 SCO	9 CAP	8 AQU	8 ARI	8 TAU	9 CAN	8 LEO	10 LIB	9 SCO	9 SAG
11 LIB	12 SAG	10 SAG	11 AQU	10 PIS	11 TAU	11 GEM	12 LEO	11 VIR	13 SCO	11 SAG	11 CAP
14 SCO	14 CAP	13 CAP	13 PIS	12 ARI	13 GEM	13 CAN	14 VIR	13 LIB	15 SAG	13 CAP	13 AQU
16 SAG	16 AQU	15 AQU	15 ARI	15 TAU	16 CAN	16 LEO	17 LIB	15 SCO	17 CAP	16 AQU	15 PIS
18 CAP	18 PIS	17 PIS	17 TAU	17 GEM	18 LEO	18 VIR	19 SCO	18 SAG	19 AQU	18 PIS	17 ARI
20 AQU	20 ARI	19 ARI	20 GEM	19 CAN	21 VIR	21 LIB	21 SAG	20 CAP	21 PIS	20 ARI	19 TAU
22 PIS	23 TAU	21 TAU	22 CAN	22 LEO	23 LIB	23 SCO	24 CAP	22 AQU	23 ARI	22 TAU	22 GEM
24 ARI	25 GEM	23 GEM	25 LEO	24 VIR	25 SCO	25 SAG	26 AQU	24 PIS	26 TAU	24 GEM	24 CAN
26 TAU	27 CAN	26 CAN	27 VIR	27 LIB	28 SAG	27 CAP	28 PIS	26 ARI	28 GEM	27 CAN	26 LEO
29 GEM		28 LEO	30 LIB	29 SCO	30 CAP	29 AQU	30 ARI	28 TAU	30 CAN	29 LEO	29 VIR
31 CAN		31 VIR		31 SAG		31 PIS		30 GEM			31 LIB

1997

JAN	FEB	MAR	APR	MAY	JUN	JUL	AUG	SEP	OCT	NOV	DEC
3 SCO	1 SAG	1 SAG	1 AQU	1 PIS	1 TAU	1 GEM	2 LEO	3 LIB	3 SCO	1 SAG	1 CAP
5 SAG	4 CAP	3 CAP	4 PIS	3 ARI	4 GEM	3 CAN	4 VIR	6 SCO	5 SAG	4 CAP	3 AQU
7 CAP	6 AQU	5 AQU	6 ARI	5 TAU	6 CAN	5 LEO	7 LIB	8 SAG	8 CAP	6 AQU	5 PIS
9 AQU	8 PIS	7 PIS	8 TAU	7 GEM	8 LEO	8 VIR	9 SCO	10 CAP	10 AQU	8 PIS	8 ARI
11 PIS	10 ARI	9 ARI	10 GEM	9 CAN	10 VIR	10 LIB	12 SAG	12 AQU	12 PIS	10 ARI	10 TAU
13 ARI	12 TAU	11 TAU	12 CAN	12 LEO	13 LIB	13 SCO	14 CAP	15 PIS	14 ARI	12 TAU	12 GEM
15 TAU	14 GEM	13 GEM	14 LEO	14 VIR	15 SCO	15 SAG	16 AQU	17 ARI	16 TAU	14 GEM	14 CAN
18 GEM	16 CAN	16 CAN	17 VIR	17 LIB	18 SAG	18 CAP	18 PIS	19 TAU	18 GEM	17 CAN	16 LEO
20 CAN	19 LEO	18 LEO	19 LIB	19 SCO	20 CAP	20 AQU	20 ARI	21 GEM	20 CAN	19 LEO	19 VIR
23 LEO	21 VIR	21 VIR	22 SCO	22 SAG	22 AQU	22 PIS	22 TAU	23 CAN	23 LEO	21 VIR	21 LIB
25 VIR	24 LIB	23 LIB	24 SAG	24 CAP	24 PIS	24 ARI	24 GEM	25 LEO	25 VIR	24 LIB	24 SCO
28 LIB	26 SCO	26 SCO	27 CAP	26 AQU	26 ARI	26 TAU	27 CAN	28 VIR	28 LIB	26 SCO	26 SAG
30 SCO		28 SAG	29 AQU	28 PIS	29 TAU	28 GEM	29 LEO	30 LIB	30 SCO	29 SAG	28 CAP
		30 CAP		30 ARI		30 CAN	31 VIR				31 AQU

1998

JAN	FEB	MAR	APR	MAY	JUN	JUL	AUG	SEP	OCT	NOV	DEC
2 PIS	2 TAU	2 TAU	2 CAN	2 LEO	3 LIB	3 SCO	2 SAG	3 AQU	2 PIS	1 ARI	2 GEM
4 ARI	4 GEM	4 GEM	4 LEO	4 VIR	5 SCO	5 SAG	4 CAP	5 PIS	4 ARI	3 TAU	4 CAN
6 TAU	7 CAN	6 CAN	7 VIR	7 LIB	8 SAG	8 CAP	6 AQU	7 ARI	6 TAU	5 GEM	6 LEO
8 GEM	9 LEO	8 LEO	9 LIB	9 SCO	10 CAP	10 AQU	8 PIS	9 TAU	8 GEM	7 CAN	9 VIR
10 CAN	11 VIR	11 VIR	12 SCO	12 SAG	13 AQU	12 PIS	11 ARI	11 GEM	10 CAN	9 LEO	11 LIB
13 LEO	14 LIB	13 LIB	14 SAG	14 CAP	15 PIS	14 ARI	13 TAU	13 CAN	13 LEO	11 VIR	14 SCO
15 VIR	16 SCO	16 SCO	17 CAP	16 AQU	17 ARI	16 TAU	15 GEM	15 LEO	15 VIR	14 LIB	16 SAG
18 LIB	19 SAG	18 SAG	19 AQU	19 PIS	19 TAU	18 GEM	17 CAN	18 VIR	17 LIB	16 SCO	19 CAP
20 SCO	21 CAP	21 CAP	21 PIS	21 ARI	21 GEM	21 CAN	19 LEO	20 LIB	20 SCO	19 SAG	21 AQU
23 SAG	23 AQU	23 AQU	23 ARI	23 TAU	23 CAN	23 LEO	21 VIR	23 SCO	23 SAG	21 CAP	23 PIS
25 CAP	25 PIS	25 PIS	25 TAU	25 GEM	25 LEO	25 VIR	24 LIB	25 SAG	25 CAP	24 AQU	25 ARI
27 AQU	27 ARI	27 ARI	27 GEM	27 CAN	28 VIR	28 LIB	26 SCO	28 CAP	27 AQU	26 PIS	28 TAU
29 PIS		29 TAU	29 CAN	29 LEO	30 LIB	30 SCO	29 SAG	30 AQU	30 PIS	28 ARI	30 GEM
31 ARI		31 GEM		31 VIR			31 CAP			30 TAU	

1999

JAN	FEB	MAR	APR	MAY	JUN	JUL	AUG	SEP	OCT	NOV	DEC
1 CAN	1 VIR	1 VIR	2 SCO	2 SAG	3 AQU	2 PIS	1 ARI	2 GEM	1 CAN	1 VIR	1 LIB
3 LEO	4 LIB	3 LIB	4 SAG	4 CAP	5 PIS	5 ARI	3 TAU	4 CAN	3 LEO	4 LIB	3 SCO
5 VIR	6 SCO	6 SCO	7 CAP	7 AQU	8 ARI	7 TAU	5 GEM	6 LEO	5 VIR	6 SCO	6 SAG
7 LIB	9 SAG	8 SAG	9 AQU	9 PIS	10 TAU	9 GEM	7 CAN	8 VIR	8 LIB	9 SAG	8 CAP
10 SCO	11 CAP	11 CAP	12 PIS	11 ARI	12 GEM	11 CAN	10 LEO	10 LIB	10 SCO	11 CAP	11 AQU
12 SAG	14 AQU	13 AQU	14 ARI	13 TAU	14 CAN	13 LEO	12 VIR	13 SCO	12 SAG	14 AQU	13 PIS
15 CAP	16 PIS	15 PIS	16 TAU	15 GEM	16 LEO	15 VIR	14 LIB	15 SAG	15 CAP	16 PIS	16 ARI
17 AQU	18 ARI	17 ARI	18 GEM	17 CAN	18 VIR	17 LIB	16 SCO	18 CAP	17 AQU	18 ARI	18 TAU
19 PIS	20 TAU	19 TAU	20 CAN	19 LEO	20 LIB	19 SCO	19 SAG	20 AQU	20 PIS	21 TAU	20 GEM
22 ARI	22 GEM	22 GEM	22 LEO	21 VIR	23 SCO	22 SAG	21 CAP	22 PIS	22 ARI	23 GEM	22 CAN
24 TAU	24 CAN	23 CAN	24 VIR	23 LIB	25 SAG	25 CAP	24 AQU	25 ARI	24 TAU	25 CAN	24 LEO
26 GEM	26 LEO	26 LEO	27 LIB	26 SCO	28 CAP	27 AQU	26 PIS	27 TAU	26 GEM	27 LEO	26 VIR
28 CAN		28 VIR	29 SCO	28 SAG		30 PIS	28 ARI	29 GEM	28 CAN	29 VIR	28 LIB
30 LEO		30 LIB		31 CAP			30 TAU		30 LEO		31 SCO

2000

JAN	FEB	MAR	APR	MAY	JUN	JUL	AUG	SEP	OCT	NOV	DEC
3 SAG	1 CAP	2 AQU	1 PIS	3 TAU	1 GEM	2 LEO	1 VIR	2 SCO	1 SAG	3 AQU	2 PIS
5 CAP	4 AQU	4 PIS	3 ARI	5 GEM	3 CAN	4 VIR	3 LIB	4 SAG	4 CAP	5 PIS	5 ARI
7 AQU	6 PIS	7 ARI	5 TAU	7 CAN	5 LEO	7 LIB	5 SCO	6 CAP	6 AQU	8 ARI	7 TAU
10 PIS	8 ARI	9 TAU	7 GEM	9 LEO	7 VIR	9 SCO	8 SAG	8 AQU	9 PIS	10 TAU	9 GEM
12 ARI	11 TAU	11 GEM	9 CAN	11 VIR	9 LIB	11 SAG	10 CAP	11 PIS	11 ARI	12 GEM	11 CAN
14 TAU	13 GEM	13 CAN	11 LEO	13 LIB	11 SCO	13 CAP	12 AQU	14 ARI	13 TAU	14 CAN	13 LEO
16 GEM	15 CAN	15 LEO	14 VIR	15 SCO	14 SAG	16 AQU	14 PIS	16 TAU	16 GEM	16 LEO	15 VIR
18 CAN	17 LEO	17 VIR	16 LIB	18 SAG	17 CAP	17 PIS	16 ARI	18 GEM	18 CAN	18 VIR	18 LIB
20 LEO	19 VIR	20 LIB	18 SCO	20 CAP	19 AQU	19 ARI	18 TAU	20 CAN	20 LEO	20 LIB	20 SCO
23 VIR	21 LIB	22 SCO	21 SAG	23 AQU	22 PIS	21 TAU	20 GEM	23 LEO	22 VIR	23 SCO	22 SAG
25 LIB	23 SCO	24 SAG	23 CAP	25 PIS	24 ARI	24 GEM	22 CAN	25 VIR	24 LIB	25 SAG	25 CAP
27 SCO	26 SAG	27 CAP	26 AQU	28 ARI	26 TAU	26 CAN	24 LEO	27 LIB	26 SCO	27 CAP	27 AQU
29 SAG	28 CAP	29 AQU	28 PIS	30 TAU	28 GEM	28 LEO	26 VIR	29 SCO	29 SAG	30 AQU	30 PIS
			30 ARI		30 CAN	30 VIR	28 LIB		31 CAP		
							30 LIB				

2001

JAN	FEB	MAR	APR	MAY	JUN	JUL	AUG	SEP	OCT	NOV	DEC
1 ARI	2 GEM	1 GEM	2 LEO	1 VIR	2 SCO	1 SAG	3 AQU	1 PIS	1 ARI	2 GEM	2 CAN
4 TAU	4 CAN	4 CAN	4 VIR	3 LIB	4 SAG	4 CAP	5 PIS	4 ARI	4 TAU	4 CAN	4 LEO
6 GEM	6 LEO	6 LEO	6 LIB	6 SCO	7 CAP	6 AQU	8 ARI	6 TAU	6 GEM	7 LEO	6 VIR
8 CAN	8 VIR	8 VIR	8 SCO	8 SAG	9 AQU	9 PIS	10 TAU	9 GEM	8 CAN	9 VIR	8 LIB
10 LEO	10 LIB	10 LIB	10 SAG	10 CAP	11 PIS	11 ARI	12 GEM	11 CAN	10 LEO	11 LIB	10 SCO
12 VIR	12 SCO	12 SCO	13 CAP	12 AQU	14 ARI	14 TAU	15 CAN	13 LEO	13 VIR	13 SCO	12 SAG
14 LIB	15 SAG	14 SAG	15 AQU	15 PIS	16 TAU	16 GEM	17 LEO	15 VIR	15 LIB	15 SAG	15 CAP
16 SCO	17 CAP	16 CAP	18 PIS	18 ARI	19 GEM	18 CAN	19 VIR	17 LIB	17 SCO	17 CAP	17 AQU
18 SAG	20 AQU	19 AQU	20 ARI	20 TAU	21 CAN	20 LEO	21 LIB	19 SCO	19 SAG	19 AQU	20 PIS
21 CAP	22 PIS	22 PIS	23 TAU	22 GEM	23 LEO	22 VIR	23 SCO	21 SAG	21 CAP	22 PIS	22 ARI
23 AQU	25 ARI	24 ARI	25 GEM	24 CAN	25 VIR	24 LIB	25 SAG	24 CAP	23 AQU	25 ARI	25 TAU
26 PIS	27 TAU	26 TAU	27 CAN	26 LEO	27 LIB	26 SCO	27 CAP	26 AQU	26 PIS	27 TAU	27 GEM
28 ARI		29 GEM	29 LEO	29 VIR	29 SCO	29 SAG	30 AQU	29 PIS	28 ARI	30 GEM	29 CAN
31 TAU		31 CAN		31 LIB		31 CAP			31 TAU		31 LEO

2002

JAN	FEB	MAR	APR	MAY	JUN	JUL	AUG	SEP	OCT	NOV	DEC
2 VIR	1 LIB	2 SCO	1 SAG	2 AQU	1 PIS	1 ARI	2 GEM	1 CAN	1 LEO	1 LIB	1 SCO
4 LIB	3 SCO	4 SAG	3 CAP	5 PIS	4 ARI	4 TAU	5 CAN	3 LEO	3 VIR	3 SCO	3 SAG
6 SCO	5 SAG	6 CAP	5 AQU	7 ARI	6 TAU	6 GEM	7 LEO	5 VIR	5 LIB	5 SAG	5 CAP
9 SAG	7 CAP	9 AQU	8 PIS	10 TAU	9 GEM	8 CAN	9 VIR	7 LIB	7 SCO	7 CAP	7 AQU
11 CAP	10 AQU	11 PIS	10 ARI	12 GEM	11 CAN	11 LEO	11 LIB	9 SCO	9 SAG	10 AQU	9 PIS
13 AQU	12 PIS	14 ARI	13 TAU	15 CAN	13 LEO	13 VIR	13 SCO	12 SAG	11 CAP	12 PIS	12 ARI
16 PIS	15 ARI	16 TAU	15 GEM	17 LEO	15 VIR	15 LIB	15 SAG	14 CAP	13 AQU	15 ARI	14 TAU
18 ARI	17 TAU	19 GEM	18 CAN	19 VIR	18 LIB	17 SCO	18 CAP	16 AQU	16 PIS	17 TAU	17 GEM
21 TAU	20 GEM	21 CAN	20 LEO	21 LIB	20 SCO	19 SAG	20 AQU	19 PIS	18 ARI	20 GEM	19 CAN
23 GEM	22 CAN	24 LEO	22 VIR	23 SCO	22 SAG	21 CAP	22 PIS	21 ARI	21 TAU	22 CAN	22 LEO
26 CAN	24 LEO	26 VIR	24 LIB	25 SAG	24 CAP	24 AQU	25 ARI	24 TAU	23 GEM	24 LEO	24 VIR
28 LEO	26 VIR	28 LIB	26 SCO	28 CAP	26 AQU	26 PIS	27 TAU	26 GEM	26 CAN	27 VIR	26 LIB
30 VIR	28 LIB	30 SCO	28 SAG	30 AQU	29 PIS	28 ARI	30 GEM	29 CAN	28 LEO	29 LIB	28 SCO
			30 CAP			31 TAU			30 VIR		30 SAG

2003

JAN	FEB	MAR	APR	MAY	JUN	JUL	AUG	SEP	OCT	NOV	DEC
1 CAP	2 PIS	1 PIS	3 TAU	2 GEM	1 CAN	1 LEO	2 LIB	2 SAG	1 CAP	2 PIS	2 ARI
3 AQU	5 ARI	4 ARI	5 GEM	5 CAN	4 LEO	3 VIR	4 SCO	4 CAP	4 AQU	5 ARI	4 TAU
6 PIS	7 TAU	6 TAU	8 CAN	7 LEO	6 VIR	5 LIB	6 SAG	6 AQU	6 PIS	7 TAU	7 GEM
8 ARI	10 GEM	9 GEM	10 LEO	10 VIR	8 LIB	7 SCO	8 CAP	9 PIS	8 ARI	10 GEM	9 CAN
11 TAU	12 CAN	11 CAN	12 VIR	12 LIB	10 SCO	8 CAP	10 AQU	11 ARI	11 TAU	12 CAN	12 LEO
13 GYM	14 LEO	14 LEO	14 LIB	14 SCO	12 SAG	10 SAG	12 PIS	13 TAU	13 GEM	15 LEO	14 VIR
16 CAN	16 VIR	16 VIR	16 SCO	16 SAG	14 CAP	12 PIS	15 ARI	16 GEM	16 CAN	17 VIR	16 LIB
18 LEO	18 LIB	18 LIB	18 SAG	18 CAP	16 AQU	14 AQU	17 TAU	18 CAN	18 LEO	19 LIB	19 SCO
20 VIR	21 SCO	20 SCO	20 CAP	20 AQU	19 PIS	16 PIS	20 GEM	21 LEO	21 VIR	21 SCO	21 SAG
22 LIB	23 SAG	22 SAG	23 AQU	22 PIS	21 ARI	18 ARI	22 CAN	23 VIR	23 LIB	23 SAG	23 CAP
24 SCO	25 CAP	24 CAP	25 PIS	25 ARI	23 TAU	21 TAU	24 LEO	25 LIB	25 SCO	25 CAP	25 AQU
26 SAG	27 AQU	26 AQU	27 ARI	27 TAU	26 GEM	23 GEM	27 VIR	27 SCO	27 SAG	27 AQU	27 PIS
29 CAP		29 PIS	30 TAU	30 GEM	28 CAN	26 CAN	29 LIB	29 SAG	29 CAP	29 PIS	29 ARI
31 AQU		31 ARI				28 LEO	31 SCO		31 AQU		
						30 VIR					

2004

JAN	FEB	MAR	APR	MAY	JUN	JUL	AUG	SEP	OCT	NOV	DEC
1 TAU	2 CAN	3 LEO	1 VIR	1 LIB	2 SAG	1 CAP	1 PIS	2 TAU	2 GEM	1 CAN	1 LEO
3 CEM	4 LEO	5 VIR	4 LIB	3 SCO	4 CAP	3 AQU	4 ARI	5 GEM	5 CAN	3 LEO	3 VIR
6 CAN	7 VIR	7 LIB	6 SCO	5 SAG	6 AQU	5 PIS	6 TAU	7 CAN	7 LEO	6 VIR	6 LIB
8 LEO	9 LIB	9 SCO	8 SAG	7 CAP	8 PIS	7 ARI	8 GEM	9 LEO	9 VIR	8 LIB	8 SCO
10 VIR	11 SCO	12 SAG	10 CAP	9 AQU	10 ARI	10 TAU	11 CAN	12 VIR	12 LIB	10 SCO	10 SAG
13 LIB	13 SAG	14 CAP	12 AQU	11 PIS	12 TAU	12 GEM	13 LEO	14 LIB	14 SCO	13 SAG	12 CAP
15 SCO	15 CAP	16 AQU	14 PIS	14 ARI	15 GEM	14 CAN	16 VIR	16 SCO	16 SAG	15 CAP	14 AQU
17 SAG	17 AQU	18 PIS	16 ARI	16 TAU	17 CAN	17 LEO	18 LIB	19 SAG	18 CAP	17 AQU	16 PIS
19 CAP	20 PIS	20 ARI	19 TAU	19 GEM	20 LEO	20 VIR	20 SCO	21 CAP	20 AQU	19 PIS	18 ARI
21 AQU	22 ARI	23 TAU	21 GEM	21 CAN	22 VIR	22 LIB	23 SAG	23 AQU	22 PIS	21 ARI	21 TAU
23 PIS	24 TAU	25 GEM	24 CAN	24 LEO	25 LIB	24 SCO	25 CAP	25 PIS	25 ARI	23 TAU	23 GEM
25 ARI	27 GEM	28 CAN	26 LEO	26 VIR	27 SCO	26 SAG	27 AQU	27 ARI	27 TAU	26 GEM	25 CAN
28 TAU	29 CAN	30 LEO	29 VIR	28 LIB	29 SAG	28 CAP	29 PIS	30 TAU	29 GEM	28 CAN	28 LEO
30 GEM				31 SCO		30 AQU	31 ARI				31 VIR

2005

JAN	FEB	MAR	APR	MAY	JUN	JUL	AUG	SEP	OCT	NOV	DEC
2 LIB	1 SCO	2 SAG	3 AQU	2 PIS	3 TAU	2 GEM	1 CAN	2 VIR	2 LIB	1 SCO	2 CAP
4 SCO	3 SAG	4 CAP	5 PIS	4 ARI	5 GEM	5 CAN	3 LEO	5 LIB	4 SCO	3 SAG	4 AQU
6 SAG	5 CAP	6 AQU	7 ARI	6 TAU	7 CAN	7 LEO	6 VIR	7 SCO	7 SAG	5 CAP	7 PIS
8 CAP	7 AQU	8 PIS	9 TAU	9 GEM	10 LEO	10 VIR	8 LIB	9 SAG	9 CAP	7 AQU	9 ARI
10 AQU	9 PIS	10 ARI	11 GEM	11 CAN	12 VIR	12 LIB	11 SCO	11 CAP	11 AQU	9 PIS	11 TAU
12 PIS	11 ARI	13 TAU	14 CAN	14 LEO	15 LIB	15 SCO	13 SAG	14 AQU	13 PIS	11 ARI	13 GEM
15 ARI	13 TAU	15 GEM	16 LEO	16 VIR	17 SCO	17 SAG	15 CAP	16 PIS	15 ARI	13 TAU	15 CAN
17 TAU	16 GEM	17 CAN	19 VIR	18 LIB	19 SAG	19 CAP	17 AQU	18 ARI	17 TAU	16 GEM	18 LEO
19 GEM	18 CAN	20 LEO	21 LIB	21 SCO	21 CAP	21 AQU	19 PIS	20 TAU	19 GEM	18 CAN	20 VIR
22 CAN	21 LEO	22 VIR	23 SCO	23 SAG	23 AQU	23 PIS	21 ARI	22 GEM	21 LEO	21 LEO	23 LIB
24 LEO	23 VIR	25 LIB	26 SAG	25 CAP	25 PIS	25 ARI	23 TAU	24 CAN	24 LEO	23 VIR	25 SCO
27 VIR	25 LIB	27 SCO	28 CAP	27 AQU	28 ARI	27 TAU	26 GEM	27 LEO	27 VIR	26 LIB	28 SAG
29 LIB	28 SCO	29 SAG	30 AQU	29 PIS	30 TAU	29 GEM	28 CAN	29 VIR	29 LIB	28 SCO	30 CAP
		31 CAP		31 ARI			31 LEO			30 SAG	

2006

JAN	FEB	MAR	APR	MAY	JUN	JUL	AUG	SEP	OCT	NOV	DEC
1 AQU	1 ARI	1 ARI	1 GEM	1 CAN	2 VIR	2 LIB	1 SCO	2 CAP	1 AQU	2 ARI	1 TAU
3 PIS	3 TAU	3 TAU	4 CAN	3 LEO	5 LIB	5 SCO	3 SAG	4 AQU	4 PIS	4 TAU	3 GEM
5 ARI	6 GEM	5 GEM	6 LEO	6 VIR	7 SCO	7 SAG	6 CAP	6 PIS	6 ARI	6 GEM	6 CAN
7 TAU	8 CAN	7 CAN	9 VIR	8 LIB	10 SAG	9 CAP	8 AQU	8 ARI	8 TAU	8 CAN	8 LEO
9 GEM	10 LEO	10 LEO	11 LIB	11 SCO	12 CAP	11 AQU	10 PIS	10 TAU	10 GEM	10 LEO	10 VIR
12 CAN	12 VIR	12 VIR	14 SCO	13 SAG	14 AQU	13 PIS	12 ARI	12 GEM	12 CAN	13 VIR	13 LIB
14 LEO	16 LIB	15 LIB	16 SAG	15 CAP	16 PIS	15 ARI	14 TAU	14 CAN	14 LEO	15 LIB	15 SCO
17 VIR	18 SCO	17 SCO	18 CAP	18 AQU	18 ARI	17 TAU	16 GEM	17 LEO	17 VIR	18 SCO	18 SAG
19 LIB	20 SAG	20 SAG	20 AQU	20 PIS	20 TAU	20 GEM	18 CAN	19 VIR	19 LIB	20 SAG	20 CAP
22 SCO	23 CAP	22 CAP	22 PIS	22 ARI	22 GEM	22 CAN	21 LEO	22 LIB	22 SCO	23 CAP	22 AQU
24 SAG	25 AQU	24 AQU	24 ARI	24 TAU	25 CAN	24 LEO	23 VIR	24 SCO	24 SAG	25 AQU	25 PIS
26 CAP	27 PIS	26 PIS	27 TAU	26 GEM	27 LEO	27 VIR	26 LIB	27 SAG	26 CAP	27 PIS	27 ARI
28 AQU		28 ARI	29 GEM	28 CAN	29 VIR	29 LIB	28 SCO	29 CAP	29 AQU	29 ARI	29 TAU
30 PIS		30 TAU		31 LEO			31 SAG		31 PIS		31 GEM

2007

JAN	FEB	MAR	APR	MAY	JUN	JUL	AUG	SEP	OCT	NOV	DEC
2 CAN	1 LEO	2 VIR	1 LIB	1 SCO	2 CAP	2 AQU	2 ARI	1 TAU	2 CAN	3 VIR	3 LIB
4 LEO	3 VIR	5 LIB	3 SCO	3 SAG	4 AQU	4 PIS	4 TAU	3 GEM	4 LEO	5 LIB	5 SCO
7 VIR	5 LIB	7 SCO	6 SAG	6 CAP	7 PIS	6 ARI	6 GEM	5 CAN	7 VIR	8 SCO	8 SAG
9 LIB	8 SCO	10 SAG	8 CAP	8 AQU	9 ARI	8 TAU	9 CAN	7 LEO	9 LIB	10 SAG	10 CAP
12 SCO	10 SAG	12 CAP	11 AQU	10 PIS	11 TAU	10 GEM	11 LEO	9 VIR	12 SCO	13 CAP	13 AQU
14 SAG	13 CAP	14 AQU	13 PIS	12 ARI	13 GEM	12 CAN	13 VIR	12 LIB	14 SAG	15 AQU	15 PIS
16 CAP	15 AQU	17 PIS	15 ARI	14 TAU	15 CAN	14 LEO	15 LIB	14 SCO	17 CAP	18 PIS	17 ARI
19 AQU	17 PIS	19 ARI	17 TAU	16 GEM	17 LEO	17 VIR	18 SCO	17 SAG	19 AQU	20 ARI	19 TAU
21 PIS	19 ARI	21 TAU	19 GEM	18 CAN	19 VIR	19 LIB	20 SAG	19 CAP	21 PIS	22 TAU	21 GEM
23 ARI	21 TAU	23 GEM	21 CAN	21 LEO	22 LIB	22 SCO	23 CAP	22 AQU	23 ARI	24 GEM	23 CAN
25 TAU	23 GEM	25 CAN	23 LEO	23 VIR	24 SCO	24 SAG	25 AQU	24 PIS	25 TAU	26 CAN	25 LEO
27 GEM	25 CAN	27 LEO	26 VIR	25 LIB	27 SAG	27 CAP	27 PIS	26 ARI	27 GEM	28 LEO	27 VIR
29 CAN	28 LEO	29 VIR	28 LIB	28 SCO	29 CAP	29 AQU	29 ARI	28 TAU	29 CAN	30 VIR	30 LIB
				31 SAG		31 PIS		30 GEM	31 LEO		

2008

JAN	FEB	MAR	APR	MAY	JUN	JUL	AUG	SEP	OCT	NOV	DEC
1 SCO	3 CAP	1 CAP	2 PIS	2 ARI	2 GEM	2 CAN	2 VIR	1 LIB	3 SAG	2 CAP	2 AQU
4 SAG	5 AQU	3 AQU	4 ARI	4 TAU	4 CAN	4 LEO	4 LIB	3 SCO	5 CAP	4 AQU	4 PIS
6 CAP	7 PIS	6 PIS	6 TAU	6 GEM	6 LEO	6 VIR	7 SCO	6 SAG	8 AQU	7 PIS	6 ARI
9 AQU	10 ARI	8 ARI	8 GEM	8 CAN	8 VIR	8 LIB	9 SAG	8 CAP	10 PIS	9 ARI	9 TAU
11 PIS	12 TAU	10 TAU	10 CAN	10 LEO	11 LIB	10 SCO	12 CAP	11 AQU	13 ARI	11 TAU	11 GEM
13 ARI	14 GEM	12 GEM	13 LEO	12 VIR	13 SCO	13 SAG	14 AQU	13 PIS	15 TAU	13 GEM	13 CAN
15 TAU	16 CAN	14 CAN	15 VIR	14 LIB	16 SAG	15 CAP	17 PIS	15 ARI	17 GEM	15 CAN	15 LEO
18 GEM	18 LEO	16 LEO	17 LIB	17 SCO	18 CAP	18 AQU	19 ARI	17 TAU	19 CAN	17 LEO	17 VIR
20 CAN	20 VIR	19 VIR	20 SCO	19 SAG	21 AQU	20 PIS	21 TAU	19 GEM	21 LEO	19 VIR	19 LIB
22 LEO	23 LIB	21 LIB	22 SAG	22 CAP	23 PIS	23 ARI	23 GEM	22 CAN	23 VIR	22 LIB	21 SCO
24 VIR	25 SCO	23 SCO	25 CAP	24 AQU	25 ARI	25 TAU	25 CAN	24 LEO	25 LIB	24 SCO	24 SAG
26 LIB	23 SAG	26 SAG	27 AQU	27 PIS	28 TAU	27 GEM	27 LEO	26 VIR	28 SCO	27 SAG	26 CAP
29 SCO		28 CAP	30 PIS	29 ARI	30 GEM	29 CAN	30 VIR	28 LIB	30 SAG	29 CAP	29 AQU
31 SAG		31 AQU		31 TAU		31 LEO		30 SCO			31 PIS

2009

JAN	FEB	MAR	APR	MAY	JUN	JUL	AUG	SEP	OCT	NOV	DEC
3 ARI	1 TAU	3 GEM	1 CAN	2 VIR	1 LIB	3 SAG	2 CAP	3 PIS	3 ARI	1 TAU	1 GEM
5 TAU	3 GEM	5 CAN	3 LEO	5 LIB	3 SCO	5 CAP	4 AQU	5 ARI	5 TAU	4 GEM	3 CAN
7 GEM	5 CAN	7 LEO	5 VIR	7 SCO	6 SAG	8 AQU	7 PIS	8 TAU	7 GEM	6 CAN	5 LEO
9 CAN	7 LEO	9 VIR	7 LIB	9 SAG	8 CAP	10 PIS	9 ARI	10 GEM	9 CAN	8 LEO	7 VIR
11 LEO	10 VIR	11 LIB	10 SCO	12 CAP	11 AQU	13 ARI	11 TAU	12 CAN	12 LEO	10 VIR	9 LIB
13 VIR	12 LIB	13 SCO	12 SAG	14 AQU	13 PIS	15 TAU	14 GEM	14 LEO	14 VIR	12 LIB	11 SCO
15 LIB	14 SCO	16 SAG	15 CAP	17 PIS	16 ARI	17 GEM	16 CAN	16 VIR	16 LIB	14 SCO	14 SAG
18 SCO	16 SAG	18 CAP	17 AQU	19 ARI	18 TAU	19 CAN	18 LEO	18 LIB	18 SCO	17 SAG	16 CAP
20 SAG	19 CAP	21 AQU	20 PIS	21 TAU	20 GEM	21 LEO	20 VIR	20 SCO	20 SAG	19 CAP	19 AQU
23 CAP	21 AQU	23 PIS	22 ARI	24 GEM	22 CAN	23 VIR	22 LIB	23 SAG	23 CAP	21 AQU	21 PIS
25 AQU	24 PIS	26 ARI	24 TAU	26 CAN	24 LEO	26 LIB	24 SCO	25 CAP	25 AQU	24 PIS	24 ARI
28 PIS	26 ARI	28 TAU	26 GEM	28 LEO	26 VIR	28 SCO	26 SAG	28 AQU	28 PIS	26 ARI	26 TAU
30 ARI	28 TAU	30 GEM	28 CAN	30 VIR	28 LIB	30 SAG	29 CAP	30 PIS	30 ARI	29 TAU	28 GEM
			30 LEO		30 SCO		31 AQU				30 CAN

2010

JAN	FEB	MAR	APR	MAY	JUN	JUL	AUG	SEP	OCT	NOV	DEC
1 LEO	2 LIB	1 LIB	2 SAG	2 CAP	1 AQU	3 ARI	2 TAU	3 CAN	2 LEO	3 LIB	2 SCO
3 VIR	4 SCO	3 SCO	4 CAP	4 AQU	3 PIS	5 TAU	4 GEM	5 LEO	4 VIR	5 SCO	4 SAG
6 LIB	6 SAG	6 SAG	7 AQU	7 PIS	6 ARI	8 GEM	6 CAN	7 VIR	6 LIB	7 SAG	6 CAP
8 SCO	9 CAP	8 CAP	9 PIS	9 ARI	8 TAU	10 CAN	8 LEO	9 LIB	8 SCO	9 CAP	9 AQU
10 SAG	11 AQU	11 AQU	12 ARI	12 TAU	10 GEM	12 LEO	10 VIR	11 SCO	11 SAG	11 AQU	11 PIS
13 CAP	14 PIS	13 PIS	14 TAU	14 GEM	12 CAN	14 VIR	12 LIB	13 SAG	12 CAP	14 PIS	14 ARI
15 AQU	16 ARI	16 ARI	17 GEM	16 CAN	14 LEO	16 LIB	14 SCO	15 CAP	15 AQU	16 ARI	16 TAU
18 PIS	19 TAU	18 TAU	19 CAN	18 LEO	17 VIR	18 SCO	17 SAG	18 AQU	17 PIS	19 TAU	18 GEM
20 ARI	21 GEM	20 GEM	21 LEO	20 VIR	19 LIB	20 SAG	19 CAP	20 PIS	20 ARI	21 GEM	21 CAN
22 TAU	23 CAN	23 CAN	23 VIR	22 LIB	21 SCO	23 CAP	21 AQU	23 ARI	22 TAU	23 CAN	23 LEO
25 GEM	25 LEO	25 LEO	25 LIB	25 SCO	23 SAG	25 AQU	24 PIS	25 TAU	25 GEM	26 LEO	25 VIR
27 CAN	27 VIR	27 VIR	27 SCO	27 SAG	25 CAP	28 PIS	26 ARI	28 GEM	27 CAN	23 VIR	27 LIB
29 LEO		29 LIB	29 SAG	29 CAP	28 AQU	30 ARI	29 TAU	30 CAN	29 LEO	30 LIB	29 SCO
31 VIR		31 SCO			30 PIS		31 GEM		31 VIR		31 SAG

HOW TO FIND THE MERCURY SIGN

Under the year of your birth, find a birth date. If birth was on the first or last day of a particular time period, it's possible that your Mercury might be posited in the preceding or following Sign. For example, if the time period is from August 6 to September 10, and you were born on September 10, then you must consider that your Mercury might be in the next Sign. The only way to be absolutely sure is to have a chart done by computer (see Appendix III for computer services) or by a professional astrologer. If you're not sure, read the adjacent Sign, and you will probably be able to decide which is applicable.

1950

Jan 1 – Jan 8	AQU
Jan 9 – Jan 14	AQU (R)
Jan 15 – Jan 29	CAP (R)
Jan 30 – Feb 14	CAP
Feb 15 – Mar 7	AQU
Mar 8 – Mar 24	PIS
Mar 25 – Apr 7	ARI
Apr 8 – May3	TAU
May 4 – May 24	TAU (R)
May 25 – Jun 14	TAU
Jun 15 – Jul 2	GEM
Jul 3 – Jul 16	CAN
Jul 17 – Aug 1	LEO
Aug 2 – Aug 27	VIR
Aug 28 – Sep 4	LIB
Sep 5 – Sep 10	LIB (R)
Sep 11– Sep 26	VIR (R)
Sep 27 – Oct 9	VIR
Oct 10– Oct 26	LIB
Oct 27– Nov 14	SCO
Nov 15 – Dec4	SAG
Dec 5 – Dec 23	CAP
Dec 24 – Dec 31	CAP (R)

1951

Jan 1 – Jan 12	CAP (R)
Jan 13 – Feb 9	CAP
Feb 10 – Feb 28	AQU
Mar 1 – Mar 15	PIS
Mar 16 – Apr 1	ARI
Apr2 – Apr 14	TAU
Apr 15 – May 1	TAU (R)
May 2– May 8	ARI (R)
May 9 – May 14	ARI
May 15 – Jun 8	TAU
Jun 9 – Jun 23	GEM
Jun.24 – Jul 8	CAN
Jul 9 – Aug 1	LEO
Aug 2 – Aug 17	VIR
Aug 18 – Sep 9	VIR (R)
Sep 10 – Oct 1	VIR
Oct 2 – Oct 19	LIB
Oct 20 – Nov 7	SCO
Nov 8 – Dec 1	SAG
Dec 2 – Dec 7	CAP
Dec 8 – Dec 12	CAP (R)
Dec 13 – Dec 27	SAG (R)
Dec 28 – Dec 31	SAG

1952

Jan 1 – Jan 12	SAG
Jan 13 – Feb 1	CAP
Feb 2 – Feb 20	AQU
Feb 21 – Mar 7	PIS
Mar 8 – Mar 26	ARI
Mar 27 – Apr 19	ARI (R)
Apr 20 – May 14	ARI
May 15 – May 31	TAU
Jun 1 – Jun 14	GEM
Jun 15 – Jun 29	CAN
Jun 30 – Jul 29	LEO
Jul 30 – Aug 22	LEO (R)
Aug 23 – Sep 6	LEO
Sep 7 – Sep 23	VIR
Sep 24 – Oct 11	LIB
Oct 12 – Oct 31	SCO
Nov 1 – Nov 20	SAG
Nov 21 – Dec 10	SAG (R)
Dec 11 – Dec 31	SAG

1953

Jan 1 – Jan 6	SAG
Jan 7 – Jan 25	CAP
Jan 26 – Feb 11	AQU
Feb 12 – Mar 2	PIS
Mar 3 – Mar 9	ARI
Mar 10 – Mar 15	ARI (R)
Mar 16 – Apr 1	PIS (R)
Apr 2 – Apr 17	PIS
Apr 18 – May 7	ARI
May 8 – May 22	TAU
May 23 – Jun 5	GEM
Jun 6 – Jun 25	CAN
Jun 26 – Jul 11	LEO
Jul 12 – Jul 28	LEO (R)
Jul 29 – Aug 4	CAN (R)
Aug 5 – Aug 11	CAN
Aug 12 – Aug 30	LEO
Aug 31– Sep 15	VIR
Sep 16 – Oct 4	LIB
Oct 5 – Oct31	SCO
Nov 1 – Nov 3	SAG
Nov 4 – Nov 6	SAG (R)
Nov 7 – Nov 23	SCO (R)
Nov 24 – Dec 10	SCO
Dec 11 – Dec 30	SAG
Dec 31 – Dec 31	CAP

1954

Jan 1 – Jan 17	CAP
Jan 18 – Feb 4	AQU
Feb 5 – Feb 20	PIS
Feb 21 – Mar 14	PIS (R)
Mar 15 – Apr 12	PIS
Apr 13 – Apr 29	ARI
Apr 30 – May 14	TAU
May 15 – May 30	GEM
May 31 – Jun 23	CAN
Jun 24 – Jul 17	CAN (R)
Jul 18 – Aug 7	CAN
Aug 8 – Aug 22	LEO
Aug 23 – Sep 7	VIR
Sep 8 – Sep 28	LIB
Sep 29 – Oct 18	SCO
Oct 19 – Nov 4	SCO (R)
Nov 5 – Nov 7	SCO
Nov 8 – Nov 10	LIB
Nov 11 – Dec 3	SCO
Dec 4 – Dec 22	SAG
Dec 23 – Dec 31	CAP

1955

Jan 1 – Jan 10	CAP
Jan 1 – Feb 3	AQU
Feb 4 – Feb 25	AQU (R)
Feb 26 – Mar 17	AQU
Mar 18 – Apr 6	PIS
Apr 7 – Apr 21	ARI
Apr 22 – May 6	TAU
May 7 – Jun 3	GEM
Jun 4 – Jun 27	GEM (R)
Jun 28 – Jul 13	GEM
Jul 14 – Jul 28	CAN
Jul 29 – Aug 14	LEO
Aug 15 – Aug 31	VIR
Sep 1 – Oct 1	LIB
Oct 2 – Oct 22	LIB (R)
Oct 23 – Nov 7	LIB
Nov 8 – Nov 26	SCO
Nov 27 – Dec 15	SAG
Dec 16 – Dec 31	CAP

1956

Jan 1 – Jan 3	CAP
Jan 3 – Jan 18	AQU
Jan 19 – Feb 2	AQU (R)
Feb 3 – Feb 7	CAP (R)
Feb 8 – Feb 14	CAP
Feb 5 – Mar 10	AQU
Mar 11 – Mar 28	PIS
Mar 29 – Apr 12	ARI
Apr 13 – Apr 29	TAU
Apr 30 – May 14	GEM
May 15 – Jun 7	GEM (R)
Jun 8 – Jul 6	GEM
Jul 7 – Jul 20	CAN
Jul 21 – Aug 5	LEO
Aug 6 – Aug 26	VIR
Aug 27 – Sep 13	LIB
Sep 14 – Sep 29	LIB (R)
Sep 30 – Oct 5	VIR (R)
Oct 6 – Oct 10	VIR
Oct 11 – Oct 30	LIB
Oct 31 – Nov 18	SCO
Nov 19 – Dec 7	SAG
Dec 8 – Dec 31	CAP

1957

Jan 1 – Jan 1	CAP
Jan 2 – Jan 21	CAP (R)
Jan 22 – Feb 12	CAP
Feb 13 – Mar 3	AQU
Mar 4 – Mar 20	PIS
Mar 21 – Apr 4	ARI
Apr 5 – Apr 25	TAU
Apr 26 – May 19	TAU (R)
May 20 – Jun 12	TAU
Jun 13 – Jul 28	GEM
Jun 29 – Jul 12	CAN
Jul 13 – Jul 29	LEO
Jul 30 – Aug 27	VIR
Aug 28 – Sep 19	VIR (R)
Sep 20 – Oct 5	VIR
Oct 6 – Oct 23	LIB
Oct 24 – Nov 11	SCO
Nov 12 – Dec 1	SAG
Dec 2 – Dec 16	CAP
Dec 17 – Dec 28	CAP (R)
Dec 29 – Dec 31	SAG (R)

1958

Jan 1 – Jan 5	SAG (R)
Jan 6 – Jan 13	SAG
Jan 14 – Feb 6	CAP
Feb 7 – Feb 24	AQU
Feb 25 – Mar 12	PIS
Mar 13 – Apr 2	ARI
Apr 3 – Apr 6	TAU
Apr 7 – Apr 10	TAU (R)
Apr 11 – May 1	ARI (R)
May 2 – May 16	ARI
May 17 – Jun 5	TAU
Jun 6 – Jun 19	GEM
Jun 20 – Jul 4	CAN
Jul 5 – Jul 25	LEO
Jul 26 – Aug 9	VIR
Aug 10 – Aug 23	VIR (R)
Aug 24 – Sep 2	LEO (R)
Sep 3 – Sep 10	LEO
Sep 11 – Sep 28	VIR
Sep 29 – Oct 15	LIB
Oct 16 – Nov 4	SCO
Nov 5 – Dec 1	SAG
Dec 2 – Dec 20	SAG (R)
Dec 21 – Dec 31	SAG

1959

Jan 1 – Jan 10	SAG
Jan 11 – Jan 30	CAP
Jan 31 – Feb 16	AQU
Feb 17 – Mar 4	PIS
Mar 5 – Mar 19	ARI
Mar 20 – Apr 12	ARI (R)
Apr 13 – May 12	ARI
May 13 – May 28	TAU
May 29 – Jun 11	GEM
Jun 12 – Jun 28	CAN
Jun 29 – Jul 22	LEO
Jul 23 – Aug 15	LEO (R)
Aug 16 – Sep 4	LEO
Sep 5 – Sep 20	VIR
Sep 21 – Oct 8	LIB
Oct 9 – Oct 30	SCO
Oct 31 – Nov 14	SAG
Nov 15 – Nov 24	SAG (R)
Nov 25 – Dec 3	SCO (R)
Dec 4 – Dec 13	SCO
Dec 14 – Dec 31	SAG

1960

Jan 1 – Jan 3	SAG
Jan 4 – Jan 22	CAP
Jan 23 – Feb 8	AQU
Feb 9 – Mar 1	PIS
Mar 2 – Mar 24	PIS (R)
Mar 25 – Apr 15	PIS
Apr 16 – May 4	ARI
May 5 – May 18	TAU
May 19 – Jun 2	GEM
Jun 3 – Jun 30	CAN
Jul 1 – Jul 3	LEO
Jul 4 – Jul 5	LEO (R)
Jul 6 – Jul 27	CAN (R)
Jul 28 – Aug 10	CAN
Aug 11 – Aug 26	LEO
Aug 27 – Sep 11	VIR
Sep 12 – Oct 1	LIB
Oct 2 – Oct 27	SCO
Oct 27 – Nov 16	SCO (R)
Nov 17 – Dec 7	SCO
Dec 8 – Dec 26	SAG
Dec 27 – Dec 31	CAP

1961

Jan 1 – Jan 14	CAP
Jan 15 – Feb 1	AQU
Feb 2 – Feb 12	PIS
Feb 13 – Feb 24	PIS (R)
Feb 25 – Mar 6	AQU (R)
Mar 7 – Apr 17	AQU
Mar 18 – Apr 9	PIS
Apr 10 – Apr 26	ARI
Apr 27 – May 10	TAU
May 11 – May 28	GEM
May 29 – Jun 14	CAN
Jun 15 – Jul 8	CAN (R)
Jul 9 – Aug 3	CAN
Aug 4 – Aug 18	LEO
Aug 19 – Sep 4	VIR
Sep 5 – Sep 27	LIB
Sep 28 – Oct 10	SCO
Oct 11 – Oct 21	SCO (R)
Oct 22 – Nov 1	LIB (R)
Nov 2 – Nov 10	LIB
Nov 11 – Nov 30	SCO
Dec 1 – Dec 19	SAG
Dec 20 – Dec 31	CAP

1962

Jan 1 – Jan 7	CAP
Jan 8 – Jan 27	AQU
Jan 28 – Feb 17	AQU (R)
Feb 18 – Mar 14	AQU
Mar 15 – Apr 2	PIS
Apr 3 – Apr 17	ARI
Apr 18 – May 2	TAU
May 3 – May 26	GEM
May 27 – Jun 19	GEM (R)
Jun 20 – Jul 10	GEM
Jul 11 – Jul 26	CAN
Jul 27 – Aug 10	LEO
Aug 11 – Aug 29	VIR
Aug 30 – Sep 24	LIB
Sep 25 – Oct 15	LIB
Oct 16 – Nov 4	VIR
Nov 5 – Nov 23	SCO
Nov 24 – Dec 12	SAG
Dec 13 – Dec 31	CAP

1963

Jan 1 – Jan 1	CAP
Jan 2 – Jan 11	AQU
Jan 12 – Jan 19	AQU (R)
Jan 20 – Feb 1	CAP (R)
Feb 2 – Feb 14	CAP
Feb 15 – Mar 8	AQU
Mar 9 – Mar 25	PIS
Mar 26 – Apr 9	ARI
Apr 10 – May 2	TAU
May 3 – May 6	GEM
May 7 – May 10	GEM (R)
May 11 – May 30	TAU (R)
May 31 – Jun 14	TAU
Jun 15 – Jul 6	GEM
Jul 7 – Jul 17	CAN
Jul 18 – Aug 2	LEO
Aug 3 – Aug 26	VIR
Aug 27 – Sep 6	LIB
Sep 7 – Sep 16	LIB (R)
Sep 17 – Sep 29	VIR (R)
Sep 30 – Oct 10	VIR
Oct 11 – Oct 28	LIB
Oct 29 – Nov 15	SCO
Nov 16 – Dec 5	SAG
Dec 6 – Dec 26	CAP
Dec 27 – Dec 31	CAP (R)

1964

Jan 1 – Jan 15	CAP (R)
Jan 16 – Feb 10	CAP
Feb 10 – Feb 29	AQU
Mar 1 – Mar 16	PIS
Mar 17 – Apr 1	ARI
Apr 2 – Apr 16	TAU
Apr 17 – May 10	TAU (R)
May 11 – Jun 9	TAU
Jun 10 – Jun 24	GEM
Jun 25 – Jul 8	CAN
Jul 9 – Jul 26	LEO
Jul 27 – Aug 19	VIR
Aug 20 – Sep 11	VIR (R)
Sep 12 – Oct 2	VIR
Oct 3 – Oct 19	LIB
Oct 20 – Nov 7	SCO
Nov 8 – Nov 30	SAG
Dec 1 – Dec 9	CAP
Dec 10 – Dec 16	CAP (R)
Dec 17 – Dec 29	SAG (R)
Dec 30 – Dec 31	SAG

1965

Jan 1 – Jan 12	SAG
Jan 13 – Feb 2	CAP
Feb 3 – Feb 20	AQU
Feb 21 – Mar 8	PIS
Mar 9 – Mar 29	ARI
Mar 30 – Apr 22	ARI (R)
Apr 23 – May 15	ARI
May 16 – Jun 1	TAU
Jun 2 – Jun 15	GEM
Jun 16 – Jul 1	CAN
Jul 2 – Jul 30	LEO
Jul 31 – Aug 1	VIR
Aug 2 – Aug 2	VIR (R)
Aug 3 – Aug 19	LEO (R)
Aug 20 – Sep 8	LEO
Sep 9 – Sep 24	VIR
Sep 25 – Oct 12	LIB
Oct 13 – Nov 4	SCO
Nov 8 – Nov 23	SAG
Nov 24 – Dec 12	SAG (R)
Dec 13 – Dec 31	SAG

1966

Jan 1 – Jan 7	SAG
Jan 8 – Jan 26	CAP
Jan 27 – Feb 12	AQU
Feb 13 – Mar 2	PIS
Mar 3 – Mar 12	ARI
Mar 13 – Mar 21	ARI (R)
Mar 22 – Apr 4	PIS (R)
Apr 5 – Apr 17	PIS
Apr 18 – May 9	ARI
May 10 – May 24	TAU
May 25 – Jun 7	GEM
Jun 8 – Jun 26	CAN
Jun 27 – Jul 14	LEO
Jul 15 – Aug 7	LEO (R)
Aug 8 – Aug 31	LEO
Sep 1 – Sep 16	VIR
Sep 17 – Oct 5	LIB
Oct 6 – Oct 29	SCO
Oct 30 – Nov 6	SAG
Nov 7 – Nov 12	SAG (R)
Nov 13 – Nov 26	SCO (R)
Nov 27 – Dec 11	SCO
Dec 12 – Dec 31	SAG

1967

Jan 1 – Jan 19	CAP
Jan 20 – Feb 5	AQU
Feb 6 – Feb 23	PIS
Feb 24 – Mar l7	PIS (R)
Mar 18 – Apr 14	PIS
Apr 15 – May 1	ARI
May 2 – May 15	TAU
May 16 – May 31	GEM
Jun 1 – Jun 26	CAN
Jun 27 – Jul 20	CAN (R)
Jul 21 – Aug 8	CAN
Aug 9 – Aug 23	LEO
Aug 24 – Sep 9	VIR
Sep 10 – Sep 29	LIB
Sep 30 – Oct 21	SCO
Oct 22 – Nov 10	SCO (R)
Nov 11 – Dec 5	SCO
Dec 6 – Dec 24	SAG
Dec 25 – Dec 31	CAP

1968

Jan 1 – Jan 11	CAP
Jan 12 – Feb 1	AQU
Feb 2 – Feb 6	PIS
Feb 7 – Feb 11	PIS (R)
Feb 12 – Feb 28	AQU (R)
Feb 29 – Mar 17	AQU
Mar 18 – Apr 6	PIS
Apr 7 – Apr 22	ARI
Apr 23 – May 6	TAU
May 7 – May 29	GEM
May 30 – Jun 6	CAN
Jun 7 – Jun 13	CAN (R)
Jun 14 – Jul 1	GEM(R)
Jun 2– Jul 12	GEM
Jul 13 – Jul 30	CAN
Jul 31 – Aug 14	LEO
Aug 15 – Sep 1	VIR
Sep 2 – Sep 28	LIB
Sep 29 – Oct 3	SCO
Oct 4 – Oct 7	SCO (R)
Oct 8 – Oct 24	LIB (R)
Oct 25 – Nov 7	LIB
Nov 8 – Nov 27	SCO
Nov 28 – Dec 16	SAG
Dec 17 – Dec 31	CAP

1969

Jan 1 – Jan 4	CAP
Jan 5 – Jan 20	AQU
Jan 21 – Feb 10	AQU (R)
Feb 11 – Mar 12	AQU
Mar 13 – Mar 29	PIS
Mar 30 – Apr 13	ARI
Apr 14 – Apr 30	TAU
May 1 – May 17	GEM
May 18 – Jun 10	GEM (R)
Jun 11 – Jul 7	GEM
Jul 8 – Jul 22	CAN
Jul 23 – Aug 6	LEO
Aug 7 – Aug 26	VIR
Aug 27 – Sep 16	LIB
Sep 17 – Oct 6	LIB (R)
Oct 7 – Oct 8	VIR (R)
Oct 9 – Oct 9	VIR
Oct 10 – Nov 1	LIB
Nov 2 – Nov 19	SCO
Nov 20 – Dec 9	SAG
Dec 10 – Dec 31	CAP

1970

Jan 1 – Jan 4	CAP
Jan 5 – Jan 24	CAP (R)
Jan 25 – Feb 13	CAP
Feb 14 – Mar 5	AQU
Mar 6 – Mar 21	PIS
Mar 22 – Apr 5	ARI
Apr 6 – Apr 28	TAU
Apr 29 – May 22	TAU (R)
May 23 – Jun 13	TAU
Jun 14 – Jun 29	GEM
Jun 30 – Jul 13	CAN
Jul 14 – Jul 30	LEO
Jul 31 – Aug 30	VIR
Aug 31 – Sep 22	VIR (R)
Sep 23 – Oct 7	VIR
Oct 8 – Oct 24	LIB
Oct 25 – Nov 12	SCO
Nov 13 – Dec 2	SAG
Dec 3 – Dec 19	CAP
Dec 20 – Dec 31	CAP (R)

1971

Jan 1 – Jan 2	CAP (R)
Jan 3 – Jan 8	SAG (R)
Jan 9 – Jan 13	SAG
Jan 14 – Feb 7	CAP
Feb 8 – Feb 25	AQU
Feb 26 – Mar 13	PIS
Mar 14 – Apr 1	ARI
Apr 2 – Apr 9	TAU
Apr 10 – Apr 18	TAU (R)
Apr 19 – May 3	ARI (R)
May 4 – May 16	ARI
May 17 – Jun 6	TAU
Jun 7 – Jun 21	GEM
Jun 22 – Jul 5	CAN
Jul 6 – Jul 26	LEO
Jul 27 – Aug 12	VIR
Aug 13 – Aug 29	VIR (R)
Aug 30 – Sep 5	LEO (R)
Sep 6 – Sep 10	LEO
Sep 11 – Sep 29	VIR
Sep 30 – Oct 17	LIB
Oct 18 – Nov 5	SCO
Nov 6 – Dec 3	SAG
Dec 4 – Dec 22	SAG (R)
Dec 23 – Dec 31	SAG

1972

Jan 1 – Jan 11	SAG
Jan 12 – Jan 31	CAP
Feb 1 – Feb 18	AQU
Feb 19 – Mar 5	PIS
Mar 6 – Mar 21	ARI
Mar 22 – Apr 14	ARI (R)
Apr 15 – May 12	ARI
May 13 – May 28	TAU
May 29 – Jun 11	GEM
Jun 12 – Jun 28	CAN
Jun 29 – Jul 24	LEO
Jul 25 – Aug 17	LEO (R)
Aug 18 – Sep 4	LEO
Sep 5 – Sep 21	VIR
Sep 22 – Oct 8	LIB
Oct 9 – Oct 30	SCO
Oct 31 – Nov 15	SAG
Nov 16 – Nov 28	SAG (R)
Nov 29 – Dec 5	SCO (R)
Dec 6 – Dec 12	SCO
Dec 13 – Dec 31	SAG

1973

Jan 1 – Jan 4	SAG
Jan 5 – Jan 23	CAP
Jan 24 – Feb 9	AQU
Feb 10 – Mar 4	PIS
Mar 5 – Mar 27	PIS (R)
Mar 28 – Apr 16	PIS
Apr 17 – May 5	ARI
May 6 – May 20	TAU
May 21 – Jun 3	GEM
Jun 4 – Jun 26	CAN
Jun 27 – Jul 6	LEO
Jul 7 – Jul 15	LEO (R)
Jul 16 – Jul 30	CAN (R)
Jul 31 – Aug 11	CAN
Aug 12 – Aug 28	LEO
Aug 29 – Sep 13	VIR
Sep 14 – Oct 2	LIB
Oct 3 – Oct 30	SCO
Oct 31 – Nov 19	SCO (R)
Nov 20 – Dec 8	SCO
Dec 9 – Dec 28	SAG
Dec 29 – Dec 31	CAP

1974

Jan 1 – Jan 15	CAP
Jan 16 – Feb 2	AQU
Feb 3 – Feb 15	PIS
Feb 16 – Mar 2	PIS (R)
Mar 3 – Mar 9	AQU (R)
Mar 10 – Mar 17	AQU
Mar 18 – Apr 11	PIS
Apr 12 – Apr 27	ARI
Apr 28 – May 11	TAU
May 12 – May 28	GEM
May 29 – Jun 17	CAN
Jun 18 – Jul 12	CAN (R)
Jul 13 – Aug 4	CAN
Aug 5 – Aug 19	LEO
Aug 20 – Sep 5	VIR
Sep 6 – Sep 27	LIB
Sep 28 – Oct 13	SCO
Oct 14 – Oct 26	SCO (R)
Oct 27 – Nov 3	LIB (R)
Nov 4 – Nov 11	LIB
Nov 12 – Dec 1	SCO
Dec 2 – Dec 20	SAG
Dec 21 – Dec 31	CAP

1975

Jan 1 – Jan 8	CAP
Jan 9 – Jan 30	AQU
Jan 31 – Feb 20	AQU (R)
Feb 21 – Mar 15	AQU
Mar 16 – Apr 4	PIS
Apr 5 – Apr 19	ARI
Apr 20 – May 3	TAU
May 4 – May 29	GEM
May 30 – Jun 22	GEM (R)
Jun 23 – Jul 12	GEM
Jul 12 – Jul 27	CAN
Jul 28 – Aug 11	LEO
Aug 12 – Aug 30	VIR
Aug 31 – Sep 26	LIB
Sep 27 – Oct 18	LIB (R)
Oct 19 – Nov 5	LIB
Nov 6 – Nov 24	SCO
Nov 25 – Dec 13	SAG
Dec 14 – Dec 31	CAP

1976

Jan 1 – Jan 2	CAP
Jan 3 – Jan 14	AQU
Jan 15 – Jan 24	AQU (R)
Jan 25 – Feb 3	CAP (R)
Feb 4 – Feb 15	CAP
Feb 16 – Mar 8	AQU
Mar 9 – Mar 26	PIS
Mar 27 – Apr 9	ARI
Apr 10 – Apr 29	TAU
Apr 30 – May 9	GEM
May 10 – May 19	GEM (R)
May 20 – Jun 2	TAU (R)
Jun 3 – Jun 13	TAU
Jun 14 – Jul 4	GEM
Jul 5 – Jul 18	CAN
Jul 19 – Aug 3	LEO
Aug 4 – Aug 25	VIR
Aug 26 – Sep 8	LIB
Sep 9 – Sep 20	LIB (R)
Sep 21 – Oct 1	VIR (R)
Oct 2 – Oct 10	VIR
Oct 11 – Oct 28	LIB
Oct 29 – Nov 16	SCO
Nov 17 – Dec 5	SAG
Dec 6 – Dec 28	CAP
Dec 29 – Dec 31	CAP (R)

1977

Jan 1 – Jan 17	CAP (R)
Jan 18 – Feb 10	CAP
Feb 11 – Mar 1	AQU
Mar 2 – Mar 17	PIS
Mar 18 – Apr 2	ARI
Apr 3 – Apr 20	TAU
Apr 21 – May 13	TAU (R)
May 14 – Jun 10	TAU
Jun 11 – Jun 25	GEM
Jun 26 – Jul 9	CAN
Jul 10 – Jul 27	LEO
Jul 28 – Aug 22	VIR
Aug 23 – Sep 14	VIR (R)
Sep 15 – Oct 3	VIR
Oct 4 – Oct 21	LIB
Oct 22 – Nov 9	SCO
Nov 10 – Nov 30	SAG
Dec 1 – Dec 12	CAP
Dec 13 – Dec 20	CAP (R)
Dec 21 – Dec 31	SAG (R)

1978

Jan 1 – Jan 1	SAG (R)
Jan 2 – Jan 13	SAG
Jan 14 – Feb 4	CAP
Feb 5 – Feb 22	AQU
Feb 23 – Mar 10	PIS
Mar 11 – Apr 1	ARI
Apr 2 – Apr 25	ARI (R)
Apr 26 – May 15	ARI
May 16 – Jun 3	TAU
Jun 4 – Jun 17	GEM
Jun 18 – Jul 2	CAN
Jul 3 – Jul 26	LEO
Jul 27 – Aug 4	VIR
Aug 5 – Aug 12	VIR (R)
Aug 13 – Aug 28	LEO (R)
Aug 29 – Sep 9	LEO
Sep 10 – Sep 26	VIR
Sep 27 – Oct 13	LIB
Oct 14 – Nov 2	SCO
Nov 3 – Nov 25	SAG
Nov 26 – Dec 15	SAG (R)
Dec 16 – Dec 31	SAG

1979

Jan 1 – Jan 8	SAG
Jan 9 – Jan 28	CAP
Jan 29 – Feb 14	AQU
Feb 15 – Mar 3	PIS
Mar 4 – Mar 15	ARI
Mar 16 – Mar 27	ARI (R)
Mar 28 – Apr 7	PIS (R)
Apr 8 – Apr 17	PIS
Apr 18 – May 10	ARI
May 11 – May 25	TAU
May 26 – Jun 8	GEM
Jun 9 – Jun 26	CAN
Jun 27 – Jul 17	LEO
Jul 18 – Aug 11	LEO (R)
Aug 12 – Sep 2	LEO
Sep 3 – Sep 18	VIR
Sep 19 – Oct 6	LIB
Oct 7 – Oct 29	SCO
Oct 30 – Nov 9	SAG
Nov 10 – Nov 17	SAG (R)
Nov 18 – Nov 29	SCO (R)
Nov 30 – Dec 12	SCO
Dec 13 – Dec 31	SAG

1980

Jan 1 – Jan 1	SAG
Jan 2 – Jan20	CAP
Jan 21 – Feb 6	AQU
Feb 7 – Feb 26	PIS
Feb 27 – Mar 19	PIS (R)
Mar 20 – Apr 14	PIS
Apr 15 – May 1	ARI
May 2 – May 16	TAU
May 17 – May 31	GEM
Jun 1 – Jun 28	CAN
Jun 29 – Jul 22	CAN (R)
Jul 23 – Aug 8	CAN
Aug 9 – Aug 24	LEO
Aug 25 – Sep 9	VIR
Sep 10 – Sep 29	LIB
Sep 30 – Oct 23	SCO
Oct 24 – Nov 12	SCO (R)
Nov 13 – Dec 5	SCO
Dec 6 – Dec 24	SAG
Dec 25 – Dec 31	CAP

1981

Jan 1 – Jan 12	CAP
Jan 13 – Jan 31	AQU
Feb 1 – Feb 8	PIS
Feb 9 – Feb 15	PIS (R)
Feb 16 – Mar 2	AQU (R)
Mar 3 – Mar 17	AQU
Mar 18 – Apr 7	PIS
Apr 8 – Apr 23	ARI
Apr 24 – May 7	TAU
May 8 – May 28	GEM
May 29 – Jun 9	CAN
Jun 10 – Jun 22	CAN (R)
Jun 23 – Jul 3	GEM (R)
Jul 4 – Jul 12	GEM
Jul 13 – Aug 1	CAN
Aug 2 – Aug 16	LEO
Aug 17 – Sep 2	VIR
Sep 3 – Sep 26	LIB
Sep 27 – Oct 6	SCO
Oct 7 – Oct 13	SCO (R)
Oct 14 – Oct 27	LIB (R)
Oct 27 – Nov 9	LIB
Nov 10 – Nov 28	SCO
Nov 29 – Dec 17	SAG
Dec 18 – Dec 31	CAP

1982

Jan 1 – Jan 5	CAP
Jan 6 – Jan 23	AQU
Jan 24 – Feb 13	AQU (R)
Feb 14 – Mar 13	AQU
Mar 14 – Mar 31	PIS
Apr 1 – Apr 15	ARI
Apr 16 – May 1	TAU
May 2 – May 21	GEM
May 22 – Jun 13	GEM (R)
Jun 14 – Jul 8	GEM
Jul 9 – Jul 23	CAN
Jul 24 – Aug 8	LEO
Aug 9 – Aug 27	VIR
Aug 28 – Sep 19	LIB
Sep 20 – Oct 11	LIB (R)
Oct 12 – Nov 18	SCO
Nov 19 – Dec 12	SAG
Dec 13 – Dec 31	CAP

1983

Jan 1 – Jan 1	CAP
Jan 2 – Jan 7	AQU
Jan 8 – Jan 11	AQU (R)
Jan 15 – Jan 27	CAP (R)
Jan 28 – Feb 13	CAP
Feb 14 – Mar 6	AQU
Mar 7 –Mar 23	PIS
Mar 24 – Apr 7	ARI
Apr 8 – May 1	TAU
May 2 – May 25	TAU (R)
May 26 – Jun 13	TAU
Jun 14 – Jul 1	GEM
Jul 2 – Jul 15	CAN
Jul 16 – Jul 31	LEO
Aug 1 – Aug 28	VIR
Aug 29 – Sep 2	LIB
Sep 3 – Sep 5	LIB (R)
Sep 6 – Sep 24	VIR (R)
Sep 25 – Oct 8	VIR
Oct 9 – Oct 26	LIB
Oct 27 – Nov 13	SCO
Nov 14 – Dec 3	SAG
Dec 4 – Dec 22	CAP
Dec 23 – Dec 31	CAP (R)

1984

Jan 1 – Jan 11	CAP (R)
Jan 12 – Feb 8	CAP
Feb 9 – Feb 27	AQU
Feb 28 – Mar 14	PIS
Mar 15 – Mar 31	ARI
Apr 1 – Apr 11	TAU
Apr 12 – Apr 24	TAU (R)
Apr 25 – May 5	ARI (R)
May 6 – May 15	ARI
May 16 – Jun 7	TAU
Jun 8 – Jun 21	GEM
Jun 22 – Jul 6	CAN
Jul 7 – Jul 25	LEO
Jul 26 – Aug 14	VIR
Aug 15 – Sep 7	VIR (R)
Sep 8 – Sep 30	VIR
Oct 1 – Oct 17	LIB
Oct 18 – Nov 5	SCO
Nov 6 – Dec 1	SAG
Dec 2 – Dec 4	CAP
Dec 5 – Dec 7	CAP (R)
Dec 8 – Dec 24	SAG (R)
Dec 25 – Dec 31	SAG

1985

Jan 1 – Jan 11	SAG
Jan 12 – Jan 31	CAP
Feb 1 – Feb 18	AQU
Feb 19 – Mar 6	PIS
Mar 7 – Mar 24	ARI
Mar 25 – Apr 17	ARI (R)
Apr 18 – May 13	ARI
May 14 – May30	TAU
May 31 – Jun 13	GEM
Jun 14 – Jun 29	CAN
Jun 30 – Jul 28	LEO
Jul 29 – Aug 20	LEO (R)
Aug 21 – Sep 6	LEO
Sep 7 – Sep 22	VIR
Sep 23 – Oct 10	LIB
Oct 11 – Oct 31	SCO
Nov 1 – Nov 18	SAG
Nov 19 – Dec 4	SAG (R)
Dec 5 – Dec 8	SCO (R)
Dec 9 – Dec 11	SCO
Dec 12 – Dec 31	SAG

1986

Jan 1 – Jan 5	SAG
Jan 6 – Jan 24	CAP
Jan 25 – Feb 10	AQU
Feb 11 –Mar 2	PIS
Mar 3 – Mar 7	ARI
Mar 8 – Mar 11	ARI (R)
Mar 12 – Mar 30	PIS (R)
Mar 31 – Apr 17	PIS
Apr 18 – May 7	ARI
May 8 – May 21	TAU
May 22 – Jun 5	GEM
Jun 6 – Jun 26	CAN
Jun 27 – Jul 9	LEO
Jul 10 – Jul 22	LEO (R)
Jul 23 – Aug 3	CAN (R)
Aug 4 – Aug 11	CAN
Aug 12 – Aug 29	LEO
Aug 30 – Sep 14	VIR
Sep 15 – Oct 3	LIB
Oct 4 – Nov 2	SCO
Nov 3 – Nov 22	SCO (R)
Nov 23 – Dec 9	SCO
Dec 10 – Dec 29	SAG
Dec 30 – Dec 31	CAP

1987

Jan 1 – Jan 17	CAP
Jan 18 – Feb 3	AQU
Feb 4 – Feb 18	PIS
Feb 19 – Mar 11	PIS (R)
Mar 12 – Mar 12	AQU (R)
Mar 13 – Mar 13	AQU
Mar 14 – Apr 12	PIS
Apr 13 – Apr 29	ARI
Apr 30 – May 13	TAU
May 14 – May 29	GEM
May 30 – Jun 21	CAN
Jun 22 – Jul 15	CAN (R)
Jul 16 – Aug 6	CAN
Aug 7 – Aug 21	LEO
Aug 22 – Sep 7	VIR
Sep 8 – Sep 28	LIB
Sep 29 – Oct 16	SCO
Oct 17 – Oct 31	SCO (R)
Nov 1 – Nov 6	LIB (R)
Nov 7 – Nov 11	LIB
Nov 12 – Dec 3	SCO
Dec 4 – Dec 22	SAG
Dec 23 – Dec 31	CAP

1988

Jan 1 – Jan 9	CAP
Jan 10 – Feb 2	AQU
Feb 3 – Feb 23	AQU (R)
Feb 24 – Mar 15	AQU
Mar 16 – Apr 4	PIS
Apr 5 – Apr 19	ARI
Apr 20 – May 4	TAU
May 5 – Jun 1	GEM
Jun 2 – Jun 24	GEM (R)
Jun 25 – Jul 11	GEM
Jul 12 – Jul 28	CAN
Jul 29 – Aug 12	LEO
Aug 13 – Aug 30	VIR
Aug 31 – Sep 28	LIB
Sep 29 – Oct 20	LIB (R)
Oct 21 – Nov 6	LIB
Nov 7 – Nov 24	SCO
Nov 25 – Dec 13	SAG
Dec 14 – Dec 31	CAP

1989

Jan 1 – Jan 2	CAP
Jan 10 – Jan 16	AQU
Jan 17 – Jan 28	AQU (R)
Jan 29 – Feb 5	CAP (R)
Feb 6 – Feb 14	CAP
Feb 15 – Mar 10	AQU
Mar 11 – Mar 27	PIS
Mar 28 – Apr 11	ARI
Apr 12 – Apr 29	TAU
Apr 30 – May 12	GEM
May 13 – May 28	GEM (R)
May 29 – Jun 5	TAU (R)
Jun 6 – Jun 11	TAU
Jun 12 – Jul 5	GEM
Jul 6 – Jul 19	CAN
Jul 20 – Aug 4	LEO
Aug 5 – Aug 25	VIR
Aug 26 – Sep 11	LIB
Sep 12 – Sep 26	LIB (R)
Sep 27 – Oct 3	VIR (R)
Oct 4 – Oct 10	VIR
Oct 11 – Oct 30	LIB
Oct 31 – Nov 17	SCO
Nov 18 – Dec 7	SAG
Dec 8 – Dec 30	CAP
Dec 31 – Dec 31	CAP (R)

1990

Jan 1 – Jan 20	CAP (R)
Jan 21 – Feb 11	CAP
Feb 12 – Mar 3	AQU
Mar 4 – Mar 19	PIS
Mar 20 – Apr 3	ARI
Apr 4 – Apr 23	TAU
Apr 24 – May 17	TAU (R)
May 18 – Jun 11	TAU
Jun 12 – Jun 27	GEM
Jun 28 – Jul 11	CAN
Jul 12 – Jul 28	LEO
Jul 29 – Aug 25	VIR
Aug 26 – Sep 17	VIR (R)
Sep 18 – Oct 5	VIR
Oct 6 – Oct 22	LIB
Oct 23 – Nov 10	SCO
Nov 11 – Dec 1	SAG
Dec 2 – Dec 14	CAP
Dec 15 – Dec 25	CAP (R)
Dec 26 – Dec 31	SAG (R)

1991

Jan 1 – Jan 3	SAG (R)
Jan 4 – Jan 13	SAG
Jan 21 – Feb 5	CAP
Feb 6 – Feb 23	AQU
Feb 24 – Mar 11	PIS
Mar 12 – Apr 4	ARI
Apr 5 – Apr 28	ARI (R)
Apr 29 – May 16	ARI
May 17 – Jun 4	TAU
Jun 5 – Jun 18	GEM
Jun 19 – Jul 3	CAN
Jul 4 – Jul 26	LEO
Jul 27 – Aug 8	VIR
Aug 9 – Aug 19	VIR (R)
Aug 20 – Sep 1	LEO (R)
Sep 2 – Sep 10	LEO
Sep 11 – Sep 27	VIR
Sep 28 – Oct 15	LIB
Oct 16 – Nov 3	SCO
Nov 4 – Nov 28	SAG
Nov 29 – Dec 18	SAG (R)
Dec 19 – Dec 31	SAG

1992

Jan 1 – Jan 9	SAG
Jan 10 – Jan 29	CAP
Jan 30 – Feb 15	AQU
Feb 16 – Mar 3	PIS
Mar 4 – Mar 17	ARI
Mar 18 – Apr 3	ARI (R)
Apr 4 – Apr 9	PIS (R)
Apr 10 – Apr 14	PIS
Aprl 5 – May 10	ARI
May 11 – May 26	TAU
May 27 – Jun 9	GEM
Jun 10 – Jun 26	CAN
Jun 27 – Jul 20	LEO
Jul 21 – Aug 13	LEO (R)
Aug 14 – Sep 2	LEO
Sep 3 – Sep 18	VIR
Sep 19 – Oct 6	LIB
Oct 7 – Oct 29	SCO
Oct 30 – Nov 11	SAG
Nov 12 – Nov 21	SAG (R)
Nov 22 – Dec 1	SCO (R)
Dec 2 – Dec 11	SCO
Dec 12 – Dec 31	SAG

1993

Jan 1 – Jan 2	SAG
Jan 3 – Jan 20	CAP
Jan 21 – Feb 7	AQU
Feb 8 – Feb 27	PIS
Feb 28 – Mar 22	PIS (R)
Mar 23 – Apr 15	PIS
Apr 16 – May 3	ARI
May 4 – May 17	TAU
May 18 – Jun 1	GEM
Jun 2 – Jul 1	CAN
Jul 2 – Jul 25	CAN (R)
Jul 26 – Aug 9	CAN
Aug 10 – Aug 25	LEO
Aug 26 – Sep 10	VIR
Sep 11 – Sep 30	LIB
Oct 1 – Oct 25	SCO
Oct 26 – Nov 15	SCO (R)
Nov 16 – Dec 6	SCO
Dec 7 – Dec 26	SAG
Dec 27 – Dec 31	CAP

1994

Date	Sign
Jan 1 – Jan 13	CAP
Jan 14 – Jan 31	AQU
Feb 1 – Feb 11	PIS
Feb 12 – Feb 21	PIS (R)
Feb 22 – Mar 5	AQU (R)
Mar 6 – Mar 17	AQU
Mar 18 – Apr 9	PIS
Apr 10 – Apr 25	ARI
Apr 26 – May 9	TAU
May 10 – May 28	GEM
May 29 – Jun 12	CAN
Jun 13 – Jul 2	CAN (R)
Jul 3 – Jul 6	GEM (R)
Jul 7 – Jul 10	GEM
Jul 11 – Aug 2	CAN
Aug 3 – Aug 17	LEO
Aug 18 – Sep 3	VIR
Sep 4 – Sep 26	LIB
Sep 27 – Oct 9	SCO
Oct 10 – Oct 18	SCO (R)
Oct 19 – Oct 30	LIB (R)
Oct 31 – Nov 10	LIB
Nov 11 – Nov 29	SCO
Nov 30 – Dec 18	SAG
Dec 19 – Dec 31	CAP

1995

Date	Sign
Jan 1 – Jan 6	CAP
Jan 7 – Jan 26	AQU
Jan 27 – Feb 16	AQU (R)
Feb 17 – Mar 14	AQU
Mar 15 – Apr 1	PIS
Apr 2 – Apr 16	ARI
Apr 17 – May 2	TAU
May 3 – May 24	GEM
May 25 – Jun 17	GEM (R)
Jun 18 – Jul 10	GEM
Jul 11 – Jul 25	CAN
Jul 26 – Aug 9	LEO
Aug 10 – Aug 28	VIR
Aug 29 – Sep 22	LIB
Sep 23 – Oct 14	LIB (R)
Oct 15 – Nov 2	LIB
Nov 3 – Nov 22	SCO
Nov 23 – Dec 11	SAG
Dec 12 – Dec 31	CAP

1996

Date	Sign
Jan 1 – Jan 1	CAP
Jan 2 – Jan 9	AQU
Jan 10 – Jan 16	AQU (R)
Jan 17 – Jan 30	CAP (R)
Jan 31 – Feb 14	CAP
Feb 15 – Mar 6	AQU
Mar 7 – Mar 23	PIS
Mar 24 – Apr 7	ARI
Apr 8 – May 3	TAU
May 4 – May 27	TAU (R)
May 28 – Jun 13	TAU
Jun 14 – Jul 1	GEM
Jul 2 – Jul 15	CAN
Jul 16 – Aug 1	LEO
Aug 2 – Aug 25	VIR
Aug 26 – Sep 4	LIB
Sep 5 – Sep 11	LIB (R)
Sep 12 – Sep 26	VIR (R)
Sep 27 – Oct 8	VIR
Oct 9 – Oct 26	LIB
Oct 27 – Nov 14	SCO
Nov 15 – Dec 4	SAG
Dec 5 – Dec 23	CAP
Dec 24 – Dec 31	CAP (R)

1997

Date	Sign
Jan 1 – Jan 12	CAP (R)
Jan 13 – Feb 8	CAP
Feb 9 – Feb 27	AQU
Feb 28 – Mar 15	PIS
Mar 16 – Apr 1	ARI
Apr 2 – Apr 15	TAU
Apr 16 – May 4	TAU (R)
May 5 – May 8	ARI (R)
May 9 – May 11	ARI
May 12 – Jun 8	TAU
Jun 9 – Jun 23	GEM
Jun 24 – Jul 7	CAN
Jul 8 – Jul 26	LEO
Jul 27 – Aug 17	VIR
Aug 18 – Sep 10	VIR (R)
Sep 11 – Oct 1	VIR
Oct 2 – Oct 18	LIB
Oct 19 – Nov 7	SCO
Nov 8 – Nov 30	SAG
Dec 1 – Dec 7	CAP
Dec 8 – Dec 13	CAP (R)
Dec 14 – Dec 27	SAG (R)
Dec 28 – Dec 31	SAG

1998

Date	Sign
Jan 1 – Jan 12	SAG
Jan 13 – Feb 2	CAP
Feb 3 – Feb 19	AQU
Feb 20 – Mar 7	PIS
Mar 8 – Mar 27	ARI
Mar 28 – Apr 20	ARI (R)
Apr 21 – May 14	TAU
May 15 – May 31	ARI
Jun 1 – Jun 14	GEM
Jun 15 – Jun 30	CAN
Jul 1 – Aug 1	LEO
Aug 2 – Aug 23	LEO (R)
Aug 24 – Sep 7	LEO
Sep 8 – Sep 23	VIR
Sep 24 – Oct 11	LIB
Oct 12 – Nov 1	SCO
Nov 2 – Nov 21	SAG
Nov 22 – Dec 11	SAG (R)
Dec 12 – Dec 31	SAG

1999

Date	Sign
Jan 1 – Jan 6	SAG
Jan 7 – Jan 25	CAP
Jan 26 – Feb 12	AQU
Feb 13 – Mar 2	PIS
Mar 3 – Mar 10	ARI
Mar 11 – Mar 17	ARI (R)
Mar 18 – Apr 2	PIS (R)
Apr 3 – Apr 19	PIS
Apr 18 – May 8	ARI
May 9 – May 23	TAU
May 24 – Jun 6	GEM
Jun 7 – Jun 26	CAN
Jun 27 – Jul 12	LEO
Jul 13 – Jul 31	LEO (R)
Aug 1 – Aug 6	CAN (R)
Aug 7 – Aug 10	CAN
Aug 11 – Aug 31	LEO
Sep 1 – Sep 16	VIR
Sep 17 – Oct 4	LIB
Oct 5 – Oct 30	SCO
Oct 31 – Nov 5	SAG
Nov 6 – Nov 9	SAG (R)
Nov 10 – Nov 25	SCO (R)
Nov 26 – Dec 10	SCO
Dec 11 – Dec 30	SAG
Dec 31 – Dec 31	CAP

2000

Date	Sign
Jan 1 – Jan 18	CAP
Jan 19 – Feb 4	AQU
Feb 5 – Feb 20	PIS
Feb 21 – Mar 13	PIS (R)
Mar 14 – Apr 12	PIS
Apr 13 – Apr 29	ARI
Apr 30 – May 13	TAU
May 14 – May 29	GEM
May 30 – Jun 22	CAN
Jun 23 – Jul 16	CAN (R)
Jul 17 – Aug 6	CAN
Aug 7 – Aug 21	LEO
Aug 22 – Sep 7	VIR
Sep 8 – Sep 28	LIB
Sep 29 – Oct 17	SCO
Oct 18 – Nov 6	SCO (R)
Nov 7 – Nov 7	LIB (R)
Nov 8 – Nov 8	LIB
Nov 9 – Dec 3	SCO
Dec 4 – Dec 22	SAG
Dec 23 – Dec 31	CAP

2001

Date	Sign
Jan 1 – Jan 10	CAP
Jan 11 – Feb 1	AQU
Feb 2 – Feb 3	PIS
Feb 4 – Feb 6	PIS (R)
Feb 7 – Feb 24	AQU (R)
Feb 25 – Mar 17	AQU
Mar 18 – Apr 6	PIS
Apr 7 – Apr 21	ARI
Apr 22 – May 6	TAU
May 7 – Jun 3	GEM
Jun 4 – Jun 27	GEM (R)
Jun 28 – Jul 12	GEM
Jul 13 – Jul 30	CAN
Jul 31 – Aug 14	LEO
Aug 15 – Sep 1	VIR
Sep 2 – Sep 30	LIB
Oct 1 – Oct 22	LIB (R)
Oct 23 – Nov 7	LIB
Nov 8 – Nov 26	SCO
Nov 27 – Dec 15	SAG
Dec 16 – Dec 31	CAP

2002

Date	Sign
Jan 1 – Jan 3	CAP
Jan 4 – Jan 17	AQU
Jan 18 – Feb 4	AQU (R)
Feb 5 – Feb 7	CAP (R)
Feb 8 – Feb 13	CAP
Feb 14 – Mar 11	AQU
Mar 12 – Mar 29	PIS
Mar 30 – Apr 13	ARI
Apr 14 – Apr 30	TAU
May 1 – May 14	GEM
May 15 – Jun 7	GEM (R)
Jun 8 – Jul 7	GEM
Jul 8 – Jul 21	CAN
Jul 22 – Aug 6	LEO
Aug 7 – Aug 26	VIR
Aug 27 – Sep 13	LIB
Sep 14 – Oct 2	LIB (R)
Oct 3 – Oct 5	VIR (R)
Oct 6 – Oct 11	VIR
Oct 12 – Oct 31	LIB
Nov 1 – Nov 19	SCO
Nov 20 – Dec 8	SAG
Dec 9 – Dec 31	CAP

2003

Date	Sign
Jan 1 – Jan 1	CAP
Jan 2 – Jan 22	CAP (R)
Jan 23 – Feb 13	CAP
Feb 14 – Mar 5	AQU
Mar 6 – Mar 21	PIS
Mar 22 – Apr 5	ARI
Apr 6 – Apr 25	TAU
Apr 26 – May 19	TAU (R)
May 20 – Jun 13	TAU
Jun 14 – Jun 29	GEM
Jun 30 – Jul 13	CAN
Jul 14 – Jul 30	LEO
Jul 31 – Aug 27	VIR
Aug 28 – Sep 19	VIR (R)
Sep 20 – Oct 7	VIR
Oct 8 – Oct 24	LIB
Oct 25 – Nov 12	SCO
Nov 13 – Dec 2	SAG
Dec 3 – Dec 16	CAP
Dec 17 – Dec 30	CAP (R)
Dec 31 – Dec 31	SAG (R)

2004

Date	Sign
Jan 1 – Jan 5	SAG (R)
Jan 6 – Jan 14	SAG
Jan 15 – Feb 7	CAP
Feb 8 – Feb 25	AQU
Feb 26 – Mar 12	PIS
Mar 13 – Apr 1	ARI
Apr 2 – Apr 5	TAU
Apr 6 – Apr 13	TAU (R)
Apr 14 – Apr 29	ARI (R)
Apr 30 – May 16	ARI
May 17 – Jun 5	TAU
Jun 6 – Jun 19	GEM
Jun 20 – Jul 4	CAN
Jul 5 – Jul 25	LEO
Jul 26 – Aug 10	VIR
Aug 11 – Aug 25	VIR (R)
Aug 26 – Sep 1	LEO (R)
Sep 2 – Sep 10	LEO
Sep 11 – Sep 28	VIR
Sep 29 – Oct 15	LIB
Oct 16 – Nov 4	SCO
Nov 5 – Nov 29	SAG
Nov 30 – Dec 18	SAG (R)
Dec 19 – Dec 31	SAG

2005

Date	Sign
Jan 1 – Jan 10	SAG
Jan 11 – Jan 30	CAP
Jan 31 – Feb 16	AQU
Feb 17 – Mar 5	PIS
Mar 6 – Mar 19	ARI
Mar 20 – Apr 11	ARI (R)
Apr 12 – May 12	ARI
May 13 – May 28	TAU
May 29 – Jun 11	GEM
Jun 12 – Jun 28	CAN
Jun 29 – Jul 22	LEO
Jul 23 – Aug 15	LEO (R)
Aug 16 – Sep 4	LEO
Sep 5 – Sep 20	VIR
Sep 21 – Oct 8	LIB
Oct 9 – Oct 30	SCO
Oct 31 – Nov 13	SAG
Nov 14 – Nov 26	SAG (R)
Nov 27 – Dec 3	SCO (R)
Dec 4 – Dec 12	SCO
Dec 13 – Dec 31	SAG

2006

Jan 1 – Jan 3	SAG
Jan 4 – Jan 22	CAP
Jan 23 – Feb 9	AQU
Feb 10 – Mar 1	PIS
Mar 2 – Mar 24	PIS (R)
Mar 25 – Apr 16	PIS
Apr 17 – May 5	ARI
May 6 – May 19	TAU
May 20 – Jun 3	GEM
Jun 4 – Jun 28	CAN
Jun 29 – Jul 3	LEO
Jul 4 – Jul 10	LEO (R)
Jul 11 – Jul 28	CAN (R)
Jul 29 – Aug 11	CAN
Aug 12 – Aug 27	LEO
Aug 28 – Sep 12	VIR
Sep 13 – Oct 2	LIB
Oct 3 – Oct 27	SCO
Oct 28 – Nov 17	SCO (R)
Nov 18 – Dec 8	SCO
Dec 9 – Dec 27	SAG
Dec 28 – Dec 31	CAP

2007

Jan 1 – Jan 15	CAP
Jan 16 – Feb 2	AQU
Feb 3 – Feb 13	PIS
Feb 14 – Feb 17	PIS (R)
Feb 18 – Mar 7	AQU (R)
Mar 8 – Mar 18	AQU
Mar 19 – Apr 10	PIS
Apr 11 – Apr 27	ARI
Apr 28 – May 11	TAU
May 12 – May 29	GEM
May 30 – Jun 14	CAN
Jun 15 – Jul 9	CAN (R)
Jul 10 – Aug 4	CAN
Aug 5 – Aug 19	LEO
Aug 20 – Sep 5	VIR
Sep 6 – Sep 27	LIB
Sep 28 – Oct 11	SCO
Oct 12 – Oct 24	SCO (R)
Oct 25 – Oct 31	LIB (R)
Nov 1 – Nov 11	LIB
Nov 12 – Dec 1	SCO
Dec 2 – Dec 20	SAG
Dec 21 – Dec 31	CAP

2008

Jan 1 – Jan 9	CAP
Jan 10 – Jan 27	AQU
Jan 28 – Feb 18	AQU (R)
Feb 19 – Mar 14	AQU
Mar 15 – Apr 2	PIS
Apr 3 – Apr 17	ARI
Apr 18 – May 2	TAU
May 3 – May 25	GEM
May 26 – Jun 18	GEM (R)
Jun 19 – Jul 10	GEM
Jul 11 – Jul 26	CAN
Jul 27 – Aug 10	LEO
Aug 11 – Aug 29	VIR
Aug 30 – Sep 23	LIB
Sep 24 – Oct 14	LIB (R)
Oct 15 – Nov 4	LIB
Nov 5 – Nov 23	SCO
Nov 24 – Dec 12	SAG
Dec 13 – Dec 31	CAP

2009

Jan 1 – Jan 1	CAP
Jan 2 – Jan 10	AQU
Jan 11 – Jan 21	AQU (R)
Jan 22 – Jan 31	CAP (R)
Feb 1 – Feb 14	CAP
Feb 15 – Mar 8	AQU
Mar 9 – Mar 25	PIS
Mar 26 – Apr 9	ARI
Apr 10 – Apr 30	TAU
May 1 – May 6	GEM
May 7 – May 13	GEM (R)
May 14 – May 30	TAU (R)
May 31 – Jun 14	TAU
Jun 15 – Jul 3	GEM
Jul 4 – Jul 17	CAN
Jul 18 – Aug 2	LEO
Aug 3 – Aug 25	VIR
Aug 26 – Sep 6	LIB
Sep 7 – Sep 18	LIB (R)
Sep 19 – Sep 28	VIR (R)
Sep 29 – Oct 10	VIR
Oct 11 – Oct 28	LIB
Oct 29 – Nov 16	SCO
Nov 17 – Dec 5	SAG
Dec 6 – Dec 25	CAP
Dec 26 – Dec 31	CAP (R)

2010

Jan 1 – Jan 14	CAP (R)
Jan 15 – Feb 10	CAP
Feb 11 – Mar 1	AQU
Mar 2 – Mar 17	PIS
Mar 18 – Apr 2	ARI
Apr 3 – Apr 17	TAU
Apr 18 – May 10	TAU (R)
May 11 – Jun 10	TAU
Jun 11 – Jun 25	GEM
Jun 26 – Jul 9	CAN
Jul 10 – Jul 27	LEO
Jul 28 – Aug 19	VIR
Aug 20 – Sep 11	VIR (R)
Sep 12 – Oct 3	VIR
Oct 4 – Oct 20	LIB
Oct 21 – Nov 8	SCO
Nov 9 – Dec 1	SAG
Dec 2 – Dec 9	CAP
Dec 10 – Dec 18	CAP (R)
Dec 19 – Dec 29	SAG (R)
Dec 30 – Dec 31	SAG (R)

HOW TO FIND THE VENUS SIGN

Under the year of birth, find birth date. If birth was on the first or last day of a particular time period, it's possible that Venus might be posited in the preceding or following Sign. For example, if the time period is from August 6 to September 10, and you were born on September 10, then you must consider that Venus might be in the next Sign. The only way to be absolutely sure is to have your chart done by computer (see Appendix III for computer services) or by a professional astrologer. If you're not sure, read the adjacent Sign, and you will probably be able to decide which is applicable.

Before checking the Venus Ephemeris, first look at the Venus Retrograde table on the next page to determine if the Planet was in retrograde motion at the time of birth. Look up the year in the left-hand column, then check the retrograde period, marked **R,** noticing the "backward" movement of the Planet from one Sign to the previous Sign. At the end of each entry, **D** indicates the Planet's return to direct motion.

Example:

> 1975 **R** Aug 6 in Virgo, into Leo Sep 3, **D** Sep 18 at which point refer to the ephemeris to find 1975 Sep 3–Oct 4 Leo. Thus, if birth occurred between Sep 3–17, Venus would be in Leo retrograde; but if birth occurred between Sep 18–Oct 4, Venus, while still in Leo, would be direct.

Venus does not go retrograde every year.

VENUS RETROGRADE TABLES

1950 *R* Jan 10 in Aqu—*D* Feb 20 1950
1951 *R* Aug 13 in Vir—*D* Sep 25 1951
1953 *R* Mar 23 in Tau,—into Ari Apr 1—*D* May 4 1953
1954 *R* Oct 25 in Sag,—into Sco Oct 28—*D* Nov 7 1954
1956 *R* May 30 in Can,—in Gem Jun 24—*D* Jul 13 1956
1958 *R* Jan 8 in Aqu—*D* Feb 18 1958
1959 *R* Aug 10 in Vir,—into Leo Sep 21—*D* Sep 22 1959
1961 *R* Mar 20 in Ari—*D* May 2 1961
1962 *R* Oct 23 in Sco—*D* Dec 3 1962
1964 *R* May29 in Can,— into Gem Jun 18—*D* Jul ll 1964
1966 *R* Jan 5 in Aqu,— into Cap Feb 7—*D* Feb 15 1966
1967 *R* Aug 8 in Vir,—into Leo Sep 10—*D* Sep 20 1967
1969 *R* Mar 18 in Ari—*D* Apr 10 1969
1970 *R* Oct 20 in Sco—*D* Dec 2 1970
1972 *R* May 27 in Can,—into Gem Jun 12—*D* Jul 9 1972
1974 *R* Jan 3 in Aqu,—into Cap Jan 30—*D* Feb 13 1974
1975 *R* Aug 6 in Vir,—into Leo Sep 3—*D* Sep 18 1975
1977 *R* Mar 16 in Ari—*D* Apr 27 1977
1978 *R* Oct 18 in Sco—*D* Nov 28 1978
1980 *R* May 24 in Can,—into Gem Jun 6—*D* Jul 6 1980
1982 *R* Jan 1 in Aqu,—into Cap Jan 24—*D* Feb 10 1982
1983 *R* Aug 3 in Vir,—into Leo Aug 28—*D* Sep 15 1983
1985 *R* Mar 13 in Ari—*D* Apr 25 1985
1986 *R* Oct 15 in Sco—*D* Nov 26 1986
1988 *R* May 22 in Can,—into Gem May 28—*D* Jul 4 1988
1989 *R* Dec 29 in Aqu,—into Cap Jan 17 1990—*D* Feb 8 1990
1991 *R* Aug 2 in Vir,—into Leo Aug 22—*D* Sep 13 1991
1993 *R* Mar 11 in Ari—*D* Apr 22 1993
1994 *R* Oct 13 in Sco—*D* Nov 23 1994
1996 *R* May 20 in Gem—*D* Jul 2 1996
1997 *R* Dec 26 in Aqu,—into Cap Jan 10 1998—*D* Feb 5 1998
1999 *R* Aug 2 in Vir,—into Leo Aug 16—*D* Sep 11 1999
2001 *R* Mar 9 in Ari—*D* Apr 20 2001
2002 *R* Oct 10 in Sco—*D* Nov 21 2002
2004 *R* May17 in Gem—*D* Jun 29 2004
2005 *R* Dec 24 in Aqu,—into Cap Jan 2 2006—*D* Feb 3 2006
2007 *R* Jul 27 in Vir,— into Leo Aug 10—*D* Sep 8 2007
2009 *R* Mar 6 in Ari,— into Pis Apr 12—*D* Apr 17 2009
2010 *R* Oct 8 in Sco,—into Lib Nov 9—*D* Nov 18 2010

VENUS EPHEMERIS

1950

Jan 1 – Apr 6	AQU
Apr 7 – May 5	PIS
May 6 – Jun 1	ARI
Jun 2 – Jun 26	TAU
Jun 27 – Jul 22	GEM
Jul 23 – Aug 16	CAN
Aug 17 – Sep 9	LEO
Sep 10 – Oct 3	VIR
Oct 4 – Oct 27	LIB
Oct 28 – Nov 20	SCO
Nov 21 – Dec 14	SAG
Dec 15 – Dec 31	CAP

1951

Jan I – Jan 6	CAP
Jan 7 – Jan 30	AQU
Jan 31 – Feb 24	PIS
Feb 25 – Mar 20	ARI
Mar 21 – Apr 14	TAU
Apr 15 – May 10	GEM
May 11 – Jun 6	CAN
Jun 7 – Jul 7	LEO
Jul 8 – Nov 7	VIR
Nov 8 – Dec 8	LIB
Dec 8 – Dec 31	SCO

1952

Jan 1	SCO
Jan 2 – Jan 26	SAG
Jan 27 – Feb 20	CAP
Feb 21 – Mar 16	AQU
Mar 17 – Apr 8	PIS
Apr 9 – May 3	ARI
May 4 – May 28	TAU
May 29 – Jun 21	GEM
Jun 22 – Jul 15	CAN
Jul 16 – Aug 8	LEO
Aug 9 – Sep 2	VIR
Sep 3 – Sep 26	LIB
Sep 27 – Oct 21	SCO
Oct 22 – Nov 15	SAG
Nov 16 – Dec 9	CAP
Dec 10 – Dec 31	AQU

1953

Jan 1 – Jan 4	AQU
Jan 5 – Feb 1	PIS
Feb 2 – Feb 14	ARI
Mar 15 – Mar 30	TAU
Mar 31 – Jun 4	ARI
Jun 5 – Jul 6	TAU
Jul 7 – Aug 3	GEM
Aug 4 – Aug 29	CAN
Aug 30 – Sop 23	LEO
Sep 24 – Oct 18	VIR
Oct 19 – Nov 11	LIB
Nov 12 – Dec 5	SCO
Dec 6 – Dec 29	SAG
Dec 30 – Dec 31	CAP

1954

Jan 1 – Jan 21	CAP
Jan 22 – Fob 14	AQU
Feb 15 – Mar 10	PIS
Mar 11 – Apr 3	ARI
Apr 4 – Apr 28	TAU
Apr 29 – May 23	GEM
May 24 – Jun 17	CAN
Jun 18 – Jul 12	LEO
Jul 13 – Aug 8	VIR
Aug 9 – Sep 6	LIB
Sep 7 – Oct 22	SCO
Oct 23 – Oct 26	SAG
Oct 27 – Dec 31	SCO

1955

Jan 1 – Jan 5	SCO
Jan 6 – Feb 5	SAG
Feb 6 – Mar 4	CAP
Mar 5 – Mar 29	AQU
Mar 30 – Apr 24	PIS
Apr 25 – May 19	ARI
May 20 – Jun 12	TAU
Jun 13 – Jul 7	GEM
Jul 8 – Jul 31	CAN
Aug I – Aug 25	LEO
Aug 26 – Sep 18	VIR
Sep 19 – Oct 12	LIB
Oct 13 – Nov 5	SCO
Nov 6 – Nov 29	SAG
Nov 30 – Dec 23	CAP
Dec 24 – Dec 31	AQU

1956

Jan 1 – Jan 17	AQU
Jan 18 – Feb 10	PIS
Feb 11 – Mar 7	ARI
Mar 8 – Apr 3	TAU
Apr 4 – May 7	GEM
May 8 – Jun 22	CAN
Jun 23 – Aug 3	GEM
Aug 4 – Sep 7	CAN
Sep 8 – Oct 5	LEO
Oct 6 – Oct 31	VIR
Nov 1 – Nov 25	LIB
Nov 26 – Dec 19	SCO
Dec 20 – Dec 31	SAG

1957

Jan 1 – Jan 12	SAG
Jan 13 – Feb 5	CAP
Feb 6 – Mar 1	AQU
Mar 2 – Mar 25	PIS
Mar 26 – Apr 18	ARI
Apr 19 – May 12	TAU
May 13 – Jun 6	GEM
Jun 7 – Jul 1	CAN
Jul 2 – Jul 25	LEO
Jul 26 – Aug 19	VIR
Aug 20 – Sep 13	LIB
Sep 14 – Oct 9	SCO
Oct 10 – Nov 5	SAG
Nov 6 – Dec 6	CAP
Dec 7 – Dec 31	AQU

1958

Jan 1 – Apr 6	AQU
Apr 7 – May 4	PIS
May 5 – May 31	ARI
Jun I – Jun 26	TAU
Jun 27 – Jul 21	GEM
Jul 22 – Aug 15	CAN
Aug 16 – Sep 9	LEO
Sep 10 – Oct 3	VIR
Oct 4 – Oct 27	LIB
Oct 28 – Nov 20	SCO
Nov 21 – Dec 13	SAG
Dec 14 – Dec 31	CAP

1959

Jan 1 – Jan 6	CAP
Jan 7 – Jan 30	AQU
Jan 31 – Feb 24	PIS
Feb 25 – Mar 20	ARI
Mar 21 – Apr 14	TAU
Apr 15 – May 10	GEM
May 11 – Jun 6	CAN
Jun 7 – Jul 8	LEO
Jul 9 – Sep 19	VIR
Sep 20 – Sep 24	LEO
Sep 25 – Nov 9	VIR
Nov 10 – Dec 7	LIB
Dec 8 – Dec 31	SCO

1960

Jan 1	SCO
Jan 2 – Jan 26	SAG
Jan 27 – Feb 20	CAP
Feb 21 – Mar 15	AQU
Mar 16 – Apr 8	PIS
Apr 9 – May 3	ARI
May 4 – May 27	TAU
May 28 – Jun 21	GEM
Jun 22 – Jul 15	CAN
Jul 16 – Aug 8	LEO
Aug 9 – Sep 2	VIR
Sep 3 – Sep 26	LIB
Sep 27 – Oct 21	SCO
Oct 22 – Nov 15	SAG
Nov 16 – Dec 9	CAP
Dec 10 – Dec 31	AQU

1961

Jan 1 – Jan 4	AQU
Jan 5 – Feb 1	PIS
Feb 2 – Jun 5	ARI
Jun 6 – Jul 6	TAU
Jul 7 – Aug 3	GEM
Aug 4 – Aug 29	CAN
Aug 30 – Sep 23	LEO
Sep 24 – Oct 17	VIR
Oct 18 – Nov 10	LIB
Nov 11 – Dec 4	SCO
Dec 5 – Dec 28	SAG
Dec 29 – Dec 31	CAP

1962

Jan 1 – Jan 21	CAP
Jan 22 – Feb 14	AQU
Feb 15 – Mar 10	PIS
Mar 11 – Apr 3	ARI
Apr 4 – Apr 27	TAU
Apr 28 – May 22	GEM
May 23 – Jun 16	CAN
Jun 17 – Jul 12	LEO
Jul 13 – Aug 8	VIR
Aug 9 – Sep 6	LIB
Sep 7 – Dec 31	SCO

1963

Jan 1 – Jan 6	SCO
Jan 7 – Feb 5	SAG
Feb 6 – Mar 3	CAP
Mar 4 – Mar 29	AQU
Mar 30 – Apr 23	PIS
Apr 24 – May 18	ARI
May 19 – Jun 11	TAU
Jun 12 – Jul 6	GEM
Jul 7 – Jul 31	CAN
Aug 1 – Aug 24	LEO
Aug 25 – Sep 17	VIR
Sep 18 – Oct 11	LIB
Oct 12 – Nov 4	SCO
Nov 5 – Nov 28	SAG
Nov 29 – Dec 23	CAP
Dec 24 – Dec 31	AQU

1964

Jan 1 – Jan 16	AQU
Jan 17 – Feb 9	PIS
Feb 10 – Mar 6	ARI
Mar 7 – Apr 3	TAU
Apr 4 – May 8	GEM
May 9 – Jun 16	CAN
Jun 17 – Aug 4	GEM
Aug 5 – Sep 7	CAN
Sep 8 – Oct 4	LEO
Oct 5 – Oct 30	VIR
Oct 31 – Nov 24	LIB
Nov 25 – Dec 18	SCO
Dec 19 – Dec 31	SAG

1965

Jan 1 – Jan 11	SAG
Jan 12 – Feb 4	CAP
Feb 5 – Feb 28	AQU
Mar 1 – Mar 24	PIS
Mar 25 – Apr 17	ARI
Apr 18 – May 11	TAU
May 12 – Jun 5	GEM
Jun 6 – Jun 30	CAN
Jul 1 – Jul 24	LEO
Jul 25 – Aug 18	VIR
Aug 19 – Sep 13	LIB
Sep 14 – Oct 8	SCO
Oct 9 – Nov 5	SAG
Nov 6 – Dec 6	CAP
Dec 7 – Dec 31	AQU

1966

Jan 1 – Feb 6	AQU
Feb 7 – Feb 25	CAP
Feb 26 – Apr 6	AQU
Apr 7 – May 5	PIS
May 6 – May 31	ARI
Jun 1 – Jun 26	TAU
Jun 27 – Jul 21	GEM
Jul 22 – Aug 15	CAN
Aug 16 – Sep 8	LEO
Sep 9 – Oct 3	VIR
Oct 4 – Oct 27	LIB
Oct 28 – Nov 20	SCO
Nov 21 – Dec 13	SAG
Dec 14 – Dec 31	CAP

1967

Jan 1 – Jan 6	CAP
Jan 7 – Jan 30	AQU
Jan 31 – Feb 23	PIS
Feb 24 – Mar 20	ARI
Mar 21 – Apr 14	TAU
Apr 15 – May 10	GEM
May 11 – Jun 6	CAN
Jun 7 – Jul 8	LEO
Jul 9 – Sep 9	VIR
Sep 10 – Oct 1	LEO
Oct 2 – Nov 9	VIR
Nov 10 – Dec 7	LIB
Dec 8 – Dec 31	SCO

1968

Jan 1 – Jan 26	SAG
Jan 27 – Feb 20	CAP
Feb 21 – Mar 15	AQU
Mar 16 – Apr 8	PIS
Apr 9 – May 3	ARI
May 4 – May 27	TAU
May 28 – Jun 21	GEM
Jun 22 – Jul 15	CAN
Jul 16 – Aug 8	LEO
Aug 9 – Sep 2	VIR
Sep 3 – Sep 26	LIB
Sep 27 – Oct 21	SCO
Oct 22 – Nov 14	SAG
Nov 15 – Dec 9	CAP
Dec 10 – Dec 31	AQU

1969

Jan 1 – Jan 4	AQU
Jan 5 – Feb 2	PIS
Feb 3 – Jun 6	ARI
Jun 7 – Jul 6	TAU
Jul 7 – Aug 3	GEM
Aug 4 – Aug 29	CAN
Aug 30 – Sep 23	LIB
Sep 24 – Oct 17	VIR
Oct 18 – Nov 10	LIB
Nov 11 – Dec 4	SCO
Dec 5 – Dec 28	SAG
Dec 29 – Dec 31	CAP

1970

Jan 1 – Jan 21	CAP
Jan 22 – Feb 14	AQU
Feb 15 – Mar 10	PIS
Mar 11 – Apr 3	ARI
Apr 4 – Apr 27	TAU
Apr 28 – May 22	GEM
May 23 – Jun 16	CAN
Jun 17 – Jul 12	LEO
Jul 13 – Aug 8	VIR
Aug 9 – Sep 7	LIB
Sep 8 – Dec 31	SCO

1971

Jan 1 – Jan 7	SCO
Jan 8 – Feb 5	SAG
Feb 6 – Mar 4	CAP
Mar 5 – Mar 29	AQU
Mar 30 – Apr 23	PIS
Apr 24 – May 18	ARI
May 19 – Jun 12	TAU
Jun 13 – Jul 6	GEM
Jul 7 – Jul 31	CAN
Aug 1 – Aug 24	LEO
Aug 25 – Sep 17	VIR
Sep 18 – Oct 11	LIB
Oct 12 – Nov 5	SCO
Nov 6 – Nov 29	SAG
Nov 30 – Dec 23	CAP
Dec 24 – Dec 31	AQU

1972

Jan 1 – Jan 16	AQU
Jan 17 – Feb 10	PIS
Feb 11 – Mar 7	ARI
Mar 8 – Apr 3	TAU
Apr 4 – May 10	GEM
May 11 – Jun 11	CAN
Jun 12 – Aug 6	GEM
Aug 7 – Sep 7	CAN
Sep 8 – Oct 5	LEO
Oct 6 – Oct 30	VIR
Oct 31 – Nov 24	LIB
Nov 25 – Dec 18	SCO
Dec 19 – Dec 31	SAG

1973

Jan 1 – Jan 11	SAG
Jan 12 – Feb 4	CAP
Feb 5 – Feb 28	AQU
Mar 1 – Mar 24	PIS
Mar 25 – Apr 18	ARI
Apr 19 – May 12	TAU
May 13 – Jun 5	GEM
Jun 6 – Jun 30	CAN
Jul 1 – Jul 25	LEO
Jul 26 – Aug 19	VIR
Aug 20 – Sep 13	LIB
Sep 14 – Oct 9	SCO
Oct 10 – Nov 5	SAG
Nov 6 – Dec 7	CAP
Dec 8 – Dec 31	AQU

1974

Jan 1 – Jan 29	AQU
Jan 30 – Feb 28	CAP
Mar 1 – Apr 6	AQU
Apr 7 – May 4	PIS
May 5 – May 31	ARI
Jun 1 – Jun 25	TAU
Jun 26 – Jul 21	GEM
Jul 22 – Aug 14	CAN
Aug 15 – Sep 8	LEO
Sep 9 – Oct 2	VIR
Oct 3 – Oct 26	LIB
Oct 27 – Nov 19	SCO
Nov 20 – Dec 13	SAG
Dec 14 – Dec 31	CAP

1975

Jan 1 – Jan 6	CAP
Jan 7 – Jan 30	AQU
Jan 31 – Feb 23	PIS
Feb 24 – Mar 19	ARI
Mar 20 – Apr 13	TAU
Apr 14 – May 9	GEM
May 10 – Jun 6	CAN
Jun 7 – Jul 9	LEO
Jul 10 – Sep 2	VIR
Sep 3 – Oct 4	LEO
Oct 5 – Nov 9	VIR
Nov 10 – Dec 7	LIB
Dec 8 – Dec 31	SCO

1976

Jan 1	SCO
Jan 2 – Jan 26	SAG
Jan 27 – Feb 19	CAP
Feb 20 – Mar 15	AQU
Mar 16 – Apr 8	PIS
Apr 9 – May 2	ARI
May 3 – May 27	TAU
May 28 – Jun 20	GEM
Jun 21 – Jun 14	CAN
Jun 15 – Aug 8	LEO
Aug 9 – Sep 1	VIR
Sep 2 – Sep 26	LIB
Sep 27 – Oct 20	SCO
Oct 21 – Nov 14	SAG
Nov 15 – Dec 9	CAP
Dec 10 – Dec 31	AQU

1977

Jan 1 – Jan 4	AQU
Jan 5 – Feb 2	PIS
Feb 3 – Jun 6	ARI
Jun 7 – Jul 6	TAU
Jul 7 – Aug 2	GEM
Aug 3 – Aug 28	CAN
Aug 29 – Sep 22	LEO
Sep 23 – Oct 17	VIR
Oct 18 – Nov 10	LIB
Nov 11 – Dec 4	SCO
Dec 5 – Dec 27	SAG
Dec 28 – Dec 31	CAP

1978

Jan 1 – Jan 20	CAP
Jan 21 – Feb 13	AQU
Feb 14 – Mar 9	PIS
Mar 10 – Apr 2	ARI
Apr 3 – Apr 27	TAU
Apr 28 – May 22	GEM
May 23 – Jun 16	CAN
Jun 17 – Jul 12	LEO
Jul 13 – Aug 8	VIR
Aug 9 – Sep 7	LIB
Sep 8 – Dec 31	SCO

1979

Jan 1 – Jan 7	SCO
Jan 8 – Feb 5	SAG
Feb 6 – Mar 3	CAP
Mar 4 – Mar 29	AQU
Mar 30 – Apr 23	PIS
Apr 24 – May 18	ARI
May 19 – Jun 11	TAU
Jun 12 – Jul 6	GEM
Jul 7 – Jul 30	CAN
Jul 31 – Aug 24	LEO
Aug 25 – Sep 17	VIR
Sep 18 – Oct 11	LIB
Oct 12 – Nov 4	SCO
Nov 5 – Nov 28	SAG
Nov 29 – Dec 22	CAP
Dec 23 – Dec 31	AQU

1980

Jan 1 – Jan 16	AQU
Jan 17 – Feb 9	PIS
Feb 10 – Mar 6	ARI
Mar 7 – Apr 3	TAU
Apr 4 – May 12	GEM
May 13 – Jun 5	CAN
Jun 6 – Aug 6	GEM
Aug 7 – Sep 7	CAN
Sep 8 – Oct 4	LEO
Oct 5 – Oct 30	VIR
Oct 31 – Nov 24	LIB
Nov 25 – Dec 18	SCO
Dec 19 – Dec 31	SAG

1981

Jan 1 – Jan 11	SAG
Jan 12 – Feb 4	CAP
Feb 5 – Feb 28	AQU
Mar 1 – Mar 24	PIS
Mar 25 – Apr 17	ARI
Apr 18 – May 11	TAU
May 12 – Jun 5	GEM
Jun 6 – Jun 29	CAN
Jun 30 – Jul 24	LEO
Jul 25 – Aug 18	VIR
Aug 19 – Sep 12	LIB
Sep 13 – Oct 9	SCO
Oct 10 – Nov 5	SAG
Nov 6 – Dec 8	CAP
Dec 9 – Dec 31	AQU

1982

Jan 1 – Jan 23	AQU
Jan 24 – Mar 2	CAP
Mar 3 – Apr 6	AQU
Apr 7 – May 4	PIS
May 5 – May 30	ARI
May 31 – Jun 25	TAU
Jun 26 – Jul 20	GEM
Jul 21 – Aug 14	CAN
Aug 15 – Sep 7	LEO
Sep 8 – Oct 2	VIR
Oct 3 – Oct 26	LIB
Oct 27 – Nov 18	SCO
Nov 19 – Dec 12	SAG
Dec 13 – Dec 31	CAP

1983

Jan 1 – Jan 5	CAP
Jan 6 – Jan 29	AQU
Jan 30 – Feb 22	PIS
Feb 23 – Mar 18	ARI
Mar 19 - Apr 12	TAU
Apr 13 – May 8	GEM
May 9 – Jun 5	CAN
Jun 6 – Jul 9	LEO
Jul 10 – Aug 26	VIR
Aug 27 – Oct 5	LEO
Oct 6 – Nov 8	VIR
Nov 14 – Dec 6	LIB
Dec 7 – Dec 31	SCO

1984

Jan 1 – Jan 25	SAG
Jan 26 – Feb 18	CAP
Feb 19 – Mar 14	AQU
Mar 15 – Apr 9	PIS
Apr 8 – May 1	ARI
May 2 – May 26	TAU
May 27 – Jun 19	GEM
Jun 20 – Jul 13	CAN
Jul 14 – Aug 7	LEO
Aug 8 – Aug 31	VIR
Sep 1 – Sep 25	LIB
Sep 26 – Oct 19	SCO
Oct 20 – Nov 13	SAG
Nov 14 – Dec 8	CAP
Dec 9 – Dec 31	AQU

1985

Jan 1 – Jan 3	AQU
Jan 4 – Feb 1	PIS
Feb 2 – Jun 5	ARI
Jun 6 – Jul 5	TAU
Jul 6 – Aug 1	GEM
Aug 2 – Aug 27	CAN
Aug 28 – Sep 21	LEO
Sep 22 – Oct 16	VIR
Oct 17 – Nov 9	LIB
Nov 10 – Dec 3	SCO
Dec 4 – Dec 26	SAG
Dec 27 – Dec 31	CAP

1986

Jan 1 – Jan 19	CAP
Jan 20 – Feb 12	AQU
Feb 13 – Mar 8	PIS
Mar 9 – Apr 1	ARI
Apr 2 – Apr 26	TAU
Apr 27 – May 21	GEM
May 22 – Jun 15	CAN
Jun 16 – Jul 11	LEO
Jul 12 – Aug 7	VIR
Aug 8 – Sep 6	LIB
Sep 7 – Dec 31	SCO

1987

Jan 1 – Jan 6	SCO
Jan 7 – Feb 4	SAG
Feb 5 – Mar 2	CAP
Mar 3 – Mar 28	AQU
Mar 29 – Apr 22	PIS
Apr 23 – May 16	ARI
May 17 – Jun 10	TAU
Jun 11 – Jul 5	GEM
Jul 6 – Jul 29	CAN
Jul 30 – Aug 23	LEO
Aug 24 – Sep 16	VIR
Sep 17 – Oct 10	LIB
Oct 11 – Nov 3	SCO
Nov 4 – Nov 27	SAG
Nov 28 – Dec 21	CAP
Dec 22 – Dec 31	AQU

1988

Jan 1 – Jan 15	AQU
Jan 16 – Feb 9	PIS
Feb 10 – Mar 5	ARI
Mar 6 – Apr 3	TAU
Apr 4 – May 17	GEM
May 18 – May 26	CAN
May 27 – Aug 6	GEM
Aug 7 – Sep 6	CAN
Sep 7 – Oct 4	LEO
Oct 5 – Oct 29	VIR
Oct 30 – Nov 23	LIB
Nov 24 – Dec 17	SCO
Dec 18 – Dec 31	SAG

1989

Jan 1 – Jan 10	SAG
Jan 11 – Feb 3	CAP
Feb 4 – Feb 27	AQU
Feb 28 – Mar 23	PIS
Mar 24 – Apr 16	ARI
Apr 17 – May 10	TAU
May 11 – Jun 4	GEM
Jun 5 – Jun 28	CAN
Jun 29 – Jul 23	LEO
Jul 24 – Aug 17	VIR
Aug 18 – Sep 12	LIB
Sep 13 – Oct 8	SCO
Oct 9 – Nov 4	SAG
Nov 5 – Dec 9	CAP
Dec 10 – Dec 31	AQU

1990

Jan 1 – Jan 16	AQU
Jan 17 – Mar 3	CAP
Mar 4 – Apr 5	AQU
Apr 6 – May 3	PIS
May 4 – May 29	ARI
May 30 – Jun 24	TAU
Jun 25 – Jul 19	GEM
Jul 20 – Aug 13	CAN
Aug 14 – Sep 6	LEO
Sep 7 – Sep 30	VIR
Oct 1 – Oct 24	LIB
Oct 25 – Nov 17	SCO
Nov 18 – Dec 11	SAG
Dec 12 – Dec 31	CAP

1991

Jan 1 – Jan 4	CAP
Jan 5 – Jan 28	AQU
Jan 29 – Feb 21	PIS
Feb 22 – Mar 18	ARI
Mar 19 – Apr 12	TAU
Apr 13 – May 8	GEM
May 9 – Jun 5	CAN
Jun 6 – Jul 10	LEO
Jul 11 – Aug 21	VIR
Aug 22 – Oct 6	LEO
Oct 7 – Nov 8	VIR
Nov 9 – Dec 5	LIB
Dec 6 – Dec 31	SCO

1992

Jan 1 – Jan 24	SAG
Jan 25 – Feb 18	CAP
Feb 19 – Mar 13	AQU
Mar 14 – Apr 6	PIS
Apr 7 – May 1	ARI
May 2 – May 25	TAU
May 26 – Jun 18	GEM
Jun 19 – Jul 13	CAN
Jul 14 – Aug 6	LEO
Aug 7 – Aug 31	VIR
Sep 1 – Sep 24	LIB
Sep 25 – Oct 19	SCO
Oct 20 – Nov 13	SAG
Nov 14 – Dec 8	CAP
Dec 9 – Dec 31	AQU

1993

Jan 1 – Jan 3	AQU
Jan 4 – Feb 2	PIS
Feb 3 – Jun 5	ARI
Jun 6 – Jul 5	TAU
Jul 6 – Aug 1	GEM
Aug 2 – Aug 27	CAN
Aug 28 – Sep 21	LEO
Sep 22 – Oct 15	VIR
Oct 16 – Nov 8	LIB
Nov 9 – Dec 2	SCO
Dec 3 – Dec 26	SAG
Dec 27 – Dec 31	CAP

1994

Jan 1 – Jan 19	CAP
Jan 20 – Feb 12	AQU
Feb 13 – Mar 8	PIS
Mar 9 – Apr 1	ARI
Apr 2 – Apr 25	TAU
Apr 26 – May 20	GEM
May 21 – Jun 14	CAN
Jun 15 – Jul 10	LEO
Jul 11 – Aug 7	VIR
Aug 8 – Sep 7	LIB
Sep 8 – Dec 31	SCO

1995

Jan 1 – Jan 7	SCO
Jan 8 – Feb 4	SAG
Feb 5 – Mar 2	CAP
Mar 3 – Mar 27	AQU
Mar 28 – Apr 21	PIS
Apr 22 – May 16	ARI
May 17 – Jun 10	TAU
Jun 11 – Jul 4	GEM
Jul 5 – Jul 29	CAN
Jul 30 – Aug 22	LEO
Aug 23 – Sep 15	VIR
Sep 16 – Oct 9	LIB
Oct 10 – Nov 2	SCO
Nov 3 – Nov 27	SAG
Nov 28 – Dec 21	CAP
Dec 22 – Dec 31	AQU

1996

Jan 1 – Jan 14	AQU
Jan 15 – Feb 8	PIS
Feb 9 – Mar 5	ARI
Mar 6 – Apr 3	TAU
Apr 4 – Aug 6	GEM
Aug 7 – Sep 6	CAN
Sep 7 – Oct 3	LEO
Oct 4 – Oct 28	VIR
Oct 29 – Nov 22	LIB
Nov 23 – Dec 16	SCO
Dec 17 – Dec 31	SAG

1997

Jan 1 – Jan 9	SAG
Jan 10 – Feb 2	CAP
Feb 3 – Feb 26	AQU
Feb 27 – Mar 22	PIS
Mar 23 – Apr 15	ARI
Apr 16 – May 10	TAU
May 11 – Jun 3	GEM
Jun 4 – Jun 28	CAN
Jun 29 – Jul 23	LEO
Jul 24 – Aug 17	VIR
Aug 18 – Sep 11	LIB
Sep 12 – Oct 7	SCO
Oct 8 – Nov 4	SAG
Nov 5 – Dec 11	CAP
Dec 12 – Dec 31	AQU

1998

Jan 1 – Jan 9	AQU
Jan 10 – Mar 4	CAP
Mar 5 – Apr 5	AQU
Apr 6 – May 3	PIS
May 4 – May 29	ARI
May 30 – Jun 24	TAU
Jun 25 – Jul 19	GEM
Jul 20 – Aug 12	CAN
Aug 13 – Sep 6	LEO
Sep 7 – Sep 30	VIR
Oct 1 – Oct 24	LIB
Oct 25 – Nov 17	SCO
Nov 18 – Dec 11	SAG
Dec 12 – Dec 31	CAP

1999

Jan 1 – Jan 4	CAP
Jan 5 – Jan 28	AQU
Jan 29 – Feb 21	PIS
Feb 22 – Mar 17	ARI
Mar 18 – Apr 12	TAU
Apr 13 – May 8	GEM
May 9 – Jun 5	CAN
Jun 6 – Jul 12	LEO
Jul 13 – Aug 15	VIR
Aug 16 – Oct 7	LEO
Oct 8 – Nov 8	VIR
Nov 9 – Dec 5	LIB
Dec 6 – Dec 30	SCO
Dec 31 – Dec 31	SAG

2000

Jan 1 – Jan 24	SAG
Jan 25 – Feb 17	CAP
Feb 18 – Mar 12	AQU
Mar 13 – Apr 6	PIS
Apr 7 – Apr 30	ARI
May 1 – May 25	TAU
May 26 – Jun 18	GEM
Jun 19 – Jul 12	CAN
Jul 13 – Aug 6	LEO
Aug 7 – Aug 30	VIR
Aug 31 – Sep 24	LIB
Sep 25 – Oct 18	SCO
Oct 19 – Nov 12	SAG
Nov 13 – Dec 7	CAP
Dec 8 – Dec 31	AQU

2001

Jan 1 – Jan 2	AQU
Jan 3 – Feb 1	PIS
Feb 2 – Jun 5	ARI
Jun 6 – Jul 4	TAU
Jul 5 – Jul 31	GEM
Aug 1 – Aug 25	CAN
Aug 26 – Sep 19	LEO
Sep 20 – Oct 14	VIR
Oct 15 – Nov 7	LIB
Nov 8 – Dec 1	SCO
Dec 2 – Dec 25	SAG
Dec 26 – Dec 31	CAP

2002

Jan 1 – Jan 17	CAP
Jan 18 – Feb 10	AQU
Feb 11 – Mar 6	PIS
Mar 7 – Mar 31	ARI
Apr 1 – Apr 24	TAU
Apr 25 – May 19	GEM
May 20 – Jun 13	CAN
Jun 14 – Jul 9	LEO
Jul 10 – Aug 6	VIR
Aug 7 – Sep 6	LIB
Sep 7 – Dec 31	SCO

2003

Jan 1 – Jan 6	SCO
Jan 7 – Feb 3	SAG
Feb 4 – Mar 1	CAP
Mar 2 – Mar 26	AQU
Mar 27 – Apr 20	PIS
Apr 21 – May 15	ARI
May 16 – Jun 8	TAU
Jun 9 – Jul 13	GEM
Jul 14 – Jul 27	CAN
Jul 28 – Aug 21	LEO
Aug 22 – Sep 14	VIR
Sep 15 – Oct 8	LIB
Oct 9 – Nov 1	SCO
Nov 2 – Nov 25	SAG
Nov 26 – Dec 20	CAP
Dec 21 – Dec 31	AQU

2004

Jan 1 – Jan 13	AQU
Jan 14 – Feb 7	PIS
Feb 8 – Mar 4	ARI
Mar 5 – Apr 2	TAU
Apr 3 – Aug 6	GEM
Aug 7 – Sep 5	CAN
Sep 6 – Oct 2	LEO
Oct 3 – Oct 27	VIR
Oct 28 – Nov 21	LIB
Nov 22 – Dec 15	SCO
Dec 16 – Dec 31	SAG

2005

Jan 1 – Jan 8	SAG
Jan 9 – Feb 1	CAP
Feb 2 – Feb 25	AQU
Feb 26 – Mar 21	PIS
Mar 22 – Apr 14	ARI
Apr 15 – May 8	TAU
May 9 – Jun 2	GEM
Jun 3 – Jun 27	CAN
Jun 28 – Jul 21	LEO
Jul 22 – Aug 15	VIR
Aug 16 – Sep 10	LIB
Sep 11 – Oct 6	SCO
Oct 7 – Nov 4	SAG
Nov 5 – Dec 14	CAP
Dec 15 – Dec 31	AQU

2006

Jan 1 – Mar 4	CAP
Mar 5 – Apr 4	AQU
Apr 5 – May 2	PIS
May 3 – May 28	ARI
May 29 – Jun 22	TAU
Jun 23 – Jul 17	GEM
Jul 18 – Aug 11	CAN
Aug 12 – Sep 5	LEO
Sep 6 – Sep 29	VIR
Sep 30 – Oct 23	LIB
Oct 24 – Nov 16	SCO
Nov 17 – Dec 10	SAG
Dec 11 – Dec 31	CAP

2007

Jan 1 – Jan 2	CAP
Jan 3 – Jan 26	AQU
Jan 27 – Feb 20	PIS
Feb 21 – Mar 16	ARI
Mar 17 – Apr 10	TAU
Apr 11 – May 7	GEM
May 8 – Jun 4	CAN
Jun 5 – Jul 13	LEO
Jul 14 – Aug 7	VIR
Aug 8 – Oct 7	LEO
Oct 8 – Nov 7	VIR
Nov 8 – Dec 4	LIB
Dec 5 – Dec 29	SCO
Dec 30 – Dec 31	SAG

2008

Jan 1 – Jan 23	SAG
Jan 24 – Feb 16	CAP
Feb 17 – Mar 11	AQU
Mar 12 – Apr 5	PIS
Apr 6 – Apr 29	ARI
Apr 30 – May 23	TAU
May 24 – Jun 17	GEM
Jun 18 – Jul 11	CAN
Jul 12 – Aug 4	LEO
Aug 5 – Aug 29	VIR
Aug 30 – Sep 22	LIB
Sep 23 – Oct 17	SCO
Oct 18 – Nov 11	SAG
Nov 12 – Dec 6	CAP
Dec 7 – Dec 31	AQU

2009

Jan 1 – Jan 2	AQU
Jan 3 – Feb 1	PIS
Feb 2 – Apr 10	PIS
Apr 11 – Apr 23	PIS
Apr 24 – Jun 5	ARI
Jun 6 – Jul 4	TAU
Jul 5 – Jul 30	GEM
Jul 31 – Aug 25	CAN
Aug 26 – Sep 19	LEO
Sep 20 – Oct 13	VIR
Oct 14 – Nov 6	LIB
Nov 7 – Nov 30	SCO
Dec 1 – Dec 24	SAG
Dec 25 – Dec 31	CAP

2010

Jan 1 – Jan 17	CAP
Jan 18 – Feb 10	AQU
Feb 11 – Mar 6	PIS
Mar 7 – Mar 30	ARI
Mar 31 – Apr 23	TAU
Apr 24 – May 18	GEM
May 19 – Jun 13	CAN
Jun 14 – Jul 9	LEO
Jul 10 – Aug 5	VIR
Aug 6 – Sep 7	LIB
Sep 8 – Nov 6	SCO
Nov 7 – Nov 28	LIB
Nov 29 – Dec 31	SCO

HOW TO FIND THE MARS SIGN

Under the year of birth, find birth date. If birth was on the first or last day of a particular time period, it's possible that Mars might be posited in the preceding or following Sign. For example, if the time period is from August 6 to September 10, and you were born on September 10, then you must consider that your Mars might be in the next Sign. The only way to be absolutely sure is to have a chart done by computer (see Appendix III for computer services) or by a professional astrologer. If you're not sure, read the adjacent Sign, and you will probably be able to decide which is applicable.

Before checking the Mars Ephemeris, first look at the Mars Retrograde table on the next page to determine if the Planet was in retrograde motion at the time of birth. Look up the year in the left-hand column, then check the retrograde period, marked **R**, noticing the "backward" movement of the Planet from one Sign to the previous Sign. At the end of each entry, **D** indicates the Planet's return to direct motion.

Example:

> 1975 **R** Nov 6 in Cancer, into Gemini Nov 26, **D** Jan 20 1976 at which point refer to the ephemeris to find 1975 Oct 18– Nov 25 Cancer.
>
> Thus, if birth occurred between Oct 18–Nov 5, Venus would be in CANCER direct; but if birth occurred between Nov 6– Nov 25, Venus, while still in Cancer, would be retrograde.

MARS RETROGRADE TABLES

1950 *R* Feb 12 in Lib, into Vir Mar 29—*D* May 3 1950
1952 *R* Mar 25 in Sco—*D* Jun 10 1952
1954 *R* May 23 in Cap, into Sag Jul 4—*D* Jul 29 1954
1956 *R* Aug 10 in Pis—*D* Oct 10 1956
1958 *R* Oct 10 in Gem, into Tau Oct 30—*D* Dec 20 1958
1960 *R* Nov 20 in Can, into Gem Feb 6 1961—*D* Feb 7 1961
1962 *R* Dec 26 in Leo—*D* Mar 16 1963
1965 *R* Jan 28 in Vir—*D* Apr 19 1965
1967 *R* Mar 8 in Sco, into Lib Apr 1—*D* May 26 1967
1969 *R* Apr 27 in Sag—*D* Jul 8 1969
1971 *R* Jul 11 in Aqu—*D* Sep 9 1971
1973 *R* Sep 19 in Tau, into Ari Oct 30—*D* Nov 26 1973
1975 *R* Nov 6 in Can, into Gem Nov 26—*D* Jan 20 1976
1977 *R* Dec 12 in Leo, into Can Jan 27 1978—*D* Mar 2 1978
1980 *R* Jan 16 in Vir, into Leo Mar 12—*D* Apr 6 1980
1982 *R* Feb 20 in Lib—*D* May 11 1982
1984 *R* Apr 5 in Sco—*D* Jun 19 1984
1986 *R* Jun 8 in Cap—*D* Aug 12 1986
1988 *R* Aug 26 in Ari, into Pis Oct 24—*D* Oct 28 1988
1990 *R* Oct 20 in Gem, into Tau Dec 15—*D* Jan 2 1991
1992 *R* Nov 28 in Can—*D* Feb 15 1993
1995 *R* Jan 2 in Vir, into Leo Jan 23—*D* Mar 24 1995
1997 *R* Feb 6 in Lib, into Vir Mar 9—*D* Apr 27 1997
1999 *R* Mar 18 in Sco, into Lib May 6—*D* Jun 4 1999
2001 *R* May 11 in Sag—*D* Jul 19 2001
2003 *R* Jul 29 in Pis—*D* Sep 27 2003
2005 *R* Oct 2 in Tau—*D* Dec 10 2005
2007 *R* Nov 15 in Can , into Gem Jan 1 2008—*D* Jan 30 2008
2009 *R* Dec 20 in Leo—*D* Mar 10 2010

MARS EPHEMERIS

1950

Jan 1 – Mar 27	LIB
Mar 28 – Jun 10	VIR
Jun 11 – Aug 9	LIB
Aug 10 – Sep 24	SCO
Sep 25 – Nov 5	SAG
Nov 6 – Dec 14	CAP
Dec 15 – Dec 31	AQU

1951

Jan 1 – Jan 21	AQU
Jan 22 – Feb 28	PIS
Mar 1 – Apr 9	ARI
Apr 10 – May 20	TAU
May 21 – Jul 2	GEM
Jul 3 – Aug 17	CAN
Aug 18 – Oct 3	LEO
Oct 4 – Nov 23	VIR
Nov 24 – Dec 31	LIB

1952

Jan 1 – Jan 19	LIB
Jan 20 – Aug 26	SCO
Aug 27 – Oct 11	SAG
Oct 12 – Nov 20	CAP
Nov 21 – Dec 29	AQU
Dec 30 – Dec 31	PIS

1953

Jan 1 – Feb 7	PIS
Feb 8 – Mar 19	ARI
Mar 20 – Apr 30	TAU
May 1 – Jun 13	GEM
Jun 14 – Jul 29	CAN
Jul 30 – Sep 14	LEO
Sep 15 – Nov 1	VIR
Nov 2 – Dec 19	LIB
Dec 20 – Doc 31	SCO

1954

Jan 1 – Feb 8	SCO
Feb 9 – Apr 11	SAG
Apr 12 – Jul 2	CAP
Jul 3 – Aug 23	SAG
Aug 24 – Oct 20	CAP
Oct 21 – Dec 3	AQU
Dec 4 – Dec 31	PIS

1955

Jan 1 – Jan 14	PIS
Jan 15 – Feb 25	ARI
Feb 26 – Apr 9	TAU
Apr 10 – May 25	GEM
May 26 – Jul 10	CAN
Jul 11 – Aug 26	LEO
Aug 27 – Oct 12	VIR
Oct 13 – Nov 28	LIB
Nov 29 – Dec 31	SCO

1956

Jan 1 – Jan 13	SCO
Jan 14 – Feb 27	SAG
Feb 28 – Apr 13	CAP
Apr 14 – Jun 2	AQU
Jun 3 – Dec 5	PIS
Dec 6 – Dec 31	ARI

1957

Jan 1 – Jan 27	ARI
Jan 28 – Mar 16	TAU
Mar 17 – May 3	GEM
May 4 – Jun 20	CAN
Jun 21 – Aug 7	LEO
Aug 8 – Sep 23	VIR
Sep 24 – Nov 7	LIB
Nov 8 – Dec 22	SCO
Dec 23 – Dec 31	SAG

1958

Jan 1 – Feb 2	SAG
Feb 3 – Mar 16	CAP
Mar 17 – Apr 26	AQU
Apr 27 – Jun 6	PIS
Jun 7 – Jul 20	ARI
Jul 21 – Sep 20	TAU
Sep 21 – Oct 28	GEM
Oct 29 – Dec 31	TAU

1959

Jan 1 – Feb 9	TAU
Feb 10 – Apr 9	GEM
Apr 10 – May 31	CAN
Jun 1 – Jul 19	LEO
Jul 20 – Sep 4	VIR
Sep 5 – Oct 20	LIB
Oct 21 – Dec 2	SCO
Dec 3 – Dec 31	SAG

1960

Jan 1 – Jan 13	SAG
Jan 14 – Feb 22	CAP
Feb 23 – Apr 1	AQU
Apr 2 – May 10	PIS
May 11 – Jun 19	ARI
Jun 20 – Aug 1	TAU
Aug 2 – Sep 20	GEM
Sep 21 – Dec 31	CAN

1961

Jan 1 – Feb 5	CAN
Feb 6 – Feb 7	GEM
Feb 8 – May 5	CAN
May 6 – Jun 27	LEO
Jun 28 – Aug 16	VIR
Aug 17 – Sep 30	LIB
Oct 1 – Nov 12	SCO
Nov 13 – Dec 23	SAG
Dec 24 – Dec 31	CAP

1962

Jan 1 – Jan 31	CAP
Feb 1 – Mar 11	AQU
Mar 12 – Apr 18	PIS
Apr 19 – May 27	ARI
Mar 28 – Jul 8	TAU
Jul 9 – Aug 21	GEM
Aug 22 – Oct 10	CAN
Oct 1 1 – Dec 31	LEO

1963

Jan 1 – Jun 2	LEO
Jun 3 – Jul 26	VIR
Jul 27 – Sep 11	LIB
Sep 12 – Oct 24	SCO
Oct 25 – Dec 4	SAG
Dec 5 – Dec 31	CAP

1964

Jan 1 – Jan 12	CAP
Jan 13 – Feb 19	AQU
Feb 20 – Mar 28	PIS
Mar 29 – May 6	ARI
May 7 – Jun 16	TAU
Jun 17 – Jul 29	GEM
Jul 30 – Sep 14	CAN
Sep 15 – Nov 5	LEO
Nov 6 – Dec 31	VIR

1961

Jan 1 – Jun 28	VIR
Jun 29 – Aug 19	LIB
Aug 20 – Oct 3	SCO
Oct 4 – Nov 13	SAG
Nov 14 – Dec 22	CAP
Dec 23 – Dec 31	AQU

1966

Jan 1 – Jan 29	AQU
Jan 30 – Mar 8	PIS
Mar 9 – Apr 16	ARI
Apr 17 – May 27	TAU
Jul 11 – Aug 24	CAN
Aug 25 – Oct 11	LEO
Oct 12 – Dec 3	VIR
Dec 4 – Dec 31	LIB

1967

Jan 1 – Feb 11	LIB
Feb 12 – Mar 31	SCO
Apr 1 – Jul 18	LIB
Jul 19 – Sep 9	SCO
Sep 10 – Oct 22	SAG
Oct 23 – Nov 30	CAP
Dec 1 – Dec 31	AQU

1968

Jan 1 – Jan 8	AQU
Jan 9 – Feb 16	PIS
Feb 17 – Mar 26	ARI
Mar 27 – May 7	TAU
May 8 – Jun 20	GEM
Jun 21 – Aug 4	CAN
Aug 5 – Sep 20	LEO
Sep 21 – Nov 8	VIR
Nov 9 – Dec 28	LIB
Dec 29 – Dec 31	SCO

1969

Jan 1 – Feb 24	SCO
Feb 25 – Sep 20	SAG
Sep 21 – Nov 3	CAP
Nov 4 – Dec 13	AQU
Dec 14 – Dec 31	PIS

1970

Jan 1 – Jan 23	PIS
Jan 24 – Mar 6	ARI
Mar 7 – Apr 17	TAU
Apr 18 – Jun 1	GEM
Jun 2 – Jul 17	CAN
Jul 18 – Sep 2	LEO
Sep 3 – Oct 19	VIR
Oct 20 – Dec 5	LIB
Dec 6 – Dec 31	SCO

1971

Jan 1 – Jan 23	SCO
Jan 24 – Mar 12	SAG
Mar 13 – May 3	CAP
May 4 – Nov 6	AQU
Nov 7 – Dec 26	PIS
Dec 27 – Dec 31	ARI

1972

Jan 1 – Feb 10	ARI
Feb 11 – Mar 27	TAU
Mar 28 – May 12	GEM
May 13 – Jun 28	CAN
Jun 29 – Aug 15	LEO
Aug 16 – Sep 30	VIR
Oct 1 – Nov 15	LIB
Nov 16 – Dec 30	SCO
Dec 31	SAG

1973

Jan 1 – Feb 12	SAG
Feb 13 – Mar 26	CAP
Mar 27 – May 8	AQU
May 9 – Jun 20	PIS
Jun 21 – Aug 12	ARI
Aug 13 – Oct 29	TAU
Oct 30 – Dec 24	ARI
Dec 25 – Dec 31	TAU

1974

Jan 1 – Feb 27	TAU
Feb 28 – Apr 20	GEM
Apr 21 – Jun 9	CAN
Jun 10 – Jul 27	LEO
Jul 28 – Sep 12	VIR
Sep 13 – Oct 28	LIB
Oct 29 – Dec 10	SCO
Dec 11 – Dec 31	SAG

1975

Jan 1 – Jan 21	SAG
Jan 22 – Mar 3	CAP
Mar 4 – Apr 11	AQU
Apr 12 – May 21	PIS
May 22 – Jul 1	ARI
Jul 2 – Aug 14	TAU
Aug 15 – Oct 17	GEM
Oct 18 – Nov 25	CAN
Nov 26 – Dec 31	GEM

1976

Jan 1 – Mar 18	GEM
Mar 19 – May 16	CAN
May 17 – Jul 6	LEO
Jul 7 – Aug 24	VIR
Aug 25 – Oct 8	LIB
Oct 9 – Nov 20	SCO
Nov 21 – Dec 31	SAG

1977

Jan 1	SAG
Jan 2 – Feb 9	CAP
Feb 10 – Mar 20	AQU
Mar 21 – Apr 27	PIS
Apr 28 – Jun 6	ARI
Jun 7 – Jul 17	TAU
Jul 18 – Sep 1	GEM
Sep 2 – Oct 26	CAN
Oct 27 – Dec 31	LEO

1978

Jan 1 – Jan 26	LEO
Jan 27 – Apr 10	CAN
Apr 11 – Jun 14	LEO
Jun 15 – Aug 3	VIR
Aug 4 – Sep 18	LIB
Sep 19 – Nov 3	SCO
Nov 4 – Dec 12	SAG
Dec 13 – Dec 31	CAP

1979

Jan 1 – Jan 20	CAP
Jan 21 – Feb 27	AQU
Feb 28 – Apr 7	PIS
Apr 8 – May 16	ARI
May 17 – Jun 26	TAU
Jun 27 – Aug 8	GEM
Aug 9 – Sep 24	CAN
Sep 25 – Nov 19	LEO
Nov 20 – Dec 31	VIR

1980

Jan 1 – Mar 11	VIR
Mar 12 – May 4	LEO
May 5 – Jul 10	VIR
Jul 11 – Aug 29	LIB
Aug 30 – Oct 12	SCO
Oct 13 – Nov 22	SAG
Nov 23 – Dec 30	CAP
Dec 31	AQU

1981

Jan 1 – Feb 6	AQU
Feb 7 – Mar 17	PIS
Mar 18 – Apr 25	ARI
Apr 26 – Jun 5	TAU
Jun 6 – Jul 18	GEM
Jul 19 – Sep 1	CAN
Sep 2 – Oct 21	LEO
Oct 22 – Dec 16	VIR
Dec 17 – Dec 31	LIB

1982

Jan 1 – Aug 3	LIB
Aug 4 – Sep 20	SCO
Sep 21 – Oct 31	SAG
Nov 1 – Dec 10	CAP
Dec 11 – Dec 31	AQU

1983

Jan 1 – Jan 17	AQU
Jan 18 – Feb 24	PIS
Feb 25 – Apr 5	ARI
Apr 6 – May 16	TAU
May 17 – Jun 28	GEM
Jun 29 – Aug 13	CAN
Aug 14 – Sep 29	LEO
Sep 30 – Nov 17	VIR
Nov 18 – Dec 31	LIB

1984

Jan 1 – Jan 10	LIB
Jan 11 – Aug 17	SCO
Aug 18 – Oct 4	SAG
Oct 5 – Nov 15	CAP
Nov 16 – Dec 24	AQU
Dec 25 – Dec 31	PIS

1985

Jan 1 – Feb 2	PIS
Feb 2 – Mar 14	ARI
Mar 15 – Apr 25	TAU
Apr 26 – Jun 8	GEM
Jun 9 – Jul 24	CAN
Jul 25 – Sep 9	LEO
Sep 10 – Oct 27	VIR
Oct 28 – Dec 14	LIB
Dec 15 – Dec 31	SCO

1986

Jan 1 – Feb 1	SCO
Feb 2 – Mar 27	SAG
Mar 28 – Oct 8	CAP
Oct 9 – Nov 25	AQU
Nov 26 – Dec 31	PIS

1987

Jan 1 – Jan 8	PIS
Jan 9 – Feb 20	ARI
Feb 21 – Apr 5	TAU
Apr 6 – May 20	GEM
May 21 – Jul 6	CAN
Jul 7 – Aug 22	LEO
Aug 23 – Oct 8	VIR
Oct 9 – Nov 23	LIB
Nov 24 – Dec 31	SCO

1988

Jan 1 – Jan 8	SCO
Jan 9 – Feb 21	SAG
Feb 22 – Apr 6	CAP
Apr 7 – May 21	AQU
May 22 – Jul 13	PIS
Jul 14 – Oct 23	ARI
Oct 24 – Nov 1	PIS
Nov 2 – Dec 31	ARI

1989

Jan 1 – Jan 18	ARI
Jan 19 – Mar 10	TAU
Mar 11 – Apr 28	GEM
Apr 29 – Jun 16	CAN
Jun 17 – Aug 3	LEO
Aug 4 – Sep 19	VIR
Sep 20 – Nov 3	LIB
Nov 4 – Dec 17	SCO
Dec 18 – Dec 31	SAG

1990

Jan 1 – Jan 29	SAG
Jan 30 – Mar 11	CAP
Mar 12 – Apr 20	AQU
Apr 21 – May 30	PIS
May 31 – Jul 12	ARI
Jul 13 – Aug 30	TAU
Aug 31 – Dec 13	GEM
Dec 14 – Dec 31	TAU

1991

Jan 1 – Jan 20	TAU
Jan 21 – Apr 2	GEM
Apr 3 – May 26	CAN
May 27 – Jul 15	LEO
Jul 16 – Aug 31	VIR
Sep 1 – Oct 16	LIB
Oct 17 – Nov 28	SCO
Nov 29 – Dec 31	SAG

1992

Jan 1 – Jan 8	SAG
Jan 9 – Feb 17	CAP
Feb 18 – Mar 27	AQU
Mar 28 – May 5	PIS
May 6 – Jun 14	ARI
Jun 15 – Jul 26	TAU
Jul 27 – Sep 11	GEM
Sep 12 – Dec 31	CAN

1993

Jan 1 – Apr 27	CAN
Apr 28 – Jun 22	LEO
Jun 23 – Aug 11	VIR
Aug 12 – Sep 26	LIB
Sep 27 – Nov 8	SCO
Nov 9 – Dec 19	SAG
Dec 20 – Dec 31	CAP

1994

Jan 1 – Jan 27	CAP
Jan 28 – Mar 6	AQU
Mar 7 – Apr 14	PIS
Apr 15 – May 23	ARI
May 24 – Jul 3	TAU
Jul 4 – Aug 16	GEM
Aug 17 – Oct 4	CAN
Oct 5 – Dec 11	LEO
Dec 12 – Dec 31	VIR

1995

Jan 1 – Jan 22	VIR
Jan 23 – Mar 25	LEO
Mar 26 – Jul 20	VIR
Jul 21 – Sep 6	LIB
Sep 7 – Oct 20	SCO
Oct 21 – Nov 30	SAG
Dec 1 – Dec 31	CAP

1996

Jan 1 – Jan 7	CAP
Jan 8 – Feb 14	AQU
Feb 15 – Mar 24	PIS
Mar 25 – May 2	ARI
May 3 – Jun 12	TAU
Jun 13 – Jul 25	GEM
Jul 26 – Sep 9	CAN
Sep 10 – Oct 29	LEO
Oct 30 – Dec 31	VIR

1997

Jan 1 – Jan 2	VIR
Jan 3 – Mar 8	LIB
Mar 9 – Jun 18	VIR
Jun 19 – Aug 13	LIB
Aug 14 – Sep 28	SCO
Sep 29 – Nov 8	SAG
Nov 9 – Dec 17	CAP
Dec 18 – Dec 31	AQU

1998

Jan 1 – Jan 24	AQU
Jan 25 – Mar 4	PIS
Mar 5 – Apr 12	ARI
Apr 13 – May 23	TAU
May 24 – Jul 5	GEM
Jul 6 – Aug 20	CAN
Aug 21 – Oct 7	LEO
Oct 8 – Nov 26	VIR
Nov 27 – Dec 31	LIB

1999

Jan 1 – Jan 25	LIB
Jan 26 – May 5	SCO
May 6 – Jul 4	LIB
Jul 5 – Sep 2	SCO
Sep 3 – Oct 16	SAG
Oct 17 – Nov 25	CAP
Nov 26 – Dec 31	AQU

2000

Jan 1 – Jan 3	AQU
Jan 4 – Feb 11	PIS
Feb 12 – Mar 22	ARI
Mar 23 – May 3	TAU
May 4 – Jun 16	GEM
Jun 17 – Jul 31	CAN
Aug 1 – Sep 16	LEO
Sep 17 – Nov 3	VIR
Nov 4 – Dec 23	LIB
Dec 24 – Dec 31	SCO

2001

Jan 1 – Feb 13	SCO
Feb 14 – Sep 7	SAG
Sep 8 – Oct 26	CAP
Oct 27 – Dec 7	AQU
Dec 8 – Dec 31	PIS

2002

Jan 1 – Jan 17	PIS
Jan 18 – Feb 28	ARI
Mar 1 – Apr 12	TAU
Apr 13 – May 27	GEM
May 28 – Jul 12	CAN
Jul 13 – Aug 28	LEO
Aug 29 – Oct 14	VIR
Oct 15 – Nov 30	LIB
Dec 1 – Dec 31	SCO

2003

Jan 1 – Jan 15	SCO
Jan 16 – Mar 3	SAG
Mar 4 – Apr 20	CAP
Apr 21 – Jun 15	AQU
Jun 16 – Dec 15	PIS
Dec 16 – Dec 31	ARI

2004

Jan 1 – Feb 2	ARI
Feb 3 – Mar 20	TAU
Mar 21 – May 6	GEM
May 7 – Jun 22	CAN
Jun 23 – Aug 9	LEO
Aug 10 – Sep 25	VIR
Sep 26 – Nov 9	LIB
Nov 10 – Dec 24	SCO
Dec 25 – Dec 31	SAG

2005

Jan 1 – Feb 5	SAG
Feb 6 – Mar 19	CAP
Mar 20 – Apr 29	AQU
Apr 30 – Jun 10	PIS
Jun 11 – Jul 26	ARI
Jul 27 – Dec 31	TAU

2006

Jan 1 – Feb 16	TAU
Feb 17 – Apr 12	GEM
Apr 13 – Jun 2	CAN
Jun 3 – Jul 21	LEO
Jul 22 – Sep 6	VIR
Sep 7 – Oct 22	LIB
Oct 23 – Dec 4	SCO
Dec 5 – Dec 31	SAG

2007

Jan 1 – Jan 15	SAG
Jan 16 – Feb 24	CAP
Feb 25 – Apr 5	AQU
Apr 6 – May 14	PIS
May 15 – Jun 23	ARI
Jun 24 – Aug 6	TAU
Aug 7 – Sep 27	GEM
Sep 28 – Dec 30	CAN
Dec 31 – Dec 31	GEM

2008

Jan 1 – Mar 3	GEM
Mar 4 – May 8	CAN
May 9 – Jun 30	LEO
Jul 1 – Aug 18	VIR
Aug 19 – Oct 2	LIB
Oct 3 – Nov 15	SCO
Nov 16 – Dec 26	SAG
Dec 27 – Dec 31	CAP

2009

Jan 1 – Feb 3	CAP
Feb 4 – Mar 13	PIS
Mar 14 – May 30	ARI
May 31 – Jul 10	TAU
Jul 11 – Aug 24	GEM
Aug 25 – Oct 15	CAN
Oct 16 – Dec 31	LEO

2010

Jan 1 – Jun 6	LEO
Jun 7 – Jul 28	VIR
Jul 29 – Sep 13	LIB
Sep 14 – Oct 27	SCO
Oct 28 – Dec 6	SAG
Dec 7 – Dec 31	CAP

INGRESSES

Because the Planets beyond Mars move so slowly, the following tables will give only the date that the Planet moves into a particular sign. As these tables use the glyph system, please refer to the following conversion table. An **R** following the glyph entry indicates retrograde.

Glyph	Sign
♈	Aries
♉	Taurus
♊	Gemini
♋	Cancer
♌	Leo
♍	Virgo
♎	Libra
♏	Scorpio
♐	Sagittarius
♑	Capricorn
♒	Aquarius
♓	Pisces

Jupiter Ingress

1950	APR	15	♓		1967	JAN	15	♋	R	1984	JAN	19	♑
1950	SEP	14	♒	R	1967	MAY	23	♌		1985	FEB	6	♒
1950	DEC	1	♓		1967	OCT	19	♍		1986	FEB	20	♓
1951	APR	21	♈		1968	FEB	26	♌	R	1987	MAR	2	♈
1952	APR	28	♉		1968	JUN	15	♍		1988	MAR	8	♉
1953	MAY	9	♊		1968	NOV	15	♎		1988	JUL	21	♊
1954	MAY	23	♋		1969	MAR	30	♍	R	1988	NOV	30	♉ R
1955	JUN	12	♌		1969	JUL	15	♎		1989	MAR	10	♊
1955	NOV	16	♍		1969	DEC	16	♏		1989	JUL	30	♋
1956	JAN	17	♌ R		1970	APR	30	♎	R	1990	AUG	18	♌
1956	JUL	7	♍		1970	AUG	15	♏		1991	SEP	12	♍
1956	DEC	12	♎		1971	JAN	14	♐		1992	OCT	10	♎
1957	FEB	19	♍ R		1971	JUN	4	♏	R	1993	NOV	10	♏
1957	AUG	6	♎		1971	SEP	11	♐		1994	DEC	9	♐
1958	JAN	13	♏		1972	FEB	6	♑		1996	JAN	3	♑
1958	MAR	20	♎ R		1972	JUL	24	♐	R	1997	JAN	21	♒
1958	SEP	7	♏		1972	SEP	25	♑		1998	FEB	4	♓
1959	FEB	10	♐		1973	FEB	23	♒		1999	FEB	12	♈
1959	APR	24	♏ R		1974	MAR	8	♓		1999	JUN	28	♉
1959	OCT	5	♐		1975	MAR	18	♈		1999	OCT	23	♈ R
1960	MAR	1	♑		1976	MAR	26	♉		2000	FEB	14	♉
1960	JUN	9	♐ R		1976	AUG	23	♊		2000	JUN	30	♊
1960	OCT	25	♑		1976	OCT	16	♉		2001	JUL	14	♋
1961	MAR	15	♒		1977	APR	3	♊		2002	AUG	2	♌
1961	AUG	12	♑ R		1977	AUG	20	♋		2003	AUG	28	♍
1961	NOV	3	♒		1977	DEC	30	♊	R	2004	SEP	26	♎
1962	MAR	25	♓		1978	APR	11	♋		2005	OCT	27	♏
1963	APR	3	♈		1978	SEP	5	♌		2006	NOV	25	♐
1964	APR	12	♉		1979	FEB	28	♋	R	2007	DEC	19	♑
1965	APR	22	♊		1979	APR	20	♌		2009	JAN	6	♒
1965	SEP	20	♋		1979	SEP	29	♍		2010	JAN	19	♓
1965	NOV	16	♊ R		1980	OCT	27	♎		2010	JUN	7	♈
1966	MAY	5	♋		1981	NOV	26	♏		2010	SEP	10	♓
1966	SEP	27	♌		1982	DEC	25	♐					

Saturn Ingress

1950	NOV	20	♎		1973	AUG	1	♋		1991	FEB	6	♒
1951	MAR	7	♍ R		1974	JAN	7	♊	R	1993	MAY	21	♓
1951	AUG	13	♎		1974	APR	18	♋		1993	JUN	30	♒ R
1953	OCT	22	♏		1975	SEP	17	♌		1994	JAN	28	♓
1956	JAN	12	♐		1976	JAN	14	♋		1996	APR	7	♈
1956	MAY	13	♏ R		1976	JUN	5	♌		1998	JUN	9	♉
1956	OCT	10	♐		1977	NOV	16	♍		1998	OCT	25	♈ R
1959	JAN	5	♑		1978	JAN	4	♌		1999	FEB	28	♉
1962	JAN	3	♒		1978	JUL	26	♍		2000	AUG	9	♊
1964	MAR	23	♓		1980	SEP	21	♎		2000	OCT	15	♉ R
1964	SEP	16	♒		1982	NOV	29	♏		2001	APR	21	♊
1964	DEC	16	♓		1983	MAY	6	♎		2003	JUN	5	♋
1967	MAR	3	♈		1983	AUG	24	♏		2005	JUL	17	♌
1969	APR	29	♉		1985	NOV	16	♐		2007	SEP	3	♍
1971	JUN	18	♊		1988	FEB	13	♑		2009	OCT	30	♎
1972	JAN	9	♉ R		1988	JUN	10	♐	R	2010	APR	8	♍
1972	FEB	21	♊		1988	NOV	12	♑		2010	JUL	22	♎

Uranus Ingress

1949	JUN	9	♋		1969	JUN	24	♎		1988	DEC	2	♑
1955	AUG	24	♌		1974	NOV	21	♏		1995	APR	1	♒
1956	JAN	27	♋ R		1975	MAY	1	♎ R		1995	JUN	8	♑ R
1956	JUN	9	♌		1975	SEP	8	♏		1996	JAN	12	♒
1961	NOV	1	♍		1981	FEB	17	♐		2003	MAR	11	♓
1962	JAN	10	♌ R		1981	MAR	20	♏ R		2003	SEP	16	♒
1962	AUG	9	♋		1981	NOV	16	♐		2003	DEC	31	♓
1968	SEP	28	♎		1988	FEB	14	♑		2010	MAY	29	♈
1969	MAY	20	♍ R		1988	MAY	26	♐		2010	AUG	15	♓

Neptune Ingress

1943	AUG	2	♎		1970	JAN	4	♐		1984	NOV	21	♑
1955	DEC	24	♏		1970	MAY	2	♑ R		1998	JAN	28	♒
1956	MAR	11	♎ R		1970	NOV	6	♐		1998	AUG	22	♑ R
1956	OCT	19	♏		1964	MAR	23	♓		1998 ⎱	None		
1957	JUN	15	♎ R		1984	JAN	18	♑		2010 ⎰			
1957	AUG	6	♏		1984	JUN	22	♐ R					

Pluto Ingress

1939	JUN	13	♌		1971	OCT	5	♎		1995	JAN	17	♐
1956	OCT	20	♍		1972	APR	17	♍ R		1995	APR	20	♏ R
1957	JAN	14	♌ R		1972	JUL	30	♎		1995	NOV	10	♐
1957	AUG	18	♍		1983	AUG	18	♍		2008	JAN	27	♑
1958	APR	11	♌ R		1984	APR	11	♌ R		2008	JUN	15	♐
1958	JUN	10	♍		1984	AUG	28	♏		2008	NOV	28	♑

HOW TO FIND THE ASCENDANT SIGN

Find the birth date in the following tables. The tables are calculated for 41° N, the median latitude for the United States and Europe. If birth was in either the northern or southern extremities, you will need either a computer chart or a professional to calculate the Ascendant accurately (see Appendix III for further information).

Though the Ascendant Sign changes approximately every two hours daily, it does not vary from year to year. So, no matter the year of birth, determine the Ascendant only from the day and month of birth. If you were born before the half-hour, pick the preceding hour (for example, if you were born at 3:12 A.M., choose 3:00 A.M.). If after the half-hour, choose the following hour.

Since there is little variation from day to day within the three-day periods listed, it is necessary only to pay attention to the exact degree given in the listing when birth date falls in the unlisted intermediate date. (This book is concerned only with the ASC sign, not the precise degree, therefore you need only know the sign for your ASC.)

If birth date is not listed, check the dates on either side. The degrees run from 0 to 29. If the sign is changing over the three-day period in which your birthday falls — that is, if it is in a late degree on one side and an early degree on the other side — you can estimate the ASC sign by adding 2 degrees to the degree of the sign on the day before your birthday. It is also a good idea to read both scripts of the two signs involved.

If estimated degree is either 0 or 29, only a professional astrologer or a computer chart can tell you for sure which is your ASC sign (see Appendix III).

JANUARY 1

AM		PM	
1	21 LIB	1	13 TAU
2	3 SCO	2	3 GEM
3	14 SCO	3	19 GEM
4	24 SCO	4	4 CAN
5	8 SAG	5	17 CAN
6	21 SAG	6	29 CAN
7	4 CAP	7	10 LEO
8	19 CAP	8	22 LEO
9	7 AQU	9	3 VIR
10	28 AQU	10	16 VIR
11	23 PIS	11	28 LIB
12 noon	19 TAU	12 midnight	10 LIB

JANUARY 4

AM		PM	
1	23 LIB	1	17 TAU
2	5 SCO	2	6 GEM
3	16 SCO	3	22 GEM
4	28 SCO	4	6 CAN
5	11 SAG	5	19 CAN
6	23 SAG	6	1 LEO
7	7 CAP	7	13 LEO
8	22 CAP	8	24 LEO
9	11 AQU	9	6 VIR
10	3 PIS	10	18 VIR
11	29 ARI	11	29 VIR
12 noon	25 ARI	12 midnight	12 LIB

JANUARY 7

AM		PM	
1	25 LIB	1	22 TAU
2	7 SCO	2	9 GEM
3	18 SCO	3	25 GEM
4	29 SCO	4	9 CAN
5	12 SAG	5	21 CAN
6	26 SAG	6	3 LEO
7	10 CAP	7	15 LEO
8	25 CAP	8	26 LEO
9	15 AQU	9	8 VIR
10	7 PIS	10	20 VIR
11	4 ARI	11	2 LIB
12 noon	29 ARI	12 midnight	14 LIB

JANUARY 10

AM		PM	
1	28 LIB	1	25 TAU
2	9 SCO	2	12 GEM
3	21 SCO	3	28 GEM
4	3 SAG	4	11 CAN
5	15 SAG	5	23 CAN
6	28 SAG	6	5 LEO
7	13 CAP	7	17 LEO
8	29 CAP	8	29 LEO
9	20 AQU	9	11 VIR
10	14 PIS	10	23 VIR
11	9 ARI	11	4 LIB
12 noon	3 TAU	12 midnight	16 LIB

JANUARY 13

AM		PM	
1	29 LIB	1	29 TAU
2	12 SCO	2	15 GEM
3	24 SCO	3	29 GEM
4	5 SAG	4	13 CAN
5	18 SAG	5	26 CAN
6	1 CAP	6	8 LEO
7	16 CAP	7	19 LEO
8	3 AQU	8	1 VIR
9	23 AQU	9	13 VIR
10	18 PIS	10	24 VIR
11	14 ARI	11	7 LIB
12 noon	8 TAU	12 midnight	18 LIB

JANUARY 16

AM		PM	
1	2 SCO	1	2 GEM
2	14 SCO	2	18 GEM
3	26 SCO	3	3 CAN
4	8 SAG	4	16 CAN
5	20 SAG	5	28 CAN
6	3 CAP	6	10 LEO
7	19 CAP	7	22 LEO
8	7 AQU	8	3 VIR
9	28 AQU	9	15 VIR
10	23 PIS	10	27 VIR
11	19 ARI	11	9 LIB
12 noon	13 TAU	12 midnight	21 LIB

JANUARY 19

AM		PM	
1	5 SCO	1	6 GEM
2	16 SCO	2	21 GEM
3	28 SCO	3	6 CAN
4	10 SAG	4	18 CAN
5	23 SAG	5	1 LEO
6	7 CAP	6	13 LEO
7	22 CAP	7	24 LEO
8	11 AQU	8	6 VIR
9	3 PIS	9	18 VIR
10	29 PIS	10	29 VIR
11	24 ARI	11	12 LIB
12 noon	17 TAU	12 midnight	23 LIB

JANUARY 22

AM		PM	
1	7 SCO	1	9 GEM
2	19 SCO	2	24 GEM
3	29 SCO	3	8 CAN
4	13 SAG	4	21 CAN
5	26 SAG	5	3 LEO
6	10 CAP	6	15 LEO
7	25 CAP	7	26 LEO
8	15 AQU	8	8 VIR
9	8 PIS	9	20 VIR
10	4 ARI	10	1 LIB
11	28 ARI	11	13 LIB
12 noon	20 TAU	12 midnight	25 LIB

JANUARY 25

AM			PM		
1	9	SCO	1	12	GEM
2	21	SCO	2	28	GEM
3	3	SAG	3	11	CAN
4	15	SAG	4	23	CAN
5	28	SAG	5	5	LEO
6	13	CAP	6	17	LEO
7	29	CAP	7	29	LEO
8	19	AQU	8	10	VIR
9	13	PIS	9	22	VIR
10	8	ARI	10	4	LIB
11	3	TAU	11	16	LIB
12 noon	24	TAU	12 midnight	28	LIB

JANUARY 28

AM			PM		
1	12	SCO	1	15	GEM
2	24	SCO	2	29	GEM
3	5	SAG	3	13	CAN
4	18	SAG	4	26	CAN
5	1	CAP	5	7	LEO
6	16	CAP	6	19	LEO
7	3	AQU	7	1	VIR
8	23	AQU	8	13	VIR
9	17	PIS	9	24	VIR
10	14	ARI	10	7	LIB
11	8	TAU	11	18	LIB
12 noon	28	TAU	12 midnight	29	LIB

JANUARY 31

AM			PM		
1	14	SCO	1	18	GEM
2	26	SCO	2	3	CAN
3	8	SAG	3	16	CAN
4	20	SAG	4	28	CAN
5	3	CAP	5	10	LEO
6	19	CAP	6	22	LEO
7	7	AQU	7	3	VIR
8	28	AQU	8	15	VIR
9	23	PIS	9	27	VIR
10	19	ARI	10	9	LIB
11	13	TAU	11	21	LIB
12 noon	2	GEM	12 midnight	2	SCO

FEBRUARY 3

AM			PM		
1	16	SCO	1	21	GEM
2	28	SCO	2	6	CAN
3	10	SAG	3	18	CAN
4	22	SAG	4	1	LEO
5	6	CAP	5	13	LEO
6	22	CAP	6	24	LEO
7	11	AQU	7	6	VIR
8	3	PIS	8	18	VIR
9	29	PIS	9	29	VIR
10	23	ARI	10	12	LIB
11	16	TAU	11	23	LIB
12 noon	6	GEM	12 midnight	5	SCO

FEBRUARY 6

AM			PM		
1	18	SCO	1	24	GEM
2	29	SCO	2	8	CAN
3	12	SAG	3	21	CAN
4	26	SAG	4	3	LEO
5	9	CAP	5	15	LEO
6	25	CAP	6	26	LEO
7	14	AQU	7	8	VIR
8	6	PIS	8	20	VIR
9	2	ARI	9	2	LIB
10	28	ARI	10	14	LIB
11	20	TAU	11	26	LIB
12 noon	9	GEM	12 midnight	7	SCO

FEBRUARY 9

AM			PM		
1	21	SCO	1	27	GEM
2	3	SAG	2	10	CAN
3	14	SAG	3	23	CAN
4	28	SAG	4	5	LEO
5	12	CAP	5	17	LEO
6	29	CAP	6	29	LEO
7	18	AQU	7	11	VIR
8	23	AQU	8	23	VIR
9	12	PIS	9	4	VIR
10	3	TAU	10	16	LIB
11	24	TAU	11	28	LIB
12 noon	12	GEM	12 midnight	9	SCO

FEBRUARY 12

AM			PM		
1	23	SCO	1	29	GEM
2	5	SAG	2	13	CAN
3	17	SAG	3	26	CAN
4	1	CAP	4	8	LEO
5	15	CAP	5	19	LEO
6	2	AQU	6	1	VIR
7	23	AQU	7	13	VIR
8	17	PIS	8	24	VIR
9	14	ARI	9	7	LIB
10	8	TAU	10	18	LIB
11	28	TAU	11	29	LIB
12 noon	15	GEM	12 midnight	12	SCO

FEBRUARY 15

AM			PM		
1	25	SCO	1	3	CAN
2	7	SAG	2	16	CAN
3	20	SAG	3	28	CAN
4	3	CAP	4	10	LEO
5	18	CAP	5	22	LEO
6	5	AQU	6	3	VIR
7	28	AQU	7	15	VIR
8	23	PIS	8	27	VIR
9	17	PIS	9	9	LIB
10	11	TAU	10	21	LIB
11	2	GEM	11	2	SCO
12 noon	18	GEM	12 midnight	14	SCO

FEBRUARY 18

AM			PM		
1	27	SCO	1	6	CAN
2	10	SAG	2	18	CAN
3	22	SAG	3	1	LEO
4	6	CAP	4	13	LEO
5	21	CAP	5	24	LEO
6	9	AQU	6	6	VIR
7	1	PIS	7	18	VIR
8	27	PIS	8	29	VIR
9	23	ARI	9	12	LIB
10	16	TAU	10	23	LIB
11	6	GEM	11	5	SCO
12 noon	21	GEM	12 midnight	17	SCO

FEBRUARY 21

AM			PM		
1	29	SCO	1	8	CAN
2	12	SAG	2	22	CAN
3	25	SAG	3	2	LEO
4	9	CAP	4	13	LEO
5	24	CAP	5	26	LEO
6	14	AQU	6	8	VIR
7	6	PIS	7	20	VIR
8	2	ARI	8	1	LIB
9	28	ARI	9	13	VIR
10	20	TAU	10	24	LIB
11	9	GEM	11	6	SCO
12 noon	24	GEM	12 midnight	18	SCO

FEBRUARY 24

AM			PM		
1	3	SAG	1	10	CAN
2	14	SAG	2	23	CAN
3	27	SAG	3	5	LEO
4	12	CAP	4	17	CAN
5	28	CAP	5	29	LEO
6	16	AQU	6	10	LEO
7	10	PIS	7	22	VIR
8	9	ARI	8	4	LIB
9	5	TAU	9	16	LIB
10	27	TAU	10	24	LIB
11	12	GEM	11	9	SCO
12 noon	27	GEM	12 midnight	21	SCO

FEBRUARY 27

AM			PM		
1	5	SAG	1	13	CAN
2	17	SAG	2	23	CAN
3	1	CAP	3	7	LEO
4	15	CAP	4	19	LEO
5	2	AQU	5	1	VIR
6	22	AQU	6	13	VIR
7	16	PIS	7	24	VIR
8	12	ARI	8	7	LIB
9	7	TAU	9	18	LIB
10	28	TAU	10	29	LIB
11	15	GEM	11	12	SCO
12 noon	29	GEM	12 midnight	24	SCO

MARCH 2

AM			PM		
1	7	SAG	1	16	CAN
2	20	SAG	2	28	CAN
3	3	CAP	3	10	LEO
4	18	CAP	4	22	LEO
5	5	AQU	5	3	VIR
6	26	AQU	6	15	VIR
7	21	PIS	7	27	VIR
8	17	ARI	8	9	LIB
9	11	TAU	9	21	LIB
10	2	GEM	10	2	SCO
11	18	GEM	11	14	SCO
12 noon	2	CAN	12 midnight	26	SCO

MARCH 5

AM			PM		
1	9	SAG	1	18	CAN
2	22	SAG	2	29	CAN
3	6	CAP	3	12	LEO
4	22	CAP	4	24	LEO
5	9	AQU	5	5	VIR
6	1	PIS	6	18	VIR
7	27	PIS	7	29	VIR
8	23	ARI	8	11	LIB
9	16	TAU	9	23	LIB
10	4	GEM	10	5	SCO
11	21	GEM	11	16	SCO
12 noon	6	CAN	12 midnight	28	SCO

MARCH 8

AM			PM		
1	12	SAG	1	20	CAN
2	25	SAG	2	2	LEO
3	9	CAP	3	14	LEO
4	24	CAP	4	26	LEO
5	14	AQU	5	8	VIR
6	6	PIS	6	19	VIR
7	2	ARI	7	1	LIB
8	28	ARI	8	13	LIB
9	20	TAU	9	25	LIB
10	8	GEM	10	7	SCO
11	24	GEM	11	18	SCO
12 noon	8	CAN	12 midnight	29	SCO

MARCH 11

AM			PM		
1	14	SAG	1	23	CAN
2	27	SAG	2	5	LEO
3	12	CAP	3	16	LEO
4	28	CAP	4	29	LEO
5	18	AQU	5	10	VIR
6	12	PIS	6	22	VIR
7	6	ARI	7	4	LIB
8	2	TAU	8	16	LIB
9	24	TAU	9	28	LIB
10	11	GEM	10	9	SCO
11	27	GEM	11	21	SCO
12 noon	10	CAN	12 midnight	3	SAG

MARCH 14

AM			PM		
1	17	SAG	1	25	CAN
2	29	SAG	2	7	LEO
3	15	CAP	3	19	LEO
4	2	AQU	4	29	LEO
5	21	AQU	5	13	VIR
6	15	PIS	6	24	VIR
7	12	ARI	7	7	LIB
8	7	TAU	8	18	LIB
9	27	TAU	9	29	LIB
10	14	GEM	10	12	SCO
11	29	GEM	11	24	SCO
12 noon	13	CAN	12 midnight	5	SAG

MARCH 17

AM			PM		
1	19	SAG	1	28	CAN
2	2	CAP	2	10	LEO
3	18	CAP	3	21	LEO
4	5	AQU	4	3	VIR
5	26	AQU	5	15	VIR
6	21	PIS	6	26	VIR
7	17	ARI	7	8	LIB
8	11	TAU	8	20	LIB
9	1	GEM	9	2	SCO
10	17	GEM	10	14	SCO
11	2	CAN	11	26	SCO
12 noon	15	CAN	12 midnight	8	SAG

MARCH 20

AM			PM		
1	21	SAG	1	29	CAN
2	5	CAP	2	12	LEO
3	21	CAP	3	23	LEO
4	8	AQU	4	5	VIR
5	1	PIS	5	17	VIR
6	27	PIS	6	29	VIR
7	22	ARI	7	11	LIB
8	16	TAU	8	23	LIB
9	4	GEM	9	5	SCO
10	20	GEM	10	16	SCO
11	5	CAN	11	28	SCO
12 noon	18	CAN	12 midnight	10	SAG

MARCH 23

AM			PM		
1	24	SAG	1	2	LEO
2	8	CAP	2	14	LEO
3	24	CAP	3	26	LEO
4	12	AQU	4	8	VIR
5	5	PIS	5	19	VIR
6	1	ARI	6	1	LIB
7	26	ARI	7	13	LIB
8	19	TAU	8	24	LIB
9	8	GEM	9	7	SCO
10	23	GEM	10	18	SCO
11	7	CAN	11	29	SCO
12 noon	20	CAN	12 midnight	12	SAG

MARCH 26

AM			PM		
1	27	SAG	1	4	LEO
2	12	CAP	2	16	LEO
3	28	CAP	3	28	LEO
4	17	AQU	4	10	VIR
5	10	PIS	5	22	VIR
6	6	ARI	6	4	LIB
7	2	TAU	7	16	LIB
8	23	TAU	8	28	LIB
9	11	GEM	9	9	SCO
10	26	GEM	10	21	SCO
11	10	CAN	11	3	SAG
12 noon	23	CAN	12 midnight	15	SAG

MARCH 29

AM			PM		
1	29	SAG	1	7	LEO
2	15	CAP	2	19	LEO
3	2	AQU	3	29	LEO
4	21	AQU	4	13	VIR
5	15	PIS	5	24	VIR
6	12	ARI	6	6	LIB
7	7	TAU	7	18	LIB
8	27	TAU	8	29	LIB
9	14	GEM	9	12	SCO
10	29	GEM	10	23	SCO
11	13	CAN	11	5	SAG
12 noon	25	CAN	12 midnight	18	SAG

APRIL 1

AM			PM		
1	2	CAP	1	10	LEO
2	18	CAP	2	21	LEO
3	5	AQU	3	3	VIR
4	26	AQU	4	14	VIR
5	21	PIS	5	26	VIR
6	17	ARI	6	8	LIB
7	11	TAU	7	20	LIB
8	1	GEM	8	2	SCO
9	17	GEM	9	14	SCO
10	2	CAN	10	25	SCO
11	15	CAN	11	8	SAG
12 noon	27	CAN	12 midnight	20	SAG

APRIL 4

AM			PM		
1	5	CAP	1	12	LEO
2	21	CAP	2	23	LEO
3	9	AQU	3	5	VIR
4	1	PIS	4	17	VIR
5	26	PIS	5	29	VIR
6	21	ARI	6	11	LIB
7	14	TAU	7	23	LIB
8	4	GEM	8	4	SCO
9	20	GEM	9	15	SCO
10	5	CAN	10	28	SCO
11	17	CAN	11	10	SAG
12 noon	29	CAN	12 midnight	22	SAG

APRIL 7

AM			PM		
1	8	CAP	1	14	LEO
2	24	CAP	2	26	LEO
3	12	AQU	3	8	VIR
4	5	PIS	4	19	VIR
5	1	ARI	5	1	LIB
6	26	ARI	6	13	LIB
7	19	TAU	7	25	LIB
8	8	GEM	8	6	SCO
9	23	GEM	9	18	SCO
10	7	CAN	10	29	SCO
11	20	CAN	11	12	SAG
12 noon	2	LEO	12 midnight	25	SAG

APRIL 10

AM			PM		
1	11	CAP	1	16	LEO
2	28	CAP	2	28	LEO
3	17	AQU	3	9	VIR
4	10	PIS	4	22	VIR
5	6	ARI	5	3	LIB
6	2	TAU	6	15	LIB
7	23	TAU	7	27	LIB
8	11	GEM	8	9	SCO
9	26	GEM	9	21	SCO
10	10	CAN	10	3	SAG
11	23	CAN	11	14	SAG
12 noon	4	LEO	12 midnight	27	SAG

APRIL 13

AM			PM		
1	14	CAP	1	19	LEO
2	29	CAP	2	29	LEO
3	21	AQU	3	12	VIR
4	15	PIS	4	24	VIR
5	12	ARI	5	6	LIB
6	7	TAU	6	18	LIB
7	27	TAU	7	29	LIB
8	14	GEM	8	12	SCO
9	29	GEM	9	23	SCO
10	13	CAN	10	5	SAG
11	25	CAN	11	17	SAG
12 noon	7	LEO	12 midnight	1	CAP

APRIL 16

AM			PM		
1	17	CAP	1	21	LEO
2	4	AQU	2	3	VIR
3	26	AQU	3	14	VIR
4	20	PIS	4	26	VIR
5	16	ARI	5	8	LIB
6	10	TAU	6	20	LIB
7	1	GEM	7	2	SCO
8	17	GEM	8	13	SCO
9	1	CAN	9	25	SCO
10	15	CAN	10	7	SAG
11	27	CAN	11	20	SAG
12 noon	9	LEO	12 midnight	3	CAP

APRIL 19

AM			PM		
1	20	CAP	1	23	LEO
2	8	AQU	2	5	VIR
3	29	AQU	3	17	VIR
4	25	PIS	4	29	VIR
5	21	ARI	5	11	LIB
6	14	TAU	6	23	LIB
7	4	GEM	7	4	SCO
8	20	GEM	8	15	SCO
9	5	CAN	9	28	SCO
l0	17	CAN	10	10	SAG
11	29	CAN	11	22	SAG
12 noon	11	LEO	12 midnight	10	CAP

APRIL 22

AM			PM		
1	24	CAP	1	26	LEO
2	14	AQU	2	7	VIR
3	5	PIS	3	19	VIR
4	1	ARI	4	1	LIB
5	26	ARI	5	13	LIB
6	19	TAU	6	24	LIB
7	8	GEM	7	6	SCO
8	23	GEM	8	18	SCO
9	7	CAN	9	29	SCO
11	20	CAN	10	13	SAG
11	2	LEO	11	25	SAG
12 noon	14	LEO	12 midnight	9	CAP

APRIL 25

AM			PM		
1	27	CAP	1	28	LEO
2	17	AQU	2	9	VIR
3	10	PIS	3	21	VIR
4	6	ARI	4	3	LIB
5	2	TAU	5	15	LIB
6	23	TAU	6	27	LIB
7	11	GEM	7	9	SCO
8	26	GEM	8	20	SCO
9	10	CAN	9	3	SAG
10	22	CAN	10	14	SAG
11	4	LEO	11	27	SAG
12 noon	16	LEO	12 midnight	12	CAP

APRIL 28

AM			PM		
1	2	AQU	1	29	LEO
2	21	AQU	2	12	VIR
3	15	PIS	3	24	VIR
4	10	ARI	4	6	LIB
5	5	TAU	5	18	LIB
6	27	TAU	6	29	LIB
7	14	GEM	7	11	SCO
8	29	GEM	8	23	SCO
9	12	CAN	9	5	SAG
10	25	CAN	10	17	SAG
11	7	LEO	11	29	SAG
12 noon	19	LEO	12 midnight	15	CAP

MAY 1

AM			PM		
1	4	AQU	1	3	VIR
2	24	AQU	2	14	VIR
3	19	PIS	3	26	VIR
4	16	ARI	4	8	LIB
5	10	TAU	5	20	LIB
6	29	TAU	6	2	SCO
7	17	GEM	7	13	SCO
8	1	CAN	8	25	SCO
9	15	CAN	9	7	SAG
10	27	CAN	10	19	SAG
11	9	LEO	11	3	CAP
12 noon	21	LEO	12 midnight	18	CAP

MAY 4

AM			PM		
1	8	AQU	1	4	VIR
2	29	AQU	2	17	VIR
3	25	PIS	3	28	VIR
4	21	ARI	4	10	LIB
5	14	TAU	5	22	LIB
6	3	GEM	6	4	SCO
7	20	GEM	7	15	SCO
8	5	CAN	8	27	SCO
9	17	CAN	9	9	SAG
10	29	CAN	10	21	SAG
11	11	LEO	11	5	CAP
12 noon	23	LEO	12 midnight	21	CAP

MAY 7

AM			PM		
1	21	AQU	1	7	VIR
2	5	PIS	2	18	VIR
3	1	ARI	3	1	LIB
4	26	ARI	4	13	LIB
5	19	TAU	5	24	LIB
6	7	GEM	6	6	SCO
7	23	GEM	7	18	SCO
8	7	CAN	8	29	SCO
9	20	CAN	9	12	SAG
10	1	LEO	10	25	SAG
11	13	LEO	11	9	CAP
12 noon	25	LEO	12 midnight	24	CAP

MAY 10

AM			PM		
1	16	AQU	1	9	VIR
2	9	PIS	2	21	VIR
3	4	ARI	3	3	LIB
4	29	ARI	4	15	LIB
5	23	TAU	5	27	LIB
6	10	GEM	6	9	SCO
7	26	GEM	7	20	SCO
8	10	CAN	8	2	SAG
9	22	CAN	9	14	SAG
10	4	LEO	10	27	SAG
11	16	LEO	11	11	CAP
12 noon	27	LEO	12 midnight	28	CAP

MAY 13

AM			PM		
1	20	AQU	1	12	VIR
2	14	PIS	2	24	VIR
3	10	ARI	3	6	LIB
4	5	TAU	4	18	LIB
5	26	TAU	5	29	LIB
6	13	GEM	6	11	SCO
7	29	GEM	7	22	SCO
8	12	CAN	8	5	SAG
9	25	CAN	9	17	SAG
10	7	LEO	10	29	SAG
11	18	LEO	11	15	CAP
12 noon	29	LEO	12 midnight	2	AQU

MAY 16

AM			PM		
1	24	AQU	1	14	VIR
2	19	PIS	2	25	VIR
3	16	ARI	3	7	LIB
4	10	TAU	4	19	LIB
5	29	TAU	5	2	SCO
6	16	GEM	6	13	SCO
7	1	CAN	7	25	SCO
8	14	CAN	8	7	SAG
9	27	CAN	9	19	SAG
10	9	LEO	10	2	CAP
11	20	LEO	11	18	CAP
12 noon	2	VIR	12 midnight	5	AQU

MAY 19

AM			PM		
1	29	AQU	1	16	VIR
2	25	PIS	2	28	VIR
3	21	ARI	3	10	LIB
4	14	TAU	4	22	LIB
5	3	GEM	5	4	SCO
6	19	GEM	6	15	SCO
7	4	CAN	7	27	SCO
8	17	CAN	8	9	SAG
9	29	CAN	9	21	SAG
10	11	LEO	10	5	CAP
11	22	LEO	11	21	CAP
12 noon	4	VIR	12 midnight	9	AQU

MAY 22

AM			PM		
1	5	PIS	1	18	VIR
2	29	PIS	2	1	LIB
3	25	ARI	3	13	LIB
4	18	TAU	4	24	LIB
5	7	GEM	5	5	SCO
6	22	GEM	6	18	SCO
7	6	CAN	7	29	SCO
8	20	CAN	8	12	SAG
9	1	LEO	9	25	SAG
10	13	LEO	10	9	CAP
11	25	LEO	11	24	CAP
12 noon	7	VIR	12 midnight	14	AQU

MAY 25

AM			PM		
1	8	PIS	1	21	VIR
2	4	ARI	2	3	LIB
3	29	ARI	3	15	LIB
4	22	TAU	4	27	LIB
5	10	GEM	5	9	SCO
6	25	GEM	6	20	SCO
7	9	CAN	7	2	SAG
8	22	CAN	8	14	SAG
9	4	LEO	9	27	SAG
10	16	LEO	10	11	CAP
11	27	LEO	11	28	CAP
12 noon	9	VIR	12 midnight	17	AQU

MAY 28

AM			PM		
1	14	PIS	1	23	VIR
2	10	ARI	2	6	LIB
3	5	TAU	3	17	LIB
4	26	TAU	4	29	LIB
5	13	GEM	5	10	SCO
6	29	GEM	6	27	SCO
7	11	CAN	7	4	SAG
8	24	CAN	8	17	SAG
9	6	LEO	9	29	SAG
10	18	LEO	10	14	CAP
11	29	LEO	11	2	AQU
12 noon	12	VIR	12 midnight	21	AQU

MAY 31

AM			PM		
1	19	PIS	1	25	VIR
2	16	ARI	2	7	VIR
3	10	TAU	3	19	LIB
4	29	TAU	4	2	SCO
5	16	GEM	5	13	SCO
6	1	CAN	6	24	SCO
7	14	CAN	7	7	SAG
8	27	CAN	8	19	SAG
9	8	LEO	9	2	CAP
10	20	LEO	10	18	CAP
11	2	VIR	11	5	AQU
12 noon	13	VIR	12 midnight	26	AQU

JUNE 3

AM			PM		
1	25	PIS	1	28	VIR
2	19	ARI	2	10	LIB
3	13	TAU	3	22	LIB
4	3	GEM	4	3	SCO
5	19	GEM	5	15	SCO
6	4	CAN	6	27	SCO
7	17	CAN	7	9	SAG
8	29	CAN	8	21	SAG
9	11	LEO	9	5	CAP
10	22	LEO	10	21	CAP
11	4	VIR	11	8	AQU
12 noon	16	VIR	12 midnight	1	PIS

JUNE 6

AM			PM		
1	29	PIS	1	1	LIB
2	25	ARI	2	13	LIB
3	17	TAU	3	24	LIB
4	7	GEM	4	5	SCO
5	22	GEM	5	18	SCO
6	6	CAN	6	29	SCO
7	19	CAN	7	11	SAG
8	1	LEO	8	24	SAG
9	13	LEO	9	8	CAP
10	25	LEO	10	23	CAP
11	7	VIR	11	12	AQU
12 noon	18	VIR	12 midnight	5	PIS

JUNE 9

AM			PM		
1	4	ARI	1	3	LIB
2	29	ARI	2	14	LIB
3	22	TAU	3	27	LIB
4	10	GEM	4	8	SCO
5	25	GEM	5	20	SCO
6	9	CAN	6	2	SAG
7	1	CAN	7	14	SAG
8	4	LEO	8	27	SAG
9	16	LEO	9	11	CAP
10	27	LEO	10	28	CAP
11	9	VIR	11	17	AQU
12 noon	21	VIR	12 midnight	10	PIS

JUNE 12

AM			PM		
1	10	ARI	1	5	LIB
2	3	TAU	2	17	LIB
3	26	TAU	3	29	LIB
4	13	GEM	4	10	SCO
5	28	GEM	5	22	SCO
6	11	CAN	6	4	SAG
7	24	CAN	7	16	SAG
8	6	LEO	8	29	SAG
9	18	LEO	9	14	CAP
10	29	LEO	10	29	CAP
11	11	VIR	11	21	AQU
12 noon	23	VIR	12 midnight	15	PIS

JUNE 15

AM			PM		
1	14	ARI	1	7	LIB
2	8	TAU	2	19	LIB
3	29	TAU	3	1	SCO
4	16	GEM	4	12	SCO
5	29	GEM	5	24	SCO
6	13	CAN	6	6	SAG
7	26	CAN	7	19	SAG
8	8	LEO	8	2	CAP
9	20	LEO	9	17	CAP
10	2	VIR	10	4	AQU
11	13	VIR	11	26	AQU
12 noon	25	VIR	12 midnight	20	PIS

JUNE 18

AM			PM		
1	19	ARI	1	10	LIB
2	13	TAU	2	22	LIB
3	3	GEM	3	3	SCO
4	19	GEM	4	15	SCO
5	3	CAN	5	27	SCO
6	17	CAN	6	8	SAG
7	28	CAN	7	21	SAG
8	10	LEO	8	5	CAP
9	22	LEO	9	20	CAP
10	4	VIR	10	8	AQU
11	16	VIR	11	29	AQU
12 noon	28	VIR	12 midnight	25	PIS

JUNE 21

AM			PM		
1	25	ARI	1	12	LIB
2	17	TAU	2	24	LIB
3	7	GEM	3	5	SCO
4	22	GEM	4	18	SCO
5	6	CAN	5	29	SCO
6	19	CAN	6	11	SAG
7	1	LEO	7	24	SAG
8	13	LEO	8	8	CAP
9	25	LEO	9	23	CAP
10	6	VIR	10	12	AQU
11	18	VIR	11	5	PIS
12 noon	1	LIB	12 midnight	1	ARI

JUNE 24

AM			PM		
1	29	ARI	1	14	LIB
2	22	TAU	2	26	LIB
3	10	GEM	3	8	SCO
4	25	GEM	4	19	SCO
5	9	CAN	5	1	SAG
6	21	CAN	6	14	SAG
7	4	LEO	7	26	SAG
8	16	LEO	8	11	CAP
9	27	LEO	9	27	CAP
10	8	VIR	10	16	AQU
11	20	VIR	11	10	PIS
12 noon	2	LIB	12 midnight	5	ARI

JUNE 27

AM			PM		
1	3	TAU	1	17	LIB
2	25	TAU	2	28	LIB
3	12	GEM	3	10	SCO
4	28	GEM	4	22	SCO
5	11	CAN	5	4	SAG
6	24	CAN	6	16	SAG
7	6	LEO	7	29	SAG
8	18	LEO	8	14	CAP
9	29	LEO	9	29	CAP
10	11	VIR	10	21	AQU
11	23	VIR	11	14	PIS
12 noon	5	LIB	12 midnight	10	ARI

JUNE 30

AM			PM		
1	8	TAU	1	19	LIB
2	29	TAU	2	1	SCO
3	16	GEM	3	12	SCO
4	29	GEM	4	24	SCO
5	13	CAN	5	6	SAG
6	26	CAN	6	18	SAG
7	8	LEO	7	1	CAP
8	20	LEO	8	17	CAP
9	2	VIR	9	4	AQU
10	13	VIR	10	24	AQU
11	25	VIR	11	19	PIS
12 noon	7	LIB	12 midnight	16	ARI

JULY 3

AM			PM		
1	13	TAU	1	22	LIB
2	2	GEM	2	3	SCO
3	18	GEM	3	15	SCO
4	3	CAN	4	27	SCO
5	17	CAN	5	8	SAG
6	28	CAN	6	21	SAG
7	10	LEO	7	5	CAP
8	22	LEO	8	20	CAP
9	3	VIR	9	8	AQU
10	16	VIR	10	29	AQU
11	28	VIR	11	25	PIS
12 noon	9	LIB	12 midnight	21	ARI

JULY 6

AM			PM		
1	17	TAU	1	24	LIB
2	6	GEM	2	5	SCO
3	22	GEM	3	17	SCO
4	6	CAN	4	29	SCO
5	19	CAN	5	11	SAG
6	1	LEO	6	24	SAG
7	13	LEO	7	8	CAP
8	25	LEO	8	23	CAP
9	6	VIR	9	12	AQU
10	18	VIR	10	5	PIS
11	29	VIR	11	1	ARI
12 noon	12	LIB	12 midnight	26	ARI

JULY 9

AM			PM		
1	22	TAU	1	26	LIB
2	9	GEM	2	8	SCO
3	25	GEM	3	19	SCO
4	9	CAN	4	2	SAG
5	21	CAN	5	14	SAG
6	3	LEO	6	26	SAG
7	15	LEO	7	11	CAP
8	26	LEO	8	27	CAP
9	8	VIR	9	17	AQU
10	20	VIR	10	8	PIS
11	2	LIB	11	5	PIS
12 noon	14	LIB	12 midnight	29	ARI

JULY 12

AM			PM		
1	24	TAU	1	29	LIB
2	12	GEM	2	10	SCO
3	28	GEM	3	21	SCO
4	11	CAN	4	3	SAG
5	23	CAN	5	16	SAG
6	6	LEO	6	29	SAG
7	17	LEO	7	14	CAP
8	29	LEO	8	29	CAP
9	11	VIR	9	20	AQU
10	23	VIR	10	14	PIS
11	5	LIB	11	10	ARI
12 noon	17	LIB	12 midnight	5	TAU

JULY 15

AM			PM		
1	28	TAU	1	1	SCO
2	15	GEM	2	12	SCO
3	29	GEM	3	24	SCO
4	13	CAN	4	6	SAG
5	26	CAN	5	18	SAG
6	8	LEO	6	1	CAP
7	20	LEO	7	16	CAP
8	1	VIR	8	4	AQU
9	13	VIR	9	24	AQU
10	25	VIR	10	19	PIS
11	7	LIB	11	16	ARI
12 noon	19	LIB	12 midnight	10	TAU

JULY 18

AM			PM		
1	2	GEM	1	3	SCO
2	18	GEM	2	15	SCO
3	3	CAN	3	27	SCO
4	16	CAN	4	8	SAG
5	28	CAN	5	21	SAG
6	10	LEO	6	4	CAP
7	22	LEO	7	20	CAP
8	3	VIR	8	8	AQU
9	15	VIR	9	29	AQU
10	27	VIR	10	25	PIS
11	10	LIB	11	19	ARI
12 noon	21	LIB	12 midnight	13	TAU

JULY 21

AM			PM		
1	6	GEM	1	5	SCO
2	21	GEM	2	17	SCO
3	6	CAN	3	29	SCO
4	18	CAN	4	11	SAG
5	1	LEO	5	24	SAG
6	13	LEO	6	7	CAP
7	24	LEO	7	23	CAP
8	6	VIR	8	12	AQU
9	18	VIR	9	3	PIS
10	29	VIR	10	29	PIS
11	12	LIB	11	25	ARI
12 noon	23	LIB	12 midnight	17	TAU

JULY 24

AM			PM		
1	9	GEM	1	8	SCO
2	24	GEM	2	19	SCO
3	8	CAN	3	1	SAG
4	21	CAN	4	13	SAG
5	3	LEO	5	26	SAG
6	15	LEO	6	11	CAP
7	26	LEO	7	27	CAP
8	8	VIR	8	16	AQU
9	20	VIR	9	8	PIS
10	2	LIB	10	4	ARI
11	14	LIB	11	29	ARI
12 noon	26	LIB	12 midnight	22	TAU

JULY 27

AM			PM		
1	12	GEM	1	9	SCO
2	27	GEM	2	21	SCO
3	11	CAN	3	3	SAG
4	23	CAN	4	16	SAG
5	5	LEO	5	29	SAG
6	17	LEO	6	13	CAP
7	29	LEO	7	29	CAP
8	11	VIR	8	20	AQU
9	23	VIR	9	14	PIS
10	5	LIB	10	10	ARI
11	16	LIB	11	5	TAU
12 noon	28	LIB	12 midnight	26	TAU

JULY 30

AM			PM		
1	15	GEM	1	12	SCO
2	29	GEM	2	24	SCO
3	13	CAN	3	5	SAG
4	26	CAN	4	18	SAG
5	7	LEO	5	1	CAP
6	19	LEO	6	16	CAP
7	1	VIR	7	3	AQU
8	13	VIR	8	24	AQU
9	24	VIR	9	19	PIS
10	7	LIB	10	15	ARI
11	18	LIB	11	8	TAU
12 noon	1	SCO	12 midnight	29	TAU

AUGUST 2

AM			PM		
1	18	GEM	1	15	SCO
2	3	CAN	2	26	SCO
3	16	CAN	3	8	SAG
4	28	CAN	4	21	SAG
5	10	LEO	5	4	CAP
6	22	LEO	6	20	CAP
7	3	VIR	7	7	AQU
8	15	VIR	8	29	AQU
9	27	VIR	9	25	PIS
10	9	LIB	10	19	ARI
11	21	LIB	11	13	TAU
12 noon	3	SCO	12 midnight	3	GEM

AUGUST 5

AM			PM		
1	21	GEM	1	17	SCO
2	6	CAN	2	28	SCO
3	18	CAN	3	11	SAG
4	1	LEO	4	23	SAG
5	13	LEO	5	7	CAP
6	24	LEO	6	22	CAP
7	6	VIR	7	11	AQU
8	18	VIR	8	3	PIS
9	29	VIR	9	29	PIS
10	12	LIB	10	25	ARI
11	23	LIB	11	17	TAU
12 noon	5	SCO	12 midnight	7	GEM

AUGUST 8

AM			PM		
1	24	GEM	1	19	SCO
2	8	CAN	2	1	SAG
3	20	CAN	3	13	SAG
4	3	LEO	4	26	SAG
5	15	LEO	5	10	CAP
6	26	LEO	6	26	CAP
7	8	VIR	7	15	AQU
8	20	VIR	8	8	PIS
9	2	LIB	9	4	ARI
10	14	LIB	10	29	ARI
11	26	LIB	11	22	TAU
12 noon	7	SCO	12 midnight	10	GEM

AUGUST 11

AM			PM		
1	27	GEM	1	21	SCO
2	10	CAN	2	3	SAG
3	23	CAN	3	15	SAG
4	5	LEO	4	28	SAG
5	17	LEO	5	13	CAP
6	29	LEO	6	29	CAP
7	11	VIR	7	20	AQU
8	22	VIR	8	14	PIS
9	4	LIB	9	10	ARI
10	16	LIB	10	4	TAU
11	28	LIB	11	26	TAU
12 noon	10	SCO	12 midnight	13	GEM

AUGUST 14

AM			PM		
1	29	GEM	1	24	SCO
2	13	CAN	2	5	SAG
3	26	CAN	3	18	SAG
4	7	LEO	4	1	CAP
5	19	LEO	5	16	CAP
6	1	VIR	6	3	AQU
7	13	VIR	7	24	AQU
8	24	VIR	8	19	PIS
9	7	LIB	9	15	ARI
10	18	LIB	10	8	TAU
11	29	LIB	11	28	TAU
12 noon	12	SCO	12 midnight	16	GEM

AUGUST 17

AM			PM		
1	13	CAN	1	5	SAG
2	26	CAN	2	18	SAG
3	7	LEO	3	1	CAP
4	19	LEO	4	16	CAP
5	1	VIR	5	3	AQU
6	13	VIR	6	23	AQU
7	24	VIR	7	17	PIS
8	7	LIB	8	14	ARI
9	18	LIB	9	8	TAU
10	29	LIB	10	29	TAU
11	12	SCO	11	16	GEM
12 noon	24	SCO	12 midnight	29	GEM

AUGUST 20

AM			PM		
1	6	CAN	1	28	SCO
2	18	CAN	2	11	SAG
3	29	CAN	3	23	SAG
4	12	LEO	4	7	CAP
5	24	LEO	5	22	CAP
6	6	VIR	6	1	AQU
7	18	VIR	7	3	PIS
8	29	VIR	8	29	PIS
9	11	LIB	9	25	ARI
10	23	LIB	10	17	TAU
11	5	SCO	11	7	GEM
12 noon	16	SCO	12 midnight	22	GEM

AUGUST 23

AM			PM		
1	8	CAN	1	1	SAG
2	20	CAN	2	13	SAG
3	2	LEO	3	26	SAG
4	15	LEO	4	10	CAP
5	26	LEO	5	25	CAP
6	8	VIR	6	15	AQU
7	20	VIR	7	8	PIS
8	1	LIB	8	4	ARI
9	13	LIB	9	29	ARI
10	25	LIB	10	22	TAU
11	7	SCO	11	9	GEM
12 noon	18	SCO	12 midnight	25	GEM

AUGUST 26

AM			PM		
1	10	CAN	1	3	SAG
2	23	CAN	2	15	SAG
3	5	LEO	3	28	SAG
4	16	LEO	4	13	CAP
5	29	LEO	5	29	CAP
6	10	VIR	6	20	AQU
7	22	VIR	7	14	PIS
8	4	LIB	8	9	ARI
9	16	LIB	9	3	TAU
10	28	LIB	10	26	TAU
11	9	SCO	11	12	GEM
12 noon	21	SCO	12 midnight	28	GEM

AUGUST 29

AM			PM		
1	13	CAN	1	5	SAG
2	26	CAN	2	18	SAG
3	7	LEO	3	1	CAP
4	19	LEO	4	16	CAP
5	1	VIR	5	3	AQU
6	13	VIR	6	23	AQU
7	24	VIR	7	17	PIS
8	7	LIB	8	14	ARI
9	18	LIB	9	8	TAU
10	29	LIB	10	29	TAU
11	12	SCO	11	16	GEM
12 noon	24	SCO	12 midnight	29	GEM

SEPTEMBER 1

AM			PM		
1	16	CAN	1	8	SAG
2	28	CAN	2	21	SAG
3	10	LEO	3	4	CAP
4	21	LEO	4	19	CAP
5	3	VIR	5	7	AQU
6	15	VIR	6	28	AQU
7	27	VIR	7	23	PIS
8	8	LIB	8	19	ARI
9	21	LIB	9	13	TAU
10	2	SCO	10	2	GEM
11	14	SCO	11	19	GEM
12 noon	26	SCO	12 midnight	3	CAN

SEPTEMBER 4

AM			PM		
1	18	CAN	1	10	SAG
2	29	CAN	2	23	SAG
3	12	LEO	3	6	CAP
4	24	LEO	4	22	CAP
5	5	VIR	5	11	ACU
6	17	VIR	6	3	PIS
7	29	VIR	7	29	PIS
8	11	LIB	8	24	ARI
9	23	LIB	9	17	TAU
10	5	SCO	10	6	GEM
11	16	SCO	11	22	GEM
12 noon	28	SCO	12 midnight	6	CAN

SEPTEMBER 7

AM			PM		
1	20	CAN	1	12	SAG
2	3	LEO	2	26	SAG
3	15	LEO	3	10	CAP
4	26	LEO	4	25	CAP
5	8	VIR	5	15	ACU
6	19	VIR	6	8	PIS
7	1	LIB	7	4	ARI
8	13	LIB	8	28	ARI
9	25	LIB	9	20	TAU
10	7	SCO	10	9	GEM
11	18	SCO	11	25	GEM
12 noon	29	SCO	12 midnight	9	CAN

SEPTEMBER 10

AM			PM		
1	23	CAN	1	15	SAG
2	5	LEO	2	28	SAG
3	16	LEO	3	13	CAP
4	28	LEO	4	29	CAP
5	10	VIR	5	19	AQU
6	22	VIR	6	13	PIS
7	4	LIB	7	8	ARI
8	16	LIB	8	3	TAU
9	28	LIB	9	24	TAU
10	9	SCO	10	12	GEM
11	21	SCO	11	28	GEM
12 noon	3	SAG	12 midnight	11	CAN

SEPTEMBER 13

AM			PM		
1	26	CAN	1	18	SAG
2	7	LEO	2	1	CAP
3	19	LEO	3	16	CAP
4	29	LEO	4	3	AQU
5	13	VIR	5	23	AQU
6	24	VIR	6	17	PIS
7	6	LIB	7	14	ARI
8	18	LIB	8	8	TAU
9	29	LIB	9	28	TAU
10	12	SCO	10	15	GEM
11	23	SCO	11	29	GEM
12 noon	5	SAG	12 midnight	13	CAN

SEPTEMBER 16

AM			PM		
1	28	CAN	1	20	SAG
2	10	LEO	2	3	CAP
3	21	LEO	3	19	CAP
4	3	VIR	4	7	AQU
5	14	VIR	5	28	AQU
6	26	VIR	6	23	PIS
7	8	LIB	7	18	ARI
8	20	LIB	8	13	TAU
9	2	SCO	9	2	GEM
10	14	SCO	10	18	GEM
11	25	SCO	11	3	CAN
12 noon	8	SAG	12 midnight	16	CAN

SEPTEMBER 19

AM			PM		
1	29	CAN	1	22	SAG
2	12	LEO	2	6	CAP
3	23	LEO	3	22	CAP
4	5	VIR	4	11	AQU
5	17	VIR	5	3	PIS
6	29	VIR	6	29	PIS
7	11	LIB	7	23	ARI
8	23	LIB	8	16	TAU
9	4	SCO	9	6	GEM
10	16	SCO	10	21	GEM
11	27	SCO	11	6	CAN
12 noon	10	SAG	12 midnight	18	CAN

SEPTEMBER 22

AM		PM		
1	2 LEO	1	26 SAG	
2	14 LEO	2	9 CAP	
3	26 LEO	3	25 CAP	
4	8 VIR	4	14 AQU	
5	19 VIR	5	7 PIS	
6	1 LIB	6	2 ARI	
7	14 LIB	7	28 ARI	
8	25 LIB	8	20 TAU	
9	7 SCO	9	9 GEM	
10	18 SCO	10	24 GEM	
11	29 SCO	11	8 CAN	
12 noon	12 SAG	12 midnight	21 CAN	

SEPTEMBER 25

AM		PM		
1	4 LEO	1	28 SAG	
2	16 LEO	2	13 CAP	
3	28 LEO	3	29 CAP	
4	10 VIR	4	18 AQU	
5	22 VIR	5	12 PIS	
6	3 LIB	6	8 ARI	
7	15 LIB	7	3 TAU	
8	27 LIB	8	24 TAU	
9	9 SCO	9	12 GEM	
10	21 SCO	10	28 GEM	
11	3 SAG	11	11 CAN	
12 noon	15 SAG	12 midnight	23 CAN	

SEPTEMBER 28

AM		PM		
1	7 LEO	1	1 CAP	
2	19 LEO	2	16 CAP	
3	29 LEO	3	3 AQU	
4	12 VIR	4	23 AQU	
5	24 VIR	5	17 PIS	
6	6 LIB	6	14 ARI	
7	18 LIB	7	8 TAU	
8	29 LIB	8	28 TAU	
9	12 SCO	9	15 GEM	
10	23 SCO	10	29 GEM	
11	5 SAG	11	13 CAN	
12 noon	18 SAG	12 midnight	26 CAN	

OCTOBER 1

AM		PM		
1	9 LEO	1	3 CAP	
2	21 LEO	2	18 CAP	
3	3 VIR	3	5 AQU	
4	14 VIR	4	27 AQU	
5	26 VIR	5	23 PIS	
6	8 LIB	6	17 ARI	
7	20 LIB	7	11 TAU	
8	2 SCO	8	2 GEM	
9	13 SCO	9	18 GEM	
10	25 SCO	10	3 CAN	
11	7 SAG	11	16 CAN	
12 noon	20 SAG	12 midnight	28 CAN	

OCTOBER 4

AM		PM		
1	11 LEO	1	6 CAP	
2	23 LEO	2	21 CAP	
3	5 VIR	3	9 AQU	
4	17 VIR	4	1 PIS	
5	29 VIR	5	27 PIS	
6	11 LIB	6	23 ARI	
7	23 LIB	7	16 TAU	
8	4 SCO	8	6 GEM	
9	16 SCO	9	21 GEM	
10	27 SCO	10	6 CAN	
11	10 SAG	11	18 CAN	
12 noon	22 SAG	12 midnight	1 LEO	

OCTOBER 7

AM		PM		
1	14 LEO	1	9 CAP	
2	26 LEO	2	24 CAP	
3	8 VIR	3	14 AQU	
4	19 VIR	4	6 PIS	
5	1 LIB	5	2 ARI	
6	13 LIB	6	28 ARI	
7	25 LIB	7	20 TAU	
8	6 SCO	8	9 GEM	
9	18 SCO	9	24 GEM	
10	29 SCO	10	8 CAN	
11	12 SAG	11	20 CAN	
12 noon	25 SAG	12 midnight	3 LEO	

OCTOBER 10

AM		PM		
1	16 LEO	1	12 CAP	
2	28 LEO	2	28 CAP	
3	10 VIR	3	18 AQU	
4	21 VIR	4	12 PIS	
5	3 LIB	5	8 ARI	
6	15 LIB	6	3 TAU	
7	27 LIB	7	24 TAU	
8	9 SCO	8	12 GEM	
9	21 SCO	9	27 GEM	
10	3 SAG	10	10 CAN	
11	14 SAG	11	23 CAN	
12 noon	27 SAG	12 midnight	5 LEO	

OCTOBER 13

AM		PM		
1	19 LEO	1	15 CAP	
2	29 LEO	2	2 AQU	
3	12 VIR	3	23 AQU	
4	24 VIR	4	17 PIS	
5	6 LIB	5	12 ARI	
6	18 LIB	6	8 TAU	
7	29 LIB	7	28 TAU	
8	11 SCO	8	15 GEM	
9	23 SCO	9	29 GEM	
10	5 SAG	10	13 CAN	
11	17 SAG	11	26 CAN	
12 noon	1 CAP	12 midnight	7 LEO	

OCTOBER 16

AM			PM		
1	21	LEO	1	18	CAP
2	3	VIR	2	5	AQU
3	14	VIR	3	26	AQU
4	26	VIR	4	22	PIS
5	8	LIB	5	17	ARI
6	20	LIB	6	11	TAU
7	2	SCO	7	2	GEM
8	13	SCO	8	18	GEM
9	25	SCO	9	2	CAN
10	7	SAG	10	16	CAN
11	19	SAG	11	28	CAN
12 noon	3	CAP	12 midnight	10	LEO

OCTOBER 19

AM			PM		
1	23	LEO	1	21	CAP
2	5	VIR	2	9	AQU
3	17	VIR	3	1	PIS
4	29	VIR	4	27	PIS
5	11	LIB	5	23	ARI
6	22	LIB	6	16	TAU
7	4	SCO	7	6	GEM
8	15	SCO	8	21	GEM
9	27	SCO	9	6	CAN
10	9	SAG	10	18	CAN
11	22	SAG	11	29	CAN
12 noon	6	CAP	12 midnight	12	LEO

OCTOBER 22

AM			PM		
1	26	LEO	1	24	CAP
2	7	VIR	2	14	AQU
3	19	VIR	3	6	PIS
4	1	LIB	4	2	ARI
5	13	LIB	5	28	ARI
6	24	LIB	6	20	TAU
7	6	SCO	7	8	GEM
8	18	SCO	8	24	GEM
9	29	SCO	9	8	CAN
10	11	SAG	10	20	CAN
11	25	SAG	11	2	LEO
12 noon	9	CAP	12 midnight	14	LEO

OCTOBER 25

AM			PM		
1	28	LEO	1	28	CAP
2	9	VIR	2	18	AQU
3	21	VIR	3	12	PIS
4	3	LIB	4	7	ARI
5	15	LIB	5	15	TAU
6	27	LIB	6	24	TAU
7	9	SCO	7	12	GEM
8	20	SCO	8	27	GEM
9	2	SAG	9	10	CAN
10	14	SAG	10	23	CAN
11	27	SAG	11	4	LEO
12 noon	12	CAP	12 midnight	16	LEO

OCTOBER 28

AM			PM		
1	29	LEO	1	2	AQU
2	12	VIR	2	21	AQU
3	24	VIR	3	16	PIS
4	6	LIB	4	12	ARI
5	18	LIB	5	7	TAU
6	29	LIB	6	27	TAU
7	11	SCO	7	14	GEM
8	22	SCO	8	29	GEM
9	5	SAG	9	13	CAN
10	17	SAG	10	25	CAN
11	29	SAG	11	7	LEO
12 noon	15	CAP	12 midnight	19	LEO

OCTOBER 31

AM			PM		
1	2	VIR	1	5	AQU
2	14	VIR	2	26	AQU
3	25	VIR	3	21	PIS
4	7	LIB	4	17	ARI
5	19	LIB	5	11	TAU
6	2	SCO	6	1	GEM
7	13	SCO	7	18	GEM
8	25	SCO	8	2	CAN
9	7	SAG	9	15	CAN
10	19	SAG	10	27	CAN
11	2	CAP	11	10	LEO
12 noon	18	CAP	12 midnight	22	LEO

NOVEMBER 3

AM			PM		
1	4	VIR	1	9	AQU
2	17	VIR	2	1	PIS
3	29	VIR	3	27	PIS
4	10	LIB	4	22	ARI
5	22	LIB	5	16	TAU
6	4	SCO	6	4	GEM
7	15	SCO	7	20	GEM
8	27	SCO	8	5	CAN
9	9	SAG	9	17	CAN
10	21	SAG	10	29	CAN
11	5	CAP	11	12	LEO
12 noon	21	CAP	12 midnight	23	LEO

NOVEMBER 6

AM			PM		
1	7	VIR	1	14	AQU
2	19	VIR	2	6	PIS
3	1	LIB	3	1	ARI
4	13	LIB	4	27	ARI
5	24	LIB	5	20	TAU
6	6	SCO	6	8	GEM
7	18	SCO	7	24	GEM
8	29	SCO	8	8	CAN
9	12	SAG	9	20	CAN
10	25	SAG	10	2	LEO
11	8	CAP	11	14	LEO
12 noon	24	CAP	12 midnight	26	LEO

NOVEMBER 9

AM			PM		
1	9	VIR	1	17	AQU
2	21	VIR	2	10	PIS
3	3	LIB	3	6	ARI
4	15	LIB	4	2	TAU
5	27	LIB	5	23	TAU
6	9	SCO	6	1	GEM
7	20	SCO	7	26	GEM
8	2	SAG	8	10	CAN
9	14	SAG	9	23	CAN
10	27	SAG	10	4	LEO
11	11	CAP	11	16	LEO
12 noon	28	CAP	12 midnight	28	LEO

NOVEMBER 12

AM			PM		
1	12	VIR	1	21	AQU
2	24	VIR	2	15	PIS
3	5	LIB	3	12	ARI
4	17	LIB	4	7	TAU
5	29	LIB	5	27	TAU
6	11	SCO	6	14	GEM
7	22	SCO	7	29	GEM
8	5	SAG	8	13	CAN
9	17	SAG	9	25	CAN
10	29	SAG	10	7	LEO
11	15	CAP	11	19	LEO
12 noon	2	AQU	12 midnight	29	LEO

NOVEMBER 15

AM			PM		
1	14	VIR	1	26	AQU
2	26	VIR	2	21	PIS
3	7	LIB	3	17	ARI
4	19	LIB	4	11	TAU
5	2	SCO	5	1	GEM
6	13	SCO	6	17	GEM
7	24	SCO	7	2	CAN
8	7	SAG	8	15	CAN
9	19	SAG	9	27	CAN
10	2	CAP	10	9	LEO
11	18	CAP	11	21	LEO
12 noon	5	AQU	12 midnight	3	VIR

NOVEMBER 18

AM			PM		
1	16	VIR	1	1	PIS
2	28	VIR	2	27	PIS
3	10	LIB	3	22	ARI
4	22	LIB	4	15	TAU
5	4	SCO	5	4	GEM
6	15	SCO	6	20	GEM
7	27	SCO	7	5	CAN
8	9	SAG	8	17	CAN
9	21	SAG	9	29	CAN
10	5	CAP	10	12	LEO
11	20	CAP	11	23	LEO
12 noon	9	AQU	12 midnight	5	VIR

NOVEMBER 21

AM			PM		
1	18	VIR	1	5	PIS
2	1	LIB	2	1	ARI
3	13	LIB	3	26	ARI
4	24	LIB	4	19	TAU
5	6	SCO	5	8	GEM
6	18	SCO	6	23	GEM
7	29	SCO	7	7	CAN
8	11	SAG	8	20	CAN
9	24	SAG	9	2	LEO
10	8	CAP	10	14	LEO
11	24	CAP	11	26	LEO
12 noon	12	AQU	12 midnight	8	VIR

NOVEMBER 24

AM			PM		
1	21	VIR	1	10	PIS
2	3	LIB	2	6	ARI
3	15	LIB	3	2	TAU
4	27	LIB	4	23	TAU
5	9	SCO	5	11	GEM
6	20	SCO	6	27	GEM
7	2	SAG	7	10	CAN
8	14	SAG	8	23	CAN
9	27	SAG	9	4	LEO
10	11	CAP	10	16	LEO
11	27	CAP	11	28	LEO
12 noon	17	AQU	12 midnight	10	VIR

NOVEMBER 27

AM			PM		
1	23	VIR	1	15	PIS
2	5	LIB	2	12	ARI
3	17	LIB	3	7	TAU
4	29	LIB	4	27	TAU
5	10	SCO	5	14	GEM
6	22	SCO	6	29	GEM
7	4	SAG	7	13	CAN
8	16	SAG	8	25	CAN
9	29	SAG	9	7	LEO
10	14	CAP	10	19	LEO
11	29	CAP	11	29	LEO
12 noon	21	AQU	12 midnight	12	VIR

NOVEMBER 30

AM			PM		
1	25	VIR	1	21	PIS
2	7	LIB	2	17	ARI
3	19	LIB	3	11	TAU
4	1	SCO	4	1	GEM
5	12	SCO	5	17	GEM
6	24	SCO	6	2	CAN
7	6	SAG	7	15	CAN
8	19	SAG	8	27	CAN
9	2	CAP	9	9	LEO
10	17	CAP	10	21	LEO
11	4	AQU	11	3	VIR
12 noon	26	AQU	12 midnight	14	VIR

DECEMBER 3

AM			PM		
1	28	VIR	1	25	PIS
2	10	LIB	2	21	ARI
3	22	LIB	3	14	TAU
4	3	SCO	4	4	GEM
5	15	SCO	5	20	GEM
6	27	SCO	6	5	CAN
7	9	SAG	7	17	CAN
8	21	SAG	8	29	CAN
9	5	CAP	9	11	LEO
10	20	CAP	10	23	LEO
11	8	AQU	11	5	VIR
12 noon	1	PIS	12 midnight	17	VIR

DECEMBER 6

AM			PM		
1	1	LIB	1	1	ARI
2	12	LIB	2	26	ARI
3	24	LIB	3	19	TAU
4	5	SCO	4	8	GEM
5	17	SCO	5	23	GEM
6	29	SCO	6	7	CAN
7	11	SAG	7	20	CAN
8	24	SAG	8	2	LEO
9	8	CAP	9	14	LEO
10	23	CAP	10	26	LEO
11	12	AQU	11	7	VIR
12 noon	5	PIS	12 midnight	18	VIR

DECEMBER 9

AM			PM		
1	2	LIB	1	6	ARI
2	14	LIB	2	2	TAU
3	26	LIB	3	23	TAU
4	8	SCO	4	11	GEM
5	20	SCO	5	26	GEM
6	1	SAG	6	10	CAN
7	14	SAG	7	23	CAN
8	26	SAG	8	4	LEO
9	11	CAP	9	16	LEO
10	27	CAP	10	28	LEO
11	16	AQU	11	9	VIR
12 noon	10	PIS	12 midnight	21	VIR

DECEMBER 12

AM			PM		
1	5	LIB	1	11	ARI
2	17	LIB	2	6	TAU
3	28	LIB	3	27	TAU
4	10	SCO	4	14	GEM
5	22	SCO	5	29	GEM
6	4	SAG	6	13	CAN
7	16	SAG	7	25	CAN
8	29	SAG	8	7	LEO
9	14	CAP	9	19	LEO
10	29	CAP	10	29	LEO
11	21	AQU	11	12	VIR
12 noon	15	PIS	12 midnight	24	VIR

DECEMBER 15

AM			PM		
1	7	LIB	1	16	ARI
2	19	LIB	2	10	TAU
3	1	SCO	3	1	GEM
4	12	SCO	4	17	GEM
5	24	SCO	5	1	CAN
6	6	SAG	6	15	CAN
7	18	SAG	7	27	CAN
8	1	CAP	8	9	LEO
9	17	CAP	9	21	LEO
10	4	AQU	10	3	VIR
11	24	AQU	11	14	VIR
12 noon	19	PIS	12 midnight	26	VIR

DECEMBER 18

AM			PM		
1	9	LIB	1	21	ARI
2	21	LIB	2	14	TAU
3	3	SCO	3	4	GEM
4	15	SCO	4	20	GEM
5	27	SCO	5	5	CAN
6	8	SAG	6	17	CAN
7	21	SAG	7	29	CAN
8	5	CAP	8	11	LEO
9	20	CAP	9	23	LEO
10	8	AQU	10	4	VIR
11	29	AQU	11	17	VIR
12 noon	25	PIS	12 midnight	29	VIR

DECEMBER 21

AM			PM		
1	12	LIB	1	26	ARI
2	23	LIB	2	19	TAU
3	5	SCO	3	7	GEM
4	17	SCO	4	23	GEM
5	29	SCO	5	7	CAN
6	11	SAG	6	20	CAN
7	24	SAG	7	2	LEO
8	8	CAP	8	13	LEO
9	23	CAP	9	25	LEO
10	12	AQU	10	7	VIR
11	5	PIS	11	19	VIR
12 noon	1	ARI	12 midnight	1	LIB

DECEMBER 24

AM			PM		
1	14	LIB	1	2	TAU
2	26	LIB	2	23	TAU
3	8	SCO	3	10	GEM
4	19	SCO	4	26	GEM
5	1	SAG	5	10	CAN
6	14	SAG	6	22	CAN
7	26	SAG	7	4	LEO
8	11	CAP	8	16	LEO
9	27	CAP	9	28	LEO
10	16	AQU	10	9	VIR
11	9	PIS	11	21	VIR
12 noon	5	ARI	12 midnight	3	LIB

DECEMBER 27

AM			PM		
1	17	LIB	1	5	TAU
2	28	LIB	2	26	TAU
3	10	SCO	3	13	GEM
4	22	SCO	4	29	GEM
5	4	SAG	5	12	CAN
6	16	SAG	6	25	CAN
7	29	SAG	7	6	LEO
8	14	CAP	8	18	LEO
9	29	CAP	9	29	LEO
10	20	AQU	10	12	VIR
11	14	PIS	11	24	VIR
12 noon	10	ARI	12 midnight	6	LIB

DECEMBER 30

AM			PM		
1	19	LIB	1	10	TAU
2	1	SCO	2	29	TAU
3	12	SCO	3	16	GEM
4	24	SCO	4	1	CAN
5	6	SAG	5	14	CAN
6	19	SAG	6	27	CAN
7	1	CAP	7	9	LEO
8	17	CAP	8	20	LEO
9	4	AQU	9	2	VIR
10	24	AQU	10	13	VIR
11	19	PIS	11	26	VIR
12 noon	16	ARI	12 midnight	7	LIB

RECOMMENDED READING

APPENDIX II

For those wishing to learn more about astrology for the gaining of insight into individual charts, or for the understanding of the dynamic relationship between charts, the following books are recommended.

Abadie, M. J. and Bader, Claudia. *Love Planets*. New York: Simon & Schuster, 1990.
A relationship book that goes beyond Sun Signs to include all the personal horoscopic points: the Sun, Moon, and Ascendant, plus Venus and Mars; can be used to determine compatibility with a very individualized reading. Useful not only for lovers and friends, but also for parent/child relationships. Basically an instant relationship diagnosis.

Arroyo, Steven. *Astrology, Psychology, and the Four Elements*. Reno, NV: CRCS Publications, 1978.
An excellent treatment of the meaning of the elements in the horoscope, which is extremely comprehensive and presents a different point of view, for Arroyo sees all astrological symbolism as springing from the elements.

Cunninghan, Donna. *An Astrological Guide to Self-Awareness*. Reno, NV: CRCS Publications, 1978.
Highly recommended, especially for beginners. Good basics, easy to read.

——. *Being a Lunar Type in a Solar World*. York, Maine: Weiser, 1982.
In this superb book, Cunningham explores the problems of the "lunar" or Moon-oriented, person in our unbalanced "solar," or male-dominated, world, and seeks solutions.

Davison, Ronald. *Synastry: Understanding Human Relationships through Astrology*. New York: ASI, 1977.
A good, basic treatment of relationships, technically termed "synastry."

Greene, Liz. *Saturn: A New Look at an Old Devil.* New York: Weiser, 1976.
No doubt the best book available on this important Planet, in which he is covered by sign, house position, aspects, and in synastry.

———. *Relating: An Astrological Guide to Living with Others on a Small Planet.* New York: Weiser, 1977.
Highly recommended for its chart comparisons; may be unsuitable for the beginner.
———. *The Astrology of Fate.* York, Maine: Weiser, 1984.
A brilliant treatise on complex family dynamics with an emphasis on difficult, generational patterns. For the advanced student.

Hand, Robert. *Horoscope Symbols*, Rockport, MA: Para Research, 1981.
Delves extensively into core meanings of Signs, Planets, Houses, Aspects. A well-written must for any astrological library.

———. *Planets in Youth.* Rockport, MA: Para Research, 1977.
Especially recommended for the extensive and detailed coverage of all possible planetary aspects, related to youth. Hand is simply one of the best astrological writers we have.

———. *Planets in Transit.* Rockport, MA: Para Research, 1976.
Though not related to children, this is a great reference book and will get you started on understanding the influence of the transiting planets.

Hickey, Isabel. *Astrology, A Cosmic Science.* Watertown, MA: Altieri Press, 1970.
One of the all-time greats, the late Isabel Hickey's works are to be treasured for their insights and humanity.

March, Marion D. and McEvers, Joan. *The Only Way To Learn Astrology.* Three volumes. San Diego, CA.: Astro Computing Services, rev. ed. 1981.
A self-teaching manual for the serious student.

Oken, Alan. *Alan Oken's Complete Astrology.* New York: Bantam, 1980.
A must for any astrological library. Thorough treatment of the many layers of astrological symbolism as well as interpretative techniques and insights.

Ruperti, Alexander. *Cycles of Becoming.* Reno, NV: CRCS Publications, 1978.

Highly recommended. Jungian influenced, Ruperti's work on cycles informs and confirms my own work and experience. Easy to read, simplified enough for beginners. Useful for all ages and learning levels. Especially good for counselors and therapists.

Sakoian, F. and Acker, L. *Astrologer's Handbook.* New York: Harper and Row, 1976.

A basic reference work. Highly recommended.

Sargent, Lois. *How to Handle Your Human Relations.* Tempe, AZ: American Federation of Astrologers, 1958.

The standard basic work on synastry. Useful.

COMPUTER SERVICES

APPENDIX III

If you are interested in having a personal computer chart calculated for your child, yourself, your spouse, or anyone else, our computer can do that for you.

In addition to the basic computer chart, we offer computerized interpretative services of various degrees of detailed complexity for the individual, from "A Child's Profile" to an "Ultimate Personal Profile."

For those interested in understanding family dynamics — relationships between parents (or between any two adults), a parent and a child, or even between two children, we offer a "Relationship Profile." Also, our computer can give you a print-out chart of the Planets of *both* people in a relationship, on one wheel. With this "bi-wheel" chart it's easy to see how all the Planets in both charts relate to each other.

We also offer *individualized* interpretations prepared by a professional astrologer *on tape* covering specific areas, such as "Child Guidance" — with a focus on talents and behavior, "Relationship Guidance — for interpersonal problems and potentials, and "Individual Guidance" — for the person who wants to focus on a particular area of life.

Telephone consultations can also be arranged.

For an informative brochure listing all services, a price list, and complete ordering information, please send a #10 *stamped, self-addressed envelope* to:

HAZELWOOD PRODUCTIONS
P.O. Box 247
Lenox Hill Station
New York, NY 10021

Requests that do not include an SASE cannot be processed.